THE MIDDLE EAST MILITARY BALANCE, 1997

Jaffee Center for Strategic Studies
TEL AVIV UNIVERSITY

THE MIDDLE EAST MILITARY BALANCE, 1997

Mark A. Heller and Yiftah Shapir
Edited by Mark A. Heller

New York
Columbia University Press

Jaffee Center for Strategic Studies
TEL AVIV UNIVERSITY

Columbia University Press
Publishers Since 1893
New York   Chichester, West Sussex

Library of Congress ISSN: 1099–5552
ISBN: 0–231–11464–8

Casebound editions of Columbia University Press books are printed
on permanent and durable acid-free paper.
Printed in the United States of America
c 10 9 8 7 6 5 4 3 2 1
p 10 9 8 7 6 5 4 3 2 1

The Jaffee Center for Strategic Studies (JCSS)

The Center for Strategic Studies was established at Tel Aviv University at the end of 1977. In 1983 it was renamed the Jaffee Center for Strategic Studies in honor of Mr. and Mrs. Mel Jaffee. The objective of the Center is to contribute to the expansion of knowledge on strategic subjects and to promote public understanding of and pluralistic thought on matters of national and international security.

The Jaffee Center relates to the concept of strategy in its broadest meaning, namely, the complex of processes involved in the identification, mobilization and application of resources in peace and war, in order to solidify and strengthen national and international security.

Contents

Preface		xi
Part I	**Strategic Developments**	1
Chapter 1	The Arab-Israeli Peace Process Mark A. Heller	3
Chapter 2	Developments in Major Armies of the Middle East Amos Gilboa	29
Chapter 3	Subnational Conflicts in the Middle East Anat Kurz	59
Chapter 4	Iraq's Strategic Arena Aharon Levran	83
Chapter 5	U.S. Dual Containment Policy in the Persian Gulf Gerald L. Sorokin	113
Part II	**Regional Military Forces**	139
Introductory Note		141
	1. Algeria	145
	2. Bahrain	159
	3. Egypt	169
	4. Iran	189
	5. Iraq	209
	6. Israel	223
	7. Jordan	245
	8. Kuwait	255
	9. Lebanon	267
	10. Libya	277
	11. Morocco	291
	12. Oman	303
	13. Palestinian Authority	315
	14. Qatar	321
	15. Saudi Arabia	331
	16. Sudan	349
	17. Syria	359
	18. Tunisia	373
	19. Turkey	383

20. United Arab Emirates 403
21. Yemen 419

Part III Data and Documentation 431
Comparative Tables 433
Table 1 Major Armies of the Middle East 435
Table 2 Major Air Forces of the Middle East (including Air Defense Forces) 436
Table 3 Major Navies of the Middle East 437
Table 4 The Israel-Syria Military Balance 438
Table 5 Eastern Front–Israeli Military Balance 440
Table 6 The Arab-Israel Military Balance (Israel vs. Arab Coalition, Including Egypt and Iraq) 442
Table 7 The Arab-Israel Military Balance, 1984–1997 444
Table 8 The Iran-Iraq Military Balance 446
Table 9 The U.S.A. in the Middle East: Financial Aid (Military), Arms Sales, Advisers, Trainees, and Facilities 448
Table 10 Russia in the Middle East: Arms Sales, Advisers, and Trainees 450
Table 11 France in the Middle East: Arms Sales, Advisers, and Trainees 450
Table 12 Britain in the Middle East: Arms Sales, Advisers, Trainees, and Cooperation in Arms Production 451
Table 13 China in the Middle East: Arms Sales, Advisers, Trainees, and Cooperation in Arms Production 452
Table 14 North Korea in the Middle East: Arms Sales, Advisers, Trainees, and Technology Transfers 452
Table 15 Surface-to-Surface Missiles and Rockets in Service of Middle Eastern Armies (by Number of Launchers) 453

Glossary of Weapons Systems 455
Army 457
Air Force 469

Chronology of Major Events 487

Abbreviations 521

Maps 525
1. South Lebanon 527
2. Gaza Strip 528
3. Olso II: The West Bank 529
4. Iran and Iraq 530

Editors and Contributors 531

Preface

As 1997 drew to a close, the Middle East lay under the shadow of the latest in a series of American-Iraqi crises that have periodically transfixed the region and the world since the end of the Gulf War in 1991. The proximate cause of this crisis was the attempt by the Iraqi government in the fall of 1997 to constrain the operations of United Nations Special Commission inspectors, and it was because of this context that the unfolding crisis intensified global awareness of the problem of weapons of mass destruction. Concern about the prospects and consequences of military escalation also provoked an unprecedented flurry of diplomatic activity, including involvement by Russia to a degree not seen since the collapse of the Soviet Union. Given the centrality and gravity of Gulf-related events in late 1997 and early 1998, it is natural that the survey of strategic developments in this year's *Middle East Military Balance* should devote two chapters to this part of the region. In one, Aharon Levran looks in considerable detail at Iraq's military capabilities and threat potential, and argues that while the threat is rather less pronounced than is widely assumed, continued vigilance is necessary to prevent events from moving in more troubling directions. In the second, Gerald L. Sorokin addresses doubts about the continuing ability of the U.S. dual containment policy to meet this challenge, and suggests that, for all the difficulties and uncertainties with which it must contend, some variant of dual containment will remain in effect until a more promising alternative presents itself.

Notwithstanding the drama associated with the Gulf crisis, other ''routine'' issues continued to preoccupy the region. One of these was the stalemate in the Israeli-Arab peace process, which is reviewed by Mark A. Heller. Another was the pervasive phenomenon of subnational conflict, in its Islamist and ethnic variants (particularly the Kurdish question), which is surveyed by Anat Kurz. In addition, Amos Gilboa provides an updated assessment of the main military forces in the region and looks at some of the developments, including the general qualitative improvements in regional orders-of-battle and the evolving Israeli-Turkish security relationship, that affect the strategic postures of Middle Eastern actors.

Once again, Yiftah Shapir has overall responsibility for the quantitative data on regional military forces and other documentation in parts II and III. This year much of this data is rearranged in what we hope is a more readable format.

As always, *The Military Balance* is a collaborative effort. I would like to thank all the contributors and my other colleagues at the Jaffee Center for Strategic Studies, with a special word of appreciation for Avi Muallem, and to express my appreciation to those at Columbia University Press, especially Kate Wittenberg, Anne McCoy, and Alex Coolman, for helping to smooth a bumpy path.

M. A. H.

THE MIDDLE EAST MILITARY BALANCE, 1997

PART I

STRATEGIC DEVELOPMENTS

1. The Arab-Israeli Peace Process

Mark A. Heller

1997 was a year of almost complete stagnation in the Arab-Israeli peace process. It began with an agreement on the long-delayed Israeli redeployment from Hebron and a brief flurry of hope that some momentum, at least on the Israeli-Palestinian track, might be revived. This optimism, however, was short-lived. The mutual undertakings to implement the Interim Agreement and move quickly to permanent status negotiations were not fulfilled. Instead, the dialogue quickly deteriorated into mutual accusations of breach of faith and exchanges of blame for the failure to move forward. The rest of the year witnessed much diplomatic motion – with intensifying American involvement – but very little movement, and it ended in acrimonious stalemate. On the Israeli-Syrian track, there was even less evidence of a viable process. Despite some halfhearted mediation efforts by third parties, neither side indicated any sense of urgency, and the contacts that had been broken off in March 1996 remained frozen. Israeli relations with Lebanon and Israeli policy in Lebanon were also essentially frozen, although growing domestic pressure for a unilateral withdrawal from southern Lebanon held the potential for some change. All in all, the peace process remained alive at the end of the year because of American artificial respiration and the reluctance of any of the parties to issue a political death certificate. But it would take more than these life-support systems to revive it from its comatose state.

The Israeli-Palestinian Track

After several months of intense American mediation and occasional involvement by others, Israel and the Palestine Liberation Organization (PLO) initialed a ''Protocol Concerning the Redeployment in Hebron'' on January 15, 1997. Because of its special character as the city of the biblical patriarchs, and particularly because it was the only West Bank city in which a Jewish community (of about 400) actually lived, Hebron had been accorded a status in the 1995 Interim Agreement rather different from that of the other six main Arab towns. Redeployment in Hebron was to be partial – about 15 percent of the city and almost 20,000 Palestinians were to remain under Israeli jurisdiction, at least until a permanent status agreement was reached – and to take place six months after the other cities had been turned over to the Palestinian Authority (PA). But after the first suicide attacks in February 1996, Prime Minister Shimon Peres announced that the Hebron redeployment, scheduled for March 28, would be contingent on the effectiveness of the Palestinian Authority's campaign to suppress Hamas, and after the bus bombings in early March, he raised even more stringent conditions, including the arrest and transfer to Israel of all individuals suspected of involvement in these terrorist attacks and named on a list provided to the PA. The latter demand was not met, but even if it had been, it is unlikely, given the emotional climate of the election campaign by then in high gear, that Peres would have been able to carry out the redeployment. Thus Hebron became the most immediate of the Interim Agreement's "unfinished business" bequeathed to Benjamin Netanyahu by the Labor government.

Netanyahu had never made any secret of his distaste for the entire Oslo Agreement. Along with his supporters in the nationalist camp and settler movement, he had been particularly critical of the idea that Hebron should be lumped into the same category as the other cities of the West Bank. Thus he was not at all eager to press forward with the redeployment that Shimon Peres had managed to defer, and there was virtually no activity on the Palestinian track in the first few months of the new government's tenure. But after the spasm of violence in September following the opening of the Hasmonean Tunnel entrance near the Western Wall, American intervention and growing international and domestic criticism precluded the possibility of entirely avoiding redeployment. For the last few months of 1996, Netanyahu therefore focused on renegotiating the terms in the hope of achieving something that could at least be described to his own supporters and constituents as a more favorable arrangement than that agreed to by the previous government, and Yasir Arafat took advantage of the reopened negotiations to try and link the Hebron redeployment more tightly to other outstanding interim issues and to permanent status talks.

The result was the Hebron Agreement, which was actually a package of several elements: the Protocol, which dealt with the security and civil arrangements regarding redeployment and slight enlargement (to 20 percent) of the area of Hebron and the number of Palestinians (20,000+) to remain under Israeli control; an Agreed Minute, which detailed American plans for the reopening (paving, litter baskets, planters, etc.) of Shuhada Street that transverses the

Jewish quarter; and a "Note for the Record," prepared by American Special Middle East Coordinator Dennis Ross, which dealt with the Israeli and Palestinian responsibilities concerning the outstanding "non-Hebron" issues and formally enshrined, at Netanyahu's insistence, the principle of reciprocity. According to the Note, Israel was obliged to carry out the first further redeployment (FRD) during the first week of March, to release Palestinian prisoners, and to resume negotiations on outstanding Interim Agreement issues and on permanent status (the latter by the middle of March); the Palestinian side was required to complete the process of revising the National Charter, fight terror and prevent violence, restrict the size of the Palestinian police force to previously agreed levels, and keep PA offices and activities within the areas specified in the Interim Agreement, i.e., outside Jerusalem. In addition, Warren Christopher, in what was virtually his last act as U.S. Secretary of State, provided separate letters to Netanyahu and Arafat in which he articulated the administration's understanding of what was left unsaid in the Hebron Protocol about the three FRDs stipulated in the Interim Agreement. In the letter to Netanyahu (the Arafat letter was not made public), Christopher stated that the last of these should take place no later than mid-1998, and that he had advised Arafat of U.S. views – without stipulating what they were – on *Israel's* [my emphasis] process of determining the extent of the redeployments and designating specified military locations; Israel's view was that this process was to be determined unilaterally by Israel.

The Hebron Agreement was widely seen as a breakthrough because it was the first time that a Likud-led government had negotiated and approved any withdrawal from the Land of Israel and transfer of territory to Palestinian control. As such, it was interpreted as at least implicit endorsement of the underlying premise of the Oslo process, despite Netanyahu's vigorous protests to the contrary. This was viewed as a positive development by Palestinians and by those in Israel committed to Oslo, particularly since the redeployment itself was carried out immediately and was promptly followed by renewed high-level Israeli-Palestinian contacts and agreement to set up the committees that would negotiate implementation of the outstanding issues of the Interim Agreement. But by the very same token, it provoked much suspicion and criticism within the Likud-led coalition and among elements of Netanyahu's public base, including the settler movement. Indeed, one of the leading Likud ministers, Science Minister Binyamin Begin, resigned in protest against what he interpreted as a betrayal of basic principles of the "national camp."

In order to allay fears that the Hebron Agreement was merely the first step on a slippery slope, Netanyahu undertook two measures that would influence the atmosphere in which subsequent events developed. The first was the decision in late February to proceed with the construction of a housing project on Har Homa (Jabal Abu Ghneim) in the southern suburbs of Jerusalem. The second was a Cabinet decision in early March to limit the first FRD to 9 percent of the West Bank, including 7 percent to be transferred from Area B (already under Palestinian civil control) to Area A (Palestinian civil and internal security control). In many cases, Palestinians were inclined to belittle the significance of Area B, since they believed that the continuing presence of Israeli security forces there compromised their authority. In this case, however, they argued that most of the proposed redeployment covered territory they already had, and that only 2 percent was "really" slated to be transferred from Israeli jurisdiction (in Area C) to the PA. This they viewed as altogether unacceptable, and the PA refused to legitimize the proposal by cooperating in arranging the logistics of the handover. Israel briefly considered withdrawing unilaterally, but then rejected that idea. Thus the first FRD was suspended, and it had still not been carried out by the end of the year. As a further sign of protest, Yasir Arafat also ordered that the negotiations on other issues, including permanent status, be suspended.

For the rest of the year, the Israeli government and the PA maintained intermittent contact, but their direct interaction was essentially confined to exchanges of accusations of noncompliance with the obligations under Oslo that had been reaffirmed in the Hebron Agreement. Israel charged the Palestinian Authority with failure to complete the process of amending the Palestinian National Covenant and, more important, of not carrying out its obligations to combat terror by confiscating unlicensed weapons, arresting and transferring to Israel or trying suspected terrorists, ensuring that convicted terrorists carried out their sentences (rather than engaging in what Israeli critics called a "revolving door" policy of passing public sentences and then quietly arranging for the convicts to be released, or to "escape," from prison), and generally cracking down on the "terrorist infrastructure" – the organizational and structural base of Hamas. The charge that Arafat was insufficiently vigilant in combating terrorism gained added resonance in March, when a Palestinian worker set off a charge in the Apropo Cafe in Tel Aviv, killing three Israelis, including the mother of a small baby, as well as himself. The PA, for its part, charged Israel with failing to implement the "safe passage" between Gaza and the West Bank, delaying completion of the Gaza port and airport, refusing to release all Palestinians jailed for offenses committed before the signing of the Declaration of Principles (DOP), attempting to reduce the Palestinian presence in East Jerusalem by confiscating resident identity cards, and continuing to confiscate land and expand settlements. To the extent that these charges were valid – and there was considerable merit to the accusations of both sides – they both reflected and contributed to a deep-seated mutual lack of confidence that pervaded any efforts either by the belligerents themselves or by would-be mediators to inject some momentum into the stalled negotiations.

It is true that the two major decision makers, whatever their real inclinations may have been, were partly hobbled by domestic problems and constrained from doing more to accommodate the concerns of the other side. Immediately after the Hebron redeployment, Netanyahu became embroiled in a scandal involving the appointment of a relatively obscure Jerusalem lawyer, Roni Bar-On, as Attorney-General, allegedly in order to protect Aryeh Der'i, the chairman of the Shas Party, whose support was indispensable to the government's Knesset majority. Although the police investigators recommended that Netanyahu, along with his Justice Minister and the Director-General of the Prime Minister's Office, be indicted for breach of public trust, the Solicitor-General and new Attorney-General (appointed following Bar-On's resignation) eventually decided that there was insufficient evidence of criminal intent to warrant an indictment. But even after the "Bar-On Affair" faded, Netanyahu was faced with a continuing series of crises – the resignation of Finance Minister Dan Meridor, the "Mash'al Affair" (see below), a controversy over the proposed enactment of a law regulating religious conversion, an internal Likud revolt over nomination procedures, and, toward the end of the year, a bruising intracoalition budget battle and the resignation of Deputy Prime Minister and Foreign Minister David Levy. For most of the year, there was a sense that the government was under siege, and in these circumstances, Netanyahu was unable to risk his fragile majority with measures that could be portrayed as appeasement of the Palestinians.

Arafat, too, came under increasing domestic criticism for his high-handed methods and lack of accountability, particularly his dismissive attitude toward the Palestinian Legislative Council (PLC). The PLC, although dominated by a large Fatah majority, viewed itself as a kind of watchdog of government procedures, and it showed increasing impatience with evidence of mismanagement and corruption. Following publication of an audit by the General Control Office in late spring that documented massive waste and misdirection of public funds, Arafat barely averted a PLC vote of no confidence in the Executive Council and a demand that all Cabinet ministers resign.

Nevertheless, domestic weakness was only a partial explanation of the paralysis. The fact is that the parties were deeply divided by genuine differences of interpretation over what was required of them by the Oslo Agreements, Christopher's letters notwithstanding. On the question of Har Homa, for example, the Israeli position was that the project in question was not a settlement, that even if it were, settlement activity was not prohibited during the interim period (the 1993 DOP defined settlements as a final status issue), and that even if it had been, agreements covering the West Bank and Gaza did not apply to Jerusalem. Indeed, the emotional resonance of the Jerusalem connection was so great – Netanyahu's election was partly due to his charge that Shimon Peres, if re-elected, would divide Jerusalem – that most of the Israeli opposition could not bring itself to criticize the decision to begin work on Har Homa and was reduced to arguing that the timing was wrong. For all these reasons, it was inconceivable that Netanyahu (who, when leader of the opposition, had himself voted against the previous government's decision to expropriate the site of the project) would resist an initiative by the mayor of Jerusalem (a Likud rival of the Prime Minister) to begin now. By contrast, the Palestinians believed that even if settlements were not explicitly mentioned in the DOP, they were precluded by the undertaking of both sides to refrain from unilateral actions during the interim period that would prejudice the outcome of permanent status negotiations. Moreover, they insisted that all of Jerusalem beyond the 1949 Armistice Line was an intrinsic part of the West Bank, and that any provisions of the Oslo process that applied to the West Bank also applied to East Jerusalem, unless stipulated otherwise.

The parties were similarly divided in their understanding of the FRDs. The Israeli position was that the "specified military locations'' to which Israel was required to redeploy during the interim period were to be specified unilaterally by Israel in accordance with its understanding of its security needs, and that almost any redeployment would therefore conform with the letter of the agreement. The Palestinians argued that the term was meant to apply to narrowly defined sites, such as bases and camps, and that these, along with the settlements and eastern Jerusalem, accounted for no more than 10 percent of the West Bank. Consequently, they expected to be in control of about 90 percent of the West Bank in advance of a permanent status agreement, and perhaps even before permanent status negotiations began.

These opposing positions barely disguised a very profound gap over the shape of a permanent status agreement and were actually pursued as part of an effort by both sides to ensure optimal opening positions if and when negotiations on such an agreement were initiated, that is, as a kind of ongoing prenegotiation. The extent of this gap was reflected internally in Israel in the ongoing confrontation between Left and Right, and it was clearly reiterated in the Knesset debate about the Hebron Agreement. In the same speech that praised the renegotiated arrangement for Hebron as ''better, more secure, more responsible than that which we inherited,'' Netanyahu also insisted that while his government was bound by the written texts bequeathed by the preceding government, it was not at all committed to the ''oral law'' of the Oslo process. This ''oral law'' Netanyahu described as ''the intention to uproot the Jewish community in Hebron'' and, in more cosmic terms, ''withdrawal to the 1967 lines, or almost; the establishment of a Palestinian state; and even the division of Jerusalem.''

This claim was somewhat exaggerated, in the sense that Labor leaders had never indicated any willingness to divide Jerusalem, and their pronouncements on the question of territorial compromise had always reflected a refusal to withdraw to the 1967 borders. But even allowing for political hyperbole, Netanyahu's statement did capture the essential fact that the Israeli government was no longer committed to what the original signatories had perceived as the underlying logic of Oslo – what Yitzhak Rabin had referred to as ''separation.'' As a result, there was no longer any implicit convergence of Israeli and Palestinian expectations with respect to permanent status, and in the absence of any mutual confidence with respect to permanent status, it was virtually impossible to bridge the gaps on implementation of interim issues.

In late March, Netanyahu proposed to cut this "Gordian knot" by accelerating permanent status negotiations. This proposal was met with studied reserve by the Americans and outright rejection by the Palestinians, on the grounds that it constituted a transparent attempt to evade the obligation of interim withdrawal. Nevertheless, Netanyahu pushed ahead with internal discussions about Israeli requirements in a permanent status agreement, either to prepare for the contingency that negotiations might actually begin, or to provide a conceptual framework from which interim redeployment plans might be logically derived, or to respond to the criticism that he could not simply reject the "oral law" of the previous government without articulating some alternative vision of his own.

The first product of this process was an idea Netanyahu termed "Allon plus," apparently in the hope of gaining bipartisan support by associating it with the territorial compromise proposed in the late 1960s by Yigal Allon, a leading Labor Party figure and Foreign Minister during Yitzhak Rabin's first government. Although "Allon plus" was discussed in the Cabinet, it was not presented as a formal government position. But its main components were represented in maps appearing in the Israeli press in mid-1997. These included: Israeli sovereignty over the Jordan Valley and northern Judaean Desert west of the Dead Sea, eastward extension of the coastal plain, expansion of metropolitan Jerusalem, broadening of the corridor connecting Jerusalem with the Mediterranean, and the creation of four east-west corridors to connect Israel with the Jordan Valley. All in all, "Allon plus" would incorporate almost all settlers and all but about twenty isolated settlements into Israel, and would leave the Palestinians with self-rule – but not sovereignty – in about 45 percent of the West Bank.

The publication of the "Allon plus" map provoked some interest in Israel but did nothing to break the Israeli-Palestinian logjam. Nor did American, European, and Egyptian mediation efforts produce anything more than intermittent contact until July, when American prodding persuaded the two parties to resume security contacts and agree to renew negotiations. But before this could happen, two suicide-bombers set off explosions in the Mahaneh Yehuda market in Jerusalem, killing 14 Israelis and wounding almost 170 others.

The bombing had two effects. The first was a drastic Israeli response. In addition to suspending the flagging negotiations again, Netanyahu imposed a complete internal and external closure on the

West Bank and Gaza (even for VIPs) and froze the transfer to the PA of tax revenues collected by Israel on its behalf. He also threatened other measures, such as the jamming of Palestinian radio and television broadcasts, demanded the arrest of 88 individuals on a list provided to the PA, and warned that there would be no further implementation by Israel until the PA fulfilled its security obligations. These measures had an immediate and painful effect, cutting short the modest economic recovery during the first half of 1997. Average unemployment in the West Bank and Gaza Strip, which had stood at about 20 percent in June, immediately jumped to more than 30 percent when workers were cut off from their jobs in Israel, and Palestinian export business owners were cut off from their production inputs and access routes to markets. By the end of September, it was estimated that the direct income losses to workers and exporters amounted to more than $110 million. In addition, the income and indirect taxes (value added, fuel excise, import and health duties) withheld by Israel represented more than 60 percent of the PA budget.

The second effect was to energize American mediation efforts. Against a backdrop of frequent Palestinian protests, riots, and clashes (during some of which Israeli and Palestinian forces came close to opening fire on each other) and an incident in which Palestinian police were accused of planning attacks on Israeli settlers, the bombing threatened to drive the diplomatic impasse over the edge into all-out war. To forestall this danger, Secretary of State Madeleine Albright, in a major policy speech at the National Press Club, declared that the immediate American priority was to ensure effective PA cooperation on security affairs, but that once this was achieved, she would consider coming to the region herself to promote a political breakthrough. Until that point, Albright, unlike her predecessors, had studiously avoided personal involvement in the peace process, presumably because she felt that the prospects of success did not justify the investment of her time and political capital. But the bombing in Mahaneh Yehuda had demonstrated both the costs and risks of continued stalemate and had the effect of eliciting a more direct and active American role.

In keeping with the priorities established by Albright, the first manifestation of this new role was in the security field. In early August, Dennis Ross established a three-way panel to coordinate cooperation on security matters; the American representative would be the CIA station chief in Israel. Thus the United States became directly involved in what, until then, had been a bilateral matter, and Palestinian compliance with security obligations, on which any further Israeli redeployments had been made contingent, could no longer be a matter of unilateral Israeli judgment. Barely had this panel been established when the second, explicitly political manifestation appeared.

Presumably satisfied that her requirement for security cooperation had been met, Albright announced that she would come to the Middle East in early September to pursue the rest of her agenda. But before she could arrive, terrorists struck again. On September 4, just after a partial easing of the Israeli measures, three suicide-bombers, who apparently maintained a line-of-sight and communicated with each other, set off their charges almost simultaneously in the Ben-Yehuda pedestrian mall in Jerusalem, killing four and wounding more than 190. The resulting mood in Israel was not conducive to further progress, but rather than postpone her trip, Albright traveled to the region in an effort to promote both the Interim Agreement and accelerated permanent status negotiations. During this trip, Albright delivered a message that consisted of two parts. The first was that the time for avoiding difficult decisions had passed, and that both sides needed to be serious about what was required from them: the Palestinians, in everything connected with security, the Israelis, in the avoidance of unilateral actions (i.e., settlements) that prejudged the outcome of permanent status. The second was that the United States would not and could not provide the will for peace if the protagonists themselves lacked it. This was a veiled threat to walk away from the problem and leave Israel and the Palestinians to live with the consequences of their actions unless they responded positively to the first part of the message.

Initially, her urgings seemed to have some effect. Israeli restrictions were eased, construction at Har Homa was essentially halted after the completion of the infrastructure work, and a private initiative to build Jewish housing in the Ras al-Amud neighborhood in East Jerusalem was blocked. Arafat, for his part, began to move more vigorously against Hamas following evidence that the suicide bombers had in fact come from PA-controlled areas. At the end of September, Albright met with Foreign Minister David Levy and PLO Executive Committee Deputy Chairman Abu Mazen at the United Nations and worked out an agreed basis on which to resume negotiations. The package contained four elements to be addressed: continued security cooperation, further redeployments in accordance with the Hebron agreement, the definition and content of a "time-out" on unilateral steps (i.e., settlements), and acceleration of permanent status negotiations. This was really a restatement of familiar agenda items rather than a conceptual breakthrough, but it sufficed to allow resumption of negotiations on October 6.

But before these negotiations could produce any movement, events were again derailed, this time by the so-called Mash'al Affair. Following the suicide bombing at the end of July, Netanyahu instructed Israeli security organs to step up active measures against terrorist organizations. One outcome of this determination was a decision to assassinate Khaled Mash'al, a leading figure in the political wing of Hamas. In September, Mossad operatives accosted Mash'al in the streets of Amman, Jordan, and sprayed him with a slow-acting agent that was intended to result in his death several days later, apparently from natural causes. However, the Israelis were unable to evade pursuit by Mash'al's bodyguard, and they were detained by Jordanian police. Jordanian authorities soon learned the details of the operation, and Israel was obliged to provide the antidote (along with its chemical formula). This was administered as Mash'al was on the brink of death.

The political aftermath was far messier. King Hussein was embarrassed by the revelation and outraged at the decision by the Mossad to operate in Amman, which he saw as a gross violation of Jordanian sovereignty. In response, he suspended security cooperation with Israel and made the release of the Israeli agents conditional on Israel's release of several dozen Jordanians and Palestinians detained in Israeli jails, most notably, Sheikh Ahmad Yassin, the founder and spiritual leader of Hamas. Israel had little choice but to comply, but the ramifications of the decision were problematic, to say the least. The release of Yassin and other Hamas detainees undermined the credibility of Israeli demands that the PA shut down the "revolving door" for Hamas convicts in its own jails. It also provided a boost to the spirits and prestige of Hamas, while implicitly signaling that Hussein had been able to extract from Israel what Yasir Arafat, despite all his public declarations over the years, had been unable to do. The point was implicitly underscored by the logistics of the release, which involved the transfer of Yassin to Hussein's care in Amman and only then to Gaza, rather than directly to Gaza.

Arafat and his supporters barely hid their distaste at the way events played out. He boycotted the reception ceremony for Yassin in Gaza, but not before his security people made sure that Yarmouk Stadium, where the ceremony was held, was draped with pictures of both Arafat and Yassin, and that Arafat's pictures were bigger. His spokesmen repeatedly insisted that Arafat and the PA were the sole authority in the territories, and Fatah staged a protest in Nablus against both Israel and Jordan. All this reflected the continuing mistrust between the PA and Hamas, notwithstanding the public professions of unity in the face of the Israeli threat and the periodic efforts to reach some understanding about the rules of the ongoing competition between them. This mistrust was further fueled by the subsequent revelation that Hussein, two days before the operation in Amman, had passed on to Netanyahu a Hamas proposal of a 10-year cease-fire and had himself offered to mediate between Hamas and Israel. All of this served to inflame Arafat's long-standing suspicion that Jordan, with tacit or active Israeli approval, was trying to revive its influence in Palestinian affairs, this time with Hamas as the possible vehicle.

The reported terms of the cease-fire offer – evacuation of all settlements, Israeli withdrawal to the 1967 lines, establishment of an independent Palestinian state – meant that the offer had no chance at all of being accepted, but even that did not necessarily mean that it might not have developed into an Israel-Hamas channel of communication and negotiation. In any event, the proliferation of conspiracy theories led both Netanyahu and Hussein to recognize that things had gone a little too far, a little too fast. Netanyahu quickly reaffirmed that he intended to negotiate only with Arafat (indeed, he held a late-night meeting with Arafat – the first direct contact in more than seven months – on the same day Yassin returned to Gaza, and made some other statements and gestures to strengthen Arafat); Hussein insisted that his ties with Arafat were very good. Still, the developments surrounding the "Mash'al Affair" accurately reflected the atmosphere of intense mistrust that virtually precluded any meeting of minds.

And the fact is that practically nothing came out of the revived negotiating forum. Following initial contacts in the area, Israel and the PA sent negotiating teams to Washington to address the four-point package agreed on at the end of September. But only the group on security cooperation made any headway at all. And though it eventually produced an agreement on procedures and actions, which provided for continuing three-way consultation – the third party being the CIA – the document was rejected by the Israeli

Cabinet in December on the grounds that it implied an unacceptable degree of symmetry between Israeli and Palestinian terrorist threats, but also because it precluded the possibility that Israel would be the sole arbiter of the security cooperation on which implementation of other Interim Agreement obligations, including further redeployments, would be contingent.

On the other issues – a "time-out" on unilateral measures, acceleration of permanent status negotiations, and implementation of outstanding Interim Agreement issues – the stalemate continued. Under the last category, there were some desultory discussions about the opening of the Dahaniyya airport and the Gaza seaport, as well as the industrial zone at the Karni crossing in Gaza and the whole question of "free passage"; these produced conflicting reports of progress. On the issue of FRDs, however, there could be no illusion that the prospects of agreement had been advanced, because there had been no direct discussion of the issue. Instead, Israel maintained its position that the extent of FRDs was a question to be determined unilaterally by Israel. Indeed, the issue remained primarily one of internal Israeli debate. But the unilateral character of the decision was belied by the frequent American urgings of Israel to move forward, and by discussions, occasionally acrimonious, with American mediators, ranging from Dennis Ross and Assistant Secretary Martin Indyk through the Secretary of State to President Clinton himself.

In response to these urgings, Netanyahu initiated a series of Cabinet discussions on Israel's territorial requirements in a permanent status agreement, from which its attitude to the FRDs would ostensibly derive. This became a map exercise, reviving the discussion initiated by Netanyahu's own "Allon plus" proposal earlier in the year. Defense Minister Yitzhak Mordechai produced two maps prepared earlier by the IDF. One, reflecting "security interests," entailed Israeli retention of slightly more than 50 percent of the West Bank; a second took into account other "national interests" (water sources and other infrastructure interests, transportation routes, archaeological and historical sites, etc.) and raised the area slated for incorporation into Israel to more than 60 percent. Infrastructure Minister Ariel Sharon introduced his own map, based on ideas he had himself proposed close to 20 years before, which reserved for Israel almost 65 percent. The main differences between these various proposals concerned the width of the eastern and western security zones, the number and width of east-west road corridors Israel would retain, and the number of isolated Jewish settlements (and access roads) to be transferred to Palestinian jurisdiction. But they all implied Israeli incorporation of most of the settlements, retention of the Jordan Valley, creation of a large Greater Jerusalem bloc, and the existence of three or four noncontiguous Palestinian cantons in the West Bank; as Sharon himself said, they differed only in their details.

Moreover, they all severely restricted Israel's room for maneuver during the interim period. The most "generous" plan ultimately envisaged a Palestinian entity containing no more than 50 percent of the West Bank – the Palestinians, of course, were not a party to this internal Israeli debate – and the PA already controlled almost 30 percent in Areas A and B. If Netanyahu intended to hold on to "bargaining chips" for any permanent status negotiations, this left very little margin for the "significant and credible" (widely understood to mean double-digit) second redeployment reported to have been demanded by Madeleine Albright, especially if that were indeed later followed by a third redeployment, as required by the Interim Agreement and reaffirmed in the Hebron Note for the Record. In addition, Netanyahu was repeatedly threatened by his coalition partners in the "Land of Israel Front" that they would abandon him if he agreed to withdraw (or, in some cases, actually withdrew) from one more inch of territory. The latter threat would not necessarily be decisive, since the opposition would almost surely support the government in a Knesset vote on redeployment, and the coalition rebels might well reconsider and return to the fold in subsequent votes, lest they topple the government and make possible the return to power of the Labor Party. But if coalition considerations played any role at all, they tended to reinforce the inclinations of the top leadership, not to neutralize them.

Thus the last few months of the year were mostly devoted to an Israeli-American dialogue. In response to American urgings, the Israeli side tried to explain its permanent status needs and stressed the Palestinian failure to comply with previous obligations – to complete the process of amending the Covenant, combat terror, reduce the size of its police force, restrict its governmental activity to areas under its legitimate control, and refrain from hostile propaganda and incitement. The Israeli government again vowed that any further redeployment would be contingent on rectification of these violations, a threat that assumed added gravity when it was revealed that the Mahaneh Yehuda and Ben-Yehuda bombers, like the one at the Apropo Cafe, had come from areas under PA jurisdiction. But it never actually committed itself, even conditionally, to a specific FRD, instead merely suggesting that the flexibility it could show, though limited, would be greater if the Americans would endorse the idea of skipping the third FRD and moving directly to permanent status negotiations. The Americans did not publicly express themselves on the idea of skipping the third FRD, focusing instead on "one thing at a time," meaning a package that would permit implementation of the second FRD. At the end of the year, the two sides remained separated by a few percentage points of territory.

The third partner in this negotiating relationship was somewhat less in evidence. In their parallel discussions with the Americans, the Palestinians brought their own list of alleged violations by the Israeli side, but did not express themselves on the extent of the second FRD, except to repeat their view of what was required by the Interim Agreement. They did strongly object to the idea of skipping the third FRD, and they made any agreement to begin permanent status negotiations conditional on Israeli agreement to carry out all specified Interim Agreement undertakings.

Only on the issue of security did these two parallel tracks merge into an active three-way discussion, producing the abortive agreement on cooperation. Intermittent discussions took place on the other "non-Hebron" issues – airport, seaport, safe passage – but these did not even lead to agreements at the technical level.

For all intents and purposes, the political process was therefore frozen. In the larger scheme of things, there was a considerable measure of irony in this. After all, the semipublic debate inside the Israeli government betrayed a transformation in Likud thinking that was really monumental but virtually ignored in the acrimonious exchanges between the two sides, except by a few ideological purists inside the ruling party. It was that the Likud-led Israeli government had abandoned its attachment to the integrity of the Land of Israel and endorsed partition, of some sort, and a constrained Palestinian state, of some sort; even Ariel Sharon acknowledged at one point during the year that a Palestinian state was inevitable. In other words, the Likud's own implicit operating premise was now that the ongoing confrontation with the Palestinians focused on the geographical extent and functional authority of the state they would inevitably have. But rather than engage the Israeli government in a direct negotiation of those issues, the Palestinian side preferred to wait, apparently in the expectation or hope that either internal developments or American pressure would somehow produce progressively more generous Israeli positions, before permanent status negotiations even began.

By the end of the year, this had not yet happened, and the result was a negotiating stalemate. This did not necessarily mean paralysis on the ground. In the absence of any diplomatic progress, a kind of fitful modus vivendi emerged, in which the two sides cooperated for short-term tactical reasons while trying to pursue their own agendas unilaterally, with varying degrees of success. Israel, for example, was unable to halt, much less roll back, the PA presence in East Jerusalem; Orient House remained open and operating, and various PA agencies (including the Education Ministry and some security officials) continued to make their presence felt among the Arab population of the city. Political considerations even thwarted some Israeli projects there: the Ras al-Amud proposal was never initiated, and even the Har Homa project, following the completion of basic infrastructure, was essentially frozen. On the other hand, Israel did resist demands for a ''time-out'' in settlement construction, and population growth in the Jewish settlements, while making no appreciable impact on the overall demographic balance in the West Bank, continued at the same pace as in previous years – about 9 percent. This further reduced the prospect, already extremely remote, that major settlement blocs across the Green Line could ever be negotiable. Meanwhile, the Palestinians continued their process of state-and regime-building, and, like Israel, they also engaged in a effort to establish ''facts on the grounds'' in the hope of prejudicing permanent status negotiations. This was particularly evident in East Jerusalem, where the PA continued to impose its curriculum in public schools, to encourage and support the construction of Arab-owned housing on empty lots, to strengthen the PA-appointed mufti at the expense of the Jordanian-appointed incumbent, to announce that its planned census in the West Bank and Gaza would also cover East Jerusalem, and to mobilize symbols and expressions of international recognition and support. Despite all these activities, however, the Palestinians could not reduce substantially their dependency on Israel for a broad range of economic, communications, and transportation needs.

This day-to-day reality warded off the explosion of which so many analysts warned, primarily because the PA itself had no interest in such an outburst and was strong enough to repress those who did. But uneasy coexistence did little to revive the political process.

That was in suspended animation, and what kept it alive was not so much the hope that it would somewhat recover consciousness as the fear of both Netanyahu and Arafat that they would be blamed for its death and forced to explain what alternative they proposed to pursue.

Israeli Relations with Jordan and Other Arab Countries

Stalemate on the Israeli-Palestinian track inevitably affected Israeli relations with other Arab countries, perhaps none more so than with Jordan. Since 1994, peace with Israel had been promoted and eagerly embraced by the Jordanian regime and some elements of the business community but had failed to generate much enthusiasm in the general public; many professional associations had boycotted any contact with their Israeli counterparts, and Islamist forces had been particularly critical. For the most part, the regime had stood firm in the face of this opposition, although it occasionally did make known its dissatisfaction with certain Israeli decisions or decision-making procedures, especially following the opening of the Hasmonean Tunnel entrance in September 1996.

The Jordanian regime faces a constant dilemma. On the one hand, it is invested in good relations with Israel, not only economically, but also in a strategic sense; it is the latter that explains the exchanges of intelligence and military delegations, the Jordanian willingness to engage in a joint naval exercise with Israel and to send an observer to a joint Israeli-Turkish-American exercise that was widely criticized throughout the rest of the Arab world, and even to explore the possibility of cooperation in military maintenance and upgrading. On the other hand, Jordan, because of its proximity to the West Bank and the large Palestinian population in the East Bank, remains particularly exposed to problems on the Israeli-Palestinian track. For the most part, the Jordanian regime has been able to manage this dilemma by maintaining the confidence of both sides and even occasionally intervening to facilitate the resolution or management of problems between them. Indeed, it was the King's direct involvement, after American and Egyptian efforts seemed to have stalled, that permitted the last hurdles in the Hebron negotiations to be overcome. But the Israeli decision to begin construction on Har Homa provoked a particularly widespread outpouring of protest in Jordan and elicited strong condemnations by the Jordanian leadership, including King Hussein himself. In early March, Hussein sent Netanyahu a strongly worded letter accusing him of acting in bad faith and undermining the foundations of the entire peace process.

The atmosphere of tension and suspicion peaked on March 13, when a Jordanian soldier stationed at Naharayyim/Baqura – the so-called Island of Peace in the middle of the Jordan River, transferred to Jordan under the terms of the 1994 Peace Treaty – opened fire on a group of touring Israeli schoolgirls, killing seven and wounding six others. The shock produced by this event led to an immediate cessation of the verbal attacks, and Hussein himself visited the families of the dead and wounded girls to express his condolences and ask for their forgiveness. But many Jordanians were critical of this gesture and flocked to visit the family of the soldier involved in the attack; when the soldier was brought up for trial before a military court, the legal associations and hundreds of independent lawyers volunteered to defend him. In Israel, the visit was seen as a reaffirmation of Hussein's noble spirit, so admired by Israelis, and it helped calm angry emotions.

Indeed, the killing and its immediate aftermath had something of a cathartic effect, and the two sides moved quickly thereafter to address some of the outstanding irritants in the Israeli-Jordanian relationship. This was particularly so with respect to water. One feature of the peace treaty was that Israel had promised to help Jordan find an additional 50 million cubic meters (mcm) of water per year. The failure to deliver on this promise had caused considerable resentment in Jordan, but at a meeting in early May, the Israeli Infrastructure Minister and the Jordanian Water Minister made some headway on this problem. Later in the month, Netanyahu and Hussein reached an agreement to pump to Jordan 25 mcm from existing sources and to redirect another 25 mcm/year of Yarmouk River floodwaters, the cost of the storage facilities to be shared by Israel and Jordan. Pumping of Lake Tiberias water to Jordan began in mid-May. Jordan and Israel also moved forward on a variety of other issues: commercial and aviation ties, tariffs, visas, pest control, release of prisoners, economic assistance, and security cooperation. But despite the desire on both sides to promote common interests, it was impossible to insulate the bilateral relationship from problems in the Israeli-Palestinian relationship.

The most dramatic manifestation of this reality was the "Mash'al Affair," which erupted because of an operational failure by the Mossad but reflected a more fundamental complication in the

Israeli-Jordanian relationship: that Jordan was unable to prevent a Hamas presence in the kingdom, and Israel was unwilling to make the kingdom ''out-of-bounds'' in its struggle against Hamas. Hussein interpreted the Mossad operation as a personal affront and froze security cooperation with Israel until some of the central characters on the Israeli side, including the head of the Mossad, were replaced. But while this particular contretemps might eventually be resolved, there would inevitably be further complications resulting from Jordan's unavoidable role as both participant in and arena for the very problematic Israeli-Palestinian relationship.

The Israeli-Palestinian impasse also adversely affected Israel's emerging relations with other Arab countries. The uproar over Har Homa elicited Arab League calls for the freezing of normalization with Israel, the reinstatement of the economic boycott, and the suspension of the multilateral peace talks. None of these recommendations was universally adopted, but there was a noticeable cooling in the economic and cultural ties with several Gulf and North African countries. Oman froze diplomatic and commercial relations, Qatar suspended plans to open a commercial office in Tel Aviv, and Morocco kept plans for direct flights between Rabat and Tel Aviv on hold. Perhaps the most noteworthy development concerned the annual Middle East/North Africa Economic (MENA) Summit, hosted by Qatar in November. Throughout the year, several Arab states, led by Syria, pressed Qatar to cancel the meeting in protest at Israeli policies. Qatar, under counterpressure by the United States, resisted these demands, but the summit itself was a pale shadow of previous meetings in Casablanca, Amman, and even Cairo the year before. Several major Arab states boycotted the gathering or made do with very low-level representation, and some, e.g., Egypt, Saudi Arabia, and Morocco, as if to add insult to injury, sent high-ranking delegations to the Islamic Conference Organization that met in Tehran the following month. In response to the diplomatic slight, Israeli Foreign Minister David Levy stayed away, even though Secretary of State Madeleine Albright did attend. The Economic Summit did produce some commercial contacts, even between Israeli businessmen and their counterparts from Arab countries, such as Lebanon, that had studiously avoided participation in any of the multilateral forums evolved since the Madrid Conference in 1991. But MENA, like the other multilateral institutions, had been originally conceived to encourage bilateral negotiations by facilitating the normalization of relations between Israel and the Arab world, and the rather sorry spectacle in Doha symbolized how much normalization remained an effect, rather than a cause, of progress in the peace process.

The Israeli-Syrian Track

If the Israeli-Palestinian track witnessed motion without movement during 1997, the Israeli-Syrian track saw no motion at all. This track had two branches, one directed at the bilateral issue of land (the Golan Heights) and peace, and one directed at Israel's presence in southern Lebanon, which was ostensibly an issue involving Lebanon and Israel but in practice could not be addressed diplomatically without Syrian approval.

On the first branch, most activity was confined to recurrent Syrian demands to resume negotiations at the point where they had been broken off in early 1996, i.e., with Israeli agreement, in principle, to complete withdrawal from the Golan Heights (in exchange for security and other conditions Syria was unwilling to meet), and recurrent Israeli offers to resume negotiations on any basis except that one. In contrast to her reluctant engagement on the Israeli-Palestinian track, Secretary of State Albright did avoid the practice of her predecessor on this track and refused to become involved. And periodic efforts by lower-level American officials and by European and Russian mediators to find some creative formula that could bridge this gap accomplished absolutely nothing, despite occasionally tantalizing reports of secret messages being carried back and forth between Jerusalem and Damascus.

There were one or two events that might have thawed the frosty climate underlying this standoff. One was the August visit to Syria by a group of Israeli Arabs, including some Knesset members, although it was used primarily as a vehicle to elicit expressions of support for Syrian demands. The other was the revelation, later in the year, that a former Mossad officer known to have attributed aggressive long-term intentions to the Syrian leadership had been charged with submitting fraudulent reports based on nonexistent sources. This news strengthened the conviction that Syrian troop movements in Lebanon in the summer of 1996 had actually been defensive in nature, and that willful misinterpretation of their character had falsely fed tensions and created a brief war scare. But if either of these events provided the potential for a Syrian "charm offensive," there was no follow-through. One reason given by the

Syrians for their demand to resume negotiations only at the point where they had been suspended by the previous Israeli government was the belief that going back to "square one" would mean a waste of the years spent on those negotiations. But after a further 18 months of stalemate, the Syrians showed no indication that they viewed a settlement with Israel as urgent enough to justify a departure from established policy. The Israeli government, of course, also saw no pressing need to accede to Syrian demands. Indeed, its only noteworthy action on the issue involved more farce than evidence of calculated strategy: in a mid-July Knesset debate on a draft bill to require approval by 80 Knesset members of any concession on the Golan Heights, several Cabinet ministers voted one way on the first reading, and the other way on the second.

Developments on the Lebanese branch were graver, but not necessarily more conclusive. One of Netanyahu's first actions after being elected Prime Minister in 1996 was to suggest "Lebanon first" – a negotiated withdrawal from southern Lebanon in advance of any agreement with Syria. But while the Lebanese government itself may have been inclined to facilitate Israel's departure from Lebanese territory, Syria had no such incentive – indeed, it had every reason to prefer that Israel not leave, except on Syrian terms – and this proposal, like similar ones by the previous government and subsequent ones by this government, ran into the brick wall of a Syrian veto over Lebanese policy.

Different individuals floated a variety of "trial balloons" intended to finesse this problem – informal understandings, an enlarged UN presence, the deployment of French or other foreign troops to replace departing Israeli forces – but none of these gathered any momentum, and Israel was left with the only real alternative to the status quo that had existed since the security zone had been established in 1985 – unilateral withdrawal. The difference was that the domestic appeal of unilateral withdrawal was rising, because the cost of remaining in Lebanon was rising. During 1997, 39 Israeli soldiers were killed in Lebanon, as opposed to an average of 24 per year over the previous four years. It is true that 15 of these fatalities were incurred in two unusually lethal incidents – a field fire in late August and a failed naval commando operation in early September. It is also true that the number of wounded actually declined. But the casualty reports, combined with the disastrous helicopter crash in northern Israel in February, in which seventy-three soldiers being airlifted to Lebanon were also killed, had a significant impact on the public debate. So, too, did the revelations that Hizbullah had acquired missiles capable of piercing the armor of the Merkava battle tank and that the Amal movement, Hizbullah's main competitor for Shi'ite loyalties in Lebanon, had also resumed activity after several years of relative military passivity.

The result was a series of more vocal and persistent demands for withdrawal, first by a public pressure group called "Four Mothers," established in midyear, and then by the "Movement for a Safe Withdrawal from Lebanon," headed by Knesset Member Yossi Beilin, which was established toward the end of the year. The public debate crossed party lines, and unilateral withdrawal was supported by several Likud Knesset members as well as by parts of the opposition. According to some leaked media reports, it was also endorsed by some senior military commanders in internal debates.

Hizbullah's contribution to this intensifying debate was a series of declarations to the effect that an Israeli withdrawal from Lebanon would not deflect it from its ultimate aims and that it would carry its holy war into "occupied northern Palestine" and on to Jerusalem. Israeli defenders of the status quo, from both sides of the government-opposition divide, seized on these statements to prove how ill-advised a unilateral withdrawal would be, discounting the possibility that they were issued precisely to reinforce that belief. But there were other weighty considerations aside from the danger posed by Hizbullah that continued to militate against unilateral withdrawal. These included the potential threat to residents of northern Israel from rejectionist Palestinians and other elements in Lebanon acting at the instigation of Syria, the possible damage to Israel's deterrent image, and concern for the postwithdrawal welfare of Israel's military and civilian partners in south Lebanon. As the impact of news from Lebanon ebbed and flowed, these counterarguments were also made with greater conviction, both by government and security establishment spokesmen and by prominent members of the opposition, including Labor Party Chairman Ehud Barak.

At the very end of 1997, Defense Minister Yitzhak Mordechai, perhaps in acknowledgment of the rising crescendo of debate and certainly as a concession to the need for a new approach, declared that Israel was prepared to withdraw in the context of UN Security Council Resolution 425 of 1978. But Mordechai went on to explain that 425 also imposed an obligation on Lebanon to reestablish security and public order in the south, and that Israel's obligation to withdraw could not be addressed in isolation from the Resolution's other requirements. In short, his articulation of government policy was that Israel would not withdraw without some prior understanding, tacit if not explicit, informal if not formal, of what would happen in south Lebanon after it withdrew. This left the Israeli-Lebanese peace process, like the other Israeli-Arab processes, essentially where it had been a year before.

At the end of 1997, the two major tracks of the Arab-Israeli peace process seemed equally blocked. But the appearance of comprehensive stalemate was somewhat misleading. The impasse on the Syrian-Israeli track was far more deeply entrenched, in the sense that neither side felt any particular urgency to break it. Nor was there was an internal dynamic in the situation that promised, or threatened, its own undoing. Neither side faced domestic or international pressure to move forward, and there was no negotiating relationship that awaited completion or implementation. No timetable hung over the heads of the parties, and although the Syrian use of the phrase "all options are open" seemed to imply a veiled threat or warning to use military force, neither side appeared to have a preferable alternative to the status quo to which it might be tempted or compelled to resort.

The depth of the freeze in Israeli-Syrian negotiations was reflected in the fact that it preceded the Israeli election of 1996. In any case, there was no direct or circumstantial evidence to confirm the Syrian argument that Israel under Rabin had formally committed itself to withdraw to the lines of 4 June 1967 (as opposed to the more vague formulation of "complete withdrawal"). Nor was there any indication that Syria had come close enough to satisfying Israel requirements for whatever withdrawal had been conditionally approved to sustain the expectation that a comprehensive agreement would have been reached in mid-1996 had Labor been returned to power. For these reasons, there was practically nothing inherent in the standoff to suggest that it might be broken.

The Lebanese spur-line of this track was slightly more fluid, though not necessarily because the chances of a negotiated Israeli withdrawal from southern Lebanon had improved. Toward the end of the year, there was growing speculation that the Lebanese government could be sufficiently encouraged by outside forces to adopt a somewhat more independent policy vis-à-vis Syria and approve the kind of undertakings that would permit Israel to withdraw on the basis of an agreement, or at least some general understandings. But while Lebanese interests, with the possible exception of Hizbullah, might well be served by such an arrangement, Syria's would not. Syria had strategic reasons to oppose the decoupling of Lebanon from the Golan Heights, and some economic and political incentives to oppose any resolution of the Lebanese issue. Moreover, there was no indication that Syria would agree, voluntarily or otherwise, to allow the divergence of interests between it and its Lebanese protectorate to be given political expression. Thus the most significant potential source of change remained the inclination in parts of Israeli society and Israel's political system to withdraw unilaterally. But this inclination had surged before, only to subside later on, and while it seemed to take on unprecedented momentum in 1997, there was no sign that it had yet passed a critical threshold.

By contrast, the Palestinian-Israeli track, for all its inertia, was characterized by greater uncertainty and potential for change. Much of this had to do with the ambiguous nature of many Israeli government actions. After 18 months in office, Netanyahu's own preferred course was still not clear, not to his supporters, critics, or interlocutors, and perhaps not even to himself. One school of thought argued that he remained true to his original approach to the Oslo process and was intent on destroying it, though in ways that minimized the damage to Israel, and to himself. The other interpretation was that, for all his original misgivings, he was reconciled to Oslo's inevitability but was determined to rehabilitate it by correcting its "flaws," especially the lack of reciprocity in fulfilling obligations and the exaggerated Palestinian expectations it had excited, and even to use the "improved Oslo" as a platform with which to pursue a grand solution of the sort implied by the Israeli "map exercise" conducted during 1997.

One problem, for both analysts and his Palestinian counterparts, was that most of Netanyahu's actions could sustain either interpretation. This was particularly the case with respect to his increasingly frequent appeals to move quickly to permanent status negotiations. A second problem, especially for the Palestinians, was that the course he had pursued for 18 months, despite its uncertainties and occasional embarrassments, had not really caused him any domestic political damage. Netanyahu's election slogan – "Secure Peace" – had failed to materialize. Peace had certainly not been achieved, and while the number of people killed by terrorists had dropped, the fact that terrorist attacks continued, along with periodic alerts and constant tension, indicated that the problem of insecurity had not been solved either. Nevertheless, for all the fluctuations in Netanyahu's political fortunes and poll standings, there was little basis for Palestinians to expect that he would soon be replaced.

This left Arafat in a very difficult dilemma. He could accept the rather unappealing invitation from Israel to accept a minimal second redeployment, skip the third one, and move directly to permanent status negotiations. This course might produce some marginal advances in terms of territorial control, but it held little promise of bringing him substantially closer to his declared objectives, while subjecting him to further accusations of compromise, or worse, by his own domestic opponents. Alternatively, he could continue to hold out in the expectation that some combination of American pressure and violence on the ground would move Israel closer to full implementation of his interpretation of Israeli obligations. But Arafat's expectations of the American input, which had in fact constituted the central pillar of Palestinian political strategy at least since the change of government in Israel, had routinely been revealed as unrealistic, and there was little, apart from faith, to indicate that a dramatic change in the nature or intensity of American involvement would work to his advantage. The primary reason for this was that broader global changes had raised growing doubts in the United States about the wisdom of investing time, effort, and political capital in the issue. And even if there was an imperative to remain actively engaged, the American administration had not been able to resolve to its own satisfaction long-standing doubts about the nature of its involvement, which stemmed (apart from domestic political calculations) from the fact that there was no self-evident formula that would bridge the gap between the parties, no obvious benefit from trying to impose some formula that fell short of that desideratum, and no clearly productive course of action if one side or the other (or both) resisted American suggestions.

As for the use of violence, it was a double-edged sword. Low-level hostilities might produce some marginal advantage (though they could also further harden Israeli public opinion already skeptical about the sincerity of the Palestinian commitment to peace). But there was also a serious risk that violence could escalate out of control. Threats of a new *intifada* were occasionally voiced, but the potential gains from actualizing the threat had to be weighed against the operational difficulties (in 1997, the bulk of the Palestinian population was under Palestinian jurisdiction and not in direct confrontation with Israeli security forces) and, even more important, against the possibility that violence could be "privatized" – which happened in 1987 – thus threatening the very foundations of Arafat's rule.

Arafat occasionally pointed to a third option: trying to buy time and control the damage until May 1999, the end of the interim period agreed to in the Declaration of Principles (DOP), at which point he would simply declare the existence of an independent Palestinian state, with its capital in Jerusalem. Such an action would certainly provide tremendous emotional gratification, far more than the Palestine National Council's symbolic Declaration of Independence in 1988, but it would not materially affect the distribution of power and territory between Israel and the Palestinians, and it might provide the Israeli government with a legal pretext to declare that the Oslo Agreement had been materially breached by the Palestinians, allowing it to annex those parts of the West Bank it still held. More important, it would end the condition of statelessness that provided much of the base for Palestinian claims on the sympathies of the world. These considerations suggested that the closer the parties came to the DOP's final status target date, the less attractive the idea of a unilateral declaration of statehood would become.

All in all, Arafat faced a rather poor menu of choices at the end of 1997. But it was not the poverty of his options as much as the general Palestinian dissatisfaction with the status quo that explained why the apparent equilibrium of stalemate was far less stable on this track than on the others in the overall peace process. Although the potential for a considered policy breakthrough here was no higher than elsewhere, the potential for spontaneous breakdown was.

2. Developments in Major Armies of the Middle East

Amos Gilboa

Four central features characterize military developments in the Middle East during 1996 and 1997:

- stagnation in the quantitative growth of the region's armies. In the past, there were several periods during which military inventories grew rapidly: after the 1973 Yom Kippur War, after the 1982 Lebanon War, and during the Iraq-Iran War. In the 1990s, there were no major increases in the order-of-battle (orbat) of regional armies. On the other hand, there has been a clear trend, especially since the 1991 Gulf War, to acquire top-of-the-line weapons systems, armaments, and support systems.
- very significant progress in Iran's drive, with Russian assistance, to acquire the capacity to produce long-range surface-to-surface missiles.
- military flare-ups and military tension. The major examples are Israel's "Grapes of Wrath" operation against the Hizbullah in South Lebanon in the spring of 1996; military tension between Israel and Syria in the fall and winter of 1996; the clash between the United States and Iraq in the summer of 1996, following the Iraqi Army's takeover of parts of Kurdistan; and the military tension between Iraq and the United States toward the end of 1997.
- growing military-strategic cooperation between Israel and Turkey, with the firm support of the United States. This is a new development, to which there are two interpretations. The first is that it is a circumstantial event, involving more public relations than substance; the second is that it involves real strategic cooperation, reflecting the basic interests of both countries. In any event, the evolving relationship has thus far withstood all the pressures of other countries in the area to erode it. Only Jordan, which has deepened its own security ties with Israel, has adopted a positive approach.

This chapter surveys the main general trends in Middle Eastern armies in 1996–1997 and then looks in greater detail at the armed forces of Egypt, Syria, Iran, Iraq, Jordan, Saudi Arabia, and Israel.

General Trends in the Area

Surface-to-Surface Missiles

Middle Eastern states are placing increasing emphasis on surface-to-surface missiles (SSMs). This is particularly the case in Iran and Syria. The former is in the advanced stages of developing a missile ("Shihab 3") with a range of about 1,300 kilometers; in late 1997, it conducted a successful engine test, and within two years, it will be able to flight-test the missile. When the missile is operational, most of the Arabian Peninsula, all countries in the Fertile Crescent (including Israel), and all of eastern and central Turkey will be within its range. Iran appears to be simultaneously developing a missile, based on the Russian SS-4, with a range of 2,000–2,500 kilometers. Syria, which previously had a facility to assemble Scud-C parts acquired from North Korea, now has an indigenous capacity to produce Scud-Cs. It also cooperates with Iran in missile production. There is, therefore, a clear trend in these states to continue developing and producing a long-range strategic arm, with conventional or nonconventional warheads, as a major element of power in the region.

Orbats and Force Buildups

In the past two years there have been no significant increases in regional orbats. There were no major procurements of main systems for ground forces. The main changes were in air forces, primarily in terms of quality but also in quantity, and in navies.

- Jordan received the first four of 16 refurbished F-16A/B jets at the end of 1997;
- Israel received the first two of 25 F-15I jets in early 1998;
- Egypt received the last of the 16 F-16C/D jets purchased from the United States;
- Saudi Arabia received another 23 F-15S, out of a total of 72, as well as 25 Tornado IDS fighter-bombers, out of a total of 48;
- Iran, Egypt, and Saudi Arabia continued to strengthen their navies: Iran got its third Kilo-class Russian submarine, Egypt took delivery of two renovated American frigates, and Saudi Arabia received an additional French missile frigate.

The most important developments in the area of ground forces were the upgrading of several hundred old Syrian T-55 tanks in Ukraine, ongoing procurement of M-1A-1 tanks by the Egyptian Army, acquisition of Merkava Mark-3 tanks by the IDF, and absorption of the last M-1A-2 tanks ordered by the Saudi Army.

Finances

Finances continue to be the major brake on military growth and development. Israel and Syria are most affected by this constraint, but even Egypt, which receives an annual grant of $1.3 billion from the U.S., is also struggling with this problem. One possible solution under consideration by the Egyptians is the ''storage'' of regular armored brigades (i.e., laying up the equipment in unit-sets and discharging most of the personnel). By contrast, wealthy oil countries like the United Arab Emirates (UAE) have no problem considering the purchase of 80 modern combat aircraft, worth about $8 billion. After a fierce competition between the advanced F-16, the Eurofighter, and the French Rafale, the UAE decided in the summer of 1997 to divide the pie, purchasing 40 Mirage 2000-9 and 40 advanced F-16s. Despite financial constraints, the defense budgets of most countries in the region did not change significantly, although Israel's budget did decline. U.S. military aid to the region was basically unchanged. Unlike Egypt, Jordan did not gain a substantial increase in U.S. assistance following its peace agreement with Israel. At the same time, Jordan, Egypt, and Israel have received indirect financial aid in the form of drawdowns – weapons from U.S. Army arsenals – at practically no cost.

In fact, Israel and Egypt enjoy U.S. defense assistance and base their procurement programs on it. But this also has a negative aspect: since they must use the aid money for American equipment, they are not free to determine their own priorities. Egypt, for example, cannot choose whatever aircraft on the world market is most suitable for its needs, and Israel cannot invest more in its own advanced armament, but must instead purchase equipment that is not necessarily at the top of its real priorities.

New Technologies

Until recently, the United States was the only country that refused to export its most advanced military technologies; France and England were prepared to sell any technology to any country that was prepared to pay for it. In the period under review, there was a significant change in the American approach, and President Clinton announced that the United States was willing to sell the AIM-120 advanced medium-range air-to-air missile, or AMRAAM, if the UAE purchased advanced F-16 aircraft. The AMRAAM, operational since 1991, is the most advanced missile in the U.S. Air Force, and Clinton made the offer in order to persuade the UAE to purchase the F-16 instead of its European competitors. Egypt and Saudi Arabia had previously tried, without success, to buy the AMRAAM, and they renewed their requests following the offer to the UAE. In the face of strong Israeli objections, they were again turned down. But other advanced technologies did reach Egypt and Saudi Arabia, including flare-resistant air-to-air missiles (AIM-9-M), electromagnetic air-to-air missiles (AIM-7-M), night-vision navigation systems (Path Finder), and laser-designator pods (Sharp Shooter). Egypt was also authorized to buy the vehicle-mounted Stinger Avenger, already supplied to the Saudis. These transfers complemented the advanced main systems that Arab states have had for some time: M1-A-1/2 tanks (Egypt, Saudi Arabia, Kuwait), Challenger-2 tanks (Oman), Bradley armored fighting vehicles (AFVs) (Saudi Arabia); Apache helicopters (Egypt, Saudi Arabia), F-16C/D aircraft (Egypt, Kuwait, Bahrain), F-15S aircraft (Saudi Arabia), and Patriot surface-to-air missiles (Saudi Arabia).

Satellites

In April 1995, Israel successfully launched the Ofek-3 satellite, thereby acquiring strategic photoreconnaissance capabilities it did not previously have. This is a clear step up in Israel's intelligence capability, giving it a qualitative edge over other countries in the region. However, current trends in commercial satellite imagery may undermine this edge; as satellite cameras acquire the capacity for higher resolution, they can make out smaller and smaller objects, giving them military significance. At the end of 1997, the Americans launched their Early Bird commercial photography satellite, with a three-meter resolution capability (as compared with five meters for earlier satellites), and in 1998, Lockheed Martin is planning to launch a Space Imaging satellite with a resolution capacity of 82 centimeters. According to an agreement between the United States and Israel, the U.S. commercial satellites will not take pictures of Israel at a level of resolution below 3.5 meters. But it is significant that high-quality satellite pictures of military targets in the area – even if not in Israel – can now be purchased commercially. The Israeli satellite launch is a stimulus for other countries in the area, especially Iran, to begin developing their own satellite launch capabilities.

Qualitative Elements of Arab Armed Forces

Arab armies began to devote more attention to qualitative aspects of force structure after the Gulf War, and this trend continues in a variety of ways:

- identifying relative weaknesses and strengths, and planning force structures and procurement accordingly;
- acquiring night-fighting and PGM/anti-PGM capabilities;
- carrying out exercises of large command formations (corps), training large armored units in deep maneuver, and adopting new concepts of defensive and offensive warfare (with each army adapting the lessons of the Gulf War to its own circumstances);
- operating the most advanced main weapon systems;
- training and exercising with Western armies, especially by Egypt (which held a "Bright Star" joint exercise with U.S., French, and Italian forces, in addition to air and naval exercises with the Americans), Jordan (which held a joint maneuver, "Moonlight," with U.S. forces), and Saudi Arabia and the Gulf states;
- introducing advanced signals and command-and-control equipment (Egypt and Saudi Arabia).

Regional Joint Training

Saudi Arabia and Egypt continued their long-standing practice of joint naval exercises. Two other naval exercises stood out. One was a small-scale search-and-rescue operation, carried out by Israel and Jordan in the Gulf of Eilat toward the end of 1997; this was the first Israeli-Arab joint military exercise, and it reflected the defense cooperation between the two countries. The other was also a search-and-rescue exercise between Israel and Turkey, with U.S. participation and Jordanian observers, held in January 1998. This was the first joint exercise between Israel and Turkey. It is important to emphasize that other military ties in the region (between Egypt, Saudi Arabia, and Syria, and between Syria and Iran) are limited in scope and have not taken on the character of a military alliance or war coalition.

Indigenous Military Production

The trend toward greater self-sufficiency is growing stronger in Egypt, Iran, and Syria. Iran, for example, has already prepared the infrastructure for producing T-72 tanks. Even Saudi Arabia has set up a factory to produce wheeled armored personnel carriers (APCs), and the UAE is pursuing contacts with a view to building shipyards for the production of combat vessels. Israel, of course, leads the region in this field.

Arms Transfers

Except for a few helicopters, Russia did not sell any main weapons systems to Arab countries in 1996–1997, but it did transfer missile technology to Iran, and it continues to host a large number of arms-purchasing missions. What particularly attracts the Arab states is the new generation of Russian antitank missiles with very high capacity to penetrate armor, including reactive armor. If these missiles enter the region in large numbers, it will have an operational impact on the armored battlefield. The United States remains the main weapons supplier to all states in the region, except Iran, Iraq, and Syria. Its largest customers are Saudi Arabia, Israel, and Egypt. Britain is the second-largest supplier. Its main clients are Saudi Arabia and the Gulf states. France is the third-largest supplier of arms. Its main clients are the Gulf states and Saudi Arabia. China is the main supplier of arms to Iran, along with Russia. If the embargo on Iraq is lifted or significantly eased, then Russia and France will be Iraq's main suppliers.

Israel's Qualitative Edge

There is a school of thought that argues that, despite all these developments, Israel's qualitative edge not only did not diminish, but actually grew. This argument is based on the following factors: Israel's growing advantage in personnel trained to operate modern technologies; its indigenous development of advanced weaponry; its growing advantage in force multipliers (good intelligence, appropriate combat doctrine, logistical support, etc.) that enable it to exploit more fully the potential of advanced weapon systems; and America's ongoing commitment to maintain Israel's qualitative edge.

Another approach argues that the qualitative gap between the IDF and Arab armies, especially the Egyptian Army, is diminishing. This thesis rests on the fact that the quality of the IDF's weaponry is no longer clearly superior to that of the Arab armies; that the Arab armies have improved in terms of their ability to train and operate forces, and that Arab armed forces, especially those of Egypt, have benefited from their joint exercises with the U.S. and other Western armies. Moreover, IDF failures in the last few years in current security operations, especially against Hizbullah in Lebanon, have exposed defects that could also influence its performance against regular Arab armies, and the budget constraints limit the IDF's ability to realize the full benefit of the armaments it has developed. Finally, it has been argued that there is a drop in Israeli society's motivation to fight.

Main Armed Forces in the Region

Syria

Between August 1996 and early 1997, a high level of military tension marked Syrian-Israeli relations. In September 1996, Syria redeployed some of its forces in Lebanon, moving a reduced division of special forces from Beirut to the Lebanon-Syria border and an armored brigade and a mechanized brigade from Beirut to the Beka' Valley and the area west of it. All the indications suggest that this was a defensive deployment, apparently provoked by fear of an Israeli attack. However, the proximity of the Syrian special forces to Mt. Hermon aroused concern on the Israeli side about a limited Syrian initiative. Israel reacted by taking steps to raise its combat readiness, and these measures, in turn, further heightened Syrian fears. The tension peaked in October, when the Syrian Army carried out a divisional exercise with forces that increased Israeli fears. Public and secret messages passed between the two countries helped to lower the tension, but it rose again at the beginning of 1997, when the Syrians (mistakenly) concluded that Israel was calling up its reserves.

This episode illustrated the constant danger of deterioration in Israeli-Syrian relations, especially in conditions of political stalemate. It was a good example of how the other side's intentions are easily misread when there are no mechanisms, such as prior notification of troop movements or a ''hotline,'' to build confidence. The tension also exposed a series of strengths and weaknesses in the Syrian Army (as well as in the IDF) and served as a catalyst for corrective measures during 1997.

During the period under review, the Syrians placed special emphasis on improving their serviceability and combat readiness.

The Syrian Army is equipped with very large quantities of obsolete weapons, some from before the 1973 Yom Kippur War: its active orbat includes more than 3,500 tanks, about 5,000 APCs and armored cars, more than 3,000 artillery tubes and mortars, thousands of anti-tank missiles and antiaircraft guns, hundreds of surface-to-air missile launchers, and more than 500 combat planes. Given the budget constraints, it is difficult for Syria to maintain and service these huge quantities, supply spare parts, and preserve reasonable levels of ammunition stocks – in a word, to maintain minimal combat readiness. It is difficult to estimate how successful Syria has been. In the air force, the readiness level appears to be quite low. In any case, in his Order of the Day on the occasion of Syrian Army Day on 1 August 1997, Chief-of-Staff Hikmat Shihabi declared that the top priority was to raise the army's fitness and readiness.

Training represents another priority. The severe financial problems of the Syrian Army have not affected the scope of its training and instruction programs. In 1996, these focused on progress in surprise offensive operations aimed at conquering all or part of the Golan Heights, or limited targets on the Golan. It is not clear whether the Syrians actually believe that they can achieve surprise, but one scenario frequently raised involves a limited attack, followed by a switch to defense, deterrence of Israel with strategic weapons, and the initiation of a political process from a position of strength. This scenario is based on the assumption that the Syrians recognize both their own limitations and the advantages of the IDF: Syria has a weak air force and outdated air defense, whereas the IDF has a very strong air force. A surprise attack on a limited target and a quick switch to defense would minimize Israel's advantages and Syria's limitations. In any event, 1997 was marked mainly by defensive exercises, and the Syrians generally give special attention to the defensive, including fortification and protection.

In building their force, the Syrians give priority to their strategic arm: long-range surface-to-surface missiles (SSMs) (18 Scud-B launchers, eight Scud-C launchers, 18 SS-21 launchers), and chemical weapons, including missile warheads. In the past two years, they have completed the local assembly of 80–90 Scud-C missiles, with parts received from North Korea, and the deep and massive fortification of Scud-C launchers in the center of Syria, including a network of tunnels connecting all the launcher- and missile-related sites. The SSMs, especially if armed with chemical warheads, undoubtedly represent Syria's response to Israel's strategic superiority and sensitivity to casualties, on the one hand, and a substitute for the inferior Syrian Air Force, on the other. However, it is not clear how the Syrians will use their missiles (if and when they do): to deter Israel from carrying out air strikes on targets deep inside Syria; to retaliate in case deterrence fails; to start a war; or some or all of the above.

There were no significant changes in the Syrian air, sea and ground orbat; Syrian procurement was limited and included no main weapon systems. There were many reports of a Syrian ''buildup'' that mentioned contracts for Mig-29 aircraft and SA-10 missiles, but nothing was actually done, primarily because of financial constraints and the fact that Syria has not yet solved the problem of its outstanding financial debts to Russia, estimated at $10 billion.

The most significant development in the ground forces was the upgrading of 200 old T-55 tanks in Ukraine. The last purchase of new tanks (700 improved T-72 tanks) took place in 1992–1993, and since then the Syrian Army has not acquired any new modern tanks. The decision to upgrade the T-55 tanks involves little cost and raises the question whether it is explained only by budgetary problems or whether it reflects a decision, in principle, not to buy any more main tank systems and to rely instead on upgrades. Whatever the answer, the Syrians will probably continue to upgrade their T-55 tanks and seek to compensate themselves with modern antitank missiles, which are relatively cheap.

At the end of 1997, the Syrian ground forces included the following main elements: three regular corps headquarters, seven regular armored divisions (each with a quadripartite structure), three regular mechanized divisions (each with a quadripartite structure), one regular division of special forces and eight independent commando groups, and one reserve armored division – for a total of twelve divisions, including one reserve. The active orbat contained more than 3,500 tanks, including 1,600 T-72s, with another 1,000 in storage. Three divisions were deployed opposite the Golan Heights, four in the Damascus area, three in central Syria, and two in Lebanon and along the Syrian-Lebanese border.

The Syrian Air Force and air defense have stagnated: weapons are in a very low state of readiness, training hours are few, the stocks of spare parts and ammunition are low. The main focus is on preserving what remains and extending the service-life of weapons and munitions. In accordance with what appears to be their order of priorities, the Syrians have started to upgrade their old SA-2/3 missile batteries. Given their emphasis on the strategic arm, it can be assumed that the Syrians will not be purchasing new planes in the near future. At the same time, it is entirely possible that they will eventually buy the SA-10 surface-to-air missile (also known as the SA-300). The Syrian Navy is practically falling apart and mothballing its ships.

Military contacts with Russia have increased, and delegations from the two countries exchanged visits. A trip by Syrian operators of SA-5 missiles to Russia in the summer of 1997 was especially noteworthy. The Syrians trained on Russian missiles and even did a live-fire exercise. This was the first trip of its kind by a Syrian military unit to Russia. Syrian security cooperation with Iran is also significant, especially in the field of SSMs and chemical weapons.

Against Israel, the Syrian Army has a good defensive capability, which relies on a very extensive system of fortifications, plenty of armored forces and a variety of weapons systems, and thoroughly exercised operational plans. Its offensive capability is less developed, and its air force is weak. It is maintaining and trying to upgrade its outdated and sometimes run-down equipment, but is not progressing in either quantitative or qualitative terms. The major stress is on the strategic arm, which further strengthens Syria's defensive capability and increases its attack options.

Jordan

The central event for the Jordanian Army was the arrival in late 1997 of four upgraded F-16s, part of a package of 16 leased aircraft (four F-16B and 12 F-16A) to be delivered during 1998. The aircraft are part of an American military aid package announced at the beginning of 1996, worth about $320 million, which also includes spare parts, auxiliary equipment, training, and other services worth $220 million. Jordan, for its part, is obliged to cover the cost – about $80 million – of preparing its air bases to absorb the aircraft. Jordan will also receive about $100 million worth of other equipment in drawdowns from American stocks: 50 M-60A3 tanks, 18 transport helicopters, and five transport airplanes.

This package does not come close to satisfying Jordanian needs. The Jordanian Army is equipped with obsolete, constantly deteriorating weapons and operates under stifling budgetary constraints. The American grant to Jordan in 1996 and 1997 remained at the same level as in previous years – $20 million a year – and only in 1998 will it rise to $45 million. Most of the grant is already tied up in preparing airfields to absorb the F-16s. But despite these constraints, the Jordanian Army manages to sustain the operational readiness of its weaponry. It continues to rely on career soldiers and officers and has extended the freeze on compulsory service. The few force-building steps it has taken include the replacement of the M-60A1 tanks with M-60A3s and the establishment of an overall command for special forces (a commando group, a paratroop group, and a special infantry brigade), with a focus on training the special forces with helicopters.

Most of the Jordanian Army's activities continued to be connected to internal and current security, with an emphasis on counterterrorism. In the domain of training, the most prominent developments were the joint exercises with the Americans: "Eagle Tiger" with the U.S. Air Force, in the spring of 1996, and the "Moonlight" series of exercises with the U.S. Marines, in the summers of 1996 and 1997.

But perhaps the greatest innovation was the significant deepening of defense-strategic cooperation with Israel. The relationship was expressed in strategic dialogue, intelligence cooperation, border defense (antiterrorism) cooperation, air and sea coordination, exchange visits by military delegations, visits of defense VIPs, coordination against terrorism, a joint naval exercise, etc. Israel even offered to upgrade the Jordanian F-16s and to provide a variety of other services related to aircraft maintenance and servicing. Before the peace treaty with Jordan, Israel had strenuously opposed every Jordanian request for F-16s, due to the danger of having advanced aircraft within several minutes' flying time of central Israel. But in a state of peace, when Jordanian territory is no longer a base for Arab forces operating against Israel, the presence of such aircraft in Jordan no longer presents the same direct dangers. Furthermore, it is doubtful whether the 16 planes will have any military significance with respect to Jordan's Arab neighbors – Syria, Iraq, and Saudi Arabia. What their arrival does represent is a qualitative step up for the Jordanian Air Force, which has a reputation for producing good pilots, and a threshold for the era of even more advanced aircraft. Of course, there is also an element of prestige in the introduction of advanced warplanes.

The Jordanians have requested another 24 warplanes, four Blackhawk helicopters, M-1A-1 tanks, improved Hawk missiles, and a long list of other items. The "traditional" Jordanian approach has been to submit inflated requests in the expectation of settling for less. It is therefore difficult to know when and to what extent the long-standing Jordanian request will be met. What is clear is that in 1998, the Jordanians will absorb the 12 F-16s already ordered, and they may receive additional M-60A3 tanks in order to continue replacing their M-60A1s. There may also be some slight improvement in the artillery deployment. Otherwise, no changes are expected in the Jordanian Army in the near future.

Iraq

The Iraqi Army has undergone greater turmoil in the past decade than any other in the region. From a force of 55 divisions at the end of the Iraq-Iran War in 1988, it grew to 68 divisions (some incomplete and with untrained personnel) on the eve of the invasion of Kuwait in 1990. It dropped to 27 divisions after the Gulf War, as the result of losses and disintegration during the war and an intentional policy to dismantle most of the infantry divisions. For the past seven years, it suffered from a total embargo on arms and ammunition. At the end of 1997, following the dismantling of additional infantry units, it had 23 divisions (six armored, four mechanized, 13 infantry), and 2,300 tanks (of which 700 were T-72s). In the army units, and especially in the air force, there is a continuous deterioration in operational readiness and technical serviceability of weapons; weapons complements are rarely full (and often fall 50% below standard), the standards are not uniform, and defections continue. This is an army with no answers, not even partial ones, to the threat of American forces, and there is serious doubt about its capacity to defend itself against Iran.

Despite its sorry state, the Iraqi Army continues to survive and to function operationally. This is explained by several factors:

- a special effort is made to maintain the operational readiness of the Republican Guard (six divisions – three armored, one mechanized, and two infantry);
- cannibalization of weapons, in addition to indigenous production of, inter alia, spare parts for T-72 tanks (conditional, of course, on the availability of raw materials), makes it possible to extend the service-life of main combat systems;
- the army is rich in experience and has always been known for its high-level logistics and its orderly staff work, drawing on British doctrine;

- the large number of tanks and AFV transporters continues to provide mobility within Iraq and outside it;
- the old array of SA-2/3 batteries has been upgraded.

The operational ability of the ground forces, within limits, was demonstrated in the summer of 1996, when Republican Guard armored divisions exploited intra-Kurdish fighting to take over the Kurdish city of Irbil. In response, the Americans launched dozens of cruise missiles on the Iraqi air defense array, hitting missile sites, radars, and command-and-control centers. The Iraqi divisions eventually withdrew, but control over Irbil and its surroundings remained in the hands of the central government. The ground forces have several missions: to protect the regime, to maintain an offensive capability against the Kurds in the north and the Shi'ite rebels in the south, and to protect the eastern border against Iran. Until now, they have proven that they can fulfill at least the first two missions.

On the other hand, the Iraqi Air Force and air defense are very weak, and helpless against the Americans. The Iraqi Air Force has about 310 combat planes (about half of them old Mig-21s). According to various assessments, only about 170–180 of the planes are fit for service, and they make up the active order-of-battle (orbat). As time passes, the number of planes in Iraq's active orbat will undoubtedly diminish (assuming the embargo will continue). The Iraqi air defenses did not manage to shoot down even a single American airplane. During the military tension between Iraq and the United States at the end of 1997, the Iraqis made a major effort to track the flight path of the American U-2 reconnaissance plane and to shoot it down, but they failed. Special stress is placed on maintaining Iraq's residual nuclear, biological and chemical (NBC) and SSM capability. Insofar as SSMs are concerned, it was estimated that Iraq has two Scud launchers and between 8 and 16 al-Hussein missiles, with a range of 500 kilometers. Moreover, the Iraqis are allowed to produce SSMs with a range of up to 150 kilometers. Iraq indeed produces such missiles (Ababil), and in the same factory it is also developing missile engines using both solid and liquid fuel. In this way, the Iraqis maintain their knowledge base for the production of long-range missiles. The assessment of UN inspectors is that if the sanctions and the embargo are removed or eased, the Iraqis will be able to begin serial production of long-range missiles within one year.

The Iraqi Army needs a general overhaul and modernization. And because Iraq has great financial potential, it is already the most appealing magnet for the global arms market. If the embargo is lifted or eased, the Iraq will almost certainly give priority to SSMs, the air force, and air defense.

Saudi Arabia

The years 1996 and 1997 were marked by the implementation of old procurement contracts. The introduction and integration of high-quality ground, air, and naval weapons made it possible to replace older systems. But no new units were added to the orbat, and ongoing Saudi efforts to increase the manpower complements of the army and the National Guard still did not meet with success.

The ground forces (three armored brigades, five mechanized brigades, one special forces brigade, and one Royal Guard brigade) absorbed about 300 M-1A-2 tanks and about 400 Bradley APCs, thereby completing a procurement deal signed following the Gulf War, and 52 M-577 command and signals APCs. As a result, Saudi Arabia now has three armored brigades equipped with the most advanced command vehicles, tanks, and APCs available anywhere in the world. Saudi Arabia's central problem is that these formations are not organized into divisional structures that can function as one large maneuver force. This significantly erodes the capabilities of the weapons systems, and it reflects Saudi Arabia's fundamental problem: the inability to recruit the manpower that would make it possible to enlarge the ground forces and create organizational force-multipliers for the high-quality weapons.

In the air force, which operates with centralized control, this problem hardly exists. The problem here is mainly one of technical personnel trained to maintain the platforms and all their support systems; in most cases, foreign companies and the manufacturers do this themselves.

The National Guard, which received about 260 Canadian LAV-25 armored cars in 1995 (part of a 1,200-vehicle deal), transformed one of its infantry brigades into a mechanized brigade. Its orbat now stands at three mechanized and five infantry brigades. But no new contracts for main weapons systems for the ground forces are known to have been signed in the period under review. It is particularly noteworthy that the Saudis ended up not buying the MLRS from the United States, despite the great interest they expressed in the system after the Gulf War and the relative ease with which they could get it.

The air force continued to absorb previously ordered equipment. By the end of 1997, the air force had received 23 F-15S aircraft (the less advanced Saudi version of the F-15E) out of a total of 72 ordered in 1992, which have been arriving at the rate of one per month since September 1995. It had also taken delivery of 25 Tornados, out of a total of 49 ordered, when Saudi Arabia exercised the option included in the 1988 al-Yamama-2 deal to purchase a second round of Tornados. The remaining aircraft are expected to arrive during 1998. Almost all 60 Hawk training aircraft from Britain were also absorbed. In the summer of 1996, the Saudis finished installing an air force command, control, and communications system worth $2.5 billion. No deals were signed in the domain of air defense, the backbone of which is 10 Patriot batteries and 16 improved Hawk batteries. During 1997, the Saudis did make an intensive effort to convince the Americans to sell them the advanced medium-range-air-to-air-missile (AMRAAM). This missile was not included with the F-15S planes now being delivered. For the time being, the Saudi requests have been denied. At the same time, the Saudis have begun to work on a plan to purchase 100 modern aircraft to replace 80 of their old F-5s. The current inclination is to purchase up-to-date F-16s, but an official request to the U.S. administration has not yet been made. As usual, the Saudis are delaying a formal request while threatening to purchase French or British planes. The anticipated scope of the purchase is $15 billion. In any case, it is clear that the main emphasis in 1998 will be on absorbing the F-15S and the Tornado attack aircraft.

The Saudi Navy has absorbed another French F-200 missile frigate (while two other French Lafayette-class frigates are expected to arrive in 1998) and three British mine sweepers. It is now the largest and most advanced navy in the Persian Gulf. Its worst enemy is the Iranian submarines.

In recent years, the Saudi Army has grown in size and improved the quality of its weapons, but it has failed in its plan for the year 2000 – to significantly increase the size of the volunteer force – given the traditional aversion to compulsory conscription (which stems from fear of instability and opposition from the religious and from the tribes). The target was a manpower complement of 120,000 in the army (there are now about 100,000 troops) and 80,000 in the National Guard (which today numbers about 55,000). The target date for reaching these goals has now been postponed to 2005.

In the spring of 1997, the Saudis opened a factory in Dammam to produce wheeled APCs. The plan was to manufacture 50 APCs in 1997 and 150 in 1998. This is the first factory for major weapons systems in Saudi Arabia (although there is local production of small-arms ammunition and a variety of electronic parts). For years there have been various plans for local production (of artillery, tank gun barrels, etc.), but none of them materialized. Moreover, even the most routine aircraft maintenance is still done by the foreign manufacturers. This has a negative effect in times of war or severe military tension, since at least some of the foreign employees are liable to leave. There are Saudi plans for self-maintenance, but these have not yet been realized, and it is doubtful whether they will be in the foreseeable future.

Joint exercises with the Americans and the Egyptians are the most prominent features of the Saudi training program. In general, military cooperation between Saudi Arabia and Egypt has grown stronger in recent years. This is expressed not only in joint exercises, but also in the frequent exchanges of delegations and the presence of Egyptian military advisers in the Saudi armed forces.

All in all, the Saudi Army is slowly but steadily growing stronger. It is the largest buyer of arms in the region – $9 billion worth in 1996. Its air, sea, and ground forces are equipped with the highest-quality arms in the world. Its main strengths lie in its advanced air force and its large and high-quality fleet. Its weakness lies in the limited manpower it can mobilize, in its dependence on foreign elements to maintain its weapons systems, especially in the air, and in the structure of its armored and mechanized maneuver formations, which does not allow it to make the optimal use of its weapons.

In the Persian Gulf military balance, the Saudi Air Force and Navy have a clear advantage over Iraq and a good capability to cope with the forces of Iran.

Iran

Iran's main priorities are its weapons of mass destruction (WMD) programs and its SSMs. Insofar as missiles are concerned, the focus is on developing a long-range capability, primarily with the assistance of various Russian factors. The main project is known as Shihab-3. It is apparently based on North Korean No Dong technology, i.e., a missile with a range of 1,300 kilometers and warhead weighing about one ton. The missile's engine has undergone several tests, the last of which was at the end of 1997. According to most estimates, the missile will be ready for production within two to three years, at the most. At the same time, the Iranians are known to be developing another missile, the Shihab-4, which is based on the Russian SS-4 missile and will have an even longer range.

These projects are a major national priority and operate with no financial constraints. Nor is Iran deterred from pursuing them by political and economic pressures. If the Iranians succeed in developing and producing the Shihab-3, they will be able to threaten Israel, parts of Egypt, most of the Arabian Peninsula, and all of eastern and central Turkey. Iran also has the capacity to build shorter-range Scud B/C missiles, as well as CSS-8, a mobile Chinese missile with a range of 150 kilometers. Iran also manufactures solid-and liquid-fuel rockets with ranges of 150 and 200 kilometers. At this stage, the entire force of missiles (16 launchers of CSS-8s and 12 launchers of Scud-Bs) and rockets is mobile, which increases their survivability. At the end of 1997, the total number of missiles was estimated at about 600 (about 220 CSS-8s, 300 Scud-Bs, and 100 Scud-Cs).

Iran's navy also receives high priority. The third Russian "Kilo-class" submarine arrived in early 1997 and was absorbed over the course of the year. Forty C-802 sea-to-sea missiles, with a 45-mile range, were purchased from China and deployed on about 20 Chinese-made missile boats in the Iranian fleet (half with the Revolutionary Guard). Many naval exercises were held. The largest, which was given full publicity, was carried out in April 1997 with the participation of ground forces and the Revolutionary Guard. With three submarines, three missile frigates, two destroyers, 20 missile boats, and a variety of auxiliary ships, this is a navy to be reckoned with.

The ground forces are at the bottom of Iran's order of priorities. There were no changes and no purchases of new main weapons systems in the period under review. On paper, the army has an impressive orbat – four armored divisions and seven infantry divisions – while the Revolutionary Guard has two armored divisions and 12 infantry divisions. But this entire orbat has no more than 1,500 tanks, of which 200–300 are T-72s. The gaps between standard and actual complements are immense; in many units, they exceed 50 percent. The Revolutionary Guard still enjoys preferential treatment, but the tension that once existed between it and the army has declined in recent years.

Like the army, the air force has signed no new deals since the purchase of two squadrons of Mig-29s and Sukhoi-24s in 1992. In 1996 an earlier deal with China for the purchase 10 F-7s was carried out. The Iranians have apparently decided, in principle, not to buy new planes in the foreseeable future, but instead to start using the Iraqi aircraft flown to Iran during the war in 1991. They started by putting into service a squadron of Sukhoi-24s and a squadron of Mig-29s, and they are now doing the same with two squadrons (24 planes) of Mirage F-1s.

No new air defense deals were contracted either. But here, as opposed to the situation in the air force, the Iranians are looking to purchase advanced systems. Their intention is to purchase the improved Russian SA-10 (with a range of 140 kilometers, compared with the 70-kilometer range of the older model). Talks are being held with the Russians, who for now are hesitating to supply the improved model, perhaps as a result of American pressure.

In general, Russia and China have been Iran's main suppliers since the early 1990s, and it is financial constraints that prevent Iran from signing huge deals with them. At the same time, the Iranians are investing much effort in the local military industry (in addition to the whole missile array). They are producing munitions, second-generation tactical operational warfare missiles, 122mm and 155mm self-propelled guns (though it is not clear that serial production of the 155mm has begun), and they have even begun testing an unmanned aerial vehicle (UAV). In the summer of 1997 they inaugurated the first stage of a project to manufacture tanks containing T-72 components. They have an assembly line for T-62 tanks and BMP-2 APCs.

All in all, Iran gives priority to its strategic array. After that comes the navy, probably because of the perception that this is the best conventional arm for projecting influence in the Persian Gulf. In the air force, the emphasis is on putting into service the Iraqi aircraft, most of which are long-range attack craft, presumably because it is felt that these complement and back up the navy in its mission of projecting influence in the Gulf. For the time being, the ground forces are being neglected. This suggests that Iran is not preparing for a ground war against Iraq in the foreseeable future.

In terms of the overall balance of forces, Iran has a sea and air advantage and very good ground defense capabilities against Iraq. But its offensive capacity is low. Against Saudi Arabia, Iran is slightly inferior in air and naval capabilities.

Egypt

Egypt today has the largest and best air, sea, and ground forces in the Arab world, and they will continue to improve in the future. Egypt also has good nonconventional capabilities, but it does not invest too much effort in that area, because they are not at the top of Egypt's priorities. Nor does Egypt invest much effort in long-range SSMs. Instead, Egypt gives priority to its conventional forces, including the air force.

In 1996 the Egyptian Air Force completed the absorption of the fourth round of F-16 deals, and it now has 160 units, 50 F-16A/Bs with improved engines, and the rest F-16C/Ds. In the summer of 1996, Egypt announced a new deal for another 21 F-16C/Ds, to be delivered by 1999. The Egyptian Air Force will then have 181 high-quality American aircraft and another 17 high-quality French Mirage 2000Cs, already part of Egypt's orbat. The Egyptians have also bought large quantities of advanced American aerial munitions and auxiliary systems. However, their request to purchase the most advanced AMRAAM missile has thus far been rejected.

No less important than the advanced equipment are the qualitative improvement in the Egyptian concept for using airpower and the ongoing internalization of Western combat doctrine. This is expressed, inter alia, in greater freedom for pilots to act independently of ground control centers, in attack and bombing techniques, in electronic counterwarfare, and in a series of long-range navigation and interception methods. All these are "brushed up" in continuing exercises with the U.S., British, Italian, and French Air Forces. Moreover, the Egyptian Air Force can train more realistically against Israel by using its F-16s to simulate Israeli aircraft in exercises. In this context, it is noteworthy that the Egyptians, in previous exercises, did not refer to the "Israeli enemy," but rather to some generic adversary, but that exercises during the past two years have made explicit public reference to Israel as the enemy in the "scenario" of the exercises (see Exercise Badr-2, below).

Egypt currently has 36 advanced Apache-A helicopters. In the past two years the Egyptians have frequently talked with the American administration about procuring another 12 Apaches – the improved D model, equipped with a Long Bow radar that can locate both ground and air targets. Moreover, the Egyptians intend to upgrade all their current Apaches to Apache-Ds. Thus far, the Americans have not acceded to the Egyptian request; if they do, Egypt will have two brigades of ultramodern attack helicopters, 24 per brigade.

In the fall of 1997, Egypt also began to take delivery of Super Seasprites, a maritime helicopter primarily designated for antisubmarine warfare but capable of a variety of other missions, including patrol, search and rescue, transport, and attack. Delivery of the 10 helicopters ordered will be completed in 1998. In addition, a deal was signed in the summer of 1997 for the purchase of four CH-47D Chinook heavy transport helicopters. These will join the 15 already in Egypt's orbat, and will increase the assault air-transport capability.

In the area of air defense, no new deals were carried out, but most of the array was and continues to be upgraded – all 12 Hawk batteries by the Americans, and the SA-2/3 batteries by the Russians. Until now, the Egyptians have not shown any particular interest in acquiring the Patriot, probably because they intend to rely on the Improved Hawk.

All in all, Egypt has good air capability, based on advanced aircraft and a sound operational concept, effective command, control, and communications systems, and a large array of modernized SAMs. All the systems are in a good state of readiness. One open question concerns the Egyptians' choice of follow-on equipment in the coming decade: a multipurpose, long-range attack aircraft (which Israel and Saudi Arabia have chosen), or an improved version of the F-16. The answer to that question also depends, of course, on the American attitude.

The Egyptian ground forces continue to undergo a process of gradual improvement in their ability to operate in depth over vast areas. They have received a variety of American equipment and weapons through drawdowns, including: munitions (artillery and small arms), command APCs, TOW under armor, recovery vehicles, artillery, etc. The armored forces also continue to absorb locally assembled/produced M-1A-1 tanks. Of the original deal covering 512 tanks, about 400 have already been absorbed into the orbat. Egypt is simultaneously converting M-60A1 tanks into M-60A3s and upgrading Russian T-62s. As a result, armored units are discarding old Russian T-54/55s, receiving more modern equipment, and building two elite divisions with M-1A-1s. Western-model tanks now make up about 70 percent of the active tank orbat. The mechanized brigades have begun to absorb about 600 new YPR-765 APCs from Holland; these are replacing older Russian vehicles. In terms of artillery, the Egyptians have introduced 24 SPH 122mm self-propelled guns produced by their own military industry. This is a Russian D-30 mounted on the chassis of an American M-109 self-propelled gun. The Egyptian military industry also started producing cluster munitions for its artillery. For some reason, the Egyptians did not purchase the American MLRS after the Gulf War in 1991. Now they have begun to inquire about the new Russian SMERCH rocket launcher with 12 barrels and a range of 70 kilometers (as opposed to the 30-kilometer range of the MLRS). The Egyptians have always placed special emphasis on antitank weaponry, and they are showing some interest in advanced Russian antitank missiles, known for their penetrating power, even of reactive armor. No deal has yet been announced. Meanwhile, during 1997, the Egyptian Army received 540 TOW-2 launchers, French Hot-3 missiles, and 1,000 Hellfire-2 laser-guided antitank missiles.

Egypt also persisted in its plans to build a long-range, deep-water navy. In 1997, it received two overhauled American frigates from drawdowns, renovated the four Chinese submarines in its possession, and ordered two Perry-class missile frigates from the United States. With a main-force orbat of eight missile frigates, 22 missile boats, four upgraded submarines, and a large number of support vessels, Egypt already has the largest and highest-quality navy in the Arab world. Nevertheless, it intends to enlarge this orbat by procuring more submarines, more advanced missile boats, and large quantities of Harpoon sea-to-sea missiles.

The most prominent development with regard to training was the concentrated series of exercises known as Badr-2, which took place in the summer of 1996 (Badr-1 was held in 1993). It included exercises with high-level formations and a command and staff exercise at the general staff level. The main outline of the exercise was as follows: the IDF initiates an attack on the Egyptian front, and the Egyptian Army, after a successful defensive battle, switches to a counterattack, takes over the Sinai Peninsula, and even crosses the international border at several points. This is actually the central motif of training in the Egyptian Army: counterattacking, taking over broad expanses in Sinai, and mounting in-depth attacks by the air force.

The army's main emphasis, reflected both in day-to-day activity and in public declarations, is on fitness and readiness. It is not clear whether this reflects a fear of regional destabilization, Egyptian intentions in the event of a military flare-up in the Syrian/Lebanese or Palestinian theaters, or some other particular expectation. But it is important to take note of the phenomenon, because it has no precedent since the Egyptian-Israeli Peace Treaty, not even during the Lebanon War. A second trend is the constant effort to enhance efficiency by streamlining, saving money wherever possible, and cutting manpower. According to various estimates, the Egyptian armed forces shrank from about 450,000 to about 415,000 during the period under review. The goal is apparently to continue cutting back until the force eliminates all the "fat" and reaches its optimal size – perhaps 350,000.

In all, this is a strong army, which has gradually but consistently changed the components of its power and improved their quality since the peace agreement with Israel. From armed forces consisting of an army that relied mainly on infantry, a weak air force, and an essentially defensive navy, the Egyptian armed forces now reflect an offensive orientation: the high-quality air force has the capacity to carry out in-depth attacks, the navy can operate over long distances in the open sea, and the armored forces have the mobility and logistics to fight in depth in the expanses of the Sinai Peninsula. The central point is that Egypt's offensive capability against Israel has significantly improved. Its main vulnerabilities are its financial constraints and the constant uncertainty about the $1.3 billion military grant from the United States.

Israel

Since the second half of 1996, there has been a fundamental change in the IDF's agenda, which has influenced its activity, its training, its procurement, and its concepts. As a result, the "Mirkam-2000" multiyear work plan, the preliminary version of which was elaborated in 1991 by Chief-of-Staff Ehud Barak and which was launched just at the beginning of 1996, has collapsed. There were three causes for the change: a change in intelligence assessments regarding Syria, cuts in the defense budget and other budgetary constraints, and a change of approach toward the Palestinian Authority and the possibility of a serious deterioration in relations with the Palestinians. Mirkam-2000's basic working assumption was that the chances of war with Syria, the main enemy, were very low. The practical meaning of this assumption was that the plan would emphasize a long-term buildup, building strength for the future, and not immediate and near-term fitness and readiness. This involved certain risks: less training, lower stocks, less ammunition, fewer spare parts, etc. But in the second half of 1996, there was a change in the basic assumption, since the assessment regarding Syria had changed and now determined that "the probability of war with Syria has risen." The assessment did not determine that war was imminent or that the

Syrians had decided on it, but it did emphasize that, in parallel with its continuing preference for the political process, Syria had also begun to prepare a military option.

Against this background, the IDF's priorities changed completely. The emphasis on long-term buildups was replaced by an emphasis on higher serviceability and readiness for war. More than NIS 1 billion intended for long-term procurement were diverted to this end. From autumn 1996 through 1997, the shift exposed the IDF's low state of readiness, a product of several years of neglect. The IDF continues to improve its readiness in 1998, but the imbalance between long-term preparations and short-term readiness is no longer as severe as it was in 1996 and 1997.

In addition to the changing assessment of the Syrian theater, the IDF was exposed to budgetary shifts. In the summer of 1996, the new Israeli government decided to cut the overall budget; the army's share in this cut was set at about NIS 750 million, followed by a further cut of more than NIS 200 million in the 1998 budget. The problem was further compounded by growing expenses in several spheres: unanticipated operational activities in Lebanon and in the territories, a rise in the cost of weapons and engine hours, the need to continue offering high wages to career military people in order to compete with the civilian market, a sharp rise in the invalid rehabilitation budget (from NIS 800 million in 1986 to NIS 2.2 billion in 1997), and the cancellation of traditional exemptions or substantial discounts in payments to civilian authorities (hospitals, municipalities, telephone company, transportation services, etc.). The IDF itself has publicly declared that it needs an additional NIS 1.5 billion a year for four years in order to carry out its missions – its 1998 budget was NIS 32 billion, including American aid. All this contributed to the collapse of Mirkam-2000.

Another factor was the bloody confrontation with the Palestinians in September 1996, following the opening of the Western Wall tunnel. The participation of Palestinian military forces brought home the realization that the IDF might again have to deal with live fire from the Palestinians or even confront situations in which it might have to take over towns under the jurisdiction of the Palestinian Authority. During 1997, the IDF formulated a variety of operational plans for a variety of situations (with code names such as "Blazing Steel" and "Thorn Field"). For these contingencies, forces had to be prepared with special equipment, exercises, training, operational concepts, intelligence, etc. Of course, all this required money, which added to the IDF's budgetary distress. One other factor influenced the security establishment, including the IDF, and contributed to the collapse of Mirkam-2000: the growing Iranian threat to produce long-range SSMs and weapons of mass destruction.

But despite the change or disruption of Mirkam-2000's component elements, the force-building emphases and objectives did not change in 1997. These continue to be:

- night and all-weather capability;
- precise destruction of targets;
- ability to operate in depth (operational and strategic); and
- reducing attrition rates on the battlefield.

The pursuit of these objectives is evident across a range of subjects and in all three service arms. The guiding principle of force construction is to preserve the power and number of formations in the orbat. The IDF is neither growing nor shrinking but new frameworks are replacing old ones (for example, an F-15I squadron in place of a Phantom squadron), and new weapons are replacing old ones. At the same time, sophisticated Israeli-developed weapons are entering service. All in all, there is a constant rise in quality.

There is also an emphasis on enlarging war stocks, especially artillery, tank, air force, and small arms munitions, as well as spare parts. This trend will continue in 1998, though at a slower pace than in 1997.

Training was generally neglected in recent years, either because of a conscious decision in favor of long-term buildups or because of the demands of current security. It received greater attention in 1997, expressed in more frequent retraining of reserve units, special exercises focused on the Palestinians, and more exercises of the orbat earmarked for the Syrian front.

Operational activity naturally focused on low-intensity warfare in south Lebanon. This refers to the struggle against trained and experienced Hizbullah guerrilla forces involved in a wide range of activities: attacking or shelling outposts, laying ambushes and setting roadside charges, and engaging in antitank fire. This confrontation is not a war of survival, but the IDF's goal is to gain a clear-cut and total victory in every encounter, with a minimal number of casualties. In pursuit of this goal, the IDF spares no expense to equip its forces with the best weapons, including special equipment that would normally be held back as a surprise in case of war. In general, and particularly in the territories, the IDF has tended to reduce the use of reservists in routine operational activity and to rely more on regular conscript forces. In the future, the intention is to set up special units of career service personnel, who will spend a few years in operational activity.

With respect to manpower, several points stand out. ''Expensive'' personnel – meaning career soldiers and civilian employees – have been cut. In some cases, recruits have filled their places. At the same time, the IDF faces a severe shortage of technically skilled recruits (e.g., mechanics, electricians), due to the declining number of vocational school graduates.

There has also been a variety of problems with reservists: about one-third of those subject, in principle, to reserve duty do not actually serve, for a number of reasons; the burden of reserve service is not equally divided; society seems not to appreciate those who are called up for reserve duty; combat reserves are called up often, etc. In 1997, several measures were taken to alleviate these problems. The Knesset passed a law significantly lowering – to 36 – the number of days per year reservists could be called up, setting the limit on operational activity by reservists at 25 days; establishing maximum ages for reserve duty, in general, and for combat reservists, in particular; and specifying a variety of financial compensations. The IDF also decided to grant more material benefits for reserves serving in combat units within battalions, especially for commanders. Finally, the total number of reserve duty days was decreased. By way of example, there were 10 million reserve duty days in 1990; in 1998 there will be only 5 million days.

The guiding principles of the ground forces are to upgrade and to introduce new systems in place of old ones. Thus Merkava-3s are replacing older tanks; the ''Doher'' self-propelled gun is replacing the M-109A1/2 ''Rohev''; Merkava-1 and Magah-7 tanks are being upgraded; antitank units have received the TOW-2A; a new ''Puma'' engineering AFV has entered operational service; and additional MLRS artillery systems have been integrated. Furthermore, a modern, computerized training facility for two-sided exercises is nearing completion.

At the beginning of 1998, the air force absorbed the first two of 25 F-15Is due to arrive during 1998 and 1999. The new F-15I squadron will replace a Phantom squadron to be taken out of service. The force is also absorbing 50 F-16A/Bs acquired from American drawdowns. In 1997, 15 Blackhawk transport helicopters were ordered, in addition to the 10 already in the orbat; these are expected to arrive during 1998. The air force is already beginning to consider the question of how to equip itself for the early years of the next century. Initial contacts have focused on two basic possibilities: another 20–40 F-15Is, or up to 70 improved F-16s.

Since the navy is already equipped with modern warships (Sa'ar 4.5 and Sa'ar 5), it is focusing on advanced munitions. The first of two Dolphin submarines being built in Germany will probably not arrive before early 1999. Panther intelligence helicopters have been integrated.

Iran's progress in developing the Shihab-3 long-range SSM has given added importance to the "Homa" (Wall) antiballistic missile program. In the period under review, there were several successful tests of the "Arrow" missile, the "Green Pine" acquisition and tracking radar, and the "Golden Citron" fire-control radar. However, the last "Arrow" test, in the summer of 1997, was a failure. Another test was scheduled for the spring of 1998. According to Israeli declarations, the first of two "Arrow" batteries was supposed to be deployed in 1998, but this target will probably not be met before 1999. Nevertheless, while the "Arrow" project was once subjected to considerable criticism by top echelons of the Israeli security establishment, including air force commanders, it now receives full support. The United States also continues to support the project and funds about 70% of the development costs. The Americans even agreed to provide $156 million for deployment of a third battery of "Arrow" missiles. Beyond "Homa," the IDF also deals with other defensive (protection, renewal of gas masks) and offensive (intelligence, air force, special forces) responses to the SSM threat.

In terms of overall Israeli deterrent power, strategic and defense cooperation with the United States is a major force multiplier, and this cooperation grew tighter in the period under review. For example, beyond its annual $1.8 billion military grant, the U.S. allocated funds to Israel for counterterrorism and for the "Arrow" missile; it raised the value of weapons and equipment prepositioned in Israel to about $300 million; a quick channel for sending emergency assistance ("Air Mark") was set up; Israel was connected directly to the "early warning system," thus increasing by several minutes its early warning of an SSM launch; a hotline between the U.S. Secretary of Defense and the Israeli Defense Minister was installed (and used during the Iraq crisis); and the U.S. and Israel were cooperating to develop the Nautilus, a system of powerful laser beams intended, in the first instance, to neutralize the threat of Hizbullah rocket attacks on towns in northern Galilee.

Two other cooperative relations were particularly noteworthy in the period under review. The first was between Israel and Turkey, which formally began in February 1996 with the signing of a military training and cooperation agreement. The agreement applied to all branches of the armed forces, but special stress was placed on the air forces: the Israeli Air Force now trains in Turkey and the Turkish Air Force in Israel. Cooperation reached a new peak in early 1998, in the form of a joint naval exercise in which U.S. forces also took part. The second relationship was with Jordan, and its prominence is due to the fact that Jordan is the first Arab state to cooperate publicly with Israel.

In early 1998, the IDF was fully engaged in a process of qualitative improvement in all branches, while trying to preserve the existing frameworks and to cope with a number of problems. The first of these was its financial constraints, stemming from budget cutbacks, rising maintenance and procurement costs, and unanticipated operational activities. The second was long-range threats, such as from Iran, that necessitate investment of resources and the formulation of appropriate responses. Third, the upgrading dimension of force construction was going to take a very long time. The IDF's infrastructure – buildings, vehicles, radios, and various other equipment – is all obsolete, and if it is not refurbished, it will eventually collapse. Fourth, stocks were still too low. Finally, the status of the IDF in Israeli society has deteriorated, and questions have been raised about its fitness and readiness, partly because of some operational failures in the period under review (the worst being the helicopter crash in early 1997, in which 73 soldiers died).

Following the collapse of the Mirkam-2000 program, the IDF is working on a new multiyear plan – "Idan 2003" – to be launched in 1999. This plan is supposed to provide solutions for the IDF's current problems, but its primary objective is to look ahead five to ten years and determine the order-of-battle, structure, weapons systems, and operational concepts the IDF will need in light of the technological possibilities and the geopolitical environment.

On balance, a variety of force-multipliers (air and naval PGMs and sophisticated ground weapons, intelligence, command and control) enabled the IDF to improve its capability against the regular armies it might face. Its ability to cope more efficiently with a variety of possible confrontations in the Palestinian arena was considerably better in 1997 than it had been in 1996. Whether this improvement (the importance of which cannot be doubted) damaged the ground forces' readiness to deal with regular armies in the region remains an open question.

Future Trends

Given the virtual freeze in the buildup of conventional forces, and on the assumption that the sanctions on Iraq will not be lifted, the most important development will certainly be Iran's development of long-range SSMs, particularly the "Shihab-3." Given Iran's slow but perceptible progress in acquiring nuclear capabilities and its existing chemical capabilities, success in the development and production of 1,300-plus-kilometer range missiles will have strategic repercussions in the region and beyond. Syria already has the ability to manufacture Scud-C missiles, but this is not yet reflected in an enlarged orbat of missile units and numbers. The reasons for this remain somewhat obscure.

The general trend in the region is one of qualitative improvement, not quantitative expansion. None of the main armies in the Middle East has added large, new formations to its orbat. This trend will probably continue, since financial constraints will prevent uncontrolled growth, except in the wealthy oil-exporting states. On the other hand, advanced technologies will continue to tempt the armies of the region. Saudi Arabia and Egypt, for example, can be expected to acquire AMRAAM missiles, and the Egyptians will probably procure the advanced Long Bow Apache helicopter. Russia, for its part, will probably supply Iran, Syria, or Egypt with third-generation laser-guided antitank missiles and advanced long-range SMERCH rocket launchers.

Contracts signed in the past will be implemented over the next few years. In 1998, Jordan will receive the balance of the 16 F-16s it ordered, Egypt will take delivery of another 21 F-16C/Ds and will absorb two more missile frigates, Israel will receive all of its F-15Is as well as 15 Black Hawk helicopters, and Saudi Arabia will continue absorbing its F-15S and Tornado attack aircraft.

In addition, Russia is expected to sell SA-10 surface-to-air missiles to Iran. It is not clear if these are the new SA-10s with a range of 140 kilometers, which the Russians have thus far refused to supply, or the old SA-10s, with a range of 70 kilometers. There will probably also be an SA-10 deal between Russia and Syria, which has been under discussion since 1991. It seems reasonable to assume that the Russians have thus far refused Syrian requests, but that Syria will persist because it believes that an advanced surface-to-air missile will complement its SSM threat in the sense that it would complicate Israeli Air Force efforts to attack SSM sites and related targets deep inside Syria, especially if the missiles were launched against Israel.

Among the armed forces of the region, the Egyptian Army and the IDF stand out in terms of their quality and operational level. Both benefit from U.S. military aid and advanced American armament. Israel has a great advantage because of its ability to develop and manufacture weapons and munitions using the most advanced technologies, but financial constraints prevent it from producing large quantities of these systems. The Syrian Army is more or less stagnant in terms of qualitative improvement, but it has lots of ground formations, good defensive capability, and a long-range strategic arm able to carry chemical warheads. The Iraqi Army has the largest potential to leap forward in conventional and nonconventional power, but that can happen only if the sanctions on it are eliminated or eased.

In assessing the balance between the IDF and other armies in the region, four points are worth mentioning:

- There is a view that Israel is gradually losing its qualitative edge, both because of improvements in the Arab armies and because of negative developments in the IDF and in Israeli society at large. But there is a different view, which argues that the qualitative gap is actually increasing, because as war becomes more technological, Israel's overall advantage in knowledge, human resources, and production capacities becomes more relevant.
- In any event, Arab states are aware of the IDF's strength.
- Jordan has ceased to be a platform for Arab expeditionary forces. Consequently, the term "Eastern Front" no longer has any strategic-military meaning.
- The threat to Israel's rear-area, which emerged during the Gulf War in 1991, has intensified.

The Israeli-Arab balance of military threats can be summarized as follows:

- If Egypt joined in a war against Israel, it would constitute the most serious Arab military threat – on land, at sea, and in the air.
- As long as Syria is not at peace with Israel, it poses a constant threat, both on the ground (primarily that of a sudden, limited land-grab on the Golan Heights, followed by a shift to the defensive), and in the air (meaning a missile strike at the Israeli rear, with either conventional or nonconventional weapons).
- Iran currently poses no conventional threat to Israel; the limited expeditionary force it might send to an active war front would have no military significance. But when it completes development and begins production of long-range SSMs, it will, at least initially, possess a conventional threat capability.
- Iraq has a minimal nonconventional threat capability. Theoretically, it could contribute an expeditionary force of two to three armored/mechanized divisions to an Arab coalition, but not under current circumstances.
- Jordan's F-16s might be significant in times of tension between Israel and Iraq, because they could threaten Israeli aircraft flying to Iraq. If Jordan were actively to join a war coalition, these aircraft would pose a clear threat to various targets in Israel.
- The Saudi Air Force could pose a threat to the Israeli Air Force in wartime if it were integrated into an Arab offensive.

3. Subnational Conflicts in the Middle East

Anat Kurz

This review of subnational conflicts in the Middle East is divided into two sections. The first focuses on the major manifestation of domestic conflict in the region – the interaction between Islamic themes and popular protest – in the Maghreb, Egypt, Jordan, and the Gulf Cooperation Council (GCC) states.[1] The second deals with the war in Kurdistan. Because the international aspects of this conflict overshadow its domestic implications, the issue is surveyed from a regional perspective.

The reason for this distinction is that subnational Islamic forces challenge the legitimacy of regimes, while nationalist struggles challenge the legitimacy and integrity of the state itself. Notwithstanding this basic difference, the various subnational conflicts share several significant features: all involve domestic power struggles that threaten existing state-systems, and all reflect – and often exacerbate – the vulnerabilities of the social and political frameworks in which they are carried out.

The Islamic Subnational Challenge

More than in any other region of the world, the politicization of religion has been perceived as a major destabilizing force in the Middle East. Since the early 1980s, the call of Islam has become the most popular expression of social and political protest. The Islamic impulse stems from core demographic, social, and economic crises common to the majority of Middle Eastern states. Throughout the modern history of the Arab nation-state, these interrelated dilemmas have undermined the perceived ability of dominant state-systems to cope with popular unrest. The challenges facing the state-systems have been widely interpreted as consequences of the influence of foreign, essentially Western, ideologies on regime policies, in both the domestic and the international spheres. Indeed, the secular nation-state has itself been the core of many grievances and the focus of tension between the ruling regimes and traditionally oriented pub-

---

The author would like to acknowledge the research assistance provided by Ori Slonim, JCSS Project on Terrorism and Low Intensity Warfare.

lics. In the early 1980s, the legitimacy of the state was increasingly challenged by Islamic militants who espoused a better, more just social order, and who sometimes promoted that vision through violent confrontation with the regime, often in the hope of provoking a harsh reaction.

But beyond these commonalities, the specific character of the Islamic challenge has been determined by cultural, historical, and political features unique to each state. In other words, the Islamic movement is not monolithic, but is rather marked by considerable diversity in the way it translates religious idioms into political activism and in the organizational forms it assumes. This diversity reflects the varied political structures and socioeconomic conditions across the Middle East. It also explains the different approaches adopted by different regimes in dealing with the challenge, which in turn generate different dynamics of confrontation.

The Islamic Challenge in the Maghreb

The Algerian crisis is the most acute subnational conflict in the Maghreb, indeed, in the entire Middle East region. Since the late 1980s, Algeria has undergone a process of social and political disintegration; since 1992 this process has been transformed into a bloody civil war. By the end of 1997, between 60,000 and 100,000 civilians and security personnel had died in clashes between security forces and Islamic militiamen and in attacks perpetrated by Islamic rebels against civilian targets.

The Algerian elections of 1991 were a symbolic culmination of the process of limited liberalization permitted by the regime in the late 1980s in response to growing social and political unrest. They were intended to reinforce support for the government. Instead, they provided an opportunity for the Islamic opposition to capitalize on the deep resentment of the regime, on the fragile base of the newly introduced democratic system, and on the Islamic identification of the Algerian society. When the Islamic Salvation Front (FIS) took a large percentage of the votes in the first round, the second round was canceled. The army took power, banned the FIS, jailed or exiled the Islamic leadership, and forced its members underground.

Since then, military rule has delineated the boundaries between two clashing orientations in Algerian society. One is that of the military, economic, and political elite; the other is that of the masses – remote from the centers of power and strongly influenced by values identified with the message of Islam.[2] The military and legal measures taken by the regime were intended to frustrate the FIS's claim to power, arguably in order to preserve Algerian democracy. Their effect, however, was to provoke a fierce struggle by radical Islamic forces determined to further delegitimize the government by confronting it directly and provoking indiscriminate reprisals.

The FIS incorporates several groupings that adhere to different, sometimes contradictory policies and methods of action. The differences within the FIS, and between it and other opposition organizations, have dramatically sharpened in the course of the war. The FIS has become a mainstream opposition, occasionally calling for national dialogue. The violent struggle has been led by the Islamic Salvation Army (AIS), the military arm of the FIS, and especially by the Islamic Armed Group (GIA), which split from the FIS following attempts by the FIS leadership to exercise control over the AIS. Both the AIS and the GIA oppose any attempt to negotiate a settlement of the conflict, and they have been the principal perpetrators of the brutal killing, which has escalated steadily since 1993. Their targets have been villages and villagers, civilians in urban centers, politicians – representatives of the regime – and intellectuals – the perceived symbols of Western influence. By 1997, the total number of militiamen was 10,000.[3]

In September 1996, Liamine Zeroual, a former general who was elected President in November 1995, convened a "National Conference of Understanding," in which trade union and political leaders drew up a pact to launch a national dialogue. Among the participants were leaders of the legal, essentially moderate Islamic parties, Hamas and Ennahda. The pact was presented as the beginning of a "new era," because it rejected violence and called for national conciliation. But it was interpreted as a means to strengthen the position of the President and the army, since the elimination of religious premises from all party platforms was a precondition for their participation in the dialogue. This conference was part of a campaign by Zeroual in advance of a referendum on a new constitution that outlawed parties based on religion or language; this practically reversed the 1989 constitution, which allowed for the participation of Islamic forces in the political process. The referendum was held in late November 1996, against the backdrop of rising violence on the part of Islamic rebels and massive offensives by the army against their strongholds. As expected, the reform was approved.

The legal ban on negotiations between the government and

the opposition was not denounced by any foreign power. The international response was confined to denunciation of the killing, mainly in reference to rebel atrocities. The United States administration ignored calls by the FIS's leadership-in-exile to intervene and put an end to the war. As the western European state most concerned about the possibility of a massive flow of refugees from Algeria across the Mediterranean, France declared a policy of noninterference in internal Algerian domestic affairs, while maintaining its economic relations with the government. This position made it a target for terrorist attacks by Islamic activists. Following the 1996 referendum, the GIA threatened to continue the violent campaign it had been waging against civilian targets in France since 1994, in order to secure the release of Islamic extremists held in French jails and to halt the economic and military aid provided to Algeria by the Chirac government.[4] In December 1996, a Paris metro station was hit by a bomb presumably planted by Islamic extremists.

Domestic violence reached new peaks in early 1997, during the month of Ramadan, which the GIA declared "the month of *Jihad*." Among the targets of this violence were schools and pupils. The intensified violence provoked criticism on the part of the GIA's allies, Egyptian and Libyan Islamic groups, who decided to withdraw their support. The army intensified its crackdown on the rebels and launched new offensives against their strongholds in the northern provinces. Meanwhile, popular support for the rebels appeared to have fallen, reflecting popular revulsion at the killing and the country's economic deterioration.

On 5 June 1997, elections for the national assembly were held for the first time since early 1992. Thirty-nine parties participated in what might have been a democratic process, had the Islamic forces not been banned. Zeroual's National Democratic Movement won 150 of the 380 seats.[5] In October 1997, candidates affiliated with the ruling party also won the majority of the positions in the elections for local councils. In both cases, opposition elements claimed that election results, as well as estimates of public participation in the voting, were falsified.

Assaults against remote villages, in which dozens and even hundreds of people were slain, became more frequent toward the end of the year. At the same time, the rebels refrained from directly confronting the army or attacking strategic facilities such as oil fields and ports. This suggests that the military had regained the upper hand, an assessment reinforced by the unilateral declaration of a cease-fire by the FIS in early October 1997. This declaration had no effect on developments on the ground; it reflected FIS criticism of the GIA and of the mounting violence for which the latter was responsible.

In the summer of 1997, the FIS, other Algerian opposition leaders, and international human rights organizations began to accuse elements associated with the security forces of involvement in the massacres. These allegations, which were strongly denied by the authorities, were primarily based on the fact that several assaults had taken place not far from army garrisons and that soldiers arrived on the scene only after the attackers had left. The fact that villages sympathetic to the rebels were also attacked lent some credence to these suspicions. Arguably, the brutal assaults of the villages and the massacres were intended to frustrate any possibility of embarking on a national dialogue that would include the political leadership of the FIS, and also reflected disputes within the security forces over this issue.

In early 1998, there was another upsurge of violence – again during the month of Ramadan – and another round of allegations that the security forces were at least partially involved in the atrocities. This weakened the case for noninterference by the international community, and demands to investigate the killings began to be heard in western Europe and in the United States. An international inquiry might be the only feasible middle ground between the demands to pressure the government into negotiations with the rebels and the demand to assist it in its war against terrorism. It would also accommodate both the concern for European and American economic interests in Algeria and the risk that Algerian terrorism would spill over into the international sphere in retaliation for measures to strengthen the regime. It was clear, however, that an end to the war would have to originate from within Algeria, and that it would have to be promoted by means other than military ones. But in early 1998, the prospect of a dialogue between the government and the militant Islamic opposition, however remote, was a challenge that extremists on both sides were determined to forestall.

The case of Algeria constitutes a constant warning for the regimes of its neighbors, Tunisia and Morocco. The search for an alternative to nationalism as the focus of collective identity has intensified in these countries, fueled by worsening economic conditions that generated riots in the 1970s and 1980s in Morocco, and during the 1980s in Tunisia. The reaction of the authorities to the riots included political and economic reforms, as well as a crackdown on Islamic militants. While not eliminating sporadic terrorism or sources of future unrest, these measures have thus far restrained potentially destabilizing forces.[6]

Firmly denouncing the Algerian mass killings, Tunisian President Zine El Abidine Ben Ali stated, "The phenomenon of fundamentalism was rooted out of the political scene in Tunisia thanks . . . to special merits of ours that go by the names of openness, of tolerance, of social justice . . . In addition, there are deep-seated reforms that have borne fruit in the fields of . . . social solidarity."[7] These reforms, however, were accompanied by firm measures against Islamic political activism. The main Islamic opposition movement, Hizb al-Nahda, was banned, and its leaders were forced into exile.

Morocco has also succeeded in keeping the Islamic trend under control, partly due to security measures, but primarily through the integration of Islam into the monarchy's base of legitimacy. The political process was liberalized, and a two-chamber parliamentary system was established. Elections for both chambers, which have the power to topple the government in a no-confidence vote, were held in November and December 1997. Reform is nevertheless tightly controlled, relying on traditional political and economic elites.

Twice during the period under review, Tunisia hosted a conference of Arab interior ministers that dealt with the issue of terrorism, "particularly that linked to the violence of Islamic groups."[8] Morocco also attended the conferences. The participants expressed concern over the influence of the Algerian crisis on their domestic opposition forces, yet their official statements emphasized the "terrorist" dimension of the war, bypassing the linkage between violence and the economic and social sources of protest. Since both Tunisia and Morocco have been undergoing the destabilizing process of adapting their economy to Western demands, they may well be facing challenges greater than the ones usually associated with terrorism.

The Algerian crisis has become a factor in the regional framework of interstate relations. Border disputes have strained relations among states in the Maghreb since they gained national independence. But during the Algerian civil war, mutual threat perceptions have eased, not only because of the preoccupation of the Algerian regime and army with internal affairs, but also because of the common concern over the actual and potential Islamic upsurge in the region. Relations between Rabat and Algiers have been influenced by Algeria's opposition to Morocco's annexation of Western Sahara and its assistance to Polisario, the organization fighting for Western Saharan independence. The Islamic challenge has somewhat defused the tension between these two states, although the rifts remained unsettled. Official Moroccan statements have reflected some degree of tolerance for the FIS, and the FIS, for its part, has declared its support for a resolution of the Western Saharan conflict through the establishment of a local Islamic government that would recognize its Algerian nationality. The preoccupation of the Algerian Army with the civil war has also eased Tunisian concerns about external threats. Tunisia's major current concern is with Libyan and Algerian Islamist backing for its own Islamic opposition.[9]

The Case of Egypt

The recent Islamic upsurge in Egypt, which dates back to 1992, is the culmination of a multifaceted crisis. Though rooted in the specific Egyptian history of confrontations between the state and various Islamist movements, its immediate determinants have been the same economic and demographic dilemmas that have polarized many Middle Eastern societies: high birth rates and economic liberalization policies (begun by Sadat) increased both income gaps and unemployment. Protest against the ruling National Democratic Party (NDP) has also focused on its corrupt and inefficient administration. It has been further inflamed by foreign policies, specifically, the conciliation with Israel and Egypt's participation in the U.S.-led coalition against Iraq. These are seen as proof of the regime's self-abasement vis-à-vis the West.[10]

The limits set by the NDP on the participation of the Muslim Brotherhood in the 1990 parliamentary elections encouraged the transformation of popular Islam into a political movement focused on mobilizing the underprivileged sectors of the society. The steps taken against the Brotherhood were accompanied by crackdowns on the infrastructure of the more radical factions – Tanzim al-Gihad (the Jihad Organization), which concentrates on the armed struggle, al-Gama'a al-Islamiyya (the Islamic Group), which pursues both social activism and political violence, and other, smaller associations, all determined to topple the regime by force. These actions seemed to complement the Algerian regime's neutralization of the FIS's electoral achievements and further reinforced the radicals' conviction that the road to a Shari'a state could be paved only by jihad.[11]

The war waged by radical Islamists dealt a heavy blow to Egypt's economy. It directly targeted the tourism industry, and it precipitated a vicious cycle of terrorism and counterterrorism, involving widespread abuses and violations of human rights: hundreds of suspects were tried by military courts, and legal measures were enacted permitting the execution of convicted terrorists as well as members of violent groups.[12] The authorities also resorted to measures of collective punishment, including curfews on problematic neighborhoods and villages during searches for terrorists' hideouts. Repression was complemented by the regime's attempts to compete with Islamic militants for the hearts and minds of the people, through a government-controlled public discussion of moderate Islamic values and promises to improve the infrastructure and services in the poverty-stricken areas of Upper Egypt and the densely populated neighborhoods of Cairo. The regime also tried to cut off external channels of support for the Islamic groups, mainly by mobilizing inter-Arab cooperation against the main sponsors, Iran and Sudan, but it achieved little more than bilateral coordination with some Arab and non-Arab governments.

In 1994, the situation appeared to be stabilizing. The security forces managed to frustrate numerous terrorist schemes, and the number of casualties from terrorism-related incidents among civilians and the security forces steadily decreased. The rebels were driven away from the Cairo area, and their activities were mainly confined to the southern and central regions of the country, where sporadic attacks against policemen and Copts took place. During 1996, there were even signs of recovery in the tourism industry. In short, a popular insurrection was prevented, and the state system was preserved.

However, the government's suppressive measures provoked intraorganizational divisions at the extreme of the Islamic spectrum and, in the case of al-Gama'a, an even greater inclination to violence. Gama'a had largely refrained from mass killings, leaving this sphere of action to al-Jihad, but in recent years it has become increasingly involved in spectacular operations of this sort. Indeed, al-Gama'a operatives have been responsible for most of major attacks since late 1995, including the abortive attempt on the life of President Husni Mubarak in Addis Ababa, in July 1995, an attack on a group of Greek tourists (apparently mistaken for Israelis) near Giza, in April 1996, the detonation of a car bomb next to a tourist bus in the center of Cairo, in September 1997, and the capture and execution of passengers thought to be working for the police near Minya, in October 1997. In November, in the most spectacular operation of all, Gama'a militants assaulted the Temple of Hatshepsut in Luxor and killed 68 people, mostly tourists. This action effectively ended the revival of Egypt's tourist industry.

Rifts over the issue of the proper response to the pressure exerted by the authorities also fractured the ranks of the Muslim Brotherhood. In February 1996, the newly nominated Supreme Guide, Mustafa Mashour, confronted a crisis precipitated by the demand of key members of the Guidance Bureau to set up a political party.[13] This demand was not met, but it reflected the ongoing search for an effective means of influence in the face of the authorities' pressure. Mashour embraced the logic underlying the idea of a party when he declared that "we will not resort to violence or underground work." He also called on the regime to embark on a dialogue, contending that "a dialogue is necessary at this stage . . . better than throwing in our lot with other militant groups."[14] In the course of 1997, the Brotherhood also made several cease-fire offers. But these gestures were all interpreted as signs of weakness, both inside and outside the movement. Younger members of the Brotherhood opposed the intention to operate only through legal means.[15] And the regime made any form of dialogue conditional on the opposition abandoning the commitment to implement Shari'a.

Although the opposition groups show continuing signs of intraorganizational weakness, much of the regime's success is due to the cohesiveness, determination, and strength of the security forces. Given the fundamental economic problems facing Egypt, it will be very difficult to resolve the social dilemmas that sustain the appeal of the "Islamic solution." And since extremists are determined to escalate the confrontation by provoking harsh reactions on the part of the security forces, it is unlikely that a mutually acceptable political settlement will forestall another upsurge of violence. Consequently, any decline in the scope and volume of terrorist attacks probably reflects temporary weaknesses of the Islamic movements, rather than the arrival of a new era in Egypt.

The Case of Jordan

Though united on the ultimate goal of the "Islamic solution," the Islamic movement in Jordan shows considerable organizational, ideological, and operational diversity. The loosely structured Muslim Brotherhood has sought to advance its objective by gradual and nonviolent means. The radical groups, dominated by the younger generation of the Islamic movement, challenge the very legitimacy of the regime.

In response, the Jordanian monarchy has tried to exploit the differences among the various groups. While moderate Islamic forces have been co-opted into the political process, radical organizations have been the target of an intensive law-enforcement campaign. In recent years, the regime has managed to expand the rifts, between the radicals and the Brotherhood and also within the Brotherhood itself, further diminishing the already remote possibility that a united Islamic front can be created.

Beyond its dedication to the ''Islamic solution,'' the Islamic movement has been united in its opposition to the regional peace process and particularly to Jordan's relations with Israel. This provides the backdrop for the recent strain in relations between the monarchy and the mainstream Islamic forces, following a short-lived rapprochement after 1989. In that year, the monarchy responded to a wave of popular unrest at economic conditions by embarking on a process of political liberalization. In the ensuing parliamentary elections, the Muslim Brotherhood won a large share of the seats.[16] In late 1991, however, King Hussein endorsed the American Middle East peace initiative, which drew sharp criticism from the Islamic movement as a whole. As a result, the Islamists were stripped of their cabinet ministries, and restrictions were imposed on the political activities of the Muslim Brotherhood. In addition, the regime cracked down on radical activists, putting several of them on trial. Parliament's ratification of the Jordanian-Israeli peace treaty attested to the eroding status of the Islamists, and the Muslim Brotherhood maintained its parliamentary representation only by adopting a new name – the Islamic Action Front (IAF) – and agreeing to participate in the political process according to the strict rules dictated by the regime.

The Islamic movement's diminished ability to capitalize on popular unrest was evident in August 1996, when reductions in wheat subsidies and an increase in the price of bread led to violent clashes between protesters and the security forces in the South. Hundreds of people were arrested, and many were charged with instigating terrorism and sabotage. But according to government spokesmen, the main party responsible for the violence was the pro-Iraqi Jordanian Arab Socialist Ba'th Party, and its role in leading the riots was depicted as part of an Iraqi campaign to destabilize the monarchy. The IAF did not contribute to the parliamentary debate and public pressure that brought about the release of most of the detainees and generated promises by the government and the King to improve social services.[17]

In March 1996, the authorities announced that approximately three dozen terrorist schemes had been frustrated during the previous year. They also exposed a plot to carry out suicide attacks against buses carrying Israeli tourists, and there were suspicions that the foiled plan was inspired by a recent wave of suicide attacks perpetrated in Israel by operatives of Izz a-Din al-Qassam, the military arm of the Palestinian Hamas. The authorities explicitly showed their disapproval of the link between the Muslim Brotherhood and Hamas by arresting Hamas supporters in the ranks of the Muslim Brotherhood.[18] And they announced that Syria had frustrated a terrorist plot against Jordan, allegedly forged by Syrian officers associated with Jordanian Islamic militants.[19] In March 1997, seven Israeli schoolgirls were killed in a shooting attack on the Israeli-Jordanian border. The attacker was a Jordanian soldier, a devoted Muslim of no known organizational affiliation. In September, the previously unknown ''Islamic Resistance in Jordan'' took responsibility for the shots fired at two guards outside the Israeli embassy in Amman.[20] The next month, a petrol bomb was thrown at the front of the Israeli embassy. These sporadic but focused attacks on Israeli targets attested to the relevance attributed by the local Islamic militants to the role played by Jordan in the regional political process. In 1997, the exposure of domestic Jordanian politics and security to the impact of the peace process was clearly demonstrated by events associated with the presence in Amman of Hamas.

Amman's proximity to the West Bank facilitates communications with operatives and institutions there. Since 1992, Hamas's political activity has been centered in Amman, where it enjoys considerable freedom of action. At the same time, the movement's position there is influence by the quality of relations between the regime and the Islamic camp. The problematic nature of Hamas's presence in Jordan was clearly evident in September 1997. Several days after Izz a-Din al-Qassam claimed responsibility for a suicide attack on a crowded Jerusalem street, a Hamas spokesman was arrested by Jordanian security forces and accused of engaging in military activities, a violation of the terms under which it is allowed to operate in Jordan.[21] Later that month, the Israeli Mossad carried out an abortive attempt on the life of Khaled Mash'al, head of Hamas's political bureau in Amman.

The incident exacerbated the already tense relations between Israel and Jordan and outraged all sectors of Jordanian society. Anti-Israeli sentiments were triggered, not so much by the attack itself, but rather by what it symbolized: a blatant breach of Jordanian sovereignty, and apparent Israeli indifference to the fragile accommodation with the pragmatic Islamic bloc that the regime has been striving to consolidate. The attack boosted popular support for Hamas in Jordan and strengthened its ties with the Muslim Brotherhood, and barring a breakthrough in the Israeli-Palestinian peace process, the challenge to the regime of both movements is likely to intensify.

Militant Islam in the Gulf States

The current Islamic resurgence in the Gulf states dates back to the 1970s. It has accelerated in the 1990s for a number of reasons: the decreasing legitimacy of the regimes, the infiltration into local societies of Western economic and cultural influences associated with the strategic alliances forged between these regimes and the West, the corruption of the ruling elites, the growing disparities of wealth, and the mounting economic problems due to increasing birth rates, rapid modernization, and declining oil revenues. Solutions to the problems phrased in Islamic terms have appealed to both Sunni and Shi'ite populations, but the politicization of Islam among Shi'ites has been particularly nourished by their rejection of Sunni political and economic dominance in the region. In reaction to this challenge, the regimes have carried out economic and political reforms and expressed a mounting commitment to Islam. The political reforms, however, were tightly controlled by the regimes. Repressive policies remained in effect, and the Islamic tendency generated radical cells that have resorted to armed struggle.

Throughout the 1980s and 1990s, links between Tehran and Islamic organizations became a constant source of tension between Iran and Gulf states. But while Tehran has indeed sponsored Islamic movements and organizations operating against regimes in the Gulf states (and beyond), popular unrest and waves of terrorism there have primarily been a reflection of local social and political discontent.

The Islamic threat has been relatively contained in Kuwait, perhaps because the opposition has legal channels for the expression of discontent; since 1994, Islamic elements have been represented in Parliament. One manifestation of the declining influence of radical

Islam has been intraorganizational disputes; in late 1996, the Iranian-sponsored Kuwaiti Hizbullah split into three branches.

In Qatar, Oman and the United Arab Emirates (UAE), the Islamic tendency has been less politically focused than in other Gulf states. Social protest has not been absent, but it has not been articulated in religious terms. The Shi'ite populations constitute the underprivileged sectors of these societies, yet they have remained loyal to the regimes.

In Saudi Arabia and Bahrain, however, the militant opposition poses a potentially greater challenge to the stability of the regimes. The Saudi opposition is comprised of radical Shi'ites, Sunni extremists, and, more recently, members of the rising middle class, as well. Criticism of the monarchy has not evolved into structured organizations and is usually focused on the problem of corruption: all opposition elements call for political, economic, and administrative reforms. The other main focus of criticism is the regime's tendency to align itself with the West. Anti-Western sentiments have also motivated violent fringes of radical Islamists. In November 1996, a cell of veterans of the war in Afghanistan, with no institutionalized affiliation, carried out a bombing attack against an American military facility in Riyadh. The perpetrators were executed, but this merely intensified Islamic criticism of the regime. In June 1996, a car bomb hit an American military base in Dhahran, killing 19 servicemen. "Afghanis" were among the hundreds apprehended after the attacks, and some of them were linked with Iran.[22] Although the targets were foreigners, the attacks were obviously intended to expose the monarchy's vulnerabilities, and thus to harm its domestic and international prestige. Indeed, the limited cooperation extended by the Saudi security forces to the FBI in its investigation of the last attack could well be interpreted as a tactical gain for the Islamic activists.

Despite these achievements, the opposition has been unable to present a united front. For one thing, it suffers from conflicting sectoral conflicts, between Shi'ite and Sunni activists and between the Islamists and the evolving class of liberal professionals. For another, the regime has been effective in its repression and its "divide and rule" tactics.[23] Still, its legitimacy is increasingly questioned, and it will have to carry out major reforms in order to neutralize the causes of popular unrest. In confronting the Islamic challenge, the monarchy must tread a fine line. Political liberalization of the political system will probably further alienate the Islamic extremists, economic reform would be difficult without a radical redistribution of wealth, and loosening strategic ties with the West in order to appease the Islamists would entail strategic risks that the monarchy is not prepared to face.

Bahrain has been a major regional focus of Islamic unrest. The militant Shi'ite opposition, composed of two movements and based in London, has focused on the Sunni minority's domination of political power and wealth. The current wave of Shi'ite unrest erupted in late 1994. Since then, there have been intermittent clashes between security forces and demonstrators calling for the release of political prisoners and protesting the violation of human rights by the authorities.

Bahrain has also been the scene of terrorist attacks on both local and foreign targets – security personnel, electricity facilities, newspaper offices, banks, international firms, and hotels – usually with improvised explosives. The Bahraini government has attributed most of the attacks to the Iranian-backed Hizbullah.[24] But while Bahrain may be a "test case" for the export of the Iranian revolution, such accusations were heard less frequently in 1997, reflecting both a drastic reduction in the number of violent incidents and the recent easing of tensions between Iran and the Gulf states.

The War in Kurdistan

In a world divided into nation-states, the Kurdish issue falls within the definition of subnational conflicts. It forms the backdrop of internal conflicts in four Middle Eastern countries: Turkey, Iraq, Syria, and Iran. But the activities of Kurdish insurgent organizations spill over international borders, producing a transnational refugee problem and complicating the foreign policies and actions of several governments. The conflict itself is manifested in several closely related spheres: power struggles within and shifting alliances among the insurgent Kurdish organizations; clashes between these and state powers; coordinated efforts by regional and Western governments to pacify the region by promoting agreements among the rival Kurdish forces; and open competition among regional powers for control of the arena. Since all aspects of the Kurdish issue have transcended domestic politics, this survey approaches the war in Kurdistan from a regional strategic perspective.

Kurdish militancy is deeply rooted in the historic conflicts between the people of Kurdistan and state powers in the region, but the current phase in northern Iraq and in southeast Turkey dates back to the fighting between Kurdish insurgents and Saddam Hussein's army in the early 1990s. In the aftermath of the Gulf War, an estimated 250,000 refugees were driven north by the fighting. Among those who crossed the Turkish border were members of the Kurdish Workers Party (PKK), the largest of the Kurdish groups fighting against Turkish rule. Turkish reprisals against PKK attacks further stirred nationalist sentiments, among the refugees in particular, and among the Kurdish community in the country as a whole.

This development took place against the backdrop of rising Kurdish expectations of greater cultural liberalization, stimulated by the emergence of a public debate in Turkey itself. The Turkish debate exposed a substantial gap between the army, which was inclined to pacify southeastern Turkey by force, and some governmental echelons, which were prepared to consider a political solution to the protracted conflict. This gap emerged during Turgut Ozal's term as Prime Minister in the early 1990s, and it increased when the Islamic party Refah took over the government and Refah's leader, Necmettin Erbakan, advocated greater cultural autonomy for the Kurds.

The Turkish debate was really about ways to curb Kurdish nationalist sentiments, but it had the effect of accelerating Kurdish political mobilization, just at a time when the Western powers, led by the United States, managed to have Iraqi Kurdistan placed under UN protection. A multinational force deployed on the Turkish side of the Turkish-Iraqi border enforced this decision, which laid the groundwork for regional autonomy and perhaps the eventual disintegration of Iraq. The mandate of the force has been extended periodically since 1991, with Ankara's consent, but Turkey's own policies toward northern Iraq have often deviated from the (increasingly unclear) strategy of the allied forces.

Concern about the consequences of the dissociation of northern Iraq from central government rule led Turkey to become actively involved in the conflict between Saddam Hussein's army and the two major Kurdish tribal organizations – the Kurdish Democratic Party (KDP), led by Massoud Barazani, and the Patriotic Union of Kurdistan (PUK), led by Jalal Talabani.[25] Contacts between Ankara and the Iraqi Kurdish leaders, which began in March 1991, fell within the framework of Turkey's persistent fight against the PKK, and fluctuated in accordance with its view of what was required to promote stability in northern Iraq.

Turkey's interest in preserving Iraq's territorial and political unity was shared by Iran and Syria. Since 1992, the three states have attempted to frustrate initiatives that might lead to the creation of a Kurdish autonomous entity that could evolve into an independent state. This common interest, of course, did not eliminate other sources of rivalry, and their limited coordination was primarily intended to enable them to monitor each other's effort to influence developments in the arena.[26]

One of Turkey's primary instruments of stabilization has been the normalization of relations with Iraq. Since 1992, the flow of Turkish exports to Iraq has increased steadily, and the Turkish-sponsored KDP has been a major beneficiary of the international aid supplied to northern Iraq via Turkey and of the "tariffs" imposed on the trade and limited oil exports from Iraq. Access to this financial resource was actually a major focus of the rivalry between the KDP and the PUK, which had turned to Tehran for assistance. Turkish support for the KDP is consistent with its dual objective of maintaining tension inside northern Iraq (in order to forestall an intra-Kurdish rapprochement that might possibly lead to autonomy), and maintaining its control over border crossings into an area that Ankara sees as a buffer zone against the PKK into southeastern Turkey.

In late 1995, according to Turkish sources, 2,600 PKK fighters were active inside Turkey, and 3,800 were operating from outside the country. Most of the militiamen, about 2,500–3,000, were said to be dispersed in northern Iraq. Several hundred were reportedly in Iran, about the same number in Syria, and the rest in Armenia. Abdullah Ocalan, leader of the PKK, was said to reside in Damascus.[27] The PKK has been supported by Kurdish front organizations located in western Europe, mainly in Germany, where the PKK is banned, and in Belgium, where the Kurdish Parliament-in-exile is located. PKK members in western Europe, and particularly in Brussels, have been implicated in criminal activities, such as money laundering, extortion, and drug trafficking, which constitute the organization's main source of funds and weapons.[28]

The period 1995–1997 witnessed a decrease in the PKK's operational capabilities, largely because of massive Turkish military assaults both in the Kurdish-populated areas of Turkey and deep inside northern Iraq. The Turkish campaign constrained the PKK's operational capabilities. This was reflected in the relative calm prevailing in the previously war-torn areas of the country, and in the PKK's growing preference for low-risk operations – abductions, suicide car-bombings, and sabotage – after years of large-scale attacks. According to Turkish sources, the organization also confronted increased difficulties in recruiting new members.[29]

Perhaps most revealing of all were the PKK's attempts to secure a cease-fire and Western backing for a negotiated settlement based on a Kurdish federation.[30] Following the major Turkish offensive against PKK positions in northern Iraq in October 1995, Ocalan issued a call for a cease-fire. Ankara rejected the initiative, using previous violations of cease-fire agreements as a pretext to continue its military campaign.[31] In late 1996, the PKK declared its desire to reach an agreement during 1997 and again suggested a cease-fire as a first step to advance this goal. Ankara also rejected this proposal.

Instead, Turkey continued to pursue the pacification of its Kurdish provinces through other means that did not involve coordination with the PKK. By mid-1997, this objective seemed more feasible than ever before. The authorities launched an intensive propaganda campaign, stressing their military successes and the evident fatigue of the region's residents, as well as their own social and economic rehabilitation plans. Military commanders reported a growing sense of security as terrorism, perceived to be the core of the problem, appeared to be in decline or, at least, under control.[32] Emergency rule was lifted in three of the region's provinces and vigilante elements – village guards – were recruited to help combat PKK guerrillas on the Turkish side of the border, as the KDP had done on the Iraqi side.

Against the backdrop of an improving situation in the southeastern provinces of Turkey, the offensives against PKK positions in northern Iraq continued. In May 1997, about 60,000 Turkish troops crossed the border. This was the largest invasion into Iraqi territory since spring 1995, and the latest in a series of offensives that had been conducted for four consecutive springs. In September 1997, another operation was mounted, albeit on a smaller scale. These operations targeted the local infrastructure of PKK and featured the same tactics used by Turkey inside its own territory: evacuation of villages, intensive searches for insurgents, and airborne attacks.

The latest spring offensive elicited threats by the PKK to escalate the struggle and attack Israeli and U.S. military facilities in Turkey, in addition to Turkish objectives. An official PKK spokesman also warned that the organization would target tourism centers in order to inflict further damage on the country's economy, already badly hurt by the ongoing fighting.[33] The threat against military installations materialized in the June bombing of an armament manufacturing installation in central Turkey.

Although the de facto establishment of a Turkish buffer zone in northern Iraq in late 1996 contradicted Iranian and Syrian strategic interests, Iran and Turkey were nevertheless drawn together by their common concern about the possible establishment of an autonomous Kurdish entity in northern Iraq and the common benefit of their joint gas pipeline project, signed in August 1996. This rapprochement was manifested in the coordination of certain anti-PKK actions. Tehran approved Turkish military operations against Kurdish guerrilla positions within its territory, and it extradited several dozen PKK fighters captured in the border area on Iranian soil.[34] Iran itself has repeatedly violated Iraqi sovereignty by conducting cross-border offensives against forces of the Mujahedin al-Khalq.

On the other hand, Syria showed less willingness to curtail the PKK's cross-border activity. This reflected the Turkish government's reluctance to reach an agreement with Damascus on the distribution of water from the Euphrates River. Ankara had intended to settle the water dispute in return for Syrian agreement to halt assistance to the PKK. But in the fall of 1995, as PKK operations began to lose momentum, the immediate and long-term benefits of such an agreement were again questioned by Turkish political and economic echelons.[35] Relations between Ankara and Damascus were also strained because of Turkey's growing military cooperation with Israel. Syria perceived this development as a potential threat to the regional strategic balance, and it exposed Ankara to harsh criticism from Tehran and Cairo, as well. It also contributed to the recent rapprochement between Damascus and Baghdad. In late December 1996, a car bomb went off in Damascus. Turkey was suspected of being behind the attack, for which no one claimed responsibility.[36]

The conflict between Kurdish insurgents and Turkey is only one aspect of the multidimensional Kurdish problem. The war in northern Iraq between the KDP and the PUK is closely connected to the war between Turkey and the PKK. The two Kurdish organizations jointly controlled Iraqi Kurdistan from the end of the Gulf War until May 1994, when the historic power struggle between them broke out again, this time over the sharing of tax revenues. More specifically, the PUK, which is logistically and sometimes operationally aided by Iran and also enjoys a considerable measure of Iraqi backing, claimed a share in the $100,000 to 150,000 in taxes levied daily by the Turkish-sponsored KDP on shipments of Iraqi oil.[37] The hostilities between them involved massive ground offensives (sometimes backed by foreign forces), assassinations of leading figures, and intensive propaganda campaigns. By March 1997, more than 2,500 people were reportedly killed in the fighting.[38] Since 1995, several international attempts have been made to reach a settlement between the rival organizations. In August of that year, representatives of the KDP and the PUK met in Dublin, under U.S. auspices, and discussed terms for a cease-fire. They agreed to demilitarize the capital of northern Iraq, Irbil, and to share tax money. They also resolved to halt the fighting for several days, until a final agreement was reached.[39] But the combat went on and the stipulations of the draft agreement were not implemented.

Other efforts to reconcile the two movements have also failed. Iran, for example, attempted to mediate an agreement while actively supporting PUK, in the hope of exerting some influence over a disputed region where Iranian dissidents have found refuge. Turkey, which sponsors the KDP, has supported U.S. efforts to promote peace talks, and has invited leaders of the rival organizations to Ankara to discuss the possibility of an agreement. Ankara apparently does not share the Western goal of restoring peace in northern Iraq as a precondition for the creation of a Kurdish autonomous region, but it hopes that hosting peace talks will provide a measure of influence over their outcome, which is bound to affect the scope of its anti-PKK campaign on Iraqi soil. In the November 1996 talks in Ankara, the two Kurdish factions agreed to try to prevent the PKK from operating in northern Iraq, and to refrain from calling on outside help, meaning assistance from Iran and Iraq, thereby addressing both Turkish and U.S. concerns. Shortly afterwards, however, KDP spokesmen stated that the agreement was not fully accepted. Besides attesting to the difficulties involved in reaching an agreement, the reservations expressed by KDP officials could also be interpreted as signs of a rift within the organization itself. The U.S.-brokered talks were periodically renewed after breakdowns caused by clashes between the two organizations. But the March 1997 assassination of a KDP leader, allegedly by the PUK, led to a major escalation just as delegations of the two organizations were meeting in Ankara. In October 1997, talks in Ankara were again interrupted, this time by a KDP attack supported by Turkish tanks and aircraft, on PUK positions. The offensive was meant to drive PUK forces out of territory they had just seized in an Iranian-backed offensive in the area of Irbil.

In April 1996, a Syrian initiative to bring together ten Iraqi opposition groups also failed, as did Egyptian efforts in April 1997 to end the involvement of outside forces. The Egyptian initiative was part of a plan to establish a dialogue with the regime in Baghdad, and it was welcomed by Talabani. But by late 1997, it was still not a viable alternative to the ongoing U.S.-led search for reconciliation between the rival movements.

All this unproductive diplomatic activity provides the setting for Iraq's moves to restore its control over the region. In September 1996, the KDP, with the help of Iraqi forces, captured Irbil and drove PUK fighters toward the Iranian border. A month later, the Iraqi forces withdrew, leaving Barazani in control of the town. In late 1997, however, Saddam Hussein chose a different path. Instead of supporting one side against the other, he assumed the role of a mediator and invited both to Baghdad, to discuss the possibility of a cease-fire.

Saddam's intervention proceeded in parallel with another initiative. In late 1996, nine rival Kurdish organizations and parties, including the KDP and the PUK, responded to a proposal by the Kurdish Parliament in exile and participated in a conference held in Irbil.[40] No foreign representatives were directly involved in these talks, and the participants drew up the outlines of a settlement. But as the fighting continued, this initiative, too, faded away.

By the end of 1997, no agreement to end the fighting in the Kurdish-populated areas appeared within reach. It is possible that any effort to reach an agreement will founder on the rocks of historical animosities between different Kurdish factions and their irreconcilable ambitions to dominate the region. In any case, the contradictory interests of the states sponsoring these organizations and trying to dictate the terms of settlement probably mean that all peace proposals are doomed to fail.

Subnational Conflicts in the Middle East: A Regional Perspective

In the early 1990s, it appeared that several Middle Eastern state-systems were on the verge of momentous transformations because of challenges emanating from below. The state-systems of Algeria, Egypt, and Iraq seemed to be under particular threat. In Algeria and Egypt, rebellious Islamic forces initiated direct confrontations with the regimes, and the regime in Baghdad was attacked by

Kurdish and Shi'ite insurgencies that threatened, with the backing of external forces, to dismantle the state. Other regimes in the region faced similar, if less immediate, threats.

The Kurdish struggle was also a component in the composite and shifting framework of relations among states in the region. Cooperation among Islamic groups and between groups and foreign governments often strained regional relations, especially when this cooperation expressed itself in the armed struggle. At the same time, incentives were created for rival states to mitigate their disputes in the face of the commonly perceived Islamic threat. The Kurdish issue was actually subordinated to the interests of other states directly involved in the struggle among the insurgent groups and in their fight against the state. Regional and international concerns focused on the possible ramifications of domestic turbulence for regional stability, particularly because of the potential "domino effect" embedded in the Islamic insurgencies and in the nationalist Kurdish struggle.

In fact, subnational conflicts revealed certain structural weaknesses of the prevailing regimes, by exposing their responsibility for the evolving crises and their inability to provide appropriate remedies. Especially instructive in this regard was the evident vulnerability of the Middle Eastern version of the nation-state to challenges emanating from the devotion of popular forces to traditional concepts and forms of social identification. Thus the rapid consolidation of opposition forces as viable political alternatives demonstrated the questionable legitimacy of ruling elites and systems in the eyes of the masses.

At the same time, the eruption and escalation of the crises also demonstrated the power of those same regimes. The mounting violent and nonviolent opposition elicited concerted shows of force and intensified security measures that ensured regime control over the populations at large. Economic and political reforms, introduced in order to calm popular unrest and preserve the existing systems, appeared to serve their purpose. It is true that profound economic constraints and the very nature of the regimes precluded the comprehensive structural changes that might have minimized present unrest and future challenges. Nevertheless, by the second half of the decade, even the most challenged regimes appear, often with the help of favorable economic developments, to have curbed and contained the most immediate threats to their survival.

As for the Islamic movements themselves, most have limited the threat to existing regimes by confining themselves to nonviolent struggle and concentrating on educational and welfare activities and other efforts to transform society from below. Their pragmatic approach reflects lessons learned from previous confrontations with the authorities and current assessments concerning the regimes' determination to preserve their power, even if their operational codes represent nothing more than interim phases in the protracted struggle for the attainment of the ultimate objective – the imposition of Islamic law over the society.

In any event, the radical factions that resort to expressive or calculated violence constitute the narrow fringes of the Islamic movement. Their strategy focuses on an attempt to provoke a direct and all-encompassing confrontation between the regimes and popular forces. Their operational capabilities are rather limited, as is their freedom of action. Violence may have drawn attention to the social grievances that presumably underlie the unrest, and it may have precipitated minor changes in the domestic political agenda; the introduction of gradual and limited reforms was almost certainly stimulated by the contest for popular support between the regimes and the Islamic movements. Nevertheless, violence also created the pretext for the regimes to exercise and intensify their control over the population at large, and it may even have alienated the masses from the objectives with which they once sympathized.

Endnotes

1 Excluded from this review are the cases of Iran and Sudan, which are ruled by Islamist regimes, and Syria and Turkey, where Islamic revival has constituted a relatively minor threat to the state. In addition, the survey does not cover the Islamic dimension of the Israeli-Palestinian conflict or the low-intensity war in south Lebanon.

2 C. Spencer, "The Roots and Future of Islamism in Algeria," in A. S. Sidahmed and A. Ehteshami, eds., *Islamic Fundamentalism* (Boulder: Westview Press, 1996), pp. 93–107; C. Spencer, "The Case of Algeria," paper prepared for the Halki International Seminar on the European Union and the Mediterranean Region (1997); R. H. Dekmejian, *Islam in Revolution: Fundamentalism in the Arab World*, 2d ed. (Syracuse: Syracuse University Press, 1995), pp. 205–208.

3 Bruce Maddy-Weitzman, "The Islamic Challenge in North Africa," http://www.biu.ac.il/soc/besa/meria/7maddy.html (July 1997).

4 *International Herald Tribune,* 26.12.96; *Ha'aretz*, 26.1.96, 25.12.96, 31.12.96.

5 *Ma'ariv*, 8.6.97.

6 See: Weitzman; Dekmejian, pp. 202–210; and C. Khosrowshahi, "Pri-

vatization in Morocco: The Politics of Development,'' *Middle East Journal*, 51, no. 2 (1997).

7 FBIS-NES-97-148, 28.5.97.

8 FBIS-NES-97-003, 4.1.97.

9 The tension between Libya and its neighbors, however, has by and large been reduced in the past several years. Significantly, it was not fear of the Islamic resurgence that triggered this shift. Libya's anti-Western posture and the rather stable state of the economy, despite the sanctions imposed in the mid-1980s by the UN, explain the absence of Islamic militancy from the scene; the tight control over society explains the absence of any effective opposition. At the same time, the international isolation of Libya, especially following the demise of the Soviet Bloc, has been identified as a probable source of future economic difficulties. Related concerns have guided the current Libyan tendency to refrain from friction in the international sphere and to seek better regional relations, starting with the neighboring Maghreb states and Egypt.

10 There are significant differences in the choice of emblems and the focus of protest among the Egyptian Islamists. The predominantly southern al-Gama'a has been preoccupied with social issues, paying lip service to the Egyptian foreign policy agenda, while the platforms of the mainly northern Muslim Brotherhood and Jihad Organization have been shaped by their focus on international matters. This diversity reflects social and class differences, determined by the culture and the political histories of the movements' regions of origin. Those differences pose major obstacles to the formation of an Islamic unified front. See M. Fandy, ''Egypt's Islamic Groups: Regional Revenge?'' *Middle East Journal*, 48, no. 4 (1994): 607–25.

11 M. Azzam, ''Egypt: The Islamists and the State under Mubarak,'' in Sidahmed and Ehteshami, *Islamic Fundamentalism*, pp. 109–22; Dekmejian, pp. 175–210; Carlyle Murphy, ''Egypt: An Uneasy Portent of Change,'' *Current History*, 93, no. 580 (February 1994): 78–82.

12 *Al-Ahram Weekly*, 19–25.6.97. Since 1992, about two-thirds of the 91 people sentenced to death for involvement in terrorism were actually executed. *The Economist*, 22.11.97, p. 57.

13 FBIS-NES-96-027, 8.2.96.

14 *Al-Ahram Weekly*, 25–31.1.96.

15 *Ha'aretz*, 6.2.96.

16 Dekmejian, p. 199.

17 FBIS-NES-96-167, 25.8.96, 26.8.96; FBIS-NES-96-173, 3.9.96, 6.9.6; FBIS-NES-96-186, 21.9.96; FBIS-NES-96-219, 12.11.96. FBIS-NES-96-119, 12.11.96, FBIS-NES-96-220, 13.11.96.

18 *Ha'aretz*, 14.3.97, 20.3.96, 31.3.96; interview with Ibrahim Gawsha, Hamas spokesman in Jordan, FBIS-NES-96-215, 4.11.96.

19 *Yediot Aharonot*, 24.6.96; *Ha'aretz*, 5.8.96.

20 *The Jerusalem Post*, 23.9.97.

21 *Ha'aretz*, 8.9.97.

22 *Ha'aretz*, 15.8.96; *The Jerusalem Post*, 3.11.96.

23 Dekmejian, pp.137–39; Joseph Kostiner, ''State, Islam and Opposition in Saudi Arabia: The Post Desert-Storm Phase,'' http://www/biu.ac.il/soc/besa/meria/8kostine.html (July 1997).

24 FBIS-TOT-96-018-L, 4.1.96.

25 Mahmut Bali Ayakan, ''Turkey's Policy in Northern Iraq, 1991–1995,'' *Middle Eastern Studies*, 32, no. 4 (October 1996): 343–66.

26 R. Olson, ''The Kurdish Question and Turkey's Foreign Policy, 1991–1995: From the Gulf War to the Incursion into Iraq,'' *Journal of South Asian and Middle Eastern Studies*, XIX, no. 1 (1995): 1–30.

27 FBIS-NES-96-002, 29.3.95.

28 FBIS-WEU-96-185, 19.9.96.

29 FBIS-TOT-96-005-2, 8.1.96.

30 FBIS-WEU-95-234, 24.11.95.

31 FBIS-WEU-06-002, 30.12.95.

32 *Time*, 7 April 1997.

33 *Ha'aretz*, 3.6.97.

34 FBIS-NES-96-156, 10.8.96. For details on the cooperation between Turkey and Iran since 1994, see Olson, ''The Kurdish Question.''

35 S. Guner, ''The Turkish-Syrian War of Attrition: The Water Dispute,'' *Studies in Conflict & Terrorism*, 20, no. 1 (Spring 1997): 105–16.

36 *Ma'ariv*, 5.1.97; *Ha'aretz*, 14.1.97. Syrian official sources blamed Israel for the attack, as well as for several others carried out against Syrian military objectives in Lebanon.

37 FBIS-NES-95-179, 9.9.95.

38 FBIS-NES-97-070, 11.3.97.

39 FBIS-NES-95-176, 9.9.95.

40 London MED TV Television, 21.12.96 (said to be linked with the PKK), cited in FBIS-WEU-96-185, 19.9.96.

4. Iraq's Strategic Arena

Aharon Levran

Iraq has initiated the two largest-scale wars in the Middle East in the last two decades, and it is therefore always appropriate to examine its strategic arena. Such a review should focus mainly on the strategic threats and challenges posed by Iraq to its neighbors, the world, and Israel.

Revelations about Iraq's strength, especially in nonconventional weaponry and missiles, obviously raise concerns about the potential threat from Baghdad, especially as long as its totalitarian ruler, Saddam Hussein, remains in power. Since the Second Gulf War, Saddam has initiated at least nine confrontations, but in each case, he has backed down in the face of political or military pressure. This suggests that the threats from Baghdad, despite the defiant rhetoric behind them, are less real than is generally assumed. The reason is that stringent economic sanctions and the intrusive inspection regime aimed at dismantling weapons of mass destruction (WMD) and long-range surface-to-surface missiles (SSM) have left Iraq weaker than it was after its ignominious defeat in 1991. Even so, Iraq's military strength remains far from negligible, and it may increase substantially if and when the sanctions and the inspections are removed or significantly eased. This dialectic – the link between Iraq's residual power and its ongoing threat potential – is the subject of this chapter.

Iraq's Residual Strength and Its Threat Potential

The intriguing questions about postwar Iraq focus, not only on what it still has, but also on what can it do with its residual military capabilities, both conventional and nonconventional. Iraq provides an interesting case study of the observation that actual and usable military power are not perfectly correlated. In any event, even after its defeat in the Second Gulf War, Iraq's military power remains impressive. Nevertheless, the range of local and regional operational threats that this power might imply should not be exaggerated.

Residual Conventional Strength

Since the Second Gulf War, Iraq's armed ground and air forces have shrunk by about half in manpower and weapon systems (a substantive naval force never existed anyway). There are now 13 infantry divisions (as compared to 50 during the war); 2,300 tanks (compared to more than 5,500); about 2,000 artillery pieces (as opposed to 4,500 then); about 170–180 serviceable aircraft out of about 310 (as compared to 600–700 before the war); and about 60 surface-to-air missile (SAM) batteries (as opposed to almost three times as many before). This shrinkage has obviously weakened Iraqi military power, but the need to adjust to lower troop levels and fewer weapons systems has also resulted in a better military organization (certainly as compared to the prewar army of some 65 divisions). Moreover, some vital force components were rather well preserved: ten tank and mechanized divisions remain (in the war there were 14); the "Republican Guard" – the hard core of Saddam's regime – remains, with five tank and mechanized divisions (although its infantry order-of-battle was reduced to three divisions); the helicopter fleet, including attack helicopters, did not decline much and continued to number about 400; and a Special Guard of ten battalions was also created.

The economic sanctions and trade embargo in effect since the war are chiefly responsible for the ongoing decline in Iraqi military power. They prevent the regime from properly maintaining its weapons (due to a lack of spare parts), much less achieving any improvement (because of poor logistics and inability to purchase new weapons). Although there are still military production lines in Iraq, they cannot really compensate for the external constraints. Thus maintenance of the existing inventory is made possible, to a great extent, by the cannibalization of equipment. Another defense element – the SAM disposition – has been further weakened since the war, due to occasional air and cruise missile attacks. Similarly, Iraq's air force (which had been severely beaten during the war) is unable to mount many training or operational sorties, because of both a shortage of equipment and the imposition of extensive no-fly zones in the north and south of the country.

Beyond these material shortcomings, Iraqi armed forces suffer from low morale, except perhaps for the Republican and Special Guard forces. Poor esprit de corps is expressed in widespread desertions, which are countered by severe decrees and punishments.

Residual Nonconventional and Missile Strength

Although nonconventional and missiles capabilities are subject to close inspection by the United Nations Special Commission (UNSCOM), it is precisely in these areas that Iraq's residual strength is most conspicuous. True, Iraq has been drastically weakened in the nuclear, chemical, and SSM fields, and UNSCOM and the International Atomic Energy Agency (IAEA) have registered major successes in detecting, dismantling, and monitoring such weapons and equipment. However, even in these fields, it is hard to establish that all of the weapons have been neutralized. In the biological area, the situation is undoubtedly even less reassuring.

At the end of the Second Gulf War, Saddam apparently decided that he must do everything possible to preserve his strength in the nonconventional and SSM fields. Therefore he adopted tactics to cheat and obstruct the work of UNSCOM inspectors, and it seems that he achieved some measure of success.

Residual Nuclear Strength

Most of Iraq's grandiose prewar nuclear program has apparently been destroyed or neutralized, and dozens of related facilities have been dismantled or put under surveillance. Following some 1,000 different inspection missions, including air and ground radiometric surveys that also periodically covered main water sources, the IAEA determined, in December 1997, that Iraq did not possess any nuclear material and was not engaged in prohibited nuclear activity. Nevertheless, some uncertainty and suspicion remain that Iraq continues to conceal several secondary nuclear components (related equipment, documents, drawings, etc.).

Iraq's nuclear program was notable, not only for its dimensions, but also for its diversity (e.g., pursuit of several different methods of uranium enrichment and plutonium production). Baghdad was working on an indigenous plan to build a 40-megawatt "research" reactor based on natural uranium and heavy water. The Iraqis were also quite advanced in their weaponization work, including the integration of nuclear devices and SSMs. Finally, the know-how and skills of some 7,500 nuclear scientists and technicians who took part in the program remain a permanent source of concern. If the inspection regime is lifted, they could revive the program in fairly short order (i.e., within a few years), but as long as it remains in effect, Iraq does not pose a nuclear threat.

The Residual Chemical Weapons (CW) Threat

It is estimated that much of Iraq's CW program has been destroyed or neutralized, and some 160 related facilities have been put under monitoring and surveillance. Still, Iraq has worked even harder in the chemical area than it has in the nuclear field to conceal some quantities and elements of its capabilities, especially its VX nerve gas.

Even by its own admission, Iraq's chemical program was huge. Baghdad admitted to producing 3,850 tons of chemical agents "that it does not possess anymore."[1] It also declared that it had produced or acquired some 247,000 chemical munitions, of which about 152,000 were filled with chemical agents, but again "none exist anymore."[2] Apart from destroying 690 tons of chemical agents and 38,537 chemical munitions, UNSCOM also destroyed 3,275 tons of chemical precursors and more than 400 chemically related items, especially in the huge Iraqi chemical plant at Muthan'a (which was heavily bombed during the Second Gulf War).

It is, of course, difficult to verify fully or rely completely on Iraq's claims of unilateral destruction, consumption during the First Gulf War, and losses in the Second Gulf War. There are particular suspicions about the concealment of some chemical missile warheads and of the most lethal nerve gas – VX. It is estimated that altogether some 80 "special" warheads were produced – 50 for CW, 25 for biological weapons (BW), and five for tests. UNSCOM destroyed 30 chemical warheads, of which 16 were filled with Sarin gas and 14 with binary gases. It is also believed that 20 of the remaining "special" warheads were destroyed. Twenty-five warheads are therefore still unaccounted for (possibly those filled with BW). The situation regarding VX is even less clear. Iraq admitted to acquiring 750 tons of precursors for this gas (and independently producing another 55 tons). Baghdad claims that half of this quantity was destroyed in the Second Gulf War, another quarter was unilaterally destroyed, and 36 tons were destroyed by UNSCOM. Regarding the VX itself, UNSCOM estimated in 1996 that Iraq had produced 3.9 tons, and not 260 kilograms, as Baghdad declared. Interestingly, until Hussein Kamal's defection to Jordan in August 1995, Iraq totally denied any offensive biological capacity, including production of this most lethal gas. After the defection, however, it became known that Iraq had intended to fill several hundred air bombs and dozens of missile warheads with VX.

Iraq has developed and produced a wide variety of gases – blister gases like mustard, blood gases like cyanide, and nerve gases like Tabun, Sarin, VX, and possibly Soman. It also has a range of delivery systems, including aerial bombs, artillery shells and rockets, missile warheads, and aerosol spray dispensers (evidence of the last two systems surfaced only after the First Gulf War) – in addition to binary and cluster warheads. Since Iraq had used some of these gases (mustard, cyanide, Tabun, and Sarin) during the First Gulf War, it could not deny the existence of a CW capability and was obliged to cooperate with UNSCOM. But even if Baghdad decided to "sacrifice" most of its chemical program, it did so as a gambit in order to preserve its most lethal component, namely the VX, and perhaps to conceal its biological program (to which it apparently attaches more importance).

Even if the CW arsenal still hidden in Iraq is no longer large, it does pose a formidable threat in terms of the ability to inflict casualties, and, more important, it reflects a strategic strength. After all, the Iraqi Army possesses the most extensive and updated experience with gas warfare in the region, and even in the entire world. Iraq also retains a chemical industrial base (pesticide plants, laboratories, etc.) with "dual-use" precursors and know-how. Thus, if the inspection regime is removed, Iraq will be able to rehabilitate its CW arsenal within a matter of months.

The Residual Biological Weapons (BW) Threat

Iraq's biological program began after the First Gulf War, when Iraq purchased, "for medical purposes," large quantities of media growth, from which it could produce sizable quantities of bacteria and toxins for BW. There is even a possibility, not yet fully confirmed, that Iraq used some BW (fungus toxins against Iranian troops, malaria-carrying mosquitoes and typhoid germs against its Kurdish citizens) during the course of that war. In any case, the core of the program was located in the al-Hakam plant, which was not bombed in the Second Gulf War. Suspicions about the BW arsenal had surfaced even before they were confirmed by Hussein Kamal. In July 1995, Iraq had to admit that it had possessed a biological program (after denying that for five years), but even then it claimed that "the program was solely for defense purposes" and that "everything was destroyed." Not only are these claims dubious, at best, but unilateral destruction (in the nonconventional domain, in general, and in BW, in particular) – if it happened – constituted a blatant violation of Security Council resolutions. In any case, there is no evidence of any actual destruction of BW by Iraq.

According to one of its six different declarations (that of November 1995), Iraq had had at least 19,000 liters of botulinum toxin (10,000 liters of which were weaponized) and 2,200 liters of aflatoxin (1,580 liters of which were weaponized). It was later revealed that Iraq had also developed other varieties of BW, including the plague, smallpox, and Ricin (which can allegedly be used on the battlefield).[3] It is worth noting that Egyptian-Iraqi cooperation in the biological field (as well as in the chemical area) continued until the Second Gulf War.

Despite the fact that some 90 related sites and about 900 biological-related equipment items have been tagged and put under surveillance, it is estimated that Iraq continues to conceal indeterminate quantities of BW. Like CW, BW development and production do not present insurmountable challenges to a country that has plants, laboratories, and equipment for medical purposes. If this is true today, it will certainly be the case when the inspection regime is lifted.

The gravity of biological warfare is that a BW attack may inflict not that many fewer casualties than a nuclear bomb: an effective biological warhead containing 30 kilograms of anthrax spores could cause tens of thousands of fatalities – not much less than a 25-kiloton nuclear device.[4] Furthermore, many of the BW do not yet have fully proven medical antidotes. On the other hand, it must be pointed out that BW have not thus far been used operationally or proven to be this effective. Nor is it a simple matter to load biological agents onto SSM warheads and be confident that they will operate properly. But for rulers like Saddam, BW may be considered not only a valid weapon of mass destruction, but also equivalent to a nuclear capability. This could be the reason why he has been so determined to maintain his biological inventory and to shield it from inspection and destruction.

The Residual SSM Capability

If UNSCOM's late 1997 version of reality is accurate, then the situation with respect to SSMs is rather encouraging. According to UNSCOM, only two missiles are unaccounted for out of the 819 Scuds that Iraq had purchased by 1988 from the former Soviet Union.[5] Unlike other Iraqi claims, the claims of unilateral destruction with respect to missiles were confirmed.[6] Insofar as missile launchers are concerned, the situation seems even better: all 14 operational mobile launchers that Iraq possessed in the war (ten imported from the USSR and four indigenously produced) have been accounted for. Even if Iraq had 19 mobile launchers, as another version insists, the accounting is still satisfactory.[7] On the other hand, some ambiguity remains with respect to missile warheads Although 48 warheads (30 chemical and 18 conventional) were destroyed by UNSCOM, some 25 "special" warheads could still not be accounted for.

UNSCOM's estimate seems fairly well grounded, but some suspicion remains that Iraq has nevertheless managed to conceal a small number of missiles. It should be pointed out that UNSCOM's estimate as of early 1997 did refer to the fact that 20–25 "Scud variants" were "missing" (although they might have been traced later on), and that Baghdad has repeatedly issued misleading statements about its SSM inventory. Thus Iraq may well have hidden at least one or two mobile launchers, without which the missiles themselves have no value. In any case, the Iraqi missile problem is more one of indigenous production potential than of sheer numbers, and the fact that much missile-related equipment has been destroyed does not eliminate this problem.

UNSCOM carries out a periodic inspection regime on more than 60 missile-related sites and some 140 missile-related items and on more than 2,000 missile systems – to make sure that their ranges were not altered. As of mid-1997, UNSCOM has also instructed Iraq to submit monthly reports regarding its missile components and inventory. Nevertheless, until the summer of 1995, Iraq had managed to conceal its missile-engines project. Moreover, the fact that Iraq was allowed to continue producing missiles up to a 150-kilometer range limit left it with a variety of options. For example, the Ibn al-Haytham facility that produces short-range Ababil-50 (or Samud) missiles is also suspected of developing Ababil-100 SSMs with a range of about 2,000 kilometers. Before the war, Iraq was working on the Tammuz-1 missile, with the same range, and on a space-launch vehicle, al-Abed (which failed in a test launch in late 1989). In addition to converting imported Scuds into longer-range al-Hussein missiles, Iraq was also producing some Scud missiles indigenously. Baghdad's aspiration to produce a long-range SSM capability was reflected, inter alia, in its attempt to import gyroscopes from Russia.[8]

The most ominous aspect of Iraq's SSM potential is its demonstrated intention to produce nuclear, biological, and chemical warheads; during the Second Gulf War, the latter type may already have been in Iraq's inventory. Needless to say, long-range SSMs with nonconventional warheads do more than any other weapon to magnify Iraq's threat potential, not only to its immediate neighbors, but also to the whole region and even the world.

Iraq's Threat Potential

Iraq's threat potential is not simply a function of its actual residual strength. Nevertheless, its capacity to threaten others, though far from negligible, remains limited. This is apparent from the outcomes of repeated standoffs with Saddam since the end of the Second Gulf War. Still, as long as Iraq remains a rogue state led by a megalomaniac, the possibility of sudden shifts in the threat assessment cannot be excluded.

Threats Emanating From Iraq's Conventional Strength

Despite all constraints with which Iraq must deal, it remains the strongest military power in the Gulf. Nevertheless, Iraq's present military power suffers from severe shortcomings that restrict its strategic freedom to challenge the status quo. There is no doubt that Iraq's present power enables it to defend itself very well. On the other hand, this power is not sufficient to sustain extensive military initiatives and adventures beyond its own borders. For years, Iraq has not had a naval force, and it is therefore unable to operate in the Gulf. Conversely, Baghdad's Gulf access can be blocked rather easily, as was demonstrated in the First Gulf War, when it had to rely on Kuwait for import and export.

The two most significant components of its current military power are the "Republican Guard" and the helicopter force. By contrast, the Iraqi Air Force is in shambles and has only about 170–180 serviceable combat aircraft. Some 115 high-quality combat aircraft, which were flown to Iran during the Second Gulf War on the misguided assumption that they would later be returned, constituted the bulk of Iraq's attack aircraft (Sukhoi-24 and Mirage F-1) and advanced interceptors (Mig-29). An army without a significant air force will be hard put to undertake large-scale military adventures outside its borders. But the Iraqi air force does not even defend its own airspace, not only against the US-led coalition, but even against Iran. Since the Second Gulf War, the Iranian air force has been able to mount occasional attacks on oppositionist Mujahedin al-Khalq bases in Iraq with virtual impunity. Indeed, Iraq did not even react to these attacks, which were a blatant violation of its sovereignty.

It is noteworthy that even during the First Gulf War, which ended when Iran was compelled to stop fighting, the Iraqi armed forces did not perform with particular distinction. In the first stage of the war, from 1980 to 1982, the Iraqi Army did not accomplish its mission of occupying Khuzistan, in spite of the severe deterioration in the Iranian Army following the 1979 Islamic revolution. After the Iraqi Army withdrew from Iranian territory in the summer of 1982, its performance improved quite considerably – defending Iraqi land and repelling repeated Iranian ground offensives (except for the Iranian capture of Fao) during the next six years. Only in the last four months of the war did the Iraqi Army also show some offensive capability, taking back all the previous territorial losses and even gaining some ground inside Iran. But even then, Iraqi accomplishments were mostly due to the weakness of the Iranian forces and the extensive use of chemical weapons. Nor did the Iraqi Air Force contribute much to Iraq's victory. Apart from some long-range strikes against Iranian targets in the vicinity of the Straits of Hormuz, its overall performance against a mediocre Iranian adversary was far from impressive.

After the Second Gulf War, Saddam's guiding principle was to preserve his military power. In the first instance, this implied not putting his armed forces in harm's way. It also meant avoiding attrition of the main pillar of his power – the Republican Guard – in missions that were not vital, i.e., that could be carried out by other forces. Thus the Guard was not massively engaged in suppressing the Shi'ite and Kurdish revolts right after the war. In October 1994, however, two Guard divisions were moved to southern Iraq and assumed a threatening profile against Kuwait. But if this deployment signaled an intention to attack, the threat was not carried out. Similarly, Saddam preserved what remained of his air force, preferring to keep it grounded rather than ordering it to take off and challenge coalition aircraft patrolling freely in Iraqi airspace.

From the technotactical aspect, Iraq's army can reconquer Kuwait or retake the Kurdish enclave (torn away in 1991). Strategically, however, these are not viable options, not only because Baghdad would encounter vigorous opposition, mainly from the United States, but also because of its overall weakness. There is even less prospect for successfully employing military force against strong opponents, such as Iran, or over long distances, e.g., in Saudi Arabia, whose real defense against Iraq is its huge territorial depth. Even against Jordan, Saddam would encounter difficulties in carrying out a significant aggressive move. Not only does he need good relations with the kingdom (inter alia, as a territorial outlet); he would probably face stiff Israeli opposition. And against Israel, Saddam would be hard put to repeat his Gulf War aggression or initiate a new one.

What Iraq can do with its conventional power is to stand fast and defend itself. But behind the periodic crises created by Iraqi rhetoric, there is not enough military power to pursue other long-range strategic goals. The proof of this is in the nine confrontations that Saddam initiated since the Second Gulf War, including the three most blatant ones – the apparent threat to reconquer Kuwait in October 1994, the short-lived invasion of Kurdistan in the summer of 1996, and the dispute over UNSCOM's composition and freedom of action in late 1997 and early 1998. In all of these crises, Saddam was forced to back down.

In sum, Saddam is capable of verbal threats, harassment, and restricted, short-term, and local or short-range adventures, but he does not possess a significant military option in the conventional sphere.

Threats Emanating From Iraq's Non-Conventional Strength

In contrast to the conventional sphere, Iraq has a somewhat greater threat potential in the nonconventional area. But this threat, too, is ultimately quite limited.

The only nonconventional Iraqi threat that is now absent is the nuclear one. This will remain true for some time even if Iraq conceals some secondary nuclear components and cumulative know-how, and even if the IAEA's close inspection is removed and Saddam revives his nuclear program. Unless it were able to acquire major ready-made nuclear components, which is not likely, it would take Iraq some three to five years to attain an independent nuclear capacity.[9] Even if the sanctions are lifted, it will be a long time before Iraq possesses the financial resources it had at its disposal before the war. Nevertheless, an easing or end to the embargo and inspections would almost certainly impel Saddam to revive the nuclear program. After all, he could easily convince himself that it was a grave blunder to invade Kuwait before acquiring at least some elementary capacity that could have deterred the United States and its allies.

The threat from Iraqi SSMs is also quite limited. Whether or not it still possesses a few 300-kilometer Scuds or 650-kilometer al-Husseins, these do not provide the underpinning for a significant military initiative. At best, they provide a weapon of last resort, to be kept for real emergencies rather than squandered on routine confrontations. Of course, the situation will change if and when the sanctions, embargo, and inspection regime are removed; Saddam will then strive to reconstruct his SSM arsenal and arm it with "special warheads." After all, SSMs, especially ones armed with nonconventional warheads, may constitute the preeminent force multiplier, since they provide the owner with a clear source of strength and an ability to project it beyond national borders.

Iraq does pose some threat in the chemical and biological spheres. Still, the main question is not Baghdad's technotactical capability, but whether Saddam will even make use of any nonconventional weapons he may have, and, if so, in what circumstances. It has been argued that Saddam would not have embarked on his grandiose nonconventional arms programs if he did not intend to use them. But the empirical record does sustain that thesis. Despite his humiliating defeat, Saddam did not use chemical or biological weapons, and certainly not nonconventional SSMs, in the Second Gulf War. Moreover, although he did make rather extensive use of chemical weapons against Iranian forces during the First Gulf War, he nevertheless exhibited considerable self-restraint. First of all, the chemical weapons were used most of the time for purely defensive purposes; from 1983 to 1988, CW were employed only in the framework of defending the vital defense lines that the Iranian Army threatened to shatter. Second, the chemical weapons that were used in the last months of the war in attacks to regain Iraqi territory captured by the Iranians were also within the framework of defensive operations, i.e., counterattacks. Third, when Baghdad used CW against its Kurdish citizens, it did so because the Kurds had collaborated closely with Iran, and were considered a "fifth column."[10] Fourth, whenever CW were used, it was only on Iraqi territory proper (except for some unintended drifting beyond the front line and border).[11] Iraq could certainly have made far more extensive use of these weapons, since Iran was considered a pariah state, against which any methods were permissible, and it did have the capacity to retaliate in kind.

It is quite possible, of course, that Iraq would have refrained from any use of CW if Iran had had an equal capacity. In any case, Iraq's self-restraint during the First Gulf War and its nonuse of CW during the Second Gulf War suggest that, even for Iraq, entirely different rules prevail in the nonconventional domain. The first rule seems to be survival, and this means that nonconventional weapons, as a general principle, are not meant to be used. It is therefore not coincidental that since World War I, apart from the use of some chemical agents in unique circumstances, such weapons have only been employed in the nuclear attack on Japan meant to end the Second World War, and, more important, they have never been employed against an adversary armed with similar or superior weapons.[12] It therefore seems that nonconventional weapons are acquired for different reasons: to deter aggressors from inflicting total defeat and devastation on a state or its armed forces; to provide a response in kind in case a state is attacked with a weapon of mass destruction; to be used as a last resort, i.e., when a total national collapse is imminent; and last, for purposes of hegemony and prestige, especially when adversaries are equipped with similar weapons.

This may explain why Saddam did not use nonconventional weapons against the Gulf War coalition or against Israel, but also why he produced such weapons and continues to do so and to hide what he has. But beyond these general principles, Iraq must have more specific considerations in mind. The first is to confront Baghdad's traditional enemy and rival for hegemony in the Gulf, Iran, with which it fought a bitter, exhausting war for eight years. Not only does Iran's overall staying power exceed Iraq's by several orders of magnitude, but it, too, now possesses CW, and perhaps also BW, and it is known to be working on its own nuclear capacity. Second, Saddam needs these weapons to deter the United States, which since the Second Gulf War has substantially increased its military presence in the Gulf and against which he strives not to remain absolutely helpless. Third, although Israel is not really a direct foe or threat to Iraq, its presumed nuclear capacity and military superiority over the Arabs may drive Saddam to counter Israel's advantages, especially since he considers himself a major Arab leader. These factors should not be ignored or belittled, and they mitigate the notion that Saddam will automatically use whatever nonconventional weapons he has in every crisis, conflict, and circumstance.

Finally, the operational readiness of Iraq's residual nonconventional weapons and SSMs is not known, but it cannot be very high. For years, this equipment has probably been hidden in unsuitable conditions or constantly moved from place to place. There may a lack of components critical to effective operations, due to the embargo and the passage of time. Moreover, Iraq has been unable to carry out efficient and comprehensive field tests of nonconventional weapons since 1991. Without some certainty that they would work properly, even a dictator like Saddam would not rush to use such weapons against stronger adversaries and risk the political and military reaction – unless it were his last act on earth.

But if overt use of nonconventional weapons by military forces is a remote possibility, there remains a fear that Saddam might equip terrorists with such devices.[13] There is particular concern about the possible use by terrorists of biological agents, which act slowly and reduce the risk that the perpetrators or those behind them would be detected. Although such a scenario cannot be totally ruled out, it is still improbable that Saddam would resort to such measures as part of a "routine" confrontation. Even for a ruler like Saddam, the risk of being exposed, with all that that implied for his personal fate, would probably deter him except in the most extreme circumstances. Besides, a serious campaign of terror requires a widespread organizational infrastructure outside Iraq, and Iraq's diplomatic ties with the rest of the world have been virtually cut off since the Second Gulf War. Furthermore, Qaddafi's repentant behavior after Libya was bombed twice by the United States in 1986 for its involvement in international terror has probably not escaped Saddam's attention. It is revealing that, apart from Baghdad's one-time involvement in the attempt on the life of former President Bush, Saddam's record on terrorist activities outside Iraq has been clean. He would need exceedingly powerful reasons to contaminate such a record.

In short, the fear that Iraq will use nonconventional weapons against adversaries in the Gulf or Israel, with either military or terrorist means, is therefore exaggerated. The fact that Saddam possesses some capability or that he has used it in the past does not automatically mean that he would use it again, particularly against superior opponents. In the nonconventional realm, the first rule is survival, and this also applies to a totalitarian ruler like Saddam Hussein.

Saddam as Rational Decision Maker

There is little doubt that the essence and dimension of the threats emanating from Iraq are directly linked to Saddam's nature and character as a decision maker. The conventional wisdom in the West and in many parts of the Middle East, which stands behind the ongoing fear of Saddam, is that he is a mentally disturbed and highly irrational ruler, who is capable of virtually any act and atrocity. This is far from the truth.

It is indeed possible to attribute to Saddam the full range of negative titles and adjectives: tyrant, dictator, megalomaniac, totalitarian, brutal, unpredictable, and dangerous. But none of these descriptions automatically makes him irrational or hopelessly, irretrievably disturbed. The test of rulers' and decision makers' rationality is in their ability to weigh various considerations, particularly cost-effectiveness, to read reality soberly, to set attainable goals, and to pursue them with logical methods or change them when confronted with evidence that they are mistaken. For the most part, Saddam passes this test.

His rationality has been proven more than once, and in a variety of difficult situations. During the First Gulf War, he did not hesitate to order a full withdrawal from Iranian territory when he realized that his army's invasion of Khuzistan had failed. And for the next six years, as the war continued to sap Iraq's strength, he pleaded for a negotiated settlement. In the political arena, he made favorable gestures – albeit of tactical nature – toward Egypt, the United States, and even Israel. He did not employ CW in the Second Gulf War and did not even make preparations to do so in Kuwait, notwithstanding blatant threats and a humiliating defeat. And after the war, he swallowed both the personal insults and the protracted violation of Iraq's sovereignty by the UN inspection regime, and he refrained from using chemical agents when he suppressed the Shi'ite and Kurdish rebellions. Finally, his subsequent deceptions of UNSCOM should not be seen as irrational, but rather as attempts to remove the severe restrictions imposed on Iraq and stand tall in the eyes of his own people.

Saddam has indeed made grave mistakes as a decision maker, but it is significant that most of them were made before the Second Gulf War. When he launched the First Gulf War in 1980, he acted on the mistaken assumption that Iran's army had fallen apart. When he invaded Kuwait, he was operating under the spell of victory over Iran and the conviction that the United States would not be ready "to sacrifice 10,000 soldiers in one battle," an outcome that even many American analysts predicted at the time. But since then, he appears to behave differently in showing a much greater aversion to risk. In any event, incorrect calculations are the daily bread of many rulers, even the best and the brightest, and they do not reflect some fundamental irrationality or mental disturbance. Saddam has shown that he is ready to go to the brink and defy his adversaries, but he has also proven that he knows when to stop, and even retreat, before he crosses a critical threshold. He is not a democratic leader in the Western mold, but neither does he suffer from a suicidal compulsion. Therefore, as long as his personal existence and his rule over Iraq are not drastically threatened and he still has something more to lose, there is little reason to expect that Saddam will lose control and act irrationally, i.e., use nonconventional weapons. Still, the risk that this will happen cannot be completely eliminated until the link between Saddam and nonconventional weapons is completely severed.

Iraq's Strategic Environment

Iraq's strategic environment needs to be examined at two levels: the external one, particularly involving the United States and the international sanctions and inspection regimes, and the neighboring one, namely, Iran, Syria, and Turkey. The Kurdish region has a special status, combining international and regional factors with domestic considerations. In addition, Iraq has a peculiar connection with Israel.

The External Environment

The United States

The United States, which led the Second Gulf War coalition to victory, is the central factor constraining Iraq's threat potential. At the same time, the United States is also largely responsible for not having reaped the political gains of the war and preventing the threat from persisting after the war.

The problematic nature of American policy toward Iraq stems from its basic ambivalence: it seeks to contain and perhaps eliminate the brutal regime in Baghdad, but it does not aim to dismantle Iraq or even weaken it to the point where it would be unable to balance the power of fundamentalist Iran in the Gulf. Removing Saddam from power, during the war or after it, would have involved immense intelligence and operational obstacles, not to mention the serious political and diplomatic constraints. Even a tough policy with less ambitious goals is complicated by the very different agendas of other key countries: Russia, France, China, many of the Arab states, and even Turkey. Russia and France, to which Iraq owes huge sums of money (about $10 billion each), look forward to extensive business ties with Baghdad and make it difficult to maintain a consistently harsh policy against it.

Notwithstanding these countervailing factors, the United States could have acted more forcefully against Saddam if it had really wanted to, either alone or with the support of Britain and perhaps even some Arab states. However, President Clinton, who at one point had expressed reservations about the stern policy of his predecessor, George Bush, did not appear to favor drastic and prolonged measures in the absence of a worldwide consensus. Saddam, whose approach to the use of force is less conservative, interpreted this as weakness, and therefore the result has been a cycle of confrontations – at least once a year since the end of the Second Gulf War. These confrontations always imply a certain potential for escalation and consume the expensive resources of the United States and its allies. In the crisis of October 1994, for example, the United States amassed a force of about 600 aircraft and about 40,000 troops in the Gulf, the estimated cost of which was about half a billion dollars; in the late 1997/early 1998 crisis, more than 250 jets, two aircraft carriers, about 30 escort and support ships, and about 40,000 troops were again deployed in the area, adding another $1 billion to the U.S. military budget.

The United States acted against Iraq within the framework of "dual containment." Much criticism has been directed against this policy, but it is difficult to envision a feasible alternative. After the policy of supporting Iraq against Iran during the First Gulf War proved a failure during the Kuwait crisis and the Second Gulf War, there was no real possibility of "changing horses," i.e., of switching to active support of Iran in the hopes of promoting a new "military balance."

True, the U.S. could have denounced Saddam as a war criminal (as it has done in the case of Serb leaders in Bosnia), thereby laying the groundwork for a sustained attempt to remove him from office. But that would have provided no immediate relief from the threat he posed. It could also have exploited the confrontations initiated by Iraq to strike hard at targets directly connected with Saddam and his regime – the Republican Guard, the Special Guard, communications and electricity sites, bridges, and, of course, palaces and property owned by Saddam and his clique. Such moves would have had a better chance of restraining Saddam's behavior and undermining his regime, without provoking either some act of last-ditch desperation on his part or the disintegration of Iraq. At the very least, they would have shown that despotism and aggression do not pay and are dangerous to their perpetrators.

Instead, the U.S. contented itself with a much weaker form of containment. In response to at least nine confrontations and crises provoked by Saddam, it carried out three or four military attacks on targets in Iraq: two in 1993 (the first following the movement of some Iraqi troops, the second in retaliation for an assassination attempt on President Bush in Kuwait in the end of 1992), and one in 1996 (in response to Saddam's brief invasion of Kurdistan and conquest of Irbil). All these strikes were on military targets proper, mostly on air defense assets in the south of Iraq but also two on an intelligence base and a ''nuclear site.'' None of the strikes was especially devastating, and only the last ones were in the area of Baghdad – close to the heart of the region. Given its location and context, the September 1996 attack on the air defense disposition in the south was a particularly curious response to Saddam's ''transgression'' in Kurdistan; it did, indeed, weaken Iraqi air defenses, but that could have no perceptible impact on Saddam's regime. It is even more noteworthy that the U.S. did not exploit the movement of two Republican Guard divisions to the south in October 1994 – or the invasion of Kurdistan, or the expulsion of American UNSCOM inspectors in late 1997 – to strike a heavy blow at the Guard.

On the other hand, the United States did take a significant step in October 1994, when it reacted to the Iraqi troop concentration by enforcing the ''no-fly zones'' in the north, beyond the 36th parallel, and in the south, up to the 32nd parallel,[14] and applying a ''no-drive zone'' in the south. These measures not only reduced the ''breathing room'' of the Iraqi air and ground forces; they also struck directly at Iraq's sovereignty, hence at Saddam's own prestige.

Sanctions and Inspections

The other main factor restraining Iraq's threat potential has been the international sanctions and inspection regime. This pillar, however, has been undermined by a lack of consistency, and particularly by the significant softening of the U.S. position and the lack of a military response during and after the crisis of November 1997. Forbearance in the face of the deportation of American inspectors, the failure to pass Security Council resolutions, accommodation of Iraq's demands to change the composition of the inspection teams, and the willingness to expand the ''oil-for-food'' deal to $6 billion instead of $4 billion all rewarded Saddam for his challenges. These actions may well have diminished the image of America in Saddam's eyes and laid the groundwork for further challenges and greater threats in the future.

Economic Sanctions and the Embargo

The trade sanctions and oil export embargo make life quite difficult for Iraq. Not only do they harm Iraq's economy and sovereignty; they also deprive it of the foreign currency it so badly needs to buy parts and equipment for the army, industry, and even agriculture. It is no wonder that Saddam has persistently fought the regime, with particular vigor since 1994. The burden of sanctions also led him to make one of his major mistakes – the massing of forces opposite Kuwait in October 1994 – for which he paid by being forced to recognize Kuwait's sovereignty and borders and to accept the ''no-drive zone'' in the south.

Various organizations around the world, especially humanitarian ones, have joined hands to pressure the UN and the United States to ease the sanctions. To this end, they have produced statistics – almost certainly exaggerated – about hundreds of thousands of Iraqi children suffering from malnutrition and a shortage of medication. Even if these statistics are based in fact, the accusatory finger should have been pointed at Saddam Hussein – who has wasted many hundreds of millions of dollars on dozens of luxurious palaces, monuments, and mosques meant to glorify himself.[15] If Saddam were really interested in the welfare of his people, he could have accepted UN Security Council Resolution 706 in the summer of 1991. This allowed him to export $1.6 billion in oil every six months and to use the proceeds for food and medicine. Instead, he rejected the offer as an infringement of Iraqi sovereignty, because the ''oil-for-food'' program was to be supervised by the UN and one-third of the projected revenue was reserved for war reparations and the financing of UN operations in Iraq, leaving only two-thirds for food and medicine. Saddam persisted in his rejection even after the oil quota was raised to $2 billion in the spring of 1995, and he finally accepted it only in May 1996.[16] By the end of 1997, 25 million tons of oil could have been exported, bringing in about $4 billion. These figures represent about one-fifth of Iraq's annual oil exports and revenues before the war. Although the sum is relatively small, it provides the Iraqi economy with some breathing room, reflected in the rising value of the Iraqi dinar.[17] The increase in oil exports to $10 billion per annum will obviously provide even greater relief.

Nevertheless, Saddam continues to struggle against the sanctions. He realizes that their elimination or easing is directly related to progress in dismantling his weapons of mass destruction. Indeed, he himself brings up clause 22 of Security Council Resolution 687 – the ''mother'' of all UN resolutions on Iraq – to strengthen the linkage. Only, in his opinion, he has already fulfilled his obligations under this clause. The UN and the United States have a decidedly different opinion. For a long time, he therefore demanded, not the immediate cancellation of the sanctions, but only a timetable for that. But when that had not been produced at the end of 1997, he himself determined that inspections would end in six months. In his campaign to end the sanctions, he was supported by Russia, France, and even China, all of which hoped to benefit from a revival of the Iraqi economy.

Parallel to the political struggle to end the regime, Saddam also sought practical ways to circumvent the sanctions. Quantities of oil and other products were smuggled in and out through a variety of routes – through Iran, through the Kurdish area and Turkey, and even through the Gulf. For example, from the end of 1994 to mid-1996, the American Fifth Fleet, operating in the Gulf within the framework of Centcom, intercepted about 70 tankers and freighters carrying prohibited cargoes through the Gulf. In 1997, Saddam also defied the embargo on air traffic when he sent pilgrims to Mecca on Iraqi airplanes.

There are those who argue that since the sanctions have failed to subdue Iraq, the benefit from them does not justify the damage they have done. The alternative, however, would have been worse. The fact that Saddam was and remains prepared to resist full exposure of his weapons of mass destruction by almost any means in order to maintain his unique source of strength – and thereby endure a revenue loss of $110 billion to $140 billion by the beginning of 1998 – reinforces the grave suspicions about his intentions. And above all, the fact that he has been fighting the sanctions in every way possible is itself evidence of their effectiveness.

If the sanctions and the embargo were removed before it was solidly confirmed that all of Iraq's weapons of mass destruction (WMD) had been eliminated, that would be a victory for despotism and aggression over international norms. It would also enable Saddam to revive his threats against Iraq's neighbors, and others further afield. As long as Saddam remains in power, this outcome is avoided by maintenance of the sanctions.

The Inspection Regime

The UN Special Commission set up to uncover and dismantle Iraq's WMD has been unable to completely fulfill its mission. Nevertheless, it has achieved a considerable measure of success, and without it, Iraq's threat potential would certainly have been greater.

There are at least two types of difficulties confronting the inspection regime. One is inherent in the work of any intelligence organization, namely, that one can never know everything in time. The second is specific to the Iraqi context, namely, the obstructive and deceptive tactics used by Iraqi authorities to mislead the UN inspectors.

Just as the intelligence on Iraq during the Second Gulf War was incomplete, so, too, does UNSCOM lack current and reliable information. True, visual intelligence is quite good; U-2 overflights, coalition air patrols in Iraqi airspace, and even UNSCOM's own helicopters can provide significant information. But "visint," alone, is inherently limited in what it can reveal. Where UNSCOM, like coalition intelligence during the Second Gulf War, falls short is in human intelligence – "humint." The most important revelations after the war came from senior Iraqi defectors – particularly Hussein Kamal, who defected to Jordan in the summer of 1995. But this is chance information, not systemic and regular. Thus the inspection teams were uninformed about two central matters: BW and VX. Another intrinsic impediment for inspectors is the existence of dual-use technologies: in chemical warfare, the pesticide plants; in biological warfare, the pharmaceutical factories; and in surface-to-surface missiles, the permitted production of missiles with a range up to 150 kilometers.

It is not surprising that Iraq, following its defeat, has done its utmost to preserve its residual WMD through whatever deception, obstruction, and harassment of inspectors it can get away with. Notwithstanding its obligation to provide information to UNSCOM, it has only done so when confronted with undeniable evidence, and then, the information has been partial, inaccurate, and delayed. For example, since 1991, Iraq has submitted three "full and final" lists of its chemical warfare inventories, each different from the other two and from what UNSCOM already knew. The same situation prevails with respect to the other inspection "files."

After the defection of Hussein Kamal, Iraq immediately admitted that it had had a BW program and had produced VX gas, but it added that "everything" had been destroyed. Shortly thereafter, it tried to bar UNSCOM from "presidential" and "sensitive" sites – where the remaining WMD are suspected of being hidden – and to single out American involvement – about 12 UNSCOM inspectors out of more than 100, and U-2 overflights – because the U.S. is the moving force behind the strict supervision regime. Beginning in October 1997, the UNSCOM center in Baghdad was also attacked three times with rocket-propelled-grenades (RPG).

Despite Iraqi harassment, and the lukewarm attitude of Russia and some other powers, UNSCOM and the IAEA registered some very significant accomplishments. They appear to have exposed and dismantled most of Iraq's nuclear, surface-to-surface missile and chemical weapon sites, even if their achievements in the BW field are less reassuring. They carried out thousands of intrusive inspection operations and, since 1994, have maintained a permanent monitoring system of about 200 cameras and dozens of sensors in about 250 Iraqi installations connected with the development and production of WMD. There is no historical precedent for this. Rolf Ekeus, UNSCOM's former chairman, rightly claimed that inspections eliminated several times more WMD and SSMs than did the 42-day bombing campaign during the Second Gulf War. Moreover, the inspections forced Iraq into a nonstop effort to conceal its weapons, by constantly moving them around from place to place. This necessarily degraded readiness and serviceability. Above all, it is clear that the inspections severely curtailed the threat that Saddam could otherwise have posed to the region and the rest of the world.

The Regional Environment

Iran

Iran is Iraq's traditional enemy and historical rival for hegemony in the Gulf. But because of its harsh defeat at the end of the Second Gulf War and the isolation imposed by the sanctions and inspections regimes, Baghdad was forced to modify its approach to Iran.

Aside from bilateral visits of senior ministers, which contribute to an improved atmosphere, this approach was primarily reflected in Iraq's withdrawal from all the Iranian territory it occupied in the final stage of the First Gulf War, even as Iran held on to the Iraqi aircraft flown to "safety" there during the Second Gulf War. Baghdad takes strong exception to occasional Iranian attacks on Mujahedin bases in Iraq. One such attack, in April 1992, actually served as a pretext for the resumption of Iraqi Air Force flights, which were forbidden at the end of the war. This action was ignored by the U.S., presumably on the assumption that a further deterioration in Iraq's capabilities would have left it even more exposed to Iranian inroads.

In fact, there is no evidence that Iran has any real aggressive designs on Iraq. Iran could have taken advantage of Saddam's suppressing the 1991–92 Shi'ite rebellions in the south, but it did not. And while this passivity may have been due to concern about American and/or Arab reactions, Iran actually has no cause to be overly concerned about the current situation: Iraq is isolated and contained strategically, and it does not compete with Iran in the oil export market. Indeed, Iran even helps to circumvent the embargo and sanctions on Iraqi trade by allowing smugglers (perhaps for a financial consideration) to use its territory and territorial waters. Nor does its support of the PUK faction in intra-Kurdish conflicts necessarily reflect any ambitions of its own in northern Iraq. Iran even solicited Saddam's personal participation in the Islamic conference in Teheran in December 1997 – the first such invitation since the outbreak of the Iran-Iraq War in 1980.

Despite these indications of reconciliation, any Iraqi regime will continue to see in Iran an untrustworthy partner and constant potential threat, and it is not coincidental that a significant part of Iraq's military remains deployed along the Iranian border. The reason for the basic rivalry and suspicion is not just ideological/religious. Strategic constants play a major role. In terms of staying power, Iran has a permanent advantage over Iraq because it is three times larger and more populous. Moreover, its geographic contours provide an edge in the competition for control of the Gulf, and the proximity to the border of Iraq's major cities increases their vulnerability. During and after the Iran-Iraq War, Iraq was able to balance these advantages with military superiority, which is one obvious reason why it strives to maintain its armed forces, and particularly its nonconventional capabilities.

Syria

Iraq's relationship with Syria is perhaps less threatening but almost as complex. The two Ba'th regimes and the two presidents have been separated by a gulf of ideological and personal hostility. Nor has Iraq forgotten Syria's political and material assistance to Iran during the First Gulf War or its participation in the second. Nevertheless, neither side seems determined or able to pose a real threat to the other. In fact, there have been signs of a thaw in bilateral ties: in the summer of 1997, the border between Syria and Iraq was reopened after being closed for two decades, and at the end of the year, the Iraqi deputy prime minister, Tareq Aziz, paid a visit to Damascus. Syria has also publicly and consistently expressed its reservations about the continuing sanctions and the possibility of further American attacks on Iraq. Assad and his leadership might not be overly dismayed at the prospect of a further weakening of Saddam, but they have no obvious interest in seeing Iraq dismantled. Syria's interest in a rapprochement is probably linked to its desire to counter the strategic rapprochement between Israel and Turkey. Damascus and Baghdad also have a common interest in opposing Turkish control or diversion of Euphrates River water and in preventing the emergence of an independent and sovereign Kurdish entity. But while these common interests might facilitate some improvement in bilateral relations, they cannot erase the history of mutual suspicion and hostility. Moreover, Syria apparently promised the United States not to breach the economic sanctions on Iraq after Iraq signaled a desire to export oil through the old Iraqi-Syrian (IPC) pipeline.

Thus the rapprochement with Syria holds out the promise of breaching Iraq's strategic isolation, and if it intensifies, it could strengthen Iraq's self-confidence and threat potential, even with respect to Israel.

Turkey

Turkey and Iraq, along with Iran and Syria, share a complex strategic challenge: the Kurdish problem. About half of all the Kurds in the Middle East (about 10 million) live in Turkey, and those in the PKK have been in a state of insurgency for many years. Turkey's Kurdish problem also spills over into northern Iraq, either because the PKK uses northern Iraq as a refuge and base area from which to attack Turkish targets, or because parts of Kurdistan have become a kind of no-man's-land between Iraq and Turkey. In any event, Turkey views the Kurdish region of northern Iraq as a buffer zone in which it can operate rather freely.

In fact, Turkish and Iraqi interests converge here: both, along with Iran and Syria, are firmly opposed to Kurdish independence and view Kurdish nationalism as a severe threat to their sovereignty. At the same time, none of these countries is really confident about the intentions of the others. Iraq fears that Turkey might be tempted to take control of the Kirkuk area, which is rich in oil and connected by pipelines to southern Turkey. And even if this does not happen,

Baghdad is certainly not pleased by Turkey's constant meddling and involvement in Iraqi Kurdistan and its efforts to build influence there. Iraq also resents Turkey's control of the sources of the Euphrates and its ability to reduce or cut off the flow of water. Turkey has signaled more than once (to Iraq as well as to Syria) that the issue of water is related to the Kurdish problem. Equally disturbing to Iraq is the presence of a small U.S.-led multinational force at Incirlik air base, in southern Turkey.

At the same time, Iraq needs Turkey as a route for its exports of oil and other legal and illegal commerce. This, together with their common Kurdish concern, precipitated some rapprochement between Turkey and Iraq (and even Iran) in the years 1992–1994. This process was slowed following Saddam's renewed threat against Kuwait in October 1994 and particularly by the takeover of Irbil in the summer of 1996. Nevertheless, the fact that Turkey was also paying a price for the sanctions and the embargo on Iraq – by Turkish accounts, about $5 billion per year – led the two countries, in 1993, to demand the resumption of oil exports through Turkish pipelines; this demand was met in 1996. Turkey also facilitated the passage of food, medicine, and some other goods through the Kurdish region.

Although Turkey shows no intention of taking over Iraqi Kurdistan, its need to fight PKK rebels dictates its activities there. Turkey believes that it has the right to operate against the PKK wherever it finds refuge and operating bases, and this is certainly the case in northern Iraq, where the writ of the central Iraqi government does not run. Nor does it expect that it will encounter harsh opposition from the United States, which needs bases in Turkey. Turkey therefore allows itself extensive freedom of action, for many years from the air, and since 1994, on the ground, as well. This has involved extensive and protracted incursions every year, often in cooperation with the PDK, one of the two major Iraqi Kurdish factions. On some occasions, these incursions have taken on the character of de facto Turkish occupation; in 1997 alone, there were two such large-scale operations. These operations have been rather expensive – estimates run to $1 billion a year – but Turkey is persistent, and it eventually brought about a significant weakening of the PKK.

There is not much that Iraq can do about this breach of its sovereignty, and perhaps it does not even disturb Iraq that much. In any case, the common Iraqi-Turkish interest on the Kurdish issue strengthens Baghdad in face of the Kurdish challenge in the north, but it also serves to constrain Iraq's threat potential.

The Kurdish Region

Iraq's long-standing and difficult problem with its Kurds (who make up about one-fifth of the population) escalated following the Second Gulf War. After the 1991 Kurdish rebellion was brutally suppressed by Saddam, the United States and its allies offered protection in the framework of "Operation Provide Comfort." This action had the effect of ending Baghdad's de facto (but not de jure) rule over Kurdistan, and a separate autonomous area was established under the supervision of the UN and the small multinational force in based in Turkey. As part of this arrangement, a ban was also placed on Iraqi flights beyond the 36th parallel.

Saddam, for his part, responded at the end of 1991 by blockading the Kurdish region and established a 500-kilometer-long fortified military line, preventing the passage of food and oil to the Kurds. Saddam's move was puzzling, even paradoxical, since he had always opposed full Kurdish independence and autonomy, but by taking this measure, he himself contributed to the practical elimination of his authority over the region, at least temporarily. If he thought he could starve the Kurds into submission, he was mistaken.

Iraq's primary interest in the Kurdish region is to prevent the disintegration of the country and a linkup of Kirkuk, with its oil resources, to the autonomous Kurdish region. In fact, the very existence of this region poses a direct affront to Iraq's sovereignty and to Saddam's prestige, and it facilitates Iranian and Turkish meddling. In addition, the multinational force in southern Turkey, though focused on protecting the Kurds, is a constant threat to Saddam. It is therefore not surprising that he deploys a significant military force in the north.

The traditionally deep rift among the Kurds (the PDK headed by Massoud Barazani, the PUK headed by Jalal Talabani, the PKK headed by Abdullah Ocalan, and others) has allowed Saddam to play different groups against each other and ease the threat to the central government. One result is that he uses the region to import and export smuggled goods and oil to and from Turkey and Iran, mainly with the assistance of the PDK. These rifts reached a peak in the summer of 1996, due to the cooperation between Jalal Talabani's PUK and Iran against the PDK. Talabani's takeover of parts of

Kurdistan created a crisis that Saddam did not initiate but that he could exploit. In response to an invitation by Barazani, he ordered his army to invade and conquer the region's capital, Irbil. But if Saddam believed that the United States would not react, perhaps because of Iran's involvement in the area or because he was assisting the pro-American PDK, then he erred. The U.S. treated this action as a violation of the cease-fire agreements and forced Saddam to withdraw, under the pressure of about 40 cruise-missile strikes. But before doing so, he cleared the area of factors hostile to him, including agents of the CIA. In any event, the invasion of Irbil indicates that Saddam did not give up his claims of sovereignty over the Kurdish region, and his defiant measure even improved his image and standing within Iraq and among his neighbors.

Israel

Since the Iraqi missile attack on Israel during the Second Gulf War, the question of Iraq's threat potential is a constant concern for the Israeli public. More specifically, is Iraq capable of initiating or joining an all-out war against Israel, and if not, in what way, if at all, can Iraq attack Israel if it decides to do so?

The establishment of an "eastern front" including Iraq was always a great danger for Israel, because it would adversely affect the balance of forces and compel Israel to fight simultaneously on more than one front. To this front, Iraq could have contributed an expeditionary air and ground force that would have been not much smaller than the Syrian order-of-battle and certainly much larger than that of Jordan. But the Iraqi Army's defeat in the Second Gulf War and its subsequent weaknesses appear to make it impossible for Iraq to play a significant role in an "eastern front" in the near future. The Iraqi Army lacks all the elements of strength – the order-of-battle, the ground and air weapons, and the appropriate logistics – needed to fight 1,000 kilometers away from its home bases. A full-fledged war against Israel therefore does not appear to be a real option for Iraq, and it is unlikely to send large forces for that purpose.

Iraq might have the option of again attacking Israel with surface-to-surface missiles, but this is also problematic. For all his provocative rhetoric, it is noteworthy that in the nine confrontations and crises following the war, Saddam did not launch even one missile against Israel. It is therefore difficult to explain recurrent Israeli fears of an Iraqi missile attack, especially one with nonconventional warheads, in the context of Saddam's confrontation with the UN and the United States.

The risk of a conventional Iraqi missile attack is low. First of all, Saddam almost certainly does not have a significant SSM capability or the ability to deploy large numbers of SSMs in western Iraq, as he did during the war. Second, even if a few launchers and al-Hussein missiles able to reach Israel have survived, Iraq would not waste them on a routine confrontation, but would prefer to save them for essential defense in a real national emergency. Third, all of Saddam's confrontations have aimed at alleviating the sanctions and inspection regimes, and launching missiles against Israel would be undeniable proof that the reasons for those regimes, notwithstanding his claims, remained valid. Indeed, the result would probably be a further tightening of the regimes. Fourth, a missile attack on Israel would serve no real purpose, since there was no longer a coalition with an Arab element to be subverted. True, he might still be seeking revenge for the Israeli bombing of the Iraqi nuclear reactor in 1981, but he knows that surface-to-surface missiles (even with stone warheads) could not close that account. Finally, Saddam could assume that Israel would not again restrain itself in response to another missile attack, and distance would not protect him from Israeli retaliation. The political constraints on an Israeli response that operated during the Second Gulf War no longer exist, and Israel's strength – unlike Iraq's – has actually grown over the years, especially in air power, weapons systems (most notably, PGMs), antimissile operations, and retaliatory capacity. Moreover, if Israel were again attacked by missiles, it would have to respond vigorously, regardless of the damage or casualties it incurred, in order to retain any deterrent power.

The risk of a nonconventional attack is even more remote, since these weapons are mainly for deterrence, prestige, and hegemony, not for routine use. Even if Iraq has a residual nonconventional SSM capability, it would not automatically be directed at Israel, especially in a noncritical confrontation with it. Besides, Israel has the capacity to retaliate. Despite its humiliating defeat, it is no coincidence that Iraq did not use nonconventional weapons with any delivery systems during the Second Gulf War, either against the coalition or against Israel. The reason was not only fear of the adversary's nuclear advantage, but also Saddam's understanding that against opponents with equal or superior nonconventional capacity, the "rules of the game" are essentially different. And for all his brutality, Saddam would not lightly risk his country's survival, much less his own. Thus, as long as he does not himself possess nuclear weapons, the risk that Saddam would use other nonconventional SSMs against Israel is low. It has been argued that he might be tempted to launch chemically armed SSMs on the assumption that his BW capabilities would deter Israel from retaliating. This is a simplistic gamble, entailing an unacceptably high risk, even for Saddam. In any event, if the Arrow ATMB and other antimissile systems are deployed in 1999, Israel's "active defense" against the Iraqi threat will significantly improve.

It is difficult to understand the value of the passive defenses – gas masks, plastic sheets, and sealed rooms – to which Israel resorted during the Second Gulf War. These measures indirectly legitimized the use of gas and other nonconventional weapons by Iraq, and Israel's other enemies. The calculated risk of forgoing such measures would have signaled that Israel was not willing to tolerate an attack on its civilian population with such weapons under any circumstances, and that such an attack would cost the perpetrators their existence. It would also have prevented the damage done to Israel's deterrent power.

Iraq's residual strength following the Second Gulf War, especially in nonconventional capabilities, is far from negligible. However, it is not a simple matter to translate this capability into usable power: with its much-reduced capabilities, Iraq's ability to endanger its neighbors and others is severely limited, and this is the key to Saddam's postwar behavior. In every confrontation since 1991, he has eventually backed down, because his brutality is not matched by suicidal irrationality, and he is aware of the limits of his power. This point should be borne in mind whenever Saddam provokes a new crisis.

At the same time, that very brutality, combined with the dangerous weapons he retains, represents a source of uncertainty and instability that will persist until the link between the ruler and the weapons is severed. Thus, as long as Saddam remains in power, Iraq can only be contained by an uncompromising insistence on the inspection and dismantling of its WMD and SSMs and by the maintenance of the sanctions and the embargo until that is fully accomplished. The Iraqi threat can also be influenced by the policies of Iraq's neighbors, and even by a more measured Israeli response to any new crisis that does erupt, but the main burden will continue to fall on the United States.

Endnotes

1 In the First Gulf War, 2,870 tons were consumed, 690 tons were destroyed by UNSCOM, and 290 tons were lost during the Second Gulf War bombardments, in tests, and due to other causes.

2 Some 101,000 munitions were consumed in the First Gulf War, about 30,000 were unilaterally destroyed by Iraq, 38,537 were destroyed by UNSCOM, and about 78,000 were destroyed in the Second Gulf War or otherwise accounted for.

3 Some 160 air bombs had been filled with anthrax, botulinum and aflatoxin, along with 25 al-Hussein missile warheads (five with anthrax, 16 with botulinum, and four with aflatoxin). It was reported that these had been deployed in airfields and missile bases (i.e., ready to be used) prior to the last war. Iraq also equipped itself with all other relevant delivery systems – air bombs, artillery shells and rockets, aerosol spray dispensers, and possibly biological cluster munitions.

4 The U.S. assessment is more far-reaching: 100 kilograms of anthrax, released from an aircraft for maximum effect, could kill 1 million to 3 million people, roughly comparable to the casualties caused by a one-megaton hydrogen bomb.

5 The accounting is as follows: 516 SSMs were consumed in the First Gulf War and 93 in the Second; 48 were destroyed by UNSCOM; 83 by Iraq itself; 69 in tests and alterations; and eight in training.

6 UNSCOM was able to trace 83 of the 85 SSM engines Iraq claimed to have destroyed.

7 UNSCOM destroyed ten and has verified Iraq's destruction of nine more.

8 One delivery was intercepted in Jordan in late 1995, but another one did reach Baghdad.

9 It took more capable countries than Iraq some 10 to 15 years to build a nuclear weapons capacity.

10 In addition to other hostile actions against Iraqi forces, the Kurds actually helped Iran to capture Halabja in March 1988.

11 UN commissions appointed to investigate Iranian charges of Iraqi use of CW could not corroborate the accusations, and Iraq was never explicitly blamed.

12 Thus Egypt could use CW against rebel tribes in Yemen in the 1960s because there was no danger to its forces of a response in kind (and because the weapons were used far away from the public eye). The same is true of gas attacks on Iraqi Kurds.

13 Fears of this sort surged after a Japanese cult perpetrated a Sarin gas attack in a Tokyo subway, resulting in a dozen deaths.

14 In September 1996, the southern ''no-fly zone'' was extended northward to the 33rd parallel, bringing it virtually to the suburbs of Baghdad.

15 Then–U.S. Ambassador to the UN Madeleine Albright at one point mentioned that some $300 million had been squandered; more recent estimates point to a figure at least five times higher.

16 Because of the invasion of Kurdistan and Iraqi delays, oil exports did not actually begin until December 1996. Incidentally, Saddam's demand to export oil through the Gulf was rejected. Instead, it was sent through pipelines from Kirkuk to Turkey, partly to compensate Turkey for the losses it had suffered from sanctions on Iraq, partly to facilitate international supervision.

17 Before the war, the prevailing exchange rate had been about three dinars to the dollar. Before the oil-for-food deal, it had skyrocketed to about 3,000 to the dollar, but then fell back to about 1,500–1,700.

5. U.S. Dual Containment Policy in the Persian Gulf

Gerald L. Sorokin

In the years that followed the Gulf War of 1990–91, United States policy with respect to the major states of the Persian Gulf was driven by a complex set of priorities and variable levels of support by its friends and allies. First the Bush and then the Clinton administrations were concerned with maintaining good relations with the Gulf Cooperation Council (GCC) states, especially Saudi Arabia, while perceiving both Iran and Iraq as threats to regional political and economic stability. Previous administrations had tried to apply balance-of-power logic to Iran and Iraq, supporting one of them in an effort to offset threats from the other, but this approach had disastrous consequences: the fall of the U.S.-supported Shah led to intense animosity between Iran and the United States beginning in the late 1970s; the U.S.-supported Iraqi military buildup during and after the Iran-Iraq War enabled Saddam Hussein to capture Kuwait and brought on the Gulf War. Iran and Iraq were both seen as outlaws, rogues, or "backlash states"[1] that could not be trusted to play by the generally accepted rules of international politics. A regional balance of power approach was thus not acceptable: supporting Iraq had been discredited by the war, and supporting Iran remained unthinkable for U.S. policymakers. The obvious alternative was to side with neither Iran nor Iraq, instead pursuing what National Security Council official Martin Indyk dubbed "dual containment" in a speech shortly after the Clinton administration took office.[2] Dual containment involved the simultaneous use of deterrent threats, alliances, and economic sanctions to isolate Iran and Iraq, in hopes of ultimately preventing both of them from projecting power and threatening regional stability.

Dual containment was not so much a coherent policy as a set of tools the Clinton administration developed largely for the benefit of domestic and foreign political audiences. It was a convenient shorthand[3] for the administration's attempt to maintain pressure on both Iran and Iraq in hopes of limiting their ability to threaten their neighbors, reducing their external influence and, if possible, effecting internal political change. A few aspects of dual containment were aimed at both target states simultaneously, while most were directed at only one of them. In a real sense, then, dual containment was neither truly ''dual'' nor exactly ''containment,'' but rather a package of parallel and sometimes overlapping deterrent and compellent strategies for addressing perceived threats from the two Gulf neighbors. To the extent that the policy relied on the presence of U.S. forces and military cooperation with other Gulf states, it had the potential to alter the behavior of both Iran and Iraq. But much of the policy depended on political and economic isolation that was necessarily aimed specifically at one or the other. And to call the policy's goal ''containment'' is to understate the level of change the Clinton administration wanted to bring about. The United States was seeking a permanent reshuffling of the power hierarchy in the Middle East, so that Iran and Iraq would lack the capability and, eventually, the desire to project force and endanger regional stability.

By advocating and coordinating a dual containment approach, the United States attempted to prolong the coalition that it assembled during the Gulf War. But therein lay the major difficulty with dual containment: it relied on other states, both in the Gulf region and elsewhere, to support U.S. aims and comply with its policies. The United States had experience in this type of international coordination. Most notably, during the cold war, the countries of the North Atlantic Treaty Organization (NATO) deferred to American political leadership and complied with the economic isolation of the Soviet Bloc in order to gain the security benefits of U.S. military allocations. The trade-offs the NATO allies made involved a large U.S. military presence on their territory and constraints on their economic contact with the Warsaw Pact in exchange for gaining a military ''free ride'' from the United States. Given those countries' interest in economic development and their shared view of the threat from the East, the trade-offs were worthwhile.

The consensus among U.S. friends and allies with regard to the dual containment of Iran and Iraq was weaker. There was little debate about the desirability of isolating Iraq and preventing it from rebuilding its military capabilities. The states of the region feared that Saddam Hussein would again try to violate their borders and understood that U.S. involvement was their best chance of insuring that he complied with the post – Gulf War settlement. But there was plenty of opposition to treating Iran in the same way. With the exception of Israel, most of the United States' friends in the Middle East and elsewhere saw Iran as a potential economic partner with a large, educated population that was interested in reducing its self-imposed isolation from the outside world. To the extent that dual containment increased Iranian alienation from the rest of the world, some U.S. friends and allies saw it as having the potential to backfire, either internally, by strengthening ultraconservative, anti-Western forces, or externally, by increasing the pace of weapons development or support for terrorism. Thus there was a concern that dual containment might provoke in Iran exactly what it was designed to deter.

Meanwhile, even in states that feared the reemergence of a military threat from Iraq and received direct deterrent benefits from dual containment, there was resistance to the U.S. presence on at least three grounds. First, the U.S. could serve as a lightning rod, bringing about an increase in tension instead of deterrence stability. The more Saddam Hussein perceived himself as an international pariah whose sovereignty was being violated, the more he might attempt to provoke a confrontation with the United States or one of his neighbors. Second, U.S. intentions were hardly altruistic; there was a fear that its presence was intended to bring about changes that were undesirable for the states it was purportedly there to help. Conspiratorial explanations for U.S. involvement – from propping up U.S.-based multinational oil companies to helping Israel gain an upper hand in the peace process with the Palestinians to increasing U.S. domination of the world arms market – appear in both Middle Eastern and Western publications. Third, relying on any ally, whether the United States or a neighbor, is inherently risky: allies do not necessarily view threats in the same way, and they often do not honor their commitments. Given the U.S. public and congressional resistance to the use of force abroad, the states of the Gulf could not be fully confident that the Clinton administration would follow up on its commitments.

But dual containment was not in the end a failure. If anything, dual containment was, in Patrick Clawson's words, "a victim of its own success."[4] By relying on modern military technologies to deter aggression, and by putting pressure on the governments of Iran and Iraq, the United States kept both countries in check militarily and enabled friendly states in the Gulf region to reach out to moderates in the backlash states. Moreover, the election of a moderate Iranian president, Muhammad Khatami, in May 1997, which set the stage for at least a potential rapprochement between the United States and Iran, may have been a partial reflection of the impact of Iran's isolation under dual containment.

Alternative policies were unlikely to produce any better results than dual containment. Short of going to war or facilitating a military coup, which would have been extremely costly militarily, economically, and, most important, politically – and which would not have been guaranteed to succeed – it is hard to imagine a better way to hinder Saddam Hussein's ambitions than the Clinton administration's approach. And while Iran's pursuit of advanced military capabilities and support for terrorism were not halted by dual containment, the progress in its relations with Europe and the Arab world, as well as its internal liberalization, were facilitated by the pressure applied by the United States.

This chapter discusses dual containment from the point of view of U.S. goals, the policies developed and implemented in pursuit of these goals, and the barriers to their achievement posed by friendly states in the region and U.S. allies elsewhere. It shows that while dual containment was often incoherent and compliance was less than perfect, its results were far better than some critics predicted and others now claim. The Clinton administration's combination of muddling through, strong-arm political pressure, and military force reinforced the United Nations sanctions regime, which kept Saddam Hussein from increasing significantly his military threat, and it enabled the moderates in Iran to reach out – all the while maintaining positive relations with the Gulf states that had been part of the U.S.-led coalition in the 1990–91 war. That neither Saddam nor the Ayatollahs were pushed out of power was, perhaps, a disappointment to the Clinton administration, but it should not be interpreted as proof that dual containment failed. The United States and most of its allies understood that they lacked the political or military capabilities to bring about major internal political changes in Iran and Iraq without incurring significant, and likely long-lasting, costs. Being willing to live with unfriendly regimes in Iran and Iraq does not imply being willing to tolerate behavior from those regimes that interferes with U.S. interests. Dual containment was a way to modify Iranian and Iraqi behavior so as to contribute to regional stability.

Rogue States and the Threat of a Regional Hegemon

In 1990, a study group of The Washington Institute for Near East Policy, which included future Clinton administration officials, such as Madeleine Albright, Les Aspin, William Cohen, and Martin Indyk, issued a report on U.S. strategy in the Persian Gulf. The report laid out U.S. interests as follows:

> The United States should seek to create a global security environment – including the maintenance of stable regional military balances in key areas – so that local bullies will be unable to determine the fate of their neighbors. The United States should attempt to prevent the proliferation of destabilizing weapons of mass destruction. At the same time the United States should continue to stand for values that may be revolutionary elsewhere, including in the Middle East, such as political freedom, human rights, and the establishment of democratic institutions.[5]

Written in the midst of the Gulf crisis – after the Iraqi invasion of Kuwait but before the U.S. bombing and ground war that defeated Iraq – this assessment of U.S. interests turned out to be the foundation on which dual containment was built. Indyk and his colleagues believed that the United States needed to focus on preventing the emergence of a heavily armed regional power with hegemonic aspirations in order to protect U.S. (and, more broadly, developed world) access to Gulf oil and other commercial and political contacts.

The goals the United States pursues in the Gulf do not fluctuate drastically with changes in political leadership or the state of the global economy. Fundamental U.S. interests are based not on Saddam Hussein or the Ayatollahs as individuals, nor on short-term changes in interest rates or oil prices, but on long-term geopolitical and geoeconomic considerations. Indeed, the goals driving dual containment were similar to the justifications for U.S. involvement in the Gulf that led to the 1990–91 war and the Bush administration's postwar Gulf policy: uninterrupted access to oil, regional stability, preventing the rise of a regional hegemon. There was a remarkable level of agreement within the U.S. government, among its international friends and allies, and even among commentators, on these needs. Differences of opinion tended to be about the means for achieving the goals, that is, on whether dual containment or some other approach was the best choice.

The end of the Gulf War had created two sets of concerns for the United States. First, a renewed military threat from Iraq or Iran had the potential to destabilize the Middle East, which could threaten regional borders and U.S. and world economic interests. Although much of Saddam Hussein's military power had been destroyed in the war, he had demonstrated not only the ability but also the willingness to use force – including weapons of mass destruction (WMD) – against both neighboring states and his own people. Iran's program of rearmament, though not as far along as Iraq's, was also continuing. It, too, included weapons of mass destruction and missiles, as well as explicit calls for the end of U.S. involvement in the Gulf.[6] Second, the cooperation between the United States and its non–Middle East allies, on the one hand, and the other states of the region, on the other, had paid great dividends during the Gulf War. The United States wanted to sustain that cooperation while maintaining its leadership position.

The difficulty in dealing with states like Iran and Iraq was not simply that they had ambitions to become militarily powerful, but that the source of those ambitions was their unwillingness to abide by the generally accepted rules of international behavior. According to former National Security Advisor, Anthony Lake, "backlash states . . . exhibit a chronic inability to engage constructively with the outside world, and they do not function effectively in alliances – even with those like-minded." Moreover, because they have "a siege mentality, . . . they [embark] on ambitious and costly military programs . . . in a misguided quest for a great equalizer to protect their regimes or advance their purposes abroad."[7] Rogue states are not irrational; if anything, they are rational to a fault, often willing to absorb high costs (military, financial, even human) in pursuit of their objectives. They are willing to take risks that other states might find unacceptable. Restricting the behavior of rogue states thus requires clarity of purpose and coordination of policies among states and international organizations.

Elements of Dual Containment

In 1996, the former Iranian foreign minister, Ali Akbar Velayati, stated that "Persian Gulf security is the sole responsibility of the states of the region . . . [and] cannot be brought from outside."[8] Velayati may have been expressing his (and his government's) preference, but he was definitely not describing what has gone on in the Persian Gulf for decades. The United States has long been involved in maintaining regional security, although the nature of that involvement has changed over time. Before the end of the cold war and the Iraqi invasion of Kuwait, the United States had aligned itself with either Iran or Iraq in order to balance threats coming from the other. In the 1990s, this was neither necessary nor desirable, in the view of

U.S. officials. In his 1993 speech introducing dual containment, Indyk summarized the U.S. view as follows:

> The coalition that fought Saddam [in 1990–91] remains together, and as long as we are able to hold that coalition together and maintain our military presence in the region, as long as we succeed in restricting the military ambitions of both Iraq and Iran, and as long as we can rely on our regional allies – Egypt, Israel, Saudi Arabia, the GCC, and Turkey – to preserve a balance of power in our favor in the wider Middle East region, we will have the means to counter both the Iraqi and Iranian regimes. We will not need to depend on one to counter the other.[9]

Thus the balance of power was to be based not on Iran versus Iraq, but rather the United States and its coalition partners versus both Iran and Iraq. The United States wanted, not simply to balance Iran and Iraq, but to maintain the capability to overwhelm them militarily.

A year later, Lake explained that the environment in which the Clinton administration operated included four major factors that had been lacking for its predecessors:[10]

1. The collapse of the Soviet Union had created a new strategic situation. The United States no longer needed to worry that the Soviets would attempt to gain a foothold in the region, nor that the Iranians and Iraqis would attempt to play the superpowers off against one another.
2. The Iran-Iraq War, Iran's isolation from the rest of the world, and the Gulf War all served to reduce the absolute level of military capabilities in the two countries, giving the United States an even greater military advantage.
3. The GCC states were now more amenable to U.S. involvement than they had been before the Gulf War.
4. Progress in the Arab-Israeli peace process improved U.S. standing in the Arab world and reduced Iran's and Iraq's abilities to make political gains through their opposition to Israel.

In short, given the circumstances of the 1990s, dual containment seemed to Clinton administration officials to be a more cost-effective approach than a regional balance-of-power policy would have been.

Like the containment of the Soviet Union and Warsaw Pact during the cold war, dual containment was a multidimensional policy that relied on U.S. leadership and willingness to pay a disproportionate share of the costs. It involved aspects of both *deterrence* (dissuading Iran and Iraq from actions they would otherwise have taken) and *compellence* (persuading Iran and Iraq to do things they otherwise would not have done). A credible deterrent to expansionist military policies in Iran and Iraq required the United States to demonstrate (1) that it had the capability to repel an attack and inflict punishment in response and (2) that it was willing to do so. To demonstrate an independent deterrent capability, it stationed troops both on the ground in Persian Gulf states and on ships in the Gulf. According to Patrick Clawson, the average U.S. presence in the Gulf was "25,000 personnel, 25 ships, 100 warplanes, and sufficient prepositioned equipment for 1⅓ heavy armored divisions (to increase to 2 divisions by 2000)."[11] The United States had the capability to increase these numbers quickly, as it did in February 1998, when its presence reached over 300 combat aircraft, including additional fighters and bombers based in Bahrain, Kuwait, and Diego Garcia; 30 ships, including two aircraft carrier groups; and roughly 35,000 personnel.[12] In raw terms, these numbers (with the exception of personnel) were close to the vastly reduced levels of conventional arms that Iran and Iraq were left with after the Iran-Iraq and Gulf wars.[13] More important than the quantitative ratio, however, was the qualitative difference between U.S. capabilities and those of Iraq or Iran: U.S. tanks, missiles, and aircraft were more modern and technologically sophisticated than anything its adversaries in the region possessed.

To increase the credibility of its containment, the United States supplemented and complemented its independent capability in the Gulf by cooperating with GCC states. In congressional testimony in 1996, former Assistant Secretary of State for Near Eastern Affairs Robert H. Pelletreau, explained that the U.S. approach had three dimensions:

> First, we help each Gulf state strengthen its own defense forces through our defense sales and training programs. Second, we encourage regional defense cooperation among the Gulf states through the GCC's collective security arrangements. Third, we promote bilateral U.S. security cooperation with individual states.[14]

While none of these steps constituted a formal alliance commitment – the United States did not declare that an attack on, say, Saudi Arabia would be treated as if it had been an attack on U.S. territory – they did add up to a substantial American effort to assist the GCC states' pursuit of security. The GCC states received military assistance, in the form of hardware and training; they paid part of the cost financially and materially; and they made political concessions to the United States, including, in many cases, U.S. personnel and matériel based on their territory. The common interests of the United States and the GCC members meant that the political costs were more than outweighed by the benefits of the military cooperation. And this high level of military cooperation increased the credibility of the U.S. deterrent threat by showing Iran and Iraq that U.S. policies were inextricably linked to the states of the region, whose security was directly affected by Iranian and Iraqi military capabilities.

The United States also tried to compel Iran and Iraq to restrict the development of weapons of mass destruction and the accumulation of large arsenals that could be used against neighboring countries friendly to the United States. One way it tried to achieve this compellence in the case of Iraq was to support the United Nations effort to inspect and dismantle Iraq's weapons programs. With respect to both of the targets of dual containment, the United States also tried to inflict pain on their economies by coordinating economic sanctions, including bans on oil sales and technology transfers. It hoped that the combination of these efforts would lead to policy changes and, ultimately, the fall of the governments of Saddam Hussein in Iraq and the hard-line Islamists in Iran.

But the containment of Iran and Iraq was starkly different from the containment of the Soviet Union and Eastern Europe in at least one fundamental way: while it was aimed simultaneously at two neighboring countries, dual containment was never intended to be a single policy with a double target; in Lake's words, " 'Dual Containment' does not mean duplicate containment."[15] Iran and Iraq were not in alliance with one another, having been longtime rivals for influence in the region and having fought an eight-year war in the 1980s. More important, each posed different challenges to U.S. interests, had different strengths and weaknesses that could be exploited by U.S. policy, and were treated differently by U.S. friends and allies. Furthermore, whereas U.S. military and economic policy toward Iraq was legitimized by a series of United Nations Security Council (UNSC) resolutions issued after the invasion of Kuwait and the Gulf War, the grounds on which actions were taken against Iran were shakier, leaving the United States with weaker international support with regard to Iran than Iraq. In addition to demonstrating a consensus among the major world powers, the UNSC resolutions provided the United States with a concrete set of criteria against which to evaluate Iraqi behavior: if Iraq violated a no-fly zone, the United States was authorized to retaliate; as long as Iraq was not granting UN weapons inspectors access to all weapons manufacturing and storage sites, the economic sanctions would not be lifted. By contrast, U.S. policy toward Iran was based on administration pronouncements, legislative initiatives, including congressional hearings and resolutions, and other unilateral means of attempting to exert pressure. The rest of the world was not quiet in its criticism of U.S. pressure on Iran, and, lacking the legitimacy of UNSC resolutions, the United States was forced to use more indirect means to exert pressure on Tehran.

Nevertheless, the Clinton administration believed that containing Iraq without simultaneously containing Iran would be self-defeating. As Indyk explained in 1993:

> Iran does not *yet* face the kind of international [sanctions] regime that has been imposed on Iraq. A structural imbalance therefore exists between the measures available to contain Iraq and Iran. To the extent that the international community, as a result, succeeds in containing Iraq but fails to contain Iran, we will have inadvertently allowed the balance of power in the Gulf to tilt in favor of Iran, with potentially dangerous consequences. That imbalance therefore argues for a more energetic effort to contain Iran and modify its behavior even as we maintain the sanctions regime against Iraq.[16]

Dual containment's architect seemed to be hinting that the United States wanted to establish a sanctions regime for Iran that was similar to the one Iraq faced. That did not happen. More important, Indyk perceived a risk that the Iraqi sanctions would enable the rise of Iranian hegemony in the region, something no less harmful to U.S. interests than Iraqi hegemony. Thus, while there were differences in the underlying rationales for containing Iraq and Iran, and while the mechanisms available to the world community were not identical, the Clinton administration believed that the success of one part of the policy was a direct function of the success of the other.

Containment of Iraq

With regard to Iraq, the U.S.'s ultimate goal was to insure that Saddam's regime would be locked within a "strategic straitjacket"[17] that would prevent him from pursuing territorial conquests and threatening or actually carrying out attacks using weapons of mass destruction. The United States focused its containment of Iraq on the implementation of UNSC resolutions issued after the Gulf War and renewed regularly since. In the most important of these, Resolution 687, adopted in April 1991, the UNSC demanded that Iraq "unconditionally accept the destruction, removal, or rendering harmless, under international supervision, of . . . [all] chemical and biological weapons and . . . [all] ballistic missiles with a range greater than 150 kilometers" and "unconditionally agree not to acquire or develop nuclear weapons or nuclear-weapons-usable material or any subsystems or components or any research, development, support, or manufacturing facilities." The resolution announced the formation of a United Nations Special Commission (UNSCOM) to "carry out immediate on-site inspection of Iraq's biological, chemical, . . . missile, [and] nuclear capabilities based on Iraq's declarations and the designation of any additional locations by the Special Commission."[18] It also reinforced the economic sanctions that had been imposed on Iraq in August 1990 after its invasion of Kuwait. Subsequent UNSC resolutions, particularly 707 (August 1991) and 715 (October 1991), reiterated Iraq's responsibility to grant UNSCOM access to inspection sites and were officially accepted by the Iraqi government. By the time the Clinton administration entered office, then, the ground rules were clearly established for evaluating the degree of Iraq's compliance.

After the Gulf War, the UNSC forbade Iraq from sending aircraft either north of the 36th parallel or south of the 32d parallel. These "no-fly zones" established concrete criteria against which to evaluate Iraqi military mobilizations and to justify military responses. The global economic sanctions against Iraq, which were issued in Resolution 661 of 6 August 1990 (just days after the invasion of Kuwait), remained in force and were reiterated in subsequent resolutions. These sanctions proscribed both the import of goods from Iraq and the export of goods to Iraq. Particular emphasis was placed on military goods and "dual-use" technologies, that is, civilian goods that could be adapted for military use.

The United States was also determined to prevent Saddam from renewing his repression of minorities, primarily the Kurds in northern Iraq, but also the Shi'ites in the south. But it did not want to permit Iraq to be split up politically. The drive for an independent Kurdistan would have violated the interests of Turkey, a U.S. ally with its own rebellious Kurdish community, and likely led to a civil war among competing Kurdish factions both within Iraq and in Turkey, Syria, and Iran. And to the extent that the Shi'ites in southern Iraq gained independence from Baghdad, that could only help the interests of Iran, which was exactly the opposite of U.S. intentions.

U.S. containment of Iraq was not based merely on threats and implementation of punishments, however. There was also a reward component, formalized in April 1995 through UNSC Resolution 986, which permitted Iraq to sell $1 billion of oil on the international market every 90 days in order to purchase "medicine, health supplies, foodstuffs, and materials and supplies for essential civilian needs."[19] The resolution gave the United States a carrot that it could withdraw – with UNSC approval – on short notice, in hopes of increasing the effectiveness of the stick. As the new secretary of state, Madeleine K. Albright, explained shortly after taking office in 1997:

> The food for oil deal . . . is not related to the larger question of when and if the overall sanctions regime will be lifted. Nor is the continuation of this arrangement automatic, however strongly we support its purpose. If we see evidence that the Government of Iraq is not living up to its promises with respect to implementation [of the conditions in Resolutions 661 and 687], the experiment will cease.[20]

The "oil-for-food" formula was a response to the valid criticism that the sanctions regime was hurting the Iraqi population more than it was hurting Saddam's regime. According to Anthony H. Cordesman and Ahmed S. Hashim, by the mid-1990s, the sanctions' cumulative effect had been to reduce Iraq's per capita income and caloric intake from the levels of upper-middle-income countries to those of the poorest states of the Middle East and Africa.[21] While the United States did not want to remove the pressure that the sanctions were causing Saddam, it needed to help improve the Iraqi standard of living so as not to lose the support of other members of the world community.

While these goals and strategies were generally consistent with the aim of containment, there was a major problem: in Richard

N. Haass's words, "Saddam is a serial prober."[22] Saddam repeatedly tried to test U.S. resolve, attempting to determine how far the United States would go to back up its demands, whether it would carry out its threats, and what kinds of costs – military, political, and economic – the United States and its allies would be willing to bear. His experience in the Gulf War, in which U.S. and coalition forces stopped fighting before reaching Basra (much less Baghdad), gave him reason to suspect that U.S. deterrent and compellent threats were not fully credible.

One of the major probes came at the end of August 1996, when Saddam took advantage of Kurdish infighting and moved as many as 40,000 troops into northern Iraq, seizing the Kurdish city of Irbil. This was an unambiguous violation of UNSC resolutions and brought about a U.S. military response. But the response was indirect: the United States hit Iraqi antiaircraft sites in the south, extended the southern no-fly zone north by one degree of latitude (closer to the Baghdad suburbs), and issued new threats that it would do whatever necessary to protect its planes patrolling the no-fly zones. In effect, the U.S. response was to reaffirm its commitment to the deterrent, but not to punish Iraq directly for the violation in the north.

Iraq apparently got the message that the United States was serious. An official Ba'th Party newspaper accused the United States of aggression, calling the no-fly zones "a dangerous precedent in international relations and conduct outside the framework of international legitimacy" and describing President Clinton as "mentally retarded, immersed in vice and without conscience."[23] Several months after Iraq's invasion of Irbil, Albright claimed that the response had "reduced further the strategic threat posted by Iraq and demonstrated [the United States'] intention to respond to Iraqi transgressions in a manner of [its] choosing."[24] Maybe so. But it also angered some U.S. allies and garnered a lukewarm reception from others. And, of course, Saddam remained in charge.

The other probes Saddam issued were aimed at the UNSCOM inspectors who were searching for weapons storage and construction sites. Repeatedly, Saddam limited the access of – and even banished – the inspectors, making a loud statement to the world community that he believed that the UN was violating Iraqi sovereignty and that the United States was the worst offender. In October 1997, in the most serious of these incidents, Iraq expelled American members of the inspection team, threatened to shoot down American

U-2 spy planes that were monitoring Iraq from above, and removed some equipment from UNSCOM video monitors. These actions brought about an increase in the U.S. military presence in the region, including the arrival of an additional aircraft carrier group. They also brought on a renewed commitment from the Security Council, which once again demanded that Iraq permit UNSCOM "unconditional and unrestricted access" to any site it decided to inspect.[25] In practical terms, Saddam was able to buy some time in order to hide weapons material from the inspectors when they finally returned. In political terms, Saddam managed to anger the world community sufficiently that the level of condemnation rose again. While the United States and the world may have been experiencing fatigue with the sanctions, inspections, and military maneuvers, Saddam's defiance helped to revive them.

Overall, although it encountered setbacks and frustrations, the Iraq half of dual containment was effective. It would have been folly to expect Saddam to drop his interest in acquiring weapons of mass destruction. The best that could have been hoped was that he would be driven from power and replaced by a friendly regime. What actually occurred was the next-best thing: Saddam was prevented from ending the sanctions regime and regaining full control over his country; UNSCOM's efforts to find and destroy Saddam's weapons of mass destruction made significant progress; and the coalition that fought against Saddam in 1990–91 remained largely unified in its support of U.S. efforts. The sanctions would not have taken hold had the United States pulled out of the Gulf physically; the GCC states were not strong enough or well enough coordinated to pose a credible deterrent, individually or as a group. That Saddam was not deposed was due more to the divisions among the Iraqi opposition groups and the U.S. fear of Iran filling the power vacuum than the ineffectiveness of the U.S. military strategy.

Containment of Iran

While the United States had clear international guidelines for organizing its containment of Iraq, its policy toward Iran was more haphazard. In part, this was a reflection of the difference in the nature of the military threat: Iran had not invaded a neighboring state, its weapons of mass destruction program was not as close to fruition as that of Iraq, it had not used poison gas on segments of its own population, and, while its rhetoric was hostile and it supported terrorist organizations that targeted Israel, it had not launched missile attacks on Israeli cities. Nevertheless, the United States considered Iran a significant adversary, whose "primary threat . . . to U.S. interests [came] from the two extremes of the threat spectrum: nonconventional weapons at one end and Tehran's capacity for subversion and terror at the other."[26] And given its fear that Iran would fill the Iraqi power vacuum, the United States believed it was necessary to take actions to reduce the threats emanating from Teheran.

A positive, conciliatory approach to Iran was not a realistic option for any U.S. president. The hostage crisis of 1979–81 had created an emotional hatred of Iran in American public opinion that was reinforced by the Iranians' repeated use of inflammatory rhetoric (e.g., calling the United States "the Great Satan"), their death sentence on Salman Rushdie, and their vocal opposition to the Israeli-Palestinian peace process. And the U.S. experience with reconciliation was a political failure both internationally and domestically: its one major attempt to court moderates in Iran, the Reagan administration's arms-for-hostages deal of the mid-1980s, failed to bring about the release of the hostages in Lebanon, produced investigations and trials of high-ranking officials, and ultimately had no positive impact on Iranian behavior. In short, the political backdrop against which U.S. policy was made meant that Iran had to be dealt with by threats and boycotts.

The problem for the Clinton administration, then, was how to express its disapproval of Iranian political rhetoric and bring about changes in Iran's weapons and terrorism policies without provoking an escalation of tension to the point of military confrontation. This was a variant of the classic problem of deterrence and compellence: showing sufficient resolve to bring about a change in the target's behavior without creating a temptation by the target to preempt. The main tool the United States adopted to produce this deterrent threat was economic isolation through sanctions. When Pelletreau explained the sanctions to a congressional committee in 1996, he argued that they were designed:

> to compel Iran to change its rogue behavior . . . [which consists of] support of terrorism, including support for groups that use violence to oppose the Middle East peace process; pursuit of weapons of mass destruction and the means to deliver them beyond Iran's borders; and meddling in the affairs of neighbors. . . . As long as Iran pursues aggressive external policies, we will continue seeking to deprive it of external financial support and

> to develop international economic pressure to change its threatening behavior.[27]

This policy was self-serving for the U.S. government, since the standards of Iranian behavior it demanded were not concrete and measurable. These standards also enabled U.S. allies to object to both the United States' reading of the Iranian threat and its responses to it.

The United States' secondary tool was its physical presence in the Gulf, which, though aimed primarily at Iraq, provided a tacit military threat that increased the credibility of the U.S. containment attempt. Some analysts even claim that U.S. military capabilities in the region were actually more salient to Iran than to Iraq. According to Clawson:

> The U.S. military presence in the Gulf is well positioned to counter any Iranian actions. Indeed, the U.S. presence could well be seen by Tehran as designed more against it than against Saddam: the Navy's Fifth Fleet (the Gulf force) is better positioned to act against Iran than Iraq, the Air Force planes (largely in Saudi Arabia) are as close to Iran as to Iraq, and the prepositioned equipment in Qatar and afloat can reach Iran faster than it could reach Iraq.[28]

Thus, whether or not the United States initially intended for its military assets to be aimed at Iran, they had the potential to be turned in that direction quickly and effectively. And Iran knew it. In effect, the United States deterred Iran in part because it already had the means to do so.

By 1996, a number of domestic political actors in the United States, including prominent congressional Republicans and the American Israel Public Affairs Committee (AIPAC), were putting pressure on the Clinton administration to tighten sanctions on Iran, thus increasing its isolation. In August 1996, Clinton signed the Iran and Libya Sanctions Act (or the D'Amato Act, after its Senate sponsor), which followed a 1995 executive order. The act not only banned U.S. firms from investing in Iran, but it also created a secondary boycott of non-American firms investing there – an ''extraterritoriality'' provision. Unlike the sanctions on Iraq, which were issued by the UNSC, these sanctions were U.S. government policy and were thus not obligatory on other states by international law.

And most other major states did not agree with the premise or the particulars of the policy. The other permanent members of the Security Council, as well as Germany and Japan, were all more interested in constructive engagement; if anything, extraterritoriality angered them, rather than pushing them to support U.S. sanctions.[29]

The sanctions law had some unanticipated (or, at least, somewhat embarrassing) implications for U.S. and foreign oil companies. Conoco, a major U.S.-based multinational, had received a $2 billion contract to develop an offshore oil field in Iranian waters. The Clinton executive order of 1995 was directly aimed at forcing Conoco to give up the contract. The contract ended up going to the French oil company, Total, which formed a consortium with the Russian firm, Gazprom, and the Malaysian firm, Petronas, to develop the oil field in defiance of U.S. preferences. The gap between U.S. and foreign political interests, together with the gap between the interests of the U.S. government and those of the oil companies, are well illustrated by this episode. The United States was already receiving significant criticism from friends like Canada and the European Union over extraterritoriality in its boycott of Cuba, where there was relatively little at stake economically. There was much more to gain by investing in and trading with Iran, and the D'Amato Act did not prove effective in deterring foreign companies – or their home governments, for that matter – from involvement in Iran's economy.

In June 1996, a U.S. military barracks in Dhahran, Saudi Arabia, was bombed. There were rumors that Iran was responsible for the bombing, but those rumors were never confirmed. That the United States never took retaliatory military action against Iran suggests that the Clinton administration was not convinced that Iran was responsible.

Because of the vagueness of the underlying criteria for assessing Iranian behavior, the Iran half of dual containment was both more and less effective than the Iraq half. On one hand, the United States did not mobilize its forces and make active military preparations in response to Iranian violations of U.S. demands. Moreover, Iranian President Khatami began to reach out to U.S. public opinion, if not directly to the Clinton administration, especially through his interview on CNN in January 1998. If dual containment was designed to soften the Iranian estrangement from the United States, then it was apparently working. On the other hand, dual containment drove a wedge between the United States and most of its friends in the Middle East, Europe, and Asia. The anti-Iraq coalition was clearly not interested in being an equally united anti-Iran coalition. The United States' friends did not perceive the military threat from Iran to be as severe, and, more important, they wanted to take advantage of the economic opportunities available from contact with Iran. The only way the United States was likely to continue to contain Iran was by acting almost unilaterally, thereby threatening the consensus that bolstered the containment of Iraq.

Tension with Allies and Regional Partners

The characteristic that made dual containment most difficult was its dependence on other states for political support, compliance with U.S. demands, and active participation. While the United States was clearly regarded as the leading state in the international system, its goals were not always shared by its friends and allies, either in the Gulf region or abroad. And even when the goals were shared, there were often significant differences in preferred policies. Just as the United States was willing to overlook shortcomings in terms of democracy and human rights in places like Saudi Arabia and Kuwait, many of its friends and allies were willing to ignore undesirable aspects of Iranian or Iraqi behavior as they pursued their own goals. In short, dual containment left economic and political opportunities that could be seized – if not quite vacuums that would automatically be filled – by Saudi Arabia, France, Russia, China, and others.

Leaders of the Gulf states, who had the greatest immediate stake in the security threats posed by Iraq and Iran, were sometimes outwardly uncomfortable with the level of the U.S. military presence, even if they were privately grateful for it. Dual containment was sensitive to this discomfort. The United States and the GCC states did not formalize U.S. obligations with treaties because of the political delicacy of their relationship. In testimony to the Senate Armed Services Committee, Gen. Binford Peay, the former head of U.S. Central Command, said, ''Sovereignty is a very sensitive issue [for Gulf countries]. They look at any kind of permanent move as being intrusive, burdensome.'' These comments were reinforced by the Saudi ambassador to the United States, who suggested that the U.S. presence could be eliminated once Saddam is out of power.[30] There are three things to note about the ambassador's comments: first, Saudi Arabia was apparently not concerned about security threats emanating from Iran; second, its perceived threat was from Saddam Hussein himself, and not Iraq in general; and third, at least outwardly, Saudi Arabia and Iran were in agreement on the need to rid the Gulf of foreign military forces.[31]

The GCC states challenged U.S. Middle East policy in two ways: the first – slowing the pace of normalization with Israel – was not connected with dual containment; the second – gradually but noticeably readmitting Iran into the regional community of nations – was. By the end of 1997, most of the states of the region chose not to attend the economic summit in Doha, in which Israel was a participant – although the fact that the conference went ahead at all suggests that the GCC states continued to see some economic and political benefits to relations with Israel and compliance with U.S. preferences. More important, all of the GCC states attended a conference of the Organization of the Islamic Conference in Tehran, which was a virtual celebration of Iran's membership in good standing. These moves sent strong political signals that U.S. military assistance was not enough to alter fundamentally their political preferences. Their loyalties to Arab brotherhood and Islam cut across the security goals they shared with the United States.

The major non–Middle East allies of the United States, especially France, Germany, and Japan, disagreed sharply with the U.S. approach to Iran. Both Europe and Japan continued to engage in several billion dollars in annual trade with Iran, where, in spite of high inflation and slow economic growth, there appeared to be a strong potential for recovery. The French/Russian/Malaysian oil exploration contract was a direct slap at the U.S. boycott that reflected those countries' desires to achieve economic gains and political influence that were not available to the United States. Japan buckled to U.S. pressure and postponed (but did not cancel entirely) the second installment of a loan it was providing to Iran for the construction of a hydroelectric dam, while it continued to purchase roughly 35 percent of Iranian oil exports.[32]

Russia and China went even further, seeing both Iran and Iraq as potential markets for sales of their weapons – something that contradicted not just the specifics of U.S. policy, but also the underlying motivation behind it. Russia and China sold conventional weapons – including missiles, aircraft, tanks, and spare parts – to Iran, although they were prevented by the UN sanctions from establishing similar deals with Iraq. Russia also became involved in completing the construction of nuclear reactors in Iran that had been begun under the Shah.[33] The line between purely civilian and dual-use technologies was so unclear that it was possible for Iran's trading partners to claim a purely benign interest in economic contact that poses no security threat.

The one state that, if anything, criticized U.S. policy for being too soft on the Gulf rogues was Israel. In a speech to the U.S. Congress in July 1996, Israeli Prime Minister Benjamin Netanyahu called on the United States to step up its pressure not only on Iran and Iraq themselves, but also on other states whose commitment to dual containment was weak:

> Europe and the countries of Asia must be made to understand that it is folly . . . to pursue short-term material gain while creating a long-term existential danger for all of us. I believe only the United States can lead this vital international effort to stop the nuclearization of terrorist states. But the deadline for attaining this goal is getting extremely close.[34]

Given the context and audience of Netanyahu's speech, and Israel's perception of its vulnerability to attacks from Iranian or Iraqi territory, it is understandable that he would treat Iran and Iraq as two sides of the same coin, requiring a coordinated policy led by the United States.

The record of U.S. dual containment since the policy's inception in 1993 illustrates well the difference between deterrence – trying to get another actor not to take an action – and compellence – trying to force it to do something. Deterrence did not fail in a major way: neither Iran nor Iraq invaded a neighboring state during this period (although Saddam did move into Kurdish territory in northern Iraq, in violation of deterrent threats). The United States, with UN, NATO, and GCC backing, also made a concerted effort to maintain a military presence in the region and repeatedly demonstrated its willingness to take actions to prevent such an invasion. Both of the backlash states received a clear message that they faced a resolute defender of the status quo. As in any deterrence situation, however, it was unclear to what extent Iraqi or Iranian invasions were prevented by the deterrence, and to what extent they were not seriously intended. What is clear is that there was no war under dual containment: the primary deterrent threats never failed, and they did not provoke preemption.

Compellence, however, was a different story. Those aspects of dual containment aimed at bringing about changes in Iranian or Iraqi governmental structure, weapons policies, and support of terrorism had mixed results. The political costs to both sides were very high. For Iran or Iraq, complying with U.S. demands meant looking weak in the international community and to domestic political audiences; for the United States, bringing to bear sufficient pressure militarily and economically to achieve changes would have entailed generating levels of congressional and international support that were not achievable. The UN sanctions regime in Iraq, and especially the UNSCOM weapons inspectors, made gradual but meaningful progress – progress that was facilitated by U.S. and allied military preparedness. The U.S. sanctions against Iran caused economic pain, but the divisions they generated in the U.S.-led coalition were substantial.

Did dual containment bring about the leadership changes in Iran? Did it provoke Saddam to continue challenging UNSCOM and the world community? More generally, did dual containment enable the United States to maintain constructive and cooperative relations with its European and Asian allies, its Middle Eastern friends, and the Gulf states whose security dual containment is most directly tied to? The answer to all of these questions is ''sort of.''

Part of the problem with sustaining a policy like dual containment is that it is costly, both in the short and long runs, to the states that are doing the containing. Eventually, they begin to place a higher value on the costs they are incurring than the benefits they might be receiving. Perhaps that is what Clawson meant when he said that dual containment was a victim of its own success: it is hard to sustain a policy that brings few concrete results – after all, deterrence success means nothing happens – but is not failing badly enough to warrant replacement. As long as the U.S. military and Clinton administration were aware of the changes in Iranian and Iraqi policy and maintained sufficient flexibility to adapt to these changes, dual containment was an acceptable approach.

But just as the global and regional context was different in 1993 than it had been during the cold war, there was strong evidence by the end of 1997 that the situation had evolved further. All four of the conditions that Lake had identified as justifying and facilitating dual containment had, to some extent, changed:

1. The Russians were treating the Middle East in general, and the Gulf region in particular, as an area of the world in which they could reestablish the political influence that the Soviet Union had once enjoyed. Their renewed interest in selling arms and provid-

ing technical assistance in the development of dual-use technologies meant that the United States faced a major-power rival with direct access to the leaders of both Iran and Iraq. Russia's veto on the Security Council could prove a potent tool if its leaders were to decide to conciliate them, rather than introduce or renew sanctions or take military action against them.

2. Although the absolute levels of arms that Iran and Iraq possessed remained lower than they had been in the 1980s, the political isolation of Iran – which had helped to sustain those low levels – was, in most respects, a thing of the past. And while the world remained committed to preventing the reemergence of a heavily-armed Iraq or Iran, the United States could no longer count on overpowering them indefinitely.
3. The GCC states were increasingly wary of U.S. intentions and resistant to U.S. leadership. They were not, however, ready to call for an end to the U.S. military presence in the Gulf. As the Kuwaiti scholar and political adviser Abdullah Al-Shayeji notes, "Even seven years after the Iraqi invasion of Kuwait, the Gulf governments [had] failed to adopt a collective-security program that would reduce the region's complete dependence on the United States for their defense."[35] As long as they perceived a significant threat from Iraq and the United States was providing a credible deterrent, the GCC states had no major incentive to bear a greater share of the security burden.
4. The Arab-Israeli peace process had stalled. The Clinton administration could no longer point to its success in mediating between the Israelis and the Palestinians as evidence of its effectiveness, which harmed U.S. credibility in the region. More important, the stagnation of the peace process enabled Iran and Iraq to gain political influence by rallying Gulf countries together in opposition to U.S. policy. To the extent that U.S. Gulf policy was connected to the peace process, that connection had changed from positive to negative.

How did this new environment affect the future of U.S. strategy in the Gulf? The differences between Iraq and Iran are worth recalling a final time. At the end of 1997, the UN sanctions regime against Iraq was proving durable – largely because Saddam was resisting full compliance. The United States could continue to hold Iraq to the explicit criteria of the UNSC resolutions knowing that, as long as it was willing to bear the overwhelming share of the military burden, the rest of the world would offer little more than verbal objections to U.S. threats of force. Even if Gulf states refused to grant access to their airfields and other facilities, the United States maintained sufficient flexibility and strength to meet its deterrence needs. Furthermore, the oil-for-food formula was proving effective in response to the criticism of the sanctions' impact on the Iraqi civilian population.

As for Iran, however, the United States was clearly losing ground in its effort to achieve international consensus. If Indyk had once hoped to establish a UN-based sanctions regime, as he implied in 1993, there was no longer any chance of that. The United States needed to decide whether it wanted to contain Iran alone by continuing its unilateral sanctions or to join the constructive engagement set. As a European envoy said late in 1997, "The United States wants to stand for what is right, which is admirable . . . But in today's world, that is not always what is either most effective or realistic."[36] If containing Iran would create new political tensions with both allies and major powers like Russia and China, then the dangers might outweigh the benefits.

While the barriers to dual containment were rising, the logic underlying it – especially the notion that deterring Iraq is facilitated by curtailing the threat of Iranian hegemony – remained plausible. But that logic did not necessarily extend to political and economic isolation. As the Clinton administration entered its sixth year, dual containment was beginning to look like a spent policy – or, perhaps, like a buzzword that had worn out its usefulness and was absorbing growing criticism from Congress, the media, and foreign governments. The Clinton administration appeared likely to modify the details of its policy toward Iraq and, especially, Iran. It might even drop the name "dual containment." But it was not yet ready to welcome Iraq or Iran back into the community of nations, and it would not risk creating a power vacuum that one of the rogues might fill.

Endnotes

1 The term is used by Anthony Lake in his article, "Confronting Backlash States," *Foreign Affairs* 73, no. 2 (March/April 1994): 45–55.

2 Martin Indyk, speech delivered to The Washington Institute's Soref Symposium, 18 May 1993. Excerpts published as "Special Report: Clinton Administration Policy Toward the Middle East," *Policywatch* 84, Washington Institute for Near East Policy, 21 May 1993.

3 Some critics call it a "slogan," but that term denotes an unwarranted

level of derision. See Zbigniew Brzezinski, Brent Scowcroft, and Richard Murphy, ''Differentiated Containment,'' *Foreign Affairs* 76, no. 3 (May/June 1997), 20–30; and Richard N. Haass, ''The United States and Iraq: A Strategy for the Long Haul,'' Brookings Policy Brief No. 7 (October 1996).

4 Patrick Clawson, ''Dual Containment – Revive It or Replace It?'' *MERIA News* (Internet publication) 2/1998 (January 1998).

5 Washington Institute Strategic Study Group, *Restoring the Balance: U.S. Strategy and the Gulf Crisis* (Washington: Washington Institute for Near East Policy, 1991), p. 3.

6 See Tarek E. Masoud, ''Misreading Iran,'' *Current History*, 97, no. 615 (January 1998): 40.

7 Lake, ''Confronting Backlash States,'' p. 46.

8 Quoted by Masoud in ''Misreading Iran,'' p. 40.

9 Indyk, ''Special Report,'' p. 2.

10 Lake, ''Confronting Backlash States,'' pp. 48–49.

11 Patrick Clawson, ''The Impacts of U.S. Sanctions on Iran,'' prepared for the Council on Foreign Relations Economic Sanctions Study Group, December 1997.

12 Bradley Graham, ''A Pentagon Dilemma: Sustaining Gulf Buildup,'' *International Herald Tribune*, 25 February 1998, p. 10.

13 Michael Eisenstadt, *Iranian Military Power: Capabilities and Intentions* (Washington: The Washington Institute for Near East Policy, 1996), p. 36. See also the chapters by Amos Gilboa and Aharon Levran in this volume.

14 Pelletreau, in statement before the House Committee on International Relations, 25 September 1996.

15 Lake, ''Confronting Backlash States,'' p. 49.

16 Indyk, ''Special Report,'' p. 3. Italics added.

17 Pelletreau, House Committee on International Relations, 25 September 1996.

18 UNSC Resolution 687, 3 April 1991, paragraphs 8, 9, 12, 13.

19 UNSC Resolution 986, 14 April 1995, paragraph 8. Previous versions of the formula had been presented by the United Nations in Resolutions 706 and 712 in 1991, but Saddam had been unwilling to accept the terms at that time.

20 Madeleine K. Albright, ''Preserving Principle and Safeguarding Stability: United States Policy toward Iraq,'' speech delivered at Georgetown University, Washington D.C., 26 March 1997.

21 Anthony H. Cordesman and Ahmed S. Hashim, *Iraq: Sanctions and Beyond* (Boulder: Westview Press, 1997), p. 127.

22 Haass, ''The United States and Iraq.''

23 Quoted by Reuters, 15 September 1996.

24 Albright, ''Preserving Principle and Safeguarding Stability.''

25 UNSC Resolution 1134, 23 October 1997, preamble. See also Robert H.

Pelletreau, ''Common Sense Regarding Security in the Gulf (Part I),'' *Al-Hayat*, 14 December 1997.

[26] Eisenstadt, *Iranian Military Power*, p. xvii.

[27] Pelletreau, House Committee on International Relations, 25 September 1996.

[28] Clawson, ''The Impacts of U.S. Sanctions on Iran.''

[29] See, for example, Robert H. Pelletreau, ''The United States and Iran: We Should Be Talking,'' *Al-Hayat*, 29 August 1997; Clawson, ''The Impacts of U.S. Sanctions on Iran.''

[30] Peay and the ambassador are cited by John Diamond, Associated Press, 30 March 1997.

[31] Masoud, ''Misreading Iran,'' p. 40.

[32] Robin Wright and Shaul Bakhash, ''The U.S. and Iran: An Offer They Can't Refuse?'' *Foreign Policy*, no. 108 (Fall 1997):132.

[33] Wright and Bakhash, ''The U.S. and Iran,'' p. 128.

[34] *Reuters*, 10 July 1996.

[35] Abdullah Al-Shayeji, ''Dangerous Perceptions: Gulf Views of the U.S. Role in the Region,'' *Middle East Policy*, V, no. 3 (September 1997): 10.

[36] Quoted in Robin Wright, ''U.S. Losing Support in 'Containing' Iraq and Iran,'' *Los Angeles Times*, October 26, 1997.

PART II

REGIONAL MILITARY FORCES

Introductory Note

This issue of the *Middle East Military Balance* is marked by a substantial change from previous issues, both in content and appearance. We have replaced the lists with spacious tables that we hope are easier to consult.

As for the content, we eliminated subsections deemed unimportant for our main subject but added some more details that were absent in the past. The changes for each country reviewed include:

- eliminating the sections dealing with small arms, and with civilian air and naval transportation.
- restructuring the sections dealing with arms transfers, arms production, and foreign security cooperation to eliminate repetition of information. We now have one table that covers all arms procurement and security assistance received (arranged by supplying country), one for arms sales and security assistance extended (arranged by receiving country), one for foreign military cooperation, and one table for arms production. Data in these tables refer to the past five years only.
- changing the organization of the tables showing the organization of each military, and adding information about subdivision of formations.
- introducing a table showing the changes in the order-of-battle for the past five years. We believe that watching the trend is much more important than the numbers for a specific year.
- introducing two columns of numbers in the tables for the different categories of weapons, showing the total quantity of each system and the quantity in active service.
- creating a new section in each country for air defense forces. In some countries in the region, the air defense is an independent branch. In others, air defense equipment is divided between the ground forces and the air forces. For the sake of consistency, we have put the data in one place, whether they belong to an independent branch or not.
- introducing a major change in the tables for navies. Since naval vessels are very different from one another, we have

decided to move the technical data on each class of ships from the glossary at the end of the book into the tables of each navy. Thus the reader will be able to see at a glance what is behind each class of ships.

The tables on "economic data" are in the new format introduced in the 1996 edition of *The Middle East Military Balance*. They now include data about GDP (in current local currency and in current U.S. dollars). No attempt was made to translate the data to a common base. Likewise, per capita GDP is given as a simple division of the GDP by the size of the population, and we have made no attempt to convert it to purchasing power parity (PPP).

Accurate data on military expenditure in the Middle East are notoriously elusive. The data given should be regarded, at best, as indicators of trends rather than accurate and reliable actual expenditure.

Definitions of the different weapon categories have not changed in this issue, with the exception of air defense equipment, where we look at the following categories:

- shoulder-launched missiles.
- light SAMs – with a range up to 12 km, self-propelled or towed.
- medium SAMs – self-propelled, with range of 12–30 km.
- heavy SAMs – stationary (or towed) systems with a range of 12–30 km, or any system with a range of more than 30 km.

The reason for this categorization is to avoid putting in one category systems as different from one another as the American Chaparral and the Russian S-300V (both self-propelled), on the one hand, and the SA-5 and British-made Rapier (both towed), on the other.

The following tanks mentioned in parts 2 and 3 have been designated high quality: T-72/improved T-72; Chieftain of Jordan and Oman (but not Chieftain Mk 5 of Iran and Kuwait); M-60 A3; and Merkava. High-quality interceptors include F-14, F-15, and MiG-25. High-quality strike and multirole aircraft include F-16, F/A-

18, Mirage 2000, Tornado, MiG-29, and Su-24. Defense expenditure figures include foreign military grants. Arms transfers to and from Middle Eastern countries cover transfers during the last five years; bombers are included in numbers of total combat aircraft.

The cut-off date for all data in this issue is 31 December 1997.

Acknowledgments

I wish to thank my colleagues at JCSS, and several others for their comments and assistance during the process of collecting and collating the data. JCSS researchers and research assistants whose aid was particularly valuable are Anat Kurz, Moshe Grundman, Jenny Brosztein, Avi Muallem and Ori Slonim. Special thanks to Maj. Gen. (ret.) Shlomo Gazit, Brig. Gen. (ret.) Aryeh Shalev, and Dr. Yehudit Ronen (from the Dayan Center), for their advice.

The new format was designed by Anat Henefeld, and the hard labor of compiling and updating the data was done by Yoel Kozak and Tamir Magal. Withal, I alone bear responsibility for any inaccuracies.

Yiftah S. Shapir
March 1998

1. ALGERIA

GENERAL DATA

Official Name of the State: Democratic and Popular Republic of Algeria
Head of State: President of the High State Council Brigadier General Liamine Zeroual (also Minister of Defense)
Prime Minister: Ahmad Ouyahyah
Chief of General Staff: Major General Muhammad Lamari
Commander of the Staff of the Ground Forces: Major General Salih Ahmad Jaid (also Deputy Chief of the General Staff)
Commander of the Air Force: Brigadier General Muhammad Ibn Suleiman
Commander of the Air Defense Force: Brigadier General Achour Laoudi
Commander of the Navy: Admiral Shabane Ghodbane

Area: 2,460,500 sq. km.
Population: 29,300,000

Demography

Ethnic Groups		
Arabs	23,000,500	78.5%
Berbers	5,684,300	19.4%
Europeans	293,000	1.0%
Others	322,300	1.1%
Religious Groups		
Sunni Muslims	29,007,000	99.0%
Christians and Jews	293,000	1.0%

Economic Data

		1992	1993	1994	1995	1996
GDP current price, local currency	AD bn	1,045	1,162	1,475	1,962	2,469
GDP (U.S.$)	$ bn	47.85	49.46	42.07	41.14	45.09
GDP per capita	$	1,819	1,838	1,524	1,438	1,539
Real GDP growth	%	1.4	−1.2	−1.1	3.9	3.4

Economic Data *(continued)*

		1992	1993	1994	1995	1996
Balance of payments						
• Exports fob	$ bn	11.44	10.44	8.88	10.25	12.42
• Imports fob	$ bn	8.34	7.99	9.15	10.20	9.44
• Account balance (Includes services and income)	$ bn	1.02	0.6	–1.8	–2.31	0.21
• External debt	$ bn	27.06	26.03	30.17	32.61	32.5
Government income and expenditure						
• Revenues, local currency	AD bn	322.70	335.60	474.10	586.50	NA
• Expenditures, local currency	AD bn	396.80	504.00	613.70	734.90	NA
• Defense expenditures	AD bn	20.12	29.81	46.80	58.84	79.52
• Defense expenditure/GDP	%	1.9	2.6	3.2	3	3.2
• Defense expenditure/CGE	%	4.82	5.91	7.63	10	
• Population		26.3	26.9	27.6	28.6	29.3
• Official exchange rate	AD: $1	21.84	23.35	35.06	47.69	54.75

Sources: EIU quarterly report, EIU country profile, IMF statistical yearbook, SIPRI Yearbook.

Arms Sales and Security Assistance Received

Country	Type	Details
Britain	• Arms transfers	naval vessels (1997)
Egypt	• Arms transfers	Fahd APCs (1993)
France	• Arms transfers	helicopters (1995)
PRC	• Arms transfers	patrol craft (1992)
Russia	• Arms transfers	helicopters (1995)

Defense Production

	M	P	A
Army equipment			
• Trucks (in collaboration with France)		√	
• Small arms		√	
Naval craft			
• Tugs	√		
• Kebir class PBs		√	√

Note: M—manufacture (indigenously developed)
P—production under license
A—assembly

NBC Technology

Nuclear capabilities

- A 1 mw nuclear research reactor (from Argentina); a second nuclear reactor of 15 mw, probably upgradable to 40 mw (from PRC); basic R&D; known/acknowleged Algerian facilities are subject to IAEA safeguards; Algeria is a signatory to the NPT

CW capabilities

- No details available

Biological warfare capabilities

- No details available

ARMED FORCES

Major Changes: No major changes occurred in the Algerian order of battle.

Order-of-Battle

Year	1993	1994	1995	1996	1997
General data					
• Personnel (regular)	198,500	155,000	152,500	152,500	124,000
• Divisions	3	13	5	5	5
• Total number of brigades	25	69	37	37	26
Ground Forces					
• Tanks	1,250–1,390	1,060–1,160	1,100	1,100	930 (1,060)
• APCs/ARVs	2,100–2,250	1,780	1,780	1,780	1,930
• Artillery (incl. MRLs)	840	985	980	980	1,070
• SSM launchers	30–35	30–35	35	35	
Air Force					
• Combat aircraft	295	305	205	205	205
• Transport aircraft	67	57	76	76	48
• Helicopters	66	84	108	108	116
Air Defense Forces					
• Heavy SAM batteries	41	41	30	30	11
• Medium SAM batteries	25	25	23	23	18
• Light SAM launchers	+	+	+	+	+

Order-of-Battle *(continued)*

Year	1993	1994	1995	1996	1997
Navy					
• Combat vessels		59	60	60	50
• Submarines		2	2	2	2

Note: Beginning with data for 1997, we refer to quantities in active serivce. The number in parentheses refers to the total.

Personnel

	Regular	Reserves	Total
Ground Forces	107,000	150,000	257,000
Air Force	10,000		10,000
Navy and Coast Guard	7,000		7,000
Total	**124,000**	**150,000**	**274,000**
Paramilitary			
• National security force	16,000		16,000
• Republican guards brigade	1,200		1,200
• Gendarmerie			20,000

Note: Air defense personnel are included in the Army and Air Force personnel.

GROUND FORCES

Formations

	Division	Independent brigade/group	Independent battalions	Brigades in division
All arms				
Armored	2	1		2 tanks, 2 mech. each
Mechanized infantry	2			2 mech., 2 tanks each
Motorized infantry		5		
Special forces/ Airborne	1			
Artillery		7		
Air Defense			5	
Engineering			4	
Total	**5**	**13**	**9**	

Tanks

Model	Quantity	In service	Since	Notes
High quality				
• T-72	300	300	1980	
Others				
• T-62	330	330	1978	
• T-55/T-54	310	approx. 300	1964	Some in storage
• AMX-13	50		1962	Possibly phased out
• PT-76	70			Possibly phased out
Subtotal	760	630		
Total	**1,060**	**approx. 930**		

APCs/ARVs

Model	Quantity	In service	Since	Notes
High quality				
• BMP-2	230	230		
• BMP-1	685	685	1982	
• Engesa EE-9	50	50	1981	
Subtotal	965	965		
Others				
• AML-60	55	55	1963	
• BRDM-2	115	115		
• BTR-50/60	445	445		
• BTR-152	100	100	1965	
• Fahd	200	200	1992	
• M-3 (Panhard)	50	50	1983	
Subtotal	965	965		
Total	**1,930**	**1,930**		
On order				
• Scorpion	700			Unconfirmed
• Fahd	50			

Artillery

Model	Quantity	In service	Since	Notes
Self-propelled guns and howitzers				
• 152mm 2S3	35	35	1966	
• 122mm 2S1	150	150		

Artillery *(continued)*

Model	Quantity	In service	Since	Notes
Towed guns and howitzers				
• 152mm ML-20	20	20		
• 130mm M-46/Type-59	10	10		
• 122mm D-74	}		1966	Refers to all types
• 122mm M-1931/37	} 180–190	180–190		Refers to all types
• 122mm M-30 (M-1938)	}			Refers to all types
• 122mm D-30	190	190		
• 85mm M-1945/D-44 field/AT	80	80		
Mortars, over 160mm				
• 160mm M-43	60	60		
Mortars, under 160mm				
• 120mm M-43	120	120		
Total	**approx. 850**	**approx. 850**		
MRLs				
• 240mm BM-24	30	30		
• 140mm BM-14-16	50	50		
• 122mm BM-21	50	50		
Total	**130**	**130**		

Antitank Weapons

Model	Quantity	In service	Since	Notes
Missiles				
• AT-1 (Snapper)				
• AT-2				
• AT-3 (Sagger)			1980	
• AT-4 (Spigot)				
• AT-5 (Spandrel)				Mounted on BMP-2 APC
• BRDM-2-borne AT-3 (Sagger)/ AT-5 (Spandrel)				
• Milan	Approx. 200	Approx. 200		
Total	**approx. 1,400**	**approx. 1,400**		

Antitank Weapons *(continued)*

Model	Quantity	In service	Since	Notes
Guns				
• 76mm AT gun	50			Possibly phased out
• 107mm B-11 recoilless rifle	40	40		Unconfirmed
Total	**90**	**40**		

AIR FORCE

Order-of-Battle

Model	Quantity	In service	Notes
• Combat	205	205	
• Transport	48	48	
• Helicopters	114	114	

Combat Aircraft

Model	Quantity	In service	Since	Notes
Interceptors				
• MiG-25 A/B/U (Foxbat)	20	20	1979	
Others				
• MiG-23MF/MS (Flogger G)	30	30	1978	
• MiG-21 MF/bis/U (Fishbed)	90	90	1978	
Subtotal	120	120		
Total	approx. 140	approx. 140		
Strike and multirole aircraft—high quality				
• Su-24 (Fencer C)	10	10		
Others				
• MiG-23BN (Flogger B/D)	40	40	1978	
• Su-20/22 (Fitter C)	15	15	1978	
Total	65	65		
Total	**205**	**205**		

Transport Aircraft

Model	Quantity	In service	Since	Notes
• An-12 (Cub)	4	4		
• Beechcraft Queen Air/Beechcraft King Air/Beechcraft Super King Air T-200T	12	12	1982	2 employed in maritime patrol role
• C-130H & L-100-30 Hercules	17	17	1981	
• Fokker F-27 Mk 400/Mk 600	3	3	1973	Employed in maritime patrol role
• Gulfstream III	3	3	1983	
• IL-76 (candid)	7	7	1994	
• Mystère-Falcon 900	2	2	1990	Unconfirmed
Total	**48**	**48**		

Training and Liaison Aircraft

Model	Quantity	In service	Since	Notes
With ground attack/ close air support capability				Not all serviceable
• CM-170 Fouga Magister	20	20	1971	
• L-39 Albatross	30	30	1987	
Subtotal	50	50		
Others				
• Beechcraft Sierra 200	18	18	1976	
• Zlin 142	30	30		
• Beechcraft T-34C (Turbo Mentor)	6		1978	Possibly phased out
Subtotal	54	48		
Total	**104**	**98**		

Helicopters

Model	Quantity	In service	Since	Notes
Attack				
• Mi-24/Mi-25 (Hind)	36	36	1978	Number unconfirmed

Helicopters *(continued)*

Model	Quantity	In service	Since	Notes
Medium transport				
• Mi-8/Mi-17 (Hip)	56	56	1978	
• SA-330 Puma	5	5	1971	
Subtotal	61	61		
Light transport				
• Alouette II/III	6	6	1984	
• Bell 206	3	3	1988	
• AS-350 Ecureuil	8	8	1995	
Subtotal	17	17		
Total	**116**	**116**		
On order				
• Mi-8/17	30			From Russia

Miscellaneous Aircraft

Model	Quantity	Notes
Maritime surveillance aircraft		
• Fokker F-27 and Super King Air T-200T		Listed under transport a/c

Advanced Armament

Air-to-air missiles
AA-2 (Atoll), AA-6 (Acrid), AA-7 (Apex), AA-11 (Archer)
Air-to-ground missiles
AT-2 (Swatter), AT-6 (Spiral), AS-10 (Karen), AS-14 (Kedge)

Air Force Infrastructure

Military airfields: 16
Ain Ousira, Algiers, Amanas, Balida, Bechar, Biskra, Boufarik, Bousfear, Laghuat, Oran, Ouargla, Tafa Aoui, Tindouf, 3 additional

AIR DEFENSE FORCES

Surface-to-Air Missiles (SAMs)

Model	Batteries	Launchers	Since	Notes
Heavy missiles				
• SA-2 (Guideline)	6	30		
• SA-3 (Goa)	5	20		
Total	11	50		
Medium missiles				
• SA-6 (Gainful)	10	40		
• SA-8 (Gecko)	8	24		
Total	18	64		
Light missiles				
• SA-9 (Gaskin)		40		
• SA-13 (Gopher)				Unconfirmed
Sholder-launched missiles				
• SA-7 (Grail)		200		
Total		200		

Other Air Defense Systems

Model	Quantity	In service	Since	Notes
Short-range guns				
• 57mm ZSU 57×2 SP				
• 57mm S-60	50	50		
• 23mm ZSU 23×4 SP (Gun Dish)	30	30		
• 23mm ZU 23×2	50	50		
• 37mm M-1939	145	145		
• 20mm				
Total	**approx. 300**	**approx. 300**		

NAVY

Combat Vessels

Type	Original Class name	Quantity	Length (m.)/ Displace-ment (t.)	Armament/ special equipment
Submarines				
• K class	Kilo	2	73.8/3,076 (dived)	6 × 533mm torpedoes or 24 mines
Total		2		
MFPBs				
• Ossa I		2	38.6/171	4 × SS-N-2A (Styx)
• Ossa II		9	38.6/171	4 × SS-N-2B (Styx)
Subtotal		11		
ASW frigates				
• Mourad rais	Koni	3	96.4/1,440	RBU 6000 a/s mortars 2 × SA-N-4 (Gecko)
Missile corvettes				
• Nanuchka II		3	59.3/660	4 × SS-N-2B (Styx) 2 × SA-N-4 (Gecko)
Gun corvettes				
• Djebel chinoise (C-58)	Type 802	2	58.4/496	76mm guns 40mm guns
Gunboats/MBTs				
• Kebir class	Brooke Marine	9	37.5/166	1 × 76mm gun 4 × 25mm guns
Mine warfare				
T 43		1	58.0/500	2 a/s mortars 16 mines 2 × 45mm guns
Patrol craft				
• El muderib	Chui-E	7	58.8/388	2 × Twin 14.5mm guns
• Baglietto mangusta		6	30/91	1 × 40mm gun 1 × 20mm gun
• Baglietto 20 GC		8	20.4/44	1 × 20mm gun
Subtotal		21		

Combat Vessels *(continued)*

Type	Original Class name	Quantity	Length (m.)/ Displacement (t.)	Armament/ special equipment
Total		**50**		
On order				
• Djebel Chinoise		1		
• Kebir class		3		

Landing Craft

Type	Original Class name	Quantity	Length (m.)/ Displacement (t.)	Armament/ special equipment
• Polnochny class		1	75/760	2 × 140mm MRLs 2 × 30mm guns
• Kalaat Beni Hammad	Brooke Marine	2	93/2,450	2× 40mm guns 2 × 25mm guns
Total		**3**		

Auxiliary Vessels

Type	Original Class name	Quantity	Length (m.)/ Displacement (t.)	Armament/ special equipment
• Armed fishery protection		12	18	
• Niryat diving tender		1	28.4/120	
• Poluchat I		1	29.6/70	
• Survey ship	Matsukara	1	540	
• Survey ship		2	16 and 20	
• Chinese support ship (with Coast Guard)	T-43	1	59.0/600	

Coastal Defense

Type	Quantity	Notes
• SS-N-2 Styx	4	

Naval Infrastructure

Naval bases: 5

Algiers, Annaba, Mers al-Kebir, Oran, Skikda

Ship maintenance and repair facilities

3 slipways belonging to Chantier Naval de Mers al-Kebir at Oran, 4,000-ton dry docks at Algiers, 3 small graving docks at Annaba, small dry dock at Beni Saf

NONGOVERNMENTAL PARAMILITARY FORCES

Personnel

	Regular	Total
• Islamic Salvation Army (AIS)		
• Armed Islamic Group (GIA)		
Total	**1,000–1,500**	**1,000–1,500**

2. BAHRAIN

GENERAL DATA

Official name of the State: State of Bahrain
Head of State: Amir Shaykh Isa ibn Salman al-Khalifa
Prime Minister Khalifa ibn Salman al-Khalifa
Minister of Defense: Lieutenant General Khalifa ibn Ahmad al-Khalifa (also Commander in Chief of the Armed Forces)
Chief of Staff of the Baharaini Defense Forces: Major General Abdallah ibn Salman al-Khalifa
Commander of the Air Force: Hamad Ibn Abdallah al-Khalifa
Commander of the Navy: Lieutenant Commander Yusuf al-Maluallah

Area: 620 sq. km. (estimate, including 32 small islands)
Population: 590,000

Demography

Ethnic Groups		
Arabs	431,000	73.0%
Persians	47,000	8.0%
Southeast Asians	77,000	13.0%
Others	35,000	6.0%
Religious Groups		
Shi'ite mulsims	413,000	70.0%
Sunni Muslims	177,000	30.0%
National Groups		
Bahrainis	372,000	63.0%
Alien Arabs	59,000	10.0%
Alien Non-Arabs		
Southeast Asians	77,000	13.0%
Iranians	47,000	8.0%
Others	35,000	6.0%

Economic Data

		1992	1993	1994	1995	1996
GDP current price, local currency	BD bn	1.670	1.750	1.800	1.870	2.020

Economic Data *(continued)*

		1992	1993	1994	1995	1996
GDP (U.S.$)	$ bn	4.441	4.654	4.787	4.973	5.372
GDP per capita	$	8,541	8,619	8,549	8,575	8,561
Real GDP growth	%	7.8	8.2	2.3	2.7	3.1
Balance of payments						
• Exports fob	$ bn	3.46	3.71	3.45	4.09	4.70
• Imports fob	$ bn	3.73	3.86	3.74	3.58	3.72
• Account balance (Include services and income)	$ bn	–0.754	0.035	0.198	0.557	0.703
• External debt	$ bn	2.55	2.31	2.42	2.69	2.71
Government income and expenditure						
• Revenues, local currency	BD bn	0.502	0.564	0.514	0.668	0.649
• Expenditures, local currency	BD bn	0.617	0.566	0.572	0.596	0.655
• Defense expenditures	BD m	94.6	94.4	96.2	95.0	NA
• Defense expenditure/GDP	%	5.66	5.39	5.34	5.08	NA
• Defense expenditure/CGE	%	15.33	16.68	16.82	15.93	NA
• Population	m	0.52	0.54	0.56	0.58	0.59
• Official exchange rate	BD: $1	0.376	0.376	0.376	0.376	0.376

Sources: EIU quarterly report, EIU country profile, IMF statistical yearbook, SIPRI Yearbook.

Arms Procurement and Security Assistance Received

Country	Type	Details
Britain	• *Arms transfers*	Patrol craft (1993), electronics
	• *Military training*	Number of retired British officers hold senior positions in Bahraini force, training the new National Guard
Germany	• *Arms transfers*	Missile corvettes, missile boats, helicopters
Netherlands	• *Arms transfers*	203mm SP howitzers, AIFVs (1996) armored CP, ARVs
	• *Military training*	Foreign advisers
Saudi Arabia	• *Military training*	Trainess abroad
Sweden	• *Arms transfers*	Early warning system (1997)
U.S.A.	• *Arms transfers*	ATGMs, APCs, combat aircraft, SAMs, helicopters (1994), tanks, artillery pieces (1992), MLRS, a missile frigate (1997), landing craft
	• *Military training*	Foreign advisers/instructors; Trainees abroad

Arms Sales and Security Assistance Extended

Country	Type	Details
U.K.	• *Facilities*	Air force facilities
U.S.A.	• *Facilities*	Naval facilities, storage facilities, prepositioning of army equipment & intelligence installations, HQ facilities for the U.S. forces in the Gulf at Mina Salman

Foreign Military Cooperation

	Details
• Foreign forces	About 1,500 U.S. soldiers
• Forces deployed abroad	Saudi Arabia (part of GCC Rapid Deployment Force)
• Joint maneuvers	U.S.A.—joint air force, navy and special forces exercises
• Security agreements	U.S.A., Britain, GCC countries

ARMED FORCES

Major Changes: New M-60 A3 tanks and some YPR 765 APCs entered service. The Bahraini Air Force was reinforced by a squadron of AH-1E attack helicopters.

Order-of-Battle

Year	1993	1994	1995	1996	1997
General data					
• Personnel (regular)	6,000	6,050	7,100	7,400	8,400
• Total number of battalions	6	6	6	6	7
Ground Forces					
• Tanks	81	81	81	81	110
• APCs/ARVs	190	195	192	192	217 (237)
• Artillery (incl. MRLs)	15	29	44	44	44 (50)
Air Force					
• Combat aircraft	24	24	24	24	24
• Transport aircraft	2–3	3–4	3–4	3–4	2
• Helicopters	26–27	28	23	23	41
Air Defense Forces					
• Heavy SAM batteries	—	1	1	1	1
• Medium SAM batteries	—	—	7	7	2
• Light SAM launchers	40–50	160	160	160	40*

Order-of-Battle *(continued)*

Year	1993	1994	1995	1996	1997
Navy					
• Combat vessels	19	19	25+	29	30

Note: Beginning with data for 1997, we refer to quantities in active serivce. The numbers in parentheses refers to the total.
*Due to change in estimate.

Personnel

	Regular	Reserves	Total
Ground Forces	7,000		7,000
Air Force	700		700
Navy	700		700
Total	**8,400**		**8,400**
Paramilitary			
• Coast Guard	250		250
• National Guard	600		600

GROUND FORCES

Formations

	Independent battalions
Armored	2
Mechanized	2
Infantry	2
Artillery	1
Air defense	1
Special Forces	1
Total	**9**

Tanks

Model	Quantity	In service	Since	Notes
High quality				
• M–60 A3	110	110	1987	
Total	**110**	**110**		
On order				
• M–60 A3	60			

APCs/ARVs (including command vehicles)

Model	Quantity	In service	Since	Notes
High quality				
• M-113	50	50	1990	
• YPR-765	25	25	1996	
Subtotal	75	75		
Others				
• M-3 (Panhard)	110	110		
• AML-90	22	22	1979	
• AT-105 Saxon	10	10		
• Ferret	10	0		Possibly phased out
• Saladin	10	0		Possibly phased out
Subtotal	162	142		
Total	**237**	**217**		

Artillery

Model	Quantity	In service	Since	Notes
Self-propelled guns and howitzers				
• 203mm M-110	13	13	1994	
Towed guns and howitzers				
• 155mm M-198 A1	20	14	1984	
• 105mm L-118	8	8		
Total	41	35		
MRLs				
• 227mm MLS	9	9	1992	

Antitank Weapons

Model	Quantity	In service	Since	Notes
Missile launchers				
• BGM-71C Improved TOW	15			
On order				
• BGM-71E (TOW 2A)				

AIR FORCE

Order-of-Battle

Model	Quantity	In service	Notes
• Combat	24	24	
• Transport	2	2	
• Helicopters	41	41	

Combat Aircraft

Model	Quantity	In service	Since	Notes
Multirole—high quality				
• F-16C/D	12	12	1990	Multirole, employed as interceptor
Multirole—others				
• F-5E/F	12	12	1985	
Total	24	24		
On order				
• 1 F 16C/D in case of attrition				
• 10 F-16 C/D or 20 F-16 A/B				

Transport Aircraft

Model	Quantity	In service	Since	Notes
• Gulfstream II	2	2	1977	

Helicopters

Model	Quantity	In service	Since	Notes
Attack				
• AH-1E	14	14	1996	
Subtotal	14	14		
Transport				
• AB-212	12	12		
• Bell 412	3	3	1982	with police
• UH-60A Black Hawk	2	2	1996	executive a/c
• 500MD	2	2		
• MBB BO-105	5	5	1976	
• S-70L	1	1		
Subtotal	25	25		

Helicopters *(continued)*

Model	Quantity	In service	Since	Notes
ASW				
• SA-365 Dauphin	2	2		
Total	**41**	**41**		

Advanced Armament

Air-to-air-missiles
- AIM-9P Sidewinder

Air-to-ground missiles
- AS-15TT antiship missile

On order
- Three Sharpshooter pods (For F-16 a/c)

AIR DEFENSE FORCES

Surface-to-Air Missiles

Model	Batteries	Launchers	Since	Notes
Heavy missiles				
• MIM-23B Improved HAWK	1		1994	
Medium missiles				
• Crotale	2	7	1995	Number unconfirmed
Light missiles				
• RBS-70		40		
Shoulder-launched missiles				
• FIM-92A Stinger		18	1987	400 missiles (number unconfirmed)
On order				
• MIM-23B Improved HAWK SAM				

Other Air Defense Systems

Short-range guns
- 35mm Oerlikon

On order
- Cossor SSR and Plessey Watchman air traffic control radars for civilian and military use; an air defense command and control system from Britain (Ferranti)

Air Force Infrastructure

Military airfields: 1
- Shaykh Isa

NAVY

Combat Vessels

Type	Original Class name	Quantity	Length (m.)/ Displace-ment (t.)	Armament/ Special Equipment
Missile frigates				
• Oliver Hazard Perry class		1	135.6/3,638	1 × Dolphine heli-copter 1 × missile launcher for 4x Harpoon SSMs 36 Standard SM-1s 6 × 324mm torpedo tubes 1 × 76mm gun 1 × Vulcan Phalanx 20mm gun
Missile corvettes				
• Al Manama	Lurssen	2	63.0/632	4 × Exocet MM-40 1 × 76mm gun 1 × twin 40mm
MFPBs				
• Ahmad al-Fateh	Lurssen FPB-45	4	44.9/259	4 × Exocet MM-40 1 × 76mm gun 1 × twin 40mm gun
Gunboat/MTBs				
• Al-Riffa	Lurrsen FPB-38	2	38.5/205	1 × twin 40mm 1 × 57mm rocket launcher
• Al-Jarim	Swift FBP-20	2	19.2/33	1 × 20mm gun
Subtotal		4		
Patrol craft (mostly with coast guard)				
• Al-Muharraq	Wasp	1	30/90	1 × 30mm gun
• Dera'a	Tracker	2	19.5/31	
• Dera'a	Halmatic	4	20.1/31.5	
• Dera'a	Wasp	2	20/36.3	

Combat Vessels *(continued)*

Type	Original Class name	Quantity	Length (m.)/ Displace-ment (t.)	Armament/ Special Equipment
• Saif	Halmatic	6	14.4/17	
• Saif	Fairey Marine Sword	4	13.7/15	
Subtotal		19		
Total		**30**		

Landing Craft

Type	Original Class name	Quantity	Length (m.)/ Displace-ment (t.)	Armament/ Special Equipment
• Safra-2	150-ton Fairey Marine LCM	1	22.5/150	
• Tiger-class hovercraft	Tiger-class hovercraft	1	7.97/4.5	
Total		**2**		

Auxiliary Vessels

Type	Original Class name	Quantity	Length (m.)/ Displace-ment (t.)	Armament/ Special Equipment
• Ajeera supply ship		4	36.9/420	
• Safra support ship		1	25.9/165	
Total		**5**		

Naval Infrastructure

Naval bases: 1

- Mina Salman

Ship maintenance and repair facilities

- Arab Shipbuilding and Repair Yard (ASRY), a 500,000 dwt drydock engaged in repairs and construction (mainly supertankers; jointly owned by Bahrain, Kuwait, Qatar, Saudi Arabia, UAE—each 18.84%; Iraq—4.7%; and Libya—1.1%)

3. EGYPT

GENERAL DATA

Official Name of the State: The Arab Republic of Egypt
Head of State: President Muhammad Husni Mubarak
Prime Minister: Kamal Ahmad al-Ganzuri
Minister of Defense and War Production: Field Marshal Muhammad Hussayn Tantawi
Chief of General Staff: General Magdi Hatata
Commander of the Air Force: Lieutenant General Ahmad Abd al-Rahman Nasser
Commander of the Navy: Vice Admiral Ahmad Ali Fadil

Area: 1,000,258 sq. km. (dispute with Sudan over ''Halaib triangle'' area)
Population: 60,130,000

Demography

Ethnic Groups		
Arabs	59,168,000	98.4%
Nubians	60,100	0.1%
Greeks, Italians, Armenians	601,000	1.0%
Others	301,000	0.5%
Religious Groups		
Sunni Muslims	56,522,000	94.0%
Copts, other Christians	3,608,000	6.0%

Economic Data

		1992	1993	1994	1995	1996
GDP current price, local currency	E£ bn	139.10	157.30	175.00	205.00	231.00
GDP (U.S.$)	$ bn	41.898	46.955	51.622	60.472	68.141
GDP per capita	$	760	831	892	1,025	1,133
Real GDP growth	%	0.3	0.5	2.3	3.2	4.9
Balance of payments						
• Exports fob	$ bn	3.67	3.55	4.04	4.67	4.78
• Imports fob	$ bn	8.90	9.92	10.00	12.27	13.17

Economic Data *(continued)*

		1992	1993	1994	1995	1996
• Account balance (Includes services and income)	$ bn	3.49	2.30	0.03	–0.25	–0.19
• External debt	$ bn	31.60	31.10	33.40	34.60	32.50
Government income and expenditure						
• Revenues, local currency	E£ bn	53.389	56.33	60.443	66.195	71.147
• Expenditures, local currency	E£ bn	62.533	65.314	65.047	71.632	77.451
• Defense expenditures	E£ bn	4.884	5.413	5.724	NA	NA
• Defense expenditure/GDP	%	3.51	3.44	3.27	NA	NA
• Defense expenditure/CGE	%	7.81	8.29	8.80	NA	NA
• Population	M	55.16	56.49	57.85	59.01	60.13
• Official exchange rate	E£: $1	3.32	3.35	3.39	3.39	3.39

Sources: EIU quarterly report, EIU country profile, IMF statistical yearbook, Sipri Yearbook.
Note: Reliable data on defense expenditure is unavailable. Some sources indicate a sharp increase in defense expenditure in 1995, to E£ 8.9 bn.

Arms Procurement and Security Assistance Received

Country	Type	Details
Britain	• *Military training*	Trainees abroad
	• *Arms transfers*	Naval radars, mortar-locating radar upgrade
Czech Republic	• *Arms transfers*	L-59 jet trainer aircraft
France	• *Military training*	Trainees abroad
	• *Cooperation in arms production, assembly, R&D*	Electronics, components of SP AA systems
Germany	• *Military training*	Trainees abroad
	• *Maintenance of equipment*	Transport aircraft
India	• *Arms transfers*	Spare parts for Soviet-made aircrafts
Italy	• *Arms transfers*	Terminally guided aerial bombs
Netherlands	• *Arms transfers*	AIFVs (1996)
North Korea	• *Arms transfers*	Assistance to Egyptian production of SSMs
PRC	• *Arms transfers*	Spare parts for F-7 combat aircraft
Russia	• *Arms transfers*	BMP turrets for Egyptian Fahd APCs
Turkey	• *Arms transfers*	U.S. designed F-16 fighter a/c, assembled in Turkey

Arms Procurement and Security Assistance Received *(continued)*

Country	Type	Details
U.S.A.	• *Financial*	$1.3 billion grant, and a few items from U.S. drawdown, worth several hundred million dollars
	• *Military training*	Foreign advisers/instructors, trainees abroad
	• *Arms transfers*	APCs, ATGMs, combat aircraft (1996), helicopters, including AH-64 (1995), AAMs, early warning aircraft, radars, SAMs, upgrading kits for SAMs and tanks, UAVs and mini-UAVs, missile frigates (1996), antiship missiles, torpedoes, fire control systems for submarines, artillery, sonars, communication and ECCM equipment
	• *Cooperation in arms production, assembly, R&D*	Upgrading M-113 APCs, AIFVs, ammunition, electronics including radars and radio transceivers, M-1 A1 tank assembly, upgrading of PRC-made submarines
	• *Construction aid*	Upgrading of airfields and dry docks
	• *Maintenance aid*	Aircraft

Arms Sales and Security Assistance Extended

Country	Type	Details
Algeria	• *Arms transfers*	Fahd APCs
Bahrain	• *Military training*	Advisers/instructors, foreign trainees
Bosnia	• *Arms transfers*	10 T-55 tanks and spare parts (1997), artillery
Brazil	• *Cooperation in arms production, assembly, R&D*	Trainer aircraft
Greece	• *Military training*	Foreign trainees
Iraq	• *Facilities*	Naval vessels anchored in Egypt since the Iran-Iraq War
Jordan	• *Military training*	Foreign trainees
Kuwait	• *Military training*	Advisers/instructors
	• *Arms transfers*	Skyguard AA systems, optronics, gas masks, surveillance radar (AN-TPS/63)
Lebanon	• *Military training*	Foreign trainees

Arms Sales and Security Assistance Extended *(continued)*

Country	Type	Details
Libya	• *Military training*	Foreign trainees
Mali	• *Arms transfers*	Fahd APCs
Oman	• *Arms transfers*	Optronics
	• *Military training*	Advisers/instructors
Palestinians	• *Military training*	Foreign trainees
Qatar	• *Arms transfers*	Optronics, gas masks
Rwanda	• *Arms transfers*	6 artillery pieces
Saudi Arabia	• *Arms transfers*	Engineering equipment
Singapore	• *Arms transfers*	Optronics
Sweden	• *Cooperation in arms production, assembly, R&D*	Radio transceivers
Turkey	• *Military training*	Foreign trainees
Uganda	• *Arms transfers*	Optronics
U.S.A.	• *Facilities*	Airfields at Cairo West, Qena, Inshas, Hurghada
Yemen	• *Military training*	Foreign trainees
Zaire	• *Military training*	Advisers/instructors
	• *Arms transfers*	Optronics
Zimbabwe	• *Military training*	Foreign trainees

Foreign Military Cooperation

	Details
• Forces deployed abroad	Troops with UN forces in Angola, Bosnia (with SFOR), Croatia, Georgia, and Liberia
• Joint maneuvers	France, Britain, Italy, U.S.A.

Defense Production

	M	P	A
Army equipment			
• 130mm artillery pieces		√	
• 122mm Saqr 18/30/36 MRLs	√		
• Conversion of 122mm D-30 howitzers to 122mm AR SP howitzers	√		
• British tank guns		√	
• Upgrading of Soviet tanks (with British assistance)		√	
• M-1 A1 tanks, with cooperation from U.S.A. (some parts will be produced in Egypt)			√
• Conversion of 23mm AAGs to Sinai 23 SP AA systems	√		

Defense Production *(continued)*

	M	P	A
• Add-on armor to M-113 APCs	√		
• Upgraded Scud B SSMs (with North Korean cooperation)	√		
• Fahd APCs (with FRG components and assistance)		√	
• MRLs (copy of Soviet models)		√	
• Short-range SAMs			√
• AAGs			√
• Tank tracks		√	
• Trucks and jeeps (with U.S.A.)		√	
• Soviet design AAGs and small arms		√	
• Minefield crossing systems (similar to Viper)		√	
• Mines, including scatterable	√	√	
• Ammunition for artillery, tanks, and small arms	√		
• Rifles (Hakim 7.92mm, Raschid 7.62mm)	√		
• Chemical agents (unconfirmed)	√		
Aircraft and air ammunition			
• CBUs (U.S. design)		√	
• Antirunway bombs		√	
• A few parts for F-16		√	
• Parts for Mirage 2000		√	
• Parts for Mystère-Falcon 50 executive aircraft		√	
• Aircraft fuel pods		√	
• Aerial bombs		√	
Electronics			
• Bassal artillery fire control system	√		
• Simulators for rifle firing	√		
• AN/TPS-63 radars (assembly, with 30% of components locally produced)		√	
• Radio transceivers (in collaboration with France, Germany, Sweden, and Britain)		√	
• SAM electronics (in collaboration with Britain)		√	
• Fire control system		√	
Optronics			
• Night vision devices		√	

Note: M—manufacture (indigenously developed)
P—production under license
A—assembly

NBC Technology

Nuclear capabilities

- R&D; a declared policy not to produce nuclear weapons; NPT signatory, all declared installations under IAEA safeguards; a 2 mw Soviet-made nuclear research reactor in operation since 1961; a 22 mw research reactor from Argentina completed 1997

CW capabilities

- Alleged continued research and possible production of chemical warfare agents
- Egypt refused to sign the chemical weapons convention (CWC)
- Personal protective equipment. Soviet type decontamination units. Stockpile of chemical agents (mustard and nerve agents)
- Fuchs (Fox) ABC detection vehicle (12)
- SPW-40 P2Ch ABC detection vehicle (small numbers)

Biological warfare capabilities

- Suspected biological warfare program; no details available

ARMED FORCES

Major Changes: The Egyptian Army received 400 out of 512 M-1 A1 MBTs being assembled in Egypt. The Egyptian Air Force received the last batch of 160 F-16 combat aircraft. The Egyptian Navy acquired two new Perry-class missile frigates. Two more are on order.

Order-of-Battle

Year	1993	1994	1995	1996	1997
General Data					
• Personnel (regular)	435,000	428,000	426,000	424,000	421,000
• Divisions	12	12	12	12	12
• Number of brigades	14	14	14	14	18
Ground Forces					
• Tanks	3,225	2,750	2,800	2,900	2,550 (3,050)
• APCs/ARVs	4,400	4,400	4,400	5,180	3,125 (5,095)
• Artillery (incl. MRLs)	2,200	2,200	2,200	3,046	3,146
• SSM launchers	24	24	24	24	21
Air Force					
• Combat aircraft	515–525	457	497	497	510
• Transport aircraft	45	47	47	43	35
• Helicopters	197	197	211	211	223
Air Defense Forces					
• Heavy SAM batteries	122	122	122	122	105
• Medium SAM batteries		48	48	48	48
• Light SAM launchers	50	50	50	50	50

Order-of-Battle *(continued)*

Year	1993	1994	1995	1996	1997
Navy					
• Submarines	8	8	8	8	6
• Combat vessels	92	125	127	129	147

Note: Beginning with data for 1997, we refer to quantities in active service. The number in parentheses refer to the total.

Personnel

	Regular	Reserves	Total
Ground Forces	300,000	150,000	450,000
Air Force	25,000	20,000	45,000
Air Defense	80,000	60,000	140,000
Navy	16,000	14,000	30,000
Total	**421,000**	**244,000**	**665,000**
Paramilitary			
• Coast Guard			2,000
• Frontier Corps			6,000
• Central Security Forces			325,000
• National Guard			60,000
• Border Guard			12,000

GROUND FORCES

Formations

	Corps/ armies	Divisions	Independent brigades/ groups	Brigades in divisions
All arms	2			
Armored		4	4	2 armored, 1 mech., 1 aty each
Mechanized		7	4	2 mech, 1 tank, 1 aty each
Infantry		1	2	1 mech., 1 tank, 1 aty each
Airborne			1	
Special Forces			7	
Artillery			15	
SSM			2	
Total	**2**	**12**	**35**	

Tanks

Model	Quantity	In service	Since	Notes
High quality				
• M-1 A1	400	400	1992	
• M-60 A3	850	850	1981	
Subtotal	1,250	1,250		
Others				
• M-60 A1	700	700	1990	
• T-62	600	600	1972	
• T-55	500	+		Most in storage
Subtotal	1,800	1,300		
Total	**3,050**	**2,550**		
On order				
• 400 M-1 A1 estimated delivered out of an order of 512				
• 340 M-60 A3, out of U.S. drawdown (under negotiation), upgrading M-60 A1 to A3 standard contemplated				

Note: Armored recovery vehicles in service—M-88 A1.

APCs/ARVs (including command vehicles)

Model	Quantity	In service	Since	Notes
High quality				
• BMP-1	200	0		In storage
• M-113 A2	1,920	1,920	1980	
• YPR-765	611	611	1996	
Subtotal	2,731	2,531		
Others				
• BMR-600	250	250	1983	
• V-150/V-300 commando	approx. 180	approx. 180		
• Fahd	165	165	1986	
• BRDM-2			1968	Storage/phased out
• BTR-40/50/60/152			1965	Older models possibly phased out
• OT-62				Older models possibly phased out
Subtotal	2,365	595		
Total	**5,096**	**3,126**		
On order				
• Fahd				

Artillery

Model	Quantity	In service	Since	Notes
Self-propelled guns and howitzers				
• 155mm M-109 A2	200	200	1984	
• 122mm SP122	76	76		
Towed guns and howitzers				
• 130mm M-46/ Type-59	440	440		
• 122mm D-30	156	156		
Mortars, over 160mm				
• 240mm				
• 160mm	60	60		
Mortars, under 160mm				
• 120mm M-43	1,800	1,800		
• 107mm (4.2") M-30 SP	100	100		On M-106 A2 carrier
Total	approx. 2,850	approx. 2,850		
Artillery/mortar-locating radars				
• AN/TPQ-37				
MRLs				
• 122mm BM-11	96	96		
• 122mm BM-21				
• 122mm Saqr 18/ 30/36	200	200		
On order				
• 24 122mm SP122 (to be delivered by 1998); AN/TPQ-37 artillery and mortar-locating radar				

Logistic and Engineering Equipment

- Bar-mine-laying system, EWK pontoon bridges, GSP self-propelled ferries, M-123 Viper minefield crossing system/Egyptian Viper-like system, designated al-Fatah, MT-55 bridging tanks, MTU-55 bridging tanks, Egyptian bridging tanks (on T-34 chasis), mine-clearing rollers, PMP folding pontoon bridges, PRP motorized bridges.

Antitank Weapons

Model	Quantity	In service	Since	Notes
Missiles				
• AT-3 (Sagger)	1,400	1,200	1972	
• BGM-71C Improved TOW/ BGM-71D TOW II	840	840		Includes some on M-901 and YPR-765
• M-901 ITV SP (TOW under armor)	52	52		Listed also under APCs/ARVs
• YPR-765 (TOW under armor)	210	210	1996	Listed also under APCs/ARVs
• MILAN	250	200		
• Swingfire	200	200	1976	
Total	**2,950**	**2,700**		

Surface-to-Surface Missiles and Rockets

Model	Launchers	Missiles	Since	Notes
• FROG-7	12			
• SS-1 (Scud B)	9		1973	Possibly some upgraded
• Saqr 80				Delivery unconfirmed
Total	**21**			
On order				
• Upgraded SS-1 Scud B, locally produced; Scud C (unconfirmed)				

AIR FORCE

Order-of-Battle

Model	Quantity	In service	Notes
• Combat	505	505	
• Transport	35	35	
• Helicopters	223	223	

Combat Aircraft

Model	Quantity	In service	Since	Notes
Interceptors—high quality				
• F-16C/D	approx. 130	approx. 130	1986	Multirole, employed as interceptors
• Mirage 2000	18	18	1986	Multirole, employed as interceptors
Subtotal	148	148		
Interceptors—others				
• F-16A/B	30	30	1982	
• F-7 Shenyang/MiG-21 MF	150	150	1981	Partly used as strike a/c; 14 additional under reconnaissance
• F-6 Shenyang/FT-6	44	44		
Subtotal	224	224		
Total	372	372		
Strike and multirole aircraft—medium and low quality				
• F-4E Phantom	32	32	1980	
• Mirage 5	59	59	1974	Including 6 Mirage 5DRs
• Alpha Jet and Alpha Jet MS-2	42	42	1983	Normally an advanced trainer; defined in Egypt as CAS a/c (allegedly 30 MS-1, 15 MS-2)
Total	133	133		
Total	**505**	**505**		
On order				
• 21 F-16C from U.S. drawdown				

Transport Aircraft

Model	Quantity	In service	Since	Notes
• Beechcraft 1900C (executive a/c)	2	2	1988	
• Boeing 707	1	1	1974	3 more to be converted to aerial tankers

Transport Aircraft *(continued)*

Model	Quantity	In service	Since	Notes
• Boeing 737	1	1		
• C-130H/C-130H-30 Hercules	19	19	1978/ 1990	Including ELINT
• DHC-5D Buffalo	5	5	1982	
• Gulfstream III/V	4	4	1985/ 1996	
• Mystère-Falcon 20	3	3		
Total	**35**	**35**		

Note: Older models partly grounded, including tankers.

Training and Liaison Aircraft

Model	Quantity	In service	Since	Notes
With ground attack/close air support capability				
• Alpha Jet and Alpha Jet MS-2			1983	Listed as strike a/c, above
• L-29 (Delfin)	40	40		
• L-39 (Albatross)	48	48	1990	
• L-59	25	25	1993	
Subtotal	113	113		
Others				
• Al-Gumhuriya	36	36		
• Embraer EMB-312 (Tucano)	54	54	1984	
Subtotal	90	90		
Total	**203**	**203**		

Helicopters

Model	Quantity	In service	Since	Notes
Attack				
• AH-64A Apache	36	36	1995	
• SA-342 L/M Gazelle	65	65	1983	
Subtotal	101	101		
Heavy transport				
• CH-47C Chinook	14	14	1981	
• Westland Commando Mk2	25	25	1974	
Subtotal	39	39		

Helicopters *(continued)*

Model	Quantity	In service	Since	Notes
Medium transport				
• Mi-8 (Hip)	approx. 40	approx. 40		some may be armed
• UH-60A Black Hawk	2	2		VIP service
Subtotal	42	42		
Liaison				
• UH-12E Hiller	17	17	1982	
ASW				
• Westland Sea King Mk 47	5	5	1976	
• SH-2G	10	10	1997	
• SA-342L Gazelle	9	9		
Subtotal	24	24		
Total	**223**	**223**		
On order				
• CH-47D Chinook				

Miscellaneous Aircraft

Model	Quantity	In service	Since	Notes
Reconnaissance				
• MiG-21R	14	14		
• Mirage 5DR	6	6	1974	
AEW/AWACS aircraft				
• E-2C Hawkeye AEW	5	5	1986	
ELINT/maritime surveillance/ASW				
• Beechcraft 1900C	4	4	1992	
• C-130H	2	2	1978	
UAVs and mini-UAVs				
• Kader				
• R4E-50 Skyeye mini-UAVs	48	48		
• Teledyne Ryan model 324 Scarab	50	50		
Target drones				
• Aerospatiale CT-20 target drone				
• Beech AQM-37A target drone				

Miscellaneous Aircraft *(continued)*

Model	Quantity	In service	Since	Notes
• Beech MQM-107B target drone				
• TTL BTT-3 Banshee target drone	Several dozens	Several dozens		
On order				
• TTL BTT-3 Banshee target drones (50); Teledyne Ryan model 324 UAVs				

Advanced Armament

Air-to-air-missiles
- AIM-7F/7M Sparrow, AIM-9 Sidewinder; AIM-9L; AIM-9P, R-550 Magique, R-530D Super

Air-to-ground missiles
- AGM-65 Maverick (1,100), AS-30L, Hellfire (AGM-114), HOT

Avionics
- LANTIRN (10 units)

Air Force Infrastructure

Aircraft shelters
In all operational airfields, for combat aircraft
Military airfields 29
Abu Hammad, Abu Suweir, Alexandria, Aswan, Beni Suef, Bilbeis, Cairo International, Cairo West, Fayid, Hurghada, Inshas, Janaklis, Jebel al-Basour, Kabrit, Kom Awshim, Luxor, al-Maza, al-Minya, Mansura, Marsah Matruh, Qena, al-Qutamiya, Saqqara, Sidi Barani, Ras Banas, Salahiya, Tanta, al-Zaqaziq, one additional airfield

AIR DEFENSE FORCES

Surface-to-Air Missiles

Model	Batteries	Launchers	Since	Notes
Heavy missiles				
• MIM-23B Improved HAWK	12		1981	
• SA-2 (Guideline)	40		1965	
• SA-3 (Goa)	53		1965	
Subtotal	105			

Surface-to-Air Missiles *(continued)*

Model	Batteries	Launchers	Since	Notes
Medium missiles				
• Crotale	16	36	1977	
• SA-6 (Gainful)	14	52	1972	
Subtotal	30	88		
Light missiles				
• MIM–72A	12	50		
Shoulder-launched missiles				
• Ain al-Saqr (Saqr Eye)				
• SA-7 (Grail)		Some 2,000	1972	
On order				
• MIM-23B Improved HAWK missiles (188); upgrading kits for 12 MIM-23B batteries				
• 237 FIM-92A Stinger under negotiation; AdSAMs, under negotiation				

Other Air Defense Systems

Model	Quantity	In service	Since	Notes
Air defense systems (missiles, radars and guns)				
• Skyguard AA system (Egyptian designation: Amoun)	18	18		
• Sinai 23mm AA system				
Short-range guns				
• 57mm ZSU 57×2 SP	40	40		
• 35mm Oerlikon-Buhrle 35×2 GDF-002	36	36		Integral part of Skyguard systems
• 23mm ZSU 23×4 SP (Gun Dish)	550	550		
• 23mm ZU 23×2	117	117		
Total	743	743		
Radars				
• AN/TPS-59				
• AN/TPS-63	42	42		
• P-15 Flat Face				

Other Air Defense Systems *(continued)*

Model	Quantity	In service	Since	Notes
• P-12 Spoon Rest				
• Tiger S (TRS-2100)	15	15		
On order				
• Trackstar L-band acquisition radar; Skyguard AA systems				

NAVY

Combat Vessels

Type	Original Class name	Quantity	Length (m.)/ Displace- ment (t.)	Armament/ special equipment
Submarines				
• R class (Romeo ex-Soviet)		2		2 nonoperational
• R class (Romeo ex-Chinese)		4	76.6/1,830	sub-Harpoon SSM 8×533mm torpedo tubes 14×Mk.37F Mod 2 torpedoes or 28 mines
Total		6		
Missile frigates				
• Descubierta class		2	88.8/1,233	8×Harpoon SSMs 24×Aspide SAMs 6×324mm torpedoes 1×375mm ASW launcher 1×76mm gun 2×40mm guns
• Jianghu class		2	103.2/1,425	4×Hai Ying-II SSMs 4×57mm guns 12×37mm guns 2 RBU 1200 ASW mortars

Combat Vessels *(continued)*

Type	Original Class name	Quantity	Length (m.)/ Displace- ment (t.)	Armament/ special equipment
• Knox class		2	134/3,011	1×Seasprite helicopter 8×Harpoon SSMs 1×127mm gun 1×20mm phalanx 4×324mm torpedoes
• Oliver Hazard Perry		2	135.6/2,750	2×Seasprite helicopters 4×Harpoon SSMs 36×Standard SAMs 1×76mm gun 1×20mm Phalanx 6×324mm torpedoes
Subtotal		8		
MFPBs				
• Hegu class		6	27.0/88	2×SY-1SSMs or 2×SS-N-2 Styx 2×23mm guns
• October	Komar	6	25.5/82.0	2×Otomat SSMs 4×30mm guns
• Ossa I		6	38.6/171	4×SS-N-24 Styx SA-N-5 Grail 4×30mm guns (plus 1 nonoperational)
• Ramadan	Vosper Thornycroft	6	52.0/307	4×Otomat SSMs 1×76mm gun 2×40mm guns SA-N-5 portable SAMS
Subtotal		24		

Combat Vessels *(continued)*

Type	Original Class name	Quantity	Length (m.)/ Displace- ment (t.)	Armament/ special equipment
Gun destroyers				
• El Fateh	Zenith, Wessex	1	110.6/1730	2×SA-N-5 SAMS 4×115mm guns 6×37mm guns 2×40mm guns 8×533mm torpedo tubes
Mine warfare vessels				
• T-43 class minesweeper		4	58.0/580	4×37mm guns 20 mines plus 2 nonoperational
• Swiftships coastal minesweep		3	33.8/203	
• Yurka class minesweeper		4	52.4/540	4×30mm guns 10 mines
• Swiftships route survey		2	27.4/165	
Subtotal		13		
Gunboat/MTBs				
• Hainan class		8	58.8/375	2–4×57mm guns 4×23mm guns 3 possibly nonoperational
• Shanghai II		4	38.8/113	4×37mm guns 4×23mm guns
• Shershen class MTB		6	34.7/145	SA-N-5 portable SAMs 4×30mm guns 2×122mm MRLs
Subtotal		18		
Patrol craft (mostly with coast guard)				
• Spectre		12	13.8/37	
• Peterson		9	13.9/18	replaced older Bertram type
• Crestitalia		6	21.0/36	2×30mm gun 1×20mm gun
• DC 35–type		29	10.7/4	
• Nisr class	de Castro	5	31.0/110	2–4×25mm guns 1×122mm RL

Combat Vessels *(continued)*

Type	Original Class name	Quantity	Length (m.)/ Displace-ment (t.)	Armament/ special equipment
• Swiftships (93-ft.)		10	28.4/102	2×23mm guns 1×20mm gun
• Timsah class		12	30.5/106	2×30mm guns or 2×20mm guns
Subtotal		83		
Total		**147**		
On order				
• U.S.-made mine-sweepers/mine-searchers from Swiftships		2		
• Oliver Hazard Perry–class missile frigates		2		For delivery in 1998
• Type-209 German submarines		2		Unconfirmed

Landing Craft

Type	Original Class name	Quantity	Length (m.)/ Displace-ment (t.)	Armament/ special equipment
• LCM		5		
• Polnochny-class LCT		3	73.0/800	2×30mm guns 2×140mm MRLs 6 tanks or 350 tons
• Vydra-class LCU		9	54.8/425	4×37mm guns 200 troops or 250 tons
Total		**17**		
On order				
• U.S.-made landing ship				

Auxiliary Vessels

Type	Original Class name	Quantity	Length (m.)/ Displacement (t.)	Armament/ special equipment
• Black Swan–class frigate (training)		1	91.2/1,925	6×102mm guns 4×37mm guns possibly no longer serviceable
• Niryat diving support		1		
• Okhtensky (tug)		6	47.6/930	
• Poluchat II torpedo recovery		2	29.6/100	
• Toplivo 2–class tanker		8	53.7/1,029	500 tons diesel
• training (1 Sekstan, 1 4,650-ton, 1 3,008-ton and 1 other)		5		

Coastal Defense

Type	Quantity	Notes
• OTOMAT coastal defense missile	3 batteries	
• HY-2 in coastal defense role		
Total	**30**	**Unconfirmed**

Naval Infrastructure

Naval bases: 8

Abu Qir (naval academy), Alexandria, Hurghada, Marsa Matruh, Port Said, Safaga, Suez, Berenice (Ras Banas)

Ship maintenance and repair facilities

Alexandria (including construction up to 20,000 dwt), Port Said, Ismailiya

4. IRAN

GENERAL DATA

Official Name of the State: Islamic Republic of Iran
Supreme Religious and Political National Leader (Rahbar): Hojatolislam Ali Khamene
Head of State (formally subordinate to national leader): President Hojatolislam Seyyed Mohammed Khatami
Minister of Defense and War Production: Rear Admiral Ali Shamkhani
Chief of Staff of the Armed Forces (including IRGC): Major General Hassan Firuzabadi
Chief of Staff of the Army: Major General Ali Shabazi
Commander of the Air Force: Assad Abadi Habiballah Baqa'i
Commander of the Navy: Rear Admiral Abbas Mohtaj
Commander-in-Chief of the Islamic Revolution Guards Corps (IRGC): Major General Yahya Rahim Safavi
Commander of the IRGC Ground Forces: Brigadier General Muhammad Ali Jafari
Commander of the IRGC Air Wing: Brigadier General Muhammad Baqr Ghalibaf
Commander of the IRGC Naval Wing: General Ali Akbar Ahmadian

Area: 1,647,240 sq. km. (not including Abu Musa Island and two Tunb islands; control disputed)
Population: approx. 62,400,000

Demography

Ethnic Groups		
Persians	31,800,000	51.0%
Azeris	15,000,000	24.0%
Gilaki and Mazandarani	5,000,000	8.0%
Kurds	4,360,000	7.0%
Arabs	1,870,000	3.0%
Balouchis	1,250,000	2.0%
Turkmens	1,250,000	2.0%

Lurs	1,250,000	2.0%
Others	620,000	1.0%
Religious Groups		
Shi'ite Muslims	59,280,000	95.0%
Sunni Muslims	2,500,000	4.0%
Christians, Zoroastrians, Jews, Bahais and others	620,000	1.0%

Economic Data

		1992	1993	1994	1995	1996
GDP current price, local currency	IR tr	66.50	93.80	130.00	186.10	233.7
GDP (U.S.$)	$ bn	1,014.5	80.161	74.339	62.033	77.9
GDP per capita	$	17,736	1,370	1,243	1,017	1,248
Real GDP growth	%	6.8	2.6	1.8	4.2	5.9
Balance of payments						
• Exports fob	$ bn	19.87	18.08	19.40	18.30	22.5
• Imports fob	$ bn	23.27	19.29	12.68	12.80	14.97
• Account balance (Includes services and income)	$ bn	–6.50	–3.90	4.80	3.20	5.3
• External debt	$ bn	12.87	20.55	22.69	30.00	16.81
Government income and expenditure						
• Revenues, local currency	IR tr	12.3	29	33.92	46.13	61.03
• Expenditures, local currency	IR tr	13.1	34.9	40.33	51.03	61.03
• Defense expenditures	IR tr	1.48	2.32	2.86	4.21	5.59
• Defense expenditure/ GDP	%	2.2	2.4	2.2	2.3	2.4
• Defense expenditure/ CGE	%	11.3	6.6	7.1	8.2	9.1
• Population	m	57.2	58.5	59.8	61	62.4
• Official exchange rate	IR: $	65.55	1,170.14	1,748.75	3,000	3,000

Sources: EIU quarterly report, EIU country profile, IMF statistical yearbook, Sipri Yearbook.

Arms Procurement and Security Assistance Received

Country	Type	Details
France	• Arms transfers	Socata training aircraft
Germany	• Arms transfers	Aircraft, missile parts, chemical and nuclear technology (unauthorized by government)
North Korea	• Arms transfers	SSMs (1992), SSM technology (1997)

Arms Procurement and Security Assistance Received *(continued)*

Country	Type	Details
Poland	• Arms transfers	T-72 tanks (1995)
PRC	• Foreign advisers	(including nuclear technicians)
	• Arms transfers	C-802 naval SSMs (1995), F-7 aircraft (1992), SAMs (1992), Houdong MFPBs (1995), missile technology (1996), Transport aircraft (1997)
Russia	• Foreign advisers	including a large group of nuclear technicians
	• Arms transfers	SSM technology (1997), tanks (1992), APCs and AIFVs (1994), Kilo submarines (1997), Mig-29 aircraft (1992), SAMs (1998)
Singapore	• Arms transfers	spare parts for American weapons
Taiwan	• Arms transfers	spare parts for American aircraft
Ukraine	• Arms transfers	SAMs (1993), Naval SSMs (1993), tanks (1996)
U.S.A.	• Arms transfers	Shoulder-launched SAMs originally supplied to Afghan rebels

Arms Sales and Security Assistance Extended

Country	Type	Details
Bosnia	• Advisers	several hundred
	• Arms transfers	Chinese ATGMs, artillery shells (1996)
Kurds	• Facilities provided	To PKK by IRGC, unconfirmed
	• Arms transfers	shoulder launched SAMs
Lebanon	• Financial aid	Hizbullah militia in Lebanon—grant estimated at tens of millions of dollars per annum
	• Military training	Hizbullah militia
	• Advisers	some IRGC instructors with Hizbullah militia in Syrian-held Beka'
	• Arms transfers	Artillery, MRLs, small arms, ATGMs, engineering equipment, SAMs, night vision equipment (1997)
North Korea	• Financial aid	funding for development of long-range missiles (No-Dong-2) (1996)
Palastinian Authority	• Military training	Palestinian Hamas and Islamic Jihad; PFLP-GC
Sri Lanka	• Arms transfers	small arms

Arms Sales and Security Assistance Extended *(continued)*

Country	Type	Details
Sudan	• Advisers	a few IRGC personnel in the Sudanese Army and with People's Defense Forces (1996)
	• Arms transfers	small arms, tanks (1996), combat aircraft (1996)
Syria	• Cooperation in arms production/ assembly/R&D	Joint development of SSMs

Foreign Military Cooperation

Pakistan	• Joint maneuvers (naval)

Defense Production

	M	P	A
Army equipment			
• Heckler & Koch G-3 AR rifles		√	
• MG-1A1 machine guns		√	
• 122, 160, and 240mm MRLs	√		
• 122mm and 155mm SP guns	√		
• 81, 120, and 320mm mortars and artillery ammunition	√		
• Spare parts, trucks	√		
• Chemical agents (mustard, attempts to produce nerve agents)	√		
• Gas masks	√		
• Laser-guided AT missiles	√		
• RPG-7, Nafez, and Saegheh ATRLs	√	√	
• Raad ATGM	√		
• Boragh, Cobra, and BMT-2 APCs	√		
• 120mm Russian artillery guns		√	
• Assembly and production of SSMs (planned, with North Korea, and possibly also Pakistan)	√		√
• Production of Russian T-72 tanks		√	
• Zulfikar and Towsan tanks, upgrading of T-55 tanks to Iranian T-72Z	√	√	
Aircraft and air ammunition			
• Parasto light aircraft (probably still under development)	√		
• Spare parts for aircraft	√		
• Dorneh training aircraft	√		
• Azarakhsh and Owaz fighter aircraft	√		
• Zafar 300 attack helicopter, sanjack light helicopter	√		
• RPVs and UAVs	√		

Defense Production *(continued)*

	M	P	A
• An 140 and IL 114 transport aircraft		√	
• ZU-23mm antiaircraft guns		√	
• SAMs (assembly of Chinese HN-5A and HQ-2, unconfirmed)			√
Electronics			
• Radio transceivers (copy of U.S. model)	√		
Naval craft and ammunition			
• Tareq patrol craft	√		
• 250-ton LCU (Foque 101)	√		
• MIG-S-1800 and MIG-S-1900 patrol crafts	√		
• Hendijan auxiliary vessels	√		
Space			
• Telecommunications satellite under development, to be launched with French cooperation	√		

Note: M—manufacture (indigenously developed)
P—production under license
A—assembly

NBC Technology

Nuclear capabilities

- A 5 mw research reactor acquired from the U.S.A. in the 1960s (in Tehran) and a small 27 kw miniature neutron source reactor (in Esfahan). A 1,000 mw VVER reactor under construction, under a contract with Russia, in Busher

CW capabilities

- Personal protective equipment for part of the armed forces; CWC signatory, but Iran is nevertheless suspected of producing and stockpiling of chemical agents and munitions decontamination units

Biological warfare capabilities

- Suspected biological warfare program; no details available

ARMED FORCES

Major Changes: No major change has been recorded in Iran's regular forces. The Iranian Army is in a slow process of receiving the indigenously built Boragh APC and Zulfikar MBT. The Iranian Navy received its third Kilo-class submarine from Russia.

Order-of-Battle

Year	1993	1994	1995	1996	1997*
General data					
• Personnel (regular)	430,000	435,000	413,000	410,000	518,000
• Divisions	40	40	32	32	32
• Total number of brigades	100	100	87	87	87
Gound Forces					
• Tanks	700–800	1,000	1,500	1,500	1,500
• APCs/ARVs	700	800	1,000	1,300	1,200
• Artillery (incl. MRLs)	1,500–2,000	1,500–2,000	1,500–2,000	1,500–2,000	1,800–2,800
• SSM launchers	15	10	15	15	26–36
Air Force					
• Combat aircraft	195	214	214	214	226 (318)
• Transport aircraft	120	120	119	119	93 (114)
• Helicopters	275	275	275	275	310 (553)
Air Defense Forces					
• Heavy SAM batteries	30–35	30–35	30–35	30–35	30–35
• Medium SAM batteries	+	+	+	+	+
• Light SAM launchers	110	110	110	110	95
Navy					
• Combat vessels	81	173	175	174	169
• Submarines	1	2	2	2	3

Note: Beginning with data for 1997, we refer to quantities in active service. The numbers in parentheses refers to the total.
*Change in estimate.

Personnel

	Regular	Reserves	Total
Ground Forces	approx. 350,000	350,000	700,000
Air Force	18,000		18,000
Air Defense	12,000		12,000
Navy	approx. 18,000		18,000
IRGC—armed forces	100,000		100,000
IRGC—navy	20,000		20,000
Total	**518,000**	**350,000**	**868,000**
Paramilitary			
• Baseej		2,000,000	

GROUND FORCES

Formations

	Corps	Divisions	Independent brigade/group	Brigades in division
All arms	4			
Armored		4	1	3 arm., 1 mech., 1 art. each
Infantry		6	1	4 inf., 1 art. each
Airborne			1	
Special forces		2	5	3 commando each
Artillery			6	
Total	**4**	**12**	**14**	

IRGC Formation

	Divisions	Independent brigades	Brigades in division
Armored	4		
Infantry	16		
Special forces		3	
Artillery		6	
SSMs		1–2	
Total	**20**	**10–11**	

Note: The IRGC has possibly reorganized as 26 divisions—without independent brigades. IRGC divisions are smaller in size than army divisions, sometimes equivalent to the strength of one brigade.

Tanks

Model	Quantity	In service	Since	Notes
High quality				
• T-72 S/M1	approx. 200	approx 200	1990	
Subtotal	200	200		
Others				
• Zulfikar	approx. 20	approx. 20	1996	
• Chieftain mk 3/mk 5	approx. 100	approx. 100	1973	
• T-62	150	150		
• M-60 A1	150	150	1972	

Tanks *(continued)*

Model	Quantity	In service	Since	Notes
• T-55/type 69/type 59	550–700	550–700	1985	
• M-48/M-47	150	150	1958	Being converted to Zulfikar
• Scorpion	50–80	50–80		
Subtotal	1,300	1,300		
Total	**1,500**	**1,500**		
On order				
• T-72S	several hundred			

APCs/ARVs

Model	Quantity	In service	Since	Notes
High quality				
• M-113	200	200		
• BMP-1	300	300	1977	
• BMP-2	100	100		
• Boragh	50	50	1996	
• Engesa EE-9 Cascavel	35	35		
Subtotal	685	685		
Others				
• BTR-50/60	500	500	1967	
• MT-LB	scores	scores		
Subtotal	approx. 500	approx. 500		
Total	**1,200**	**1,200**		

Artillery

Model	Quantity	In service	Since	Notes
Self-propelled guns and howitzers				
• 203mm M-110	20–30	20–30	1976	
• 175mm/170mm Koksan M-1978	10–30	10–30		
• 175mm M-107	25	25	1972	
• 155mm M-109	440	120–150		
• 122mm 2S1	60	30–60		

Artillery *(continued)*

Model	Quantity	In service	Since	Notes
Towed guns and howitzers				
• 203mm (8") M-115	20–300	20–300		
• 155mm G-5	30	30		
• 155mm GHN-45	100	100		
• 155mm M-114	80–120	80–120		
• 152mm (PRC)	30	30		
• 130mm M-46/Type 59	500–1,000	500–1,000		
• 122mm D-30	400–500	400–500		
• 122mm Type 54/60	80–100	80–100		
• 105mm M-101	150–200	150–200		
Mortars, over 160mm				
• 320mm	some	some		
Mortars, under 160mm				
• 120mm M-65				
• 107mm (4.2") M-30				
Total	1,600–2,600	1,600–2,600		
MRLs				
• 355mm Nazeat				
• 333mm Shahin 2				
• 240mm Fajr-3				
• 230mm Oghab				
• 122mm BM-21	50–100	50–100		
• 122mm Hadid/Azrash/Nur	50	50		
• 107mm Type 63	100	100		

Logistic and Engineering Equipment

Pontoon bridges, light infantry assault boats, self-propelled pontoons, AFV transporters (several hundred)

Antitank Weapons

Missiles

AT-11 (Spandrel), AT-4 (Spigot), AT-3 (Sagger), BGM-71A TOW, SS-11/SS-12

Guns

106mm M-40 A1C recoilless rifle (200)

Surface-to-Surface Missiles and Rockets

Model	Launchers	Missiles	Notes
• SS-1 (Scud B/ Scud C)	10–20	300 scud B, 100 Scud C	
• CSS-8	16		
Total	**26–36**		
On order			
• Nodong			unconfirmed; possibly abandoned

Note: Longer-range missiles for ranges of 1,300–1,500 km are being developed indigenously (Shihab-3, Shihab-4).

AIR FORCE

Order-of-Battle

Model	Quantity	In service	Notes
• Combat	318	226	
• Transport	114	93	
• Helicopters	553	310	

Note: about 60% serviceable, not counting most of the 115 combat aircraft and the transport and civilian aircraft brought from Iraq during the 1991 Gulf War; the only Iraqi a/c integrated into the Iranian force are 24 Su-24s and a few MiG-29s; all figures include aircraft with army aviation and navy.

Combat Aircraft

Model	Quantity	In service	Since	Notes
Interceptors—high quality				
• F-14A tomcat	60	25	1972	
• MiG-29	35	35	1990	
Subtotal	95	60		
Interceptors—others				
• F-7	25	25	1987	
Total	120	85		
Strike and multirole aircraft—high quality				
• Su-24	24	24	1991	
Others				
• F-4 D/E/RF Phantom	70	40	1968	
• Mirage F1E	24	12	1991	
• F-6	20	20	1982	
• F-5 A/B/E	60	45	1974	

Combat Aircraft *(continued)*

Model	Quantity	In service	Since	Notes
Subtotal	174	117		
Total	198	141		
Total	**318**	**226**		
On order				
• MiG-29				Unconfirmed
• Su-24				Unconfirmed
• Su-25				Negotiations with Georgia
• Su-27				Negotiations
• F-1				Plans to integrate into air force

Transport Aircraft

Model	Quantity	In service	Since	Notes
• Aero Commander 690	3	3		
• Boeing 747	9	9		
• Boeing 707 and KC-707 tanker-refueling	14–15	14–15	1973	Including Boeing 707s in electronic surveillance/EW/CEW role
• C-130 E/H Hercules	50	25–35		Including 2–3 in electronic surveillance role
• Dornier Do-228	4	4		Possibly civilian, or employed in maritime surveillance role
• Fokker F-27-400M/ F-27-600	18	18	1972	
• Mystère-Falcon 20	14	14	1991	
• Jetstar	1	1		
Total	**114**	**approx. 93**		

Training and Liaison Aircraft

Model	Quantity	In service	Since	Notes
• Beechcraft Bonanza F-33	20–25	20–25		

Training and Liaison Aircraft *(continued)*

Model	Quantity	In service	Since	Notes
• Cessna 185/180/150	45	45		
• Mushshak (PAC Mushshak)	25	25	1991	
• Embraer EMB-312 (Tucano)	25	25	1989	
• Socata TB 21/TB 200 (Trinidad/Tobago)	12	12		
• Pilatus PC-7 Turbo-trainer	45	45	1983	
• Pilatus PC-6	15	15	1982	
• T-33	9	9		
Total	**201**	**201**		
On order				
• EMB-312				

Helicopters

Model	Quantity	In service	Since	Notes
Attack				
• AH-1J Cobra	100	70	1974	
Heavy transport				
• CH-47C Chinook	45	35	1973	
• RH-53D/SH-53D	20–25	20–25	1976	
Subtotal	approx. 70	approx. 55		
Medium transport				
• AB-214A	180–200	50–70	1974	
• AB-205	50	50	1969	
• AB-212	28	28	1971	
• SA-330/IAR-330 Puma	small number	small number		
• AS-61	2	2		
Subtotal	280	150		
Light transport				
• AB-206 JetRanger	90	small number	1969	
• IAR-316				
• IAR-317				
Subtotal	100	small number		

Helicopters *(continued)*

Model	Quantity	In service	Since	Notes
ASW				
• SH-3D	3	small number	1977	
Total	**553**	**approx. 310**		
On order				
• CH-47D	30			
• AS-61	10			2 out of 12 delivered
• A-109A				
• NAS-330 Puma	5–7			Possibly delivered to civilian industry

Miscellaneous Aircraft

Model	Quantity	In service	Since	Notes
Maritime surveillance aircraft				
• P-3 Orion	5	2	1984	
Electronic surveillance				
• RC-130				Listed under Transport

Advanced Armament

Air-to-air missiles

AA-10 (Alamo), AA-11 (Archer), AIM-54A Phoenix, AIM-9 Sidewinder, AIM-7 Sparrow

Air-to-ground missiles

AGM-65 Maverick, AS-10 (Karen), AS-12, C-801 antiship missile

On order

AS-1, AS-5, AS-6, AA-11 (Archer AAM), AA-12

Air Force Infrastructure

Aircraft shelters

In all operational airfields

Military airfields: 20

Bandar Abbas, Birjand, Bushehr, Ghaleh-Marghi, Isfahan, Kerman, Kharg Island, Mehrabad, Qeshm, Shiraz, Tabriz, Teheran, at least 8 additional

AIR DEFENSE FORCES

Surface-to-Air Missiles (SAMs)

Model	Batteries	Launchers	Since	Notes
Heavy missiles				
• HAWK/MIM-23B Improved HAWK	12–15		1964	
• SA-2 (Guideline)/ HQ-2J	8–10	45–60		May be under control of IRGC
• SA-5 (Gammon)				
Total	30–35			
Medium missiles				
• SA-6 (Gainful)	+			
Light missiles				
• Rapier		30	1971	
• RBS-70		50	1984	
• Tigercat		15	1968	
Total		95		
Shoulder-launched missiles				
• FIM-92A Stinger (with IRGC)		small number	1987	
• SA-7 (Grail)/HN-5A/ SA-14/SA-16		hundreds		
On order				
• SA-10/(S-300-P)	6			
• SA-5 (Gammon)				
• C^3I system				Upgrading air defense C^3I by Russia (unconfirmed)
• SA-6				

Other Air Defense Systems

Model	Quantity	In service	Since	Notes
Air defense systems (including radars, missiles, and guns)				
• 35mm Contraves Skyguard ADS	100	24		
Short-range guns				
• 57mm ZSU–57×2 SP	100	100		
• 57mm S-60	50	50		
• 40mm L-70	95	95		
• 40mm M1	20	20		

Other Air Defense Systems *(continued)*

Model	Quantity	In service	Since	Notes
• 23mm ZSU 23×4 SP (Gun Dish)	75	75		
• 23mm ZU 23×2	500	500		
Total	**840**	**840**		
Radars				
• AR-3D				

Navy

Combat Vessels

Type	Original Class name	Quantity	Length (m.)/ Displace- ment (t.)	Armament/ special equipment
Submarines				
• K class (Kilo)	Type 877	3	73.8/3,076	6 × 533 torpedoes 24 mines
• Iranian midget submarines		3	9.2/90	
Total		6		
MFPBs				
• Kaman class	Combattante II	10	47.0/249	4 × C-801/Harpoon SSMs (several without SSMs) 1 × 76mm guns 1 × 40mm guns
• Ossa II (ex-Iraqi)		1	38.6/245	4 × SS-N-2B (Styx) SSMs (probably has no SSMs) 4 × 30mm guns
• Houdong		10	36.6/171	4 × C-802 SSMs 2 × 30mm guns
Subtotal		21		

Combat Vessels *(continued)*

Type	Original Class name	Quantity	Length (m.)/ Displace-ment (t.)	Armament/ special equipment
Missile frigates				
• Alvand class	Vosper Mk 5	3	94.5/1,100	1 Seakiller II SSM 1 MK-10 a/s mortar 1 × 114mm gun 2 × 35mm guns 3 × 20mm guns
Missile destroyers				
• Badr class	Summer	2	114.8/2,388	4 × Standard SAMs 6 × 324mm torpedoes 4 × 127mm MRLs AB 204AS Helicopter
Gun corvettes				
• Bayandor class	PF-103	2	84/900	2 × 76mm guns 2 × 40mm guns 2 × 20mm guns
Mine warfare vessels				
• MSC 292 and MSC 268 class		3	44.5/384	Acoustic and magnetic sweep 2 × 20mm guns
• Cape class		2	33.9/239	Mechanical, acoustic and magnetic sweep 1 × 12.7mm MG
Subtotal		5		
Patrol craft				
• Parvin class	PGM-71	3	30.8/98	4 depth charges 1 × 40mm gun 2 × 20mm guns
• Zafan class	Chaho	3	26/70	1 BM-21 122mm MRL 2 × 20mm guns
• PBI	Peterson	60	15.2/20.1	1 Tigercat SSM 2 × 12.7mm MG
• Peterson—MK IIs		6	15.2/22.9	4 × 12.7mm MG

Combat Vessels *(continued)*

Type	Original Class name	Quantity	Length (m.)/ Displace- ment (t.)	Armament/ special equipment
• U.S. Mk III coastal patrol craft		8	19.8/41.6	3 × 12.7mm MG (some with 20mm gun)
• MIG-S-1800		6	18.7/60	1 × 20mm gun
• MIG-G-1900		8	19.5/30	2 × 23mm guns
• Boghammar		22	13/6.4	1 × 107mm MRL 1 × 106mm RCL 1 × 12.7mm MG RPG 7 (with IRGC)
• Boston Whaler craft type 1		20	6.7/1.3	1 × 107mm MRL 1 × 12.7mm MG
• Bertram Enforcer and various other small crafts		numerous	5–7m	some with 12.7mm MG
Subtotal		136		
Total		**169**		
On order				
• EM-52 mines				

Landing Craft

Type	Original Class name	Quantity	Length (m.)/ Displace- ment (t.)	Armament/ special equipment
• Wellington class hovercraft	BH-7	6	23.9/53.6	
• Winchester class hovercraft	SRN-6 class	4	14.8/10.9	50 troops and 5 tons
• Hengam class landing ship		4	93/2,540	Up to 9 tanks or 227 troops 1 × 122mm MRL 4 × 40mm guns 8 × 23mm guns
• Iran Ajr class		2	53.7/2,274	65 tons 2 × 12.7mm MG

Landing Craft *(continued)*

Type	Original Class name	Quantity	Length (m.)/ Displace-ment (t.)	Armament/ special equipment
• Iran Hormuz 24 class		3	73.1/2,014	9 tanks or 140 troops
• Iran Hormuz 21 class		5	65/1,280	600 tons
• Fouque class	Mig-S-3700	1	37/276	140 tons
• Rotork 412 class		4	12.7/9	30 troops
Total		**32**		

Auxiliary Vessels

Type	Original Class name	Quantity	Length (m.)/ Displace-ment (t.)	Armament/ special equipment
• Delvar-class support ship		7	64/890	765 dwt 2 × 23mm guns
• Luhring Yard supply ship		2	108/4,673	3,250 dwt 1AB 212 helicopter 3 × 20mm guns
• Kangan-class water tanker	Mazagon	4	148/12,000	9,430 dwt 2 × 23mm guns
• Swan Hunter replenishment ship		1	207.2/ 33,014	9,367 dwt 3 SeaKing helicopters 1 × 76mm gun
• Hendijan	Mig-S-4700	13	50.8/460	40 ton on deck and 95m^3 liquid
• Damen 1550		10	16/25	

Coastal Defense

Type	Batteries	Missiles	Notes
• HY-2 (Silkworm) SSMs	approx. 12	300	
• C-802	15–25	approx. 100	
• SS-N-22 (Sunburn)			alleged; probably not extant
Total	**approx. 25–30**	**approx. 400**	

Naval Infrastructure

Naval bases: 9

Bandar Abbas, Bandar Anzelli, Bandar Khomeini, Bandar Lengeh, Bushehr, Chah Bahar, Farsi Island, Jask, Kharg Island, Abu Island (under construction)

IRGC naval bases: 10

Abadan oil terminal, Abu Musa Island, al-Fayisiyah Island, Cyrus oilfield, Halul Island platform (unconfirmed), Larak Island, Qeshm Island, Rostam Island oilfield, Sir Abu Nuair, Sirri Island

Ship maintenance and repair facilities: 2

MAN Nordhaman 28,000-ton floating dock

NONGOVERNMENTAL PARAMILITARY FORCES

Personnel

	Regular
Democratic Party of Iranian Kurdistan (DPIK)	10,000

5. IRAQ

GENERAL DATA

Official Name of the State: The Republic of Iraq
Head of State: President Saddam Hussein (also Prime Minister and Supreme Commander of the Armed Forces)
Minister of Defense: Lieutenant General Sultan Hashim Ahmad Al-Jabburi Tai
Commander of the Air Force: Lieutenant General Khaldoun Khatab Bakr
Commander of the Navy: Rear Admiral Khalid Baqer Khadar

Area: 432,162 sq. km. (no effective control over autonomous Kurdish region in northern Iraq)
Population: 21,420,000 (estimate)

Demography

Ethnic Groups		
Arabs	15,743,000	73.5%
Kurds	4,627,000	21.6%
Turkmens	515,000	2.4%
Assyrians and others	535,000	2.5%
Religious Groups		
Shi'ite Muslims	11,780,000	55.0%
Sunni Muslims	8,997,000	42.0%
Christians, Yazidis, and others	643,000	3.0%

Economic Data

		1992	1993	1994	1995	1996
GDP current price, local currency	ID bn					
GDP (U.S.$)	$ bn	NA	NA	NA	NA	NA
GDP per capita	$	NA	NA	NA	NA	NA
Real GDP growth	%					
Balance of payments						
• Exports fob	$ bn	0.401	0.444		NA	NA
• Imports fob	$ bn	0.477	1.5		NA	NA

Economic Data *(continued)*

		1992	1993	1994	1995	1996
• Account balance (Includes services and income)	$ bn				NA	NA
• External debt	$ bn				NA	NA
Government income and expenditure						
• Revenues, local currency	ID bn				NA	NA
• Expenditures, local currency	ID bn				NA	NA
• Defense expenditures	ID bn				NA	NA
• Defense expenditure/GDP	%	NA	NA	NA	NA	NA
• Defense expenditure/CGE	%	NA	NA	NA	NA	NA
• Population	m		19.45		20.6	21.42
• Official exchange rate	ID: $		3.217	3.217	3.217	3.217

Sources: EIU quarterly report, EIU country profile, IMF statistical yearbook, Sipri Yearbook.

Arms Procurment and Security Assistance Received

Country	Type	Details
No data is available on the last seven years.		

Arms Sales and Security Assistance Extended

Country	Type	Details
No data available		

Defense Production

	M	P	A
Army equipment			
• Small arms and artillery ammunition	√		
• Electronics	√		
• Chemical agents	√		
• Biological weapons	√		
• SSMs under development	√		
• Upgrading of Soviet-designed Scud B SSMs performed in the past	√		
• Land mines, including scatterable	√		
• ATRLs		√	
• Artillery (Brazilian, Yugoslav, and South African license)		√	
• MRLs (Brazilian and Yugoslav license)		√	
• Tanks		√	
• Artillery ammunition (Spanish and South African license)		√	

Defense Production *(continued)*

	M	P	A
Aircraft and air ammunition			
• Chilean-designed Cardoen aerial CBU and FAE bombs		√	
• Aerial bombs	√	√	
• UAVs	√		
• AEW aircraft (Soviet aircraft, with French electronics and Indian assistance)		√	
Naval craft and ammunition			
• Small PBs	√		
• Rubber boats	√		
• Copy of Soviet-designed naval mines		√	

Note: All information is outdated.
M—manufacture (indigenously developed)
P—production under license
A—assembly

NBC Technology

Nuclear capabilities
- Since the Gulf War, all known Iraqi efforts have been stalled by UN and IAEA facility destruction and monitoring regimes.

CW capabilities
- Personal protective equipment. Soviet-type unit decontamination equipment
- Stockpile of chemical agents: until 1991 Iraq had mustard (sulfur mustard and purified mustard), Sarin, Tabun; Soman; VX; hydrogen cyanide (unconfirmed); a large portion of chemical agents were destroyed by UN missions, though Iraq has the know-how to renew CW production
- Delivery systems (SSM warheads, thousands of artillery shells, mortar bombs, MRL rockets, aerial bombs and land mines)

Biological warfare capabilities
- Some capability, hidden from UN supervisors; Iraq now admits having had biological weapons, but claims to have destroyed them in October 1990; there are claims BW was not destroyed
- Toxins and other biological weapons, specifically anthrax and typhoid; botulinium; BW capability largely unaffected by UN observer activity, though currently inspected; Iraq now admits having had BW, but claims it destroyed it in October 1990; there are claims BW still exists in large quantities

ARMED FORCES

Major Changes: No changes have been recorded in the order-of-battle of the Iraqi forces, due to the embargo on Iraq.

Order-of-Battle

Year	1993	1994	1995	1996	1997
General data					
• Personnel (regular)	500,000	500,000	450,000	400,000	391,800
• Divisions	28	28	26	23	23
Ground Forces					
• Tanks	2,500	2,200	2,100	2,100	2,000
• APCs/ARVs	3,500	3,500	3,300	3,300	2,000 (3,300)
• Artillery (incl. MRLs)	(1,500)	1,650	1,800	1,800	2,050
• SSM launchers	small number	small number	34	34	34
Air Force					
• Combat aircraft	400	400	380	380	210 (331)
• Transport aircraft	small number	small number	small number	small number	small number
• Helicopters	400	400	400	400	370 (465)
Air Defense Forces					
• Heavy SAM batteries	NA	NA	NA	NA	60
• Medium SAM batteries	NA	NA	NA	NA	NA
• Light SAM launchers	NA	NA	NA	NA	NA
Navy					
• Combat vessels	9	16	16	86	88

Note: Beginning with data for 1997, we refer to quantities in active service. The numbers in parentheses refers to the total.

Personnel

	Regular	Reserves	Total
Ground Forces	350,000	650,000	1,000,000
Air Force	25,000		25,000
Air Defense	15,000		15,000
Navy	1,800		1,800
Total	**391,800**	**650,000**	**1,041,800**
Paramilitary			
• Border guards	20,000		
• Security forces	25,000–45,000		
• Special Republican guard	26,000		
• Security troops	4,800		

GROUND FORCES

Formations

	Corps	Divisions	Independent brigade/group	Brigades in division
All Arms	5+2			
• Armored		6		
• Mecanized		4		
• Infantry		13		
• Special Forces			2	
Total	**5**	**23**	**2**	

Note: 4 armored/mechanized divisions and 2 infantry divisions constitute the elite Republican Guard.

Tanks

Model	Quantity	In service	Since	Notes
High quality				
• T-72/T-72M	700	700	1982	
• Assad Babil	small number	small number	1989	
Subtotal	approx. 800	approx. 800		
Others				
• T-62			1973	
• T-55/Type 59/ Type 69/M-77			1982	
Subtotal	1,200	1,200		
Total	**approx. 2,000**	**approx. 2,000**		

APCs/ARVs

Model	Quantity	In service	Since	Notes
High quality				
• BMP-1}	900			
• BMP-2}				
• YW-531				
• Engesa EE-9/11			1979	
Others				
• AML-90/60				
• BRDM-2				

APCs/ARVs *(continued)*

Model	Quantity	In service	Since	Notes
• BTR-40/50/60				
• FUG-70/PSZH-IV				
• K-63				
• M-60P				
• M-3 (Panhard)				
• OT-62/OT-64				
• BMD				
• MT-LB				An artillery prime-mover, employed also as APC
Total	**3,300**	**2,000**		

Artillery

Model	Quantity	In service	Since	Notes
Self-propelled guns and howitzers				
• 155mm M-109				
• 155mm GCT			1982	
• 155mm Majnoon				
• 152mm M-1973				
• 122mm M-1974				
Subtotal	150	150		
Towed guns and howitzers				
• 180mm S-23				
• 155mm G-5				
• 155mm GHN-45				
• 155mm M-114 A1				
• 152mm D-20				
• 152mm M-1976 (2A36)				
• 152mm M-1943 (D-1)				
• 130mm M-46/ 130mm Type 59				
• 122mm D-30/Saddam				
• 122mm M-1938				
• 105mm M-56				
• 105mm M-102				
• 85mm field/AT				
Subtotal	1,800	1,800		

Artillery *(continued)*

Model	Quantity	In service	Since	Notes
Mortars, over 160mm				
• 160mm mortar				
Mortars, under 160mm				
• 120mm × 4 SP				
• 120mm M-43				
Total	**approx. 1,950**	**approx. 1,950**		
Artillery/mortar-locating radars				
• Thomson-CSF				
• Cymbeline				
MRLs				
• Ababil (262mm Ababil-50, 400mm Ababil-100)				
• Astros II (127mm SS-30, 180mm SS-40, 300mm SS-60)				
• 132mm BM-13				
• 130mm, 128mm M-63				
• 122mm BM-21/BM-11				
• 122mm Firos-25				
• 107mm				
Total	**100**	**100**		

Logistic and Engineering Equipment

BLG-60, MTU-55 bridging tanks, GSP self-propelled ferries, mine-clearing rollers, minefield crossing system, PMP pontoon bridges, TPP pontoon bridges, Soviet-model tank-towed bridges, AFV transporters (1,500–2,000).

Antitank Weapons

Missiles

AT-3 (Sagger), AT-4 (Spigot), BGM-71A TOW, MILAN, AT-5 (Spandrel)
Mounted on BMP-2, BRDM-2 (carrying AT-3 Sagger) SP, M-3 (carrying HOT) SP, VCR/TH (carrying HOT) SP, M-901 ITV (TOW under armor).

Total **1,500**

Guns

107mm B-11

Surface-to-Surface Missiles and Rockets

Model	Launchers	Missiles	Notes
• FROG-7	29		
• Al-Hussein mobile	up to 5	20–30	Concealed
• Laith 90			
Total	**up to 34**		

AIR FORCE

Order-of-Battle

Model	Quantity	In service	Notes
Combat	331	180–230	119 additional planes flown to Iran during the Gulf War (1991)
Transport	small number	small number	
Helicopters	465	370	

Combat Aircraft

Model	Quantity	In service	Since	Notes
Interceptors—high quality				
• MiG-25 (Foxbat)	15	8–10	1982	Additional 4 in Iran
• MiG-29 (Fulcrum)	15	8–10	1988	Additional 4 in Iran
Subtotal	30	16–20		
Interceptors—others				
• MiG-21 MF/bis/U (Fishbed)/F-7	130	40–80	1974	
• MiG-23 MF/ML	30	approx. 20	1976	
Subtotal	160	60–100		
Total	190	80–120		
Strike and multirole aircraft—high quality				
• Su-24 (Fencer C)	6	0	1989	Not serviceable, additional 24 in Iran
Others				
• MiG-23 B (Flogger)/ MiG-27	30	25		Additional 12 in Iran
• Mirage F-1B/EQ5/ EQ2/EQ4	30	30	1980	Additional 24 in Iran
• Su-20/22 (Fitter C/H)	45	30	1974	Additional 24 in Iran
• Su-25 (Frogfoot)	25	10–20	1985	Additional 7 in Iran

Combat Aircraft *(continued)*

Model	Quantity	In service	Since	Notes
• Su-7b (Fitter A)				Possibly not serviceable
Subtotal	130	95–105		
Total	136	95–105		
Bombers				
• Tu-22 (Blinder)	6	approx. 4	1973	Additional 20 in Iran
• Tu-16 (Badger)/An-6 (B-6D)	1	1	1987	
Subtotal	5	5		
Total	**331**	**180–230**		

Transport Aircraft

Model	Quantity	In service	Since	Notes
• An-12 (Cub)	5	5		
• An-24 (Coke)				
• An-26 (Curl)			1977	
• Il-76 (Candid)			1989	Some tankers
• Mystère-Falcon 20/ Falcon 50				
• Tu-124A/Tu-134 (Crusty)				
Total	**small number**	**small number**		

Note: Additional 15 aircraft in Iran, 6 in Kuwait.

Training and Liaison Aircraft

Model	Quantity	In service	Since	Notes
With ground attack/close air support capability				
• L-29 (Delfin)	approx. 20	approx. 20		
• L-39 (Albatross)	approx. 30	approx. 30	1975	
Subtotal	50	50		
Others				
• Embraer EMB-312 (Tucano)	50–80	50–80	1985	
• MBB-223 Flamingo/ AS 202 Braud/Zlin 326	20–50	20–50	1979	

Training and Liaison Aircraft *(continued)*

Model	Quantity	In service	Since	Notes
• Pilatus PC-7	25	25	1980	
• Pilatus PC-9	30	30	1987	
Subtotal	approx. 165	approx. 165		
Total	**approx. 210**	**approx. 210**		

Helicopters

Model	Quantity	In service	Since	Notes
Attack				
• Alouette III (Armed)	30	30	1971	
• Mi-24/Mi-25 (Hind)	30	30	1982	
• SA-342 Gazelle	50	50	1977	
• MBB BO-105	40	40	1979	Number unconfirmed
Subtotal	150	150		
Heavy transport				
• AS 61	5	3	1982	
• SA-321 Super Frelon	10	10	1976	Also employed in maritime attack role
• Mi-6 (Hook)	15	10–15		
Subtotal	30	25		
Medium transport				
• AS-332 Super Puma	small number	small number		
• BK-117	20–25	10–20	1988	
• Mi-8/Mi-17 (Hip)	100	100		
• SA-330 Puma	20	10	1977	
• Bell 214	40	10–20	1985	
• Mi-2 (Hoplite)	small number	small number		
Subtotal	approx. 200	approx. 160		
Light transport				
• Hughes 500D	30	10	1983	
• Hughes 300C	30	10	1983	
• Hughes 530F	25	16	1985	
Subtotal	85	36		

Helicopters *(continued)*

Model	Quantity	In service	Since	Notes
Total	**approx. 465**	**approx. 370**		

Miscellaneous Aircraft

Model	Quantity	In service	Notes
AEW/AWACS aircraft			
• Adnan 1/Adnan 2 AEW	2	1–2	2 Adnan 2 flown to Iran
UAVs and mini-UAVs			
• Mirach 100			

Advanced Armament

Air-to-air-missiles

AA-2 (Atoll), AA-6 (Acrid), AA-7 (Apex), AA-8 (Aphid), AA-11 (Archer), R-530, R-550 Magique, Super 530D/F.

Air-to-ground missiles

AM-39 Exocet, Armat (Anti-radar), AS-2 (Kipper), AS-4 (Kitchen), AS-5 (Kelt), AS-6 (Kingfish), AS-7 (Kerry), AS-9 (Kyle), AS-10 laser-guided, AS-12, AS-14 (Kedge), AS-15TT anti-ship missile, AS-20, AS-30L laser-guided, AT-2 (Swatter), C-601, HOT, LX anti-ship missile, X-23 anti-radiation missile

Bombs

Belouga CBU, Cardoen CBU, fuel-air explosive (FAE)

Air Force Infrastructure

Aircraft shelters:

For all combat aircraft (some damaged)

Military airfields: 38

Abu-Ajal, al-Assad, al Bakr, Balad, Basra, H-2, H-3, Habbaniyah, Irbil, Jalibah, Khalid, Kirkuk, Kut al-Amarah, Kut al-Amarah new field, Mosul, Mudaysis, Muthanah, al-Nasiriyah, al-Qadisiyah, al-Rashid, al-Rumaylah, Saddam, Salman, al-Shuaiba, al-Tallil, al-Taqaddum, al-Tuz, Wadi al-Khir, 10 additional

AIR DEFENSE FORCES

Surface-to-Air Missiles (SAMs)

Model	Batteries	Launchers	Since	Notes
Heavy missiles				
• SA-2 (Guideline)/ SA-3 (Goa)	60			
Total	60			
Medium missiles				
• SA-6 (Gainful)			1987	
• SA-8 (Gecko)		20		
Light missiles				
• Roland I/II		100		
• SA-9 (Gaskin)				
• SA-13 (Gopher)		30		
Total				
Shoulder-launched missiles				
• SA-7 (Grail)		400		
• SA-14 (Gremlin)				
• SA-16 (Gimlet)				
Total				

Other Air Defense Systems

Model	Quantity	In service
Short-range guns		
• 57mm ZSU 57 × 2 SP		
• 57mm S-60		
• 37mm M-1939		
• 23mm ZSU 23 × 4 SP (Gun Dish)		
• 23mm ZU 23 × 2		
Total		2,000–3,000
Radars		
• P-35/37 Barlock		
• P-15/P-18 Flat Face		
• P-15M Squat Eye		
• P-14 Tall King		
• P-12 Spoon Rest		
• TRS-2215		
• TRS-2230		

NAVY

Combat Vessels

Type	Original Class name	Quantity	Length (m.)/ Displace- ment (t.)	Armament/ special equipment
Corvettes				
• Assad		2	62.3/658	2 × Otomat Mk 2 SSMs 1 × Aspide SAM launcher 1 × AB 212 helicopter 1 × 76mm gun (Weapons systems not serviceable)
MFPBs				
• Ossa I	Type 205	1	38.5/210	SS-N-2A (Styx) SSM 4 × 30mm guns
Mine warfare vessels				
• Nestin		2	27/72	Magnetic, acoustic, and explosive sweeping gear 2 or 3 220mm guns up to 24 mines
Patrol craft (mostly with coast guard)				
• PB-90		3	30.5/90	1 × 40mm gun 2 × 20mm guns, 2 × 128mm MRLs
• Sawari	various types	80	11–25/4–7	some with 12.7mm MGs or MRLs
Subtotal		83		
Total		**88**		

Auxiliary Vessels

Type	Original Class name	Quantity	Length (m.)/ Displace- ment (t.)	Armament/ special equipment
• Stromboli class support ship		1	129/3,556	3,000 ton Cargo 1 × 76mm gun

Advanced Armament

Surface-to-surface missiles
SS-N-2 Styx
Naval mines
Soviet models, Italian Manta mines

Coastal Defense

Hy-2 (Silkworm):	5 batteries

Naval Infrastructure

Naval bases: **4**
Basra, Umm Qasr, Faw, Al-Zubayir
Ship maintenance and repair facilities: **1**
6,000-ton capacity floating dock, held in Egypt

NONGOVERNMENTAL PARAMILITARY FORCES

Personnel

	Active	Reserves	Total
Kurdish Democratic party (KDP)	25,000	30,000	55,000
Kurdish Workers Party (KWP)	20,000		
Patriotic Union of Kurdistan (PUK)	18,000		
Supreme Assembly of the Islamic Revolutin (SAIRI)	2,000		
National Liberation Army (NLA—Mujahedin Khalq)	15,000		
Total	**80,000**	**30,000**	**110,000**

Equipment

Organization	System	Model	Notes
NLA	Helicopters	• Mi–17	
		• MD 530	
	Tanks	• chieftain	
PUK	Tanks	• T-54/55	

6. ISRAEL

GENERAL DATA

Official Name of the State: State of Israel
Head of State: President Ezer Weizman
Prime Minister: Binyamin Netanyahu
Defense Minister: Itzchak Mordechay
Chief of General Staff: Lieutenant General Amnon Shahak
Commander of the Air Force: Major General Eytan Ben-Eliyahu
Commander of Field Forces HQ: Major General Amos Malka
Commander of the Navy: Rear Admiral Alex Tal

Area: 20,770 sq. km., including East Jerusalem and vicinity, annexed in 1967 (not including Golan Heights, 1,176 sq. km., to which Israeli law was applied in 1981)
Population: 5,700,000

Demography

Ethnic Groups		
Jews	4,640,000	81.4%
Arabs, Druze, and others	1,060,000	18.6%
Religious Groups		
Jews	4,640,000	81.4%
Muslims	804,000	14.1%
Christians	160,000	2.8%
Druze and others	97,000	1.7%

Economic Data

		1992	1993	1994	1995	1996
GDP current price, local currency	Nis bn	161.300	184.100	223.100	261.100	301.3
GDP (U.S.$)	$ bn	65.60	64.98	73.92	86.72	94.51
GDP per capita	Nis	12,625	12,198	13,511	15,433	16,580
Real GDP growth	%	6.6	3.4	6.5	7.1	4.3
Balance of payments						
• Exports fob	$ bn	12.429	14.804	16.562	19.046	20.300
• Imports fob	$ bn	18.564	20.38	22.538	29.768	27.940

Economic Data *(continued)*

		1992	1993	1994	1995	1996
• Account balance (Includes services and income)	$ bn	0.1	–1.4	–2.5	–4.1	–4.5
• External debt	$ bn	22.5	24.3	27.2	28.9	30.8
Government income and expenditure						
• Revenues, local currency	Nis bn	98.641	105.309	130.871	145.227	177.029
• Expenditures, local currency	Nis bn	98.641	105.309	130.871	145.227	177.029
• Defense expenditures	Nis bn	18.542	19.164	21.944	25.297	27.598
• Defense expenditure/ GDP	%	11.50	10.41	9.84	9.69	9.15
• Defense expenditure/ CGE	%	18.79	18.19	16.76	17.41	15.58
• Population	m	5.1959	5.3276	5.4715	5.619	5.700
• Official exchange rate	Nis: $1	2.459	2.833	3.018	3.011	3.188

Arms Procurement and Security Assistance Received

Country	Type	Details
Belgium	• *Arms transfers*	LMGs (1993)
France	• *Arms transfers*	Spare parts, Socata training aircraft
	• *Military training*	Trainees abroad
Germany	• *Arms transfers*	ABC detection vehicles; submarines on order
	• *Financial*	A commitment for approx. $140 million per year over five years, to cover the cost of a MIM-104 battery and current construction of 2 submarines in Germany, and part of the cost of a third submarine
	• *Military training*	Trainees abroad
Netherlands	• *Cooperation in arms production, assembly, R&D*	Cooperation in building patrol boats
South Africa	• *Arms transfers*	Patrol boats (1997)
Turkey	• *Facilities*	use of airfields and airspace for training
U.S.A.	• *Arms transfers*	SP artillery, naval SSMs, SAMs, F-15I combat aircraft, MLRS, helicopters, tank transporters, missile corvettes ATGMs, AAMs

Arms Procurement and Security Assistance Received *(continued)*

Country	Type	Details
	• *Financial aid*	$1.8 billion grant (1996); a gift of surplus weapons from European drawdown arsenal worth approximately $700 million spread over several years
	• *Cooperation in arms production, assembly, R&D*	Finance and assistance for Hetz TMD and Nautilus laser defense
	• *Military training*	Trainees abroad

Arms Sales and Security Assistance Extended

Country	Type	Details
Argentina*	• *Arms transfers*	Upgrading Boeing 707 transport a/c, HUD for Pampas trainers (1997)
Australia	• *Arms transfers*	Radars for upgraded P-3C, jointly with a U.S. company; ESM for Australian C-130 aircraft, Popeye AGMs
Brazil*	• *Arms transfers*	HUD and avionics for trainer a/c (1997)
Britain	• *Arms transfers*	Artillery and infantry ammunition (1996), CATS and ACE simulators, ESM for Nimrod 2000
Cambodia	• *Arms transfers*	Upgrading of MiG-21 a/c (1997); avionics for L-39 trainer a/c
Chile*	• *Arms transfers*	Patrol boats, AAMs, AAGs, artillery, Barak shipborne antimissile missile, mini-UAVs, components for upgrading of F-5 combat a/c, AEW a/c, tanker a/c
Colombia*	• *Arms transfers*	Radio transceivers
	• *Military training*	Advisers/instructors/technicians, foreign trainees
	• *Cooperation in arms production, assembly, R&D*	Assistance in upgrading combat aircraft in Colombia, co-production of Galil assault rifle
Cyprus	• *Arms transfers*	Torpedo boats
Czech Republic	• *Arms transfers*	Avionics for L-39 trainer aircraft, ground forces radar, jointly produced

**Note:* According to foreign publications, as indicated by Israeli publications.

Arms Sales and Security Assistance Extended *(continued)*

Country	Type	Details
	• *Cooperation in arms production, assembly, R&D*	Cooperation in upgrading T-72 tanks
Ecuador*	• *Arms transfers*	Kfir combat aircraft (1997), AAMs, naval SSMs
	• *Military training*	Advisers/instructors/technicians
Eritrea*	• *Arms transfers*	Fast patrol boats (1997)
Estonia	• *Arms transfers*	Small arms, AAGs
Ethiopia	• *Arms transfers*	Upgrading MiG-21 combat a/c
Finland	• *Arms transfers*	AD command and control system (1996)
France	• *Arms transfers*	protective vests, Hunter UAVs, hand-held SAR systems (1997)
	• *Cooperation in arms production, assembly, R&D*	Cooperation with Alcatel in military communications (1997).
Germany	• *Arms transfers*	Electronic equipment, ECMs, a/c warning systems, protective vests, Litening designators for combat a/c, EHUD combat air debriefing system (1996)
	• *Cooperation in arms production, assembly, R&D*	Joint production in Germany of mini-UAVs, joint development of an antiradiation attack drone, joint production of Panzerfaust 3LR light ATRL, joint development of a satellite, joint venture to upgrade Greek F-4s
Greece	• *Arms transfers*	Ground radar (1996)
India*	• *Arms transfers*	Upgrading of fighter aircraft, upgrading of artillery, UAVs, ammunition; on order: early warning technology, Harpy anti-radiation drone,* upgrading of tanks, executive jets, EL/M-2032 radar for Jaguar a/c, Litening pods, Super-Dvora patrol boats.
Indonesia	• *Arms transfers*	Mini-UAVs (1996)
Italy	• *Arms transfers*	Enhanced add-on armor kit for some Italian M-113 family APCs, Opher guiding kit for bombs, airborne SAR system

**Note:* According to foreign publications, as cited by Israeli publications.

Arms Sales and Security Assistance Extended *(continued)*

Country	Type	Details
Lebanese Militia (SLA)	• *Arms transfers*	Small arms, tanks, artillery pieces
	• *Military training*	Advisers/instructors/technicians, foreign trainees
	• *Financial aid*	$23 million for infrastructure (1997), and approx. $70 million for salaries of SLA personnel
Lithuania	• *Arms transfers*	Submachine guns
Nepal	• *Arms transfers*	Galil assault rifles
Netherlands	• *Arms transfers*	Aircraft warning systms, Ranger mini-UAVs, under negotiation, artillery C&C systems, aircraft debriefing system
	• *Cooperation in arms production, assembly, R&D*	
Nicaragua	• *Arms transfers*	Dabur patrol boats (1997)
Poland	• *Cooperation in arms production, assembly, R&D*	Night vision for tanks, tank upgrading, upgrading Huzar attack helicopters and supply of AT missiles (1997—currently suspended)
Portugal	• *Arms transfers*	EHUD air combat debriefing systems
PRC*	• *Arms transfers*	Python-3 AAMs; radio sets; night vision systems; additional items; a/c radars; thermal-imaging tank sights, IL-76 AEW aircraft with Russia
	• *Military training*	Advisers/instructors/technicians
	• *Cooperation in arms production, assembly, R&D**	Contribution to Chinese combat a/c avionics, joint development of an AGM/cruise missile; thermal-imaging tank sights
Romania	• *Arms transfers*	OWS-25 weapons system for APCs

**Note:* According to foreign publications, as cited by Israeli publications.

Arms Sales and Security Assistance Extended *(continued)*

Country	Type	Details
	• *Cooperation in arms production, assembly, R&D*	Joint production of night vision equipment for Romanian IAR-330 Puma helicopters, upgrading Dracula attack helicopters, cooperation on ATGM production in Romania, cooperation in upgrading 100 MiG-21s in Romania, cooperation in upgrading IAR-99/109 trainer a/c (under negotiation)
Russia	• *Cooperation in arms production, assembly, R&D*	IL-76 AEW for China
Singapore*	• *Arms transfers*	Electronic warfare systems, Searcher UAVs, aerial refueling aircraft, electronic components for F-5 combat a/c, Barak shipborne antimissile missile, AAMs, naval tactical training center, air combat debriefing system
	• *Military training*	Advisers/instructors/technicians
	• *Cooperation in arms production, assembly, R&D*	Cooperation in upgrading Turkish F-5 combat a/c
Slovakia	• *Cooperation in arms production, assembly, R&D*	Upgrading T-72 tanks, developing Strop light air defense system
Slovenia	• *Arms transfers*	155mm canons, 120mm mortars
South Africa	• *Arms transfers*	Avionics for upgrading Cheetah combat a/c; upgrading Boeing 707 to SIGINT configuration
South Korea*	• *Arms transfers*	Popeye-2 ASM, Harpy antiradar drones (1997), night vision systems
	• *Cooperation in arms production, assembly, R&D*	A joint venture civilian aircraft; upgrading Korean F-4 and F-5 under negotiation
Spain*	• *Arms transfers*	Griffin guided bombs; upgrading tanks and aircraft; upgrading Boeing 707 to SIGINT configuration, UAVs, military communications (1995)

**Note:* According to foreign publications, as cited by Israeli publications.

Arms Sales and Security Assistance Extended *(continued)*

Country	Type	Details
Sri Lanka	• *Arms transfers*	Kfir aircraft, Superhawk UAVs, mine detection radar
Sweden	• *Arms transfers*	120mm ammunition for tanks, ground-penetrating radar
	• *Cooperation in arms production, assembly, R&D*	Joint development of NBC protection for civilians
Switzerland	• *Arms transfers*	Communication intelligence systems
	• *Cooperation in arms production, assembly, R&D**	Ranger UAVs and ADS-95 systems (1998–2000), C^3I simulators
Taiwan*	• *Arms transfers*	Naval SSMs
Thailand	• *Arms transfers*	Searcher mini-UAVs, Python 3 AAMs, naval SSMs, upgrading avionics in Czech L-39 trainer aircraft, VHF tactical radios
Turkey	• *Arms transfers*	Upgrading F-4 and F-5 a/c, AGMs EHUD debriefing systm for air combat training, mine detection and ground-penetrating radar
	• *Cooperation in arms production, assembly, R&D*	Joint production of Popeye AGMs, production of Delila Anti Radar Air launched drone
Ukraine	• *Cooperation in arms production, assembly, R&D*	Joint upgrading of AN-72P maritime surveillance aircraft, joint upgrading of MiG-21 a/c for Ethiopia
U.S.A.	• *Arms transfers*	Parts, Pioneer and Hunter UAVs (being phased out), tactical air-launched decoys, AGMs jointly produced, joint venture enhanced appliqué armor kits for APCs (1997), 120mm mortars, tactical communication, crashworthy troop seats for helicopters, Astra SPX a/c, central computer for Bradley AFVs

**Note:* According to foreign publicaitons, as cited by Israeli publications.

Arms Sales and Security Assistance Extended *(continued)*

Country	Type	Details
	• *Cooperation in arms production, assembly, R&D*	Aircraft components, electronics, naval vessels, terminal guidance bombs, tactical air-launched decoys, UAVs, upgrading UH-1 helicopters, joint production of Have Nap AGMs, joint research on Arrow ATBM, APC appliqué armor, joint research on Nautilus laser weapon, remote sensing satellites, helmet-mounted cueing system for U.S. Air Force
Venezuela	• *Arms transfers*	MRLs, aerial tanker a/c
Zambia	• *Military training*	Advisers/instructors/technicians, foreign trainees
	• *Arms transfers*	Upgrading MiG-21 a/c (1997)

* *Note:* According to foreign publications, as cited by Israeli publications.

Foreign Military Cooperation

	Details
• Forces deployed in Lebanon	Units in the southern Lebanese security zone
• Joint maneuvers	With the U.S.A. joint naval exercise with Turkey, joint naval SAR exercise with Jordan

Defense Production

	M	P	A
Ground Forces equipment			
• Artillery pieces	√		
• Small arms	√		
• ATGMs	√		
• ATRLs	√		
• Artillery, mortar, and small arms ammunition	√		
• Mines	√		
• Mine-clearing rollers	√		
• Tanks	√		
• Tank guns	√		
• Tread-width mine plows for tanks (TWMP)	√		
• SP AAGs (Soviet gun, U.S.A. carrier)			√
• Tank-towed bridges (TAB)	√		
• Upgrading of tanks	√		

Defense Production *(continued)*

	M	P	A
Aircraft and air ammunition (some joint venturs with U.S. companies)			
• AAMs	√		
• AGMs	√		
• CBUs	√		
• TV and laser terminal guidance bombs	√		
• Mini-UAVs	√		
• Operational flight trainer systems	√		
• Radars	√		
• Upgrading of combat aircraft	√		
• Arrow ATBM, under development	√		
• Cruise missiles	√		
• Refueling system for aircraft	√		
• Helicopter parts		√	
• Combat aircraft parts		√	
Naval craft and ammunition			
• LCTs	√		
• MFPBs	√	√	
• PBs	√		
• SSMs	√		
• Torpedo components		√	
Electronics			
• Radars	√		
• Direction finders	√		
• Pilot rescue radio sets	√		
• ELINT equipment	√		
• EW jammers	√		
• Radio transceivers	√		
• Audio/video microwave transceivers	√		
• Radio voice scramblers and encryption units	√		
• Air-launched decoys	√		
• AEW a/c conversion	√		
• Aircraft warning systems	√		
Optronics			
• Night vision devices	√		
• Laser rangefinders and target designators	√		
Space			
• Experimental military satellites including Ofeq-3 Shavit launching capability	√		
• Amos communications satellite launched in May 1996	√		

Note: M = Manufacture (indigenously developed)
P = Production under license
A = Assembly

NBC Technology

Nuclear capabilities
- Two nuclear research reactors

CW capabilities
- Personal protective equipment
- Unit decontamination equipment
- Fuchs (Fox) ABC detection vehicles (8 vehicles)
- SPW-40 P2Ch ABC detection vehicles (50 vehicles)

ARMED FORCES

Major Changes: There has been no major change in the order-of-battle of the IDF. The air force received its first F-15I by the end of 1997, and the navy's first Dolphin class submarine was launched. (It would enter service only in 1998.)

Order-of-Battle

Year	1993	1994	1995	1996	1997
General data					
• Personnel (regular)	176,000	177,500	177,500	187,000	187,000
• Divisions	16	16	16	16	16
• Total number of brigades	13	13	13	13	13
Ground Forces					
• Tanks	3,850	3,850	3,845	3,870	3,900
• APCs/ARVs	8,100	8,100	8,000	8,010	8,010
• Artillery (incl. MRLs)	1,300	1,300	1,300	1,292	1,392 (1,912)
• SSM launchers	12	12	12	12	12
Air Force					
• Combat aircraft	694	742	677	640	613 (780)
• Transport aircraft	97	93	83	83	83 (93)
• Helicopters	224	253	269	285	278 (288)
Air Defense Forces					
• Heavy SAM batteries	3+	4+	4+	4+	21
• Light SAM launchers	50	50	50	50	50
Navy					
• Submarines	3	3	3	3	4
• Combat vessels	67	59	58	58	56

Note: Beginning with data for 1997, we refer to quantities in active service. The number in parentheses refers to the total.

Personnel

	Regular	Reserves	Total
Ground Forces	141,000	380,000	521,000
Air Force	36,500	54,000	90,500
Navy	9,500	10,000	19,500
Total	**187,000**	**444,000**	**631,000**
Paramilitary			
• Border police	6,000		6,000

GROUND FORCES

Formations (including reserves)

	Corps/HQ	Divisions	Independent brigades/groups	Brigades in divisions
All arms	3*			
Armored		12		2–3 Armored each 1 Mechanized each 1 Artillery each
Mechanized/ infantry/ territorial		4	8	
Airborne			5	
Total		**16**	**13**	

Note: Antiguerrilla HQ: 3 divisional HQ for control of units engaged in antiguerrilla activities in Samaria and Gaza (after May 1994, Gaza HQ stationed in Jewish settlements) and on the Lebanese border. In emergency, the HQ will be reinforced by armor, infantry, engineering, and antitank forces.

**Note:* According to foreign publications, as cited by Israeli publications.

Tanks

Model	Quantity	In service	Since	Notes
High quality				
• Merkava Mk 1/Mk 2/Mk 3	1,140	1,140	1979/1983/ 1989	
• M-60A3-/ upgraded M-60/ Magach 7	980	980	1980	
Subtotal	2,120	2,120		

Tanks *(continued)*

Model	Quantity	In service	Since	Notes
Others				
• Centurion/ugraded Centurion	1,025	1,025		
• M-60/M-60 A1	420	420		
• M-48 A5	285	285		
• T-62	50	50		
Subtotal	1,780	1,780		
Total	**3,900**	**3,900**		
On order				
• Merkava Mk 3				

APCs/ARVs (including command vehicles)

Model	Quantity	In service	Since	Notes
High quality				
• Achzarit, Israeli APC	+	+	1994	
• M-113 (various marks)	+	+		
• Nagmashot*	100	100	1989	
• Nagmachon	+	+		
• Nakpadon	15	15		
• RBY	+	+		
Subtotal	5,325	5,325		
Others				
• M-2 and M-3 half-track	2,685	2,685		Some phased out
Subtotal	2,685	2,685		
Total	**8,010**	**8,010**		

**Note:* According to foreign publications, as citd by Israeli publications.

Artillery

Model	Quantity	In service	Since	Notes
Self-propelled guns and howitzers				
• 203mm M-110 SP	+	+		
• 175mm M-107 SP	+	+		
• 155mm M-109 A1 and A2 SP				
• 155mm M-109 Doher	600	600		

Artillery *(continued)*

Model	Quantity	In service	Since	Notes
• 155mm M-50	+	+		
• 155mm L-33 SP	+	+		
Subtotal	900	900		
Towed guns and howitzers				
• 155mm M-71	+	+		
• 130mm M-46 gun	+	+		
• 122mm D-30	+	+		
Mortars, over 160mm				
• 160mm SP	+	+		
Mortars, under 160mm				
• 120mm	250	250		
Total	1,900	1,300		
Artillery/mortar-locating radars				
• AN/TPQ-37	+	+		
• AN/PPS-15	+	+		
• Elta Shilem artillery-ranging radar	+	+		
MRLs				
• 290mm MAR 290	+	+		
• 240mm	+	+		
• 140mm	+	+		
• 122mm BM-21	+	+		
• Keres antiradar rocket	+	+		
• Kachlilit antiradar rocket	+	+		
• 227mm MLRS	12	12		
On order				
• 227mm MLRS launchers	36			Delivery 1998

Logistic and Engineering Equipment

Gilois motorized bridges, M-123 Viper minefield crossing system, M-60 AVLB, mine-clearing rollers, mine layers, Pomins II portable mine neutralization system,* Puma vehicle, TAB (Towed assault bridge, towed by tanks), TLB (trailer-launched bridge), TWMP (treated with mine ploughs), M-1000 heavy equipment transporters

* *Note:* According to foreign publications, as cited by Israeli publications.

Antitank Weapons

Missiles
- AT-3 (Sagger), BGM-71A TOW and BGM-71C Improved TOW, M-47 Dragon (1980), Mapats SP, Nimrod, Israeli BGM-71C Improved TOW SP, Spike AT missile/Gil*

On order
- BGM-71E (TOW 2A)

**Note:* According to foreign publications, as cited by Israeli publications.

Surface-to-Surface Missiles and Rockets

Model	Launchers	Missiles	Since	Notes
• MGM-52C (Lance)	12		1974	
• Jericho Mk 1/2/3 SSM*	+			
Total	**12**			

*According to foreign publications, as cited by Israeli publications.

AIR FORCE

Order-of-Battle

Model	Quantity	In service	Notes
• Combat	780	613	Including aircraft in operational storage
• Transport	93	83	
• Helicopters	288	278	

Combat Aircraft

Model	Quantity	In service	Since	Notes
Interceptors—high quality				
• F-15 Eagle	73	73	1976	
Subtotal	73	73		
Strike and multirole aircraft—high quality				
• F-16A/B/C/D	245	245	1980/ 1986	Most F-16A/C may be employed as interceptors

Combat Aircraft *(continued)*

Model	Quantity	In service	Since	Notes
Others				
• F-4E/RF-4E Phantom and Phantom 2000	140	140	1969	
• A-4 Skyhawk	177	120	1967	57 in storage, for sale/emergency
• Kfir C-2/TC-2/C-7/TC-7	145	35	1976	110 in storage, for sale/emergency
Subtotal	462	295		
Total	707	540		
Total	**780**	**613**		
On order				
• F-15I	25			Delivery 1998 and later

Transport Aircraft (including tankers)

Model	Quantity	In service	Since	Notes
• Arava	10	10	1984	
• Beechcraft Queen Air/King	12	12	1990	
• Boeing 707	10	10	1973	
• Boeing 707 tanker (refueling)	3	3		
• C-130H Hercules	22	22	1970	
• DC-3 Dakota (C-47)	18	8	1948	10 in storage for sale
• Dornier Do-28	15	15	1971	
• KC-130 tanker (refueling)	3	3	1976	
Total	**93**	**83**		

Training and Liaison Aircraft

Model	Quantity	In service	Since	Notes
With ground attack/close air support capability				
• CM-170 Fouga Magister/Tzukit	80	80	1960	Some in storage
Subtotal	80	80		

Training and Liaison Aircraft *(continued)*

Model	Quantity	In service	Since	Notes
Others				
• Socata Trinidad TB-21	22	22	1995	
• Cessna U-206 (Stationair-6)	21	0		In storage, for sale
• Piper Cub	35	35		
Subtotal	78	57		
Total	**158**	**137**		

Helicopters

Model	Quantity	In service	Since	Notes
Attack				
• AH-64A Apache	42	42	1990	
• AH-1G/1S Cobra	65	65	1981	
• 500MD Defender	33	33	1979	
Subtotal	140	140		
Heavy transport				
• CH-53	39	39	1970	Including CH-53-2000
Medium transport				
• Bell 212	55	45		10 in storage for sale
• UH-60A Black Hawk	10	10	1994	
Subtotal	65	55		
Light transport				
• AB-206 JetRanger/ Bell 206L	39	39		
Naval attack/search and rescue				
• AS 536 Panther	5	5	1995	
Total	**288**	**278**		
On order				
• UH-60L Black Hawk	15			Delivery in 1998

Miscellaneous Aircraft

Model	Quantity	In service	Since	Notes
AEW/AWACS aircraft				
• E-2C Hawkeye AEW	4	4	1978	

Miscellaneous Aircraft *(continued)*

Model	Quantity	In service	Since	Notes
• Boeing 707 AEW*				Several
ELINT and EW				
• Boeing 707 ELINT*				
• Boeing 707 EW*				
Maritime surveillance aircraft				
• Seascan (Westwind 1124N)	3	3		
UAVs and mini-UAVs				
• Hermes 450S, Hermes 450 High Altitude, Mastif mini-UAV, Pioneer mini-UAV, Scout mini-UAV, Searcher mini-UAV, MQM-74C Chuckar II UAV, Teledyne Ryan 1241 UAV				
Target drones				
• Beech AQM-37A; Beech BQM-107B				
On order				
• Hunter UAV; Heron UAV				

* *Note:* According to foreign publications, as cited by Israeli publications.

Advanced Armament

Air-to-air-missiles

- AIM-9 Sidewinder, AIM-9L, AIM-7 Sparrow, Python 3, Phyton 4, Shafrir

Air-to-ground missiles

- AGM-78D Standard ARM, AGM-65 Maverick, AGM-62A Walleye, AGM-45 A/B Shrike, Hellfire, Delilah antiradar air-launched drone/cruise missile, Popeye (equivalent to AGM-142)*

Bombs

- CBU (including Tal-1, ATA-1000, ATA-500), runway-penetration bombs, Pyramid TV terminal-guidance bombs, Griffin laser guided bomb, Harpy antiradar drone,* NTD AT missile,* Guillotine laser terminal-guidance bombs, Opher terminal-guidance bombs

On order

- AIM-9M AAM, Hellfire 2, Star 1AGM/cruise missile (under development)

EW and CEW

- Chaff and flare dispensers for combat aircraft, Samson AN/ADM-141 TALD, EL/L-8202 ECM pod, EL/L-8230 ECM system, EL/L-8231 ECM system, EL/L-8240 ECM system, EL/M-2160 warning system, LWS-20 system, SRS-25 airborne receiver, SPS-20 self-protection system, SPS-65 self-protection system, SPS-200 airborne self-protection system, SPS-1000 EW system, SPS-2000 self-protection system, Sky-Jam 200 jammer

On order

- AN/ALQ 131 electronic countermeasure systems (20)

* *Note:* According to foreign publications, as cited by Israeli publications

Air Force Infrastructure

Aircraft shelters
In all operational airfields, for combat aircraft
Military airfields: 11
Haifa, Hatzerim, Hatzor, Lod, Nevatim, Palmachim, Ramat David, Ramon, Tel Aviv, Tel Nof, Uvda
Aircraft maintenance and repair capability
Maintenance on all models in service, partly in airfields, partly at Israel Aircraft Industries facilities

AIR DEFENSE FORCES

Surface-to-Air Missiles

Model	Batteries	Launchers	Since	Notes
Heavy missiles				
• MIM-23B Improved HAWK	17		1965	
• MIM-104 Patriot	4		1991	
Total	21			
Light missiles				
• MIM-72A Chaparral		approx. 50		
• Mahbet				
Shoulder-launched missiles				
• FIM-92C Stinger		500 missiles		
• MIM-43A Redeye				
On order				
• Hetz ATBMs	3			First battery to be deployed 1999

Other Air Defense Systems

Model	Quantity	In service	Since	Notes
Short-range guns				
• 40mm Bofors L-70				
• 23mm ZU 23×2				
• 20mm M-163 A1 Vulcan SP	20	20		
• 20mm TCM-20 Hispano Suiza SP				

Other Air Defense Systems *(continued)*

Model	Quantity	In service	Since	Notes
• 20mm Hispano Suiza				
Total	900	900		
Radars				
• Elta-Ramit, FPS-100, AN/TPS-43, Oren Yarok, Alufa-3				
Aerostats with airborne radars				
• ‘‘Status’’				
On order				
• ADAMS system; 20mm M-163 from U.S. drawdown				

NAVY

Combat Vessels

Type	Original Class name	Quantity	Length (m.)/ Displace-ment (t.)	Armament/ special equipment
Submarines				
• GAL	IKL/Vickers Type 540	3	45/600	sub-Harpoon SSMs 8 × 533mm torpedoes (to be sold)
• Dolphin (Thyssen)		1	57.3/1,900	sub-Harpoon SSMs 6 × 533mm torpedoes
Total		4		
Missile corvettes				
• Eilat class	Sa’ar 5	3	86.4/1,075	1 × SA-536 helicopter 8 × Harpoon SSMs 8 × Gabriel II SSMs 64 × Barak-1 SAM launchers 1 × 76mm gun 2 × 25mm Sea Vulcans 6 × 324mm torpedoes

Combat Vessels *(continued)*

Type	Original Class name	Quantity	Length (m.)/ Displace- ment (t.)	Armament/ special equipment
MFPBs				
• Aliya class	Sa'ar 4.5	2	61.7/498	1 × SA 536 helicop- ter 8 × Harpoon SSMs 4 × Gabriel II SSMs 2 × 20mm guns 1× Vulcan Phalanx 2 × 12.7mm MGs
• Hetz class	Sa'ar 4.5	7	61.7/488	8 × Harpoon SSMs 6 × Gabriel II SSMs 32 × Barak I SAMs 1 × 76mm 1 × Vulcan Phalanx 2 × 12.7 MGs
• Reshef class	Sa'ar 4	7	58/415	4 × Harpoon SSMs 4–6 × Gabriell II SSMs 1–2 × 76mm guns 1 × Vulcan Phalanx 2 × 20mm guns 2 × 12.7 mm MGs some are used for ASW with 2×3×324 torpe- does with sonar
• Mivtach class	Sa'ar 2	2	45/250	5 × Gabriel II SSM 2×3×324mm torpe- does Sonar used for ASW
Subtotal		18		
Patrol craft				
• Super Dvora		14	21.6/54	2 × 20mm guns or 2 × 25mm guns 2 × 12.7mm MGs 1 × 84mm MRL depth charges

Combat Vessels *(continued)*

Type	Original Class name	Quantity	Length (m.)/ Displace-ment (t.)	Armament/ special equipment
• Dabur		18	19.8/39	2 × 20mm guns 2 × 12.7mm MGs 2 × 324mm torep-does 1 × 84mm MRL depth charges
• Nahshol		3		2 × 12.7mm MGs
Subtotal		35		
Total		56		
On order				
• Dolphin subma-rines		2		Delivery 1997–1999
• upgrading of Sa'ar 4 class to improved Sa'ar 4.5/Nirit level				
• Super Dvora		2		

Landing Craft

Type	Original Class name	Quantity	Length (m.)/ Displace-ment (t.)	Armament/ special equipment
• Ashdod class LCT		3	62.7/400	In reserve
• LCM type		3		
• Bat Sheva sup-port ship		1	95.1/1,150	4 × 20mm gun 4 × 12.7 MG
Total		**7**		

Auxiliary Vessels

Type	Original Class name	Quantity	Length (m.)/ Displace-ment (t.)	Armament/ special equipment
• Ro-Ro		1		

Special Maritime Forces

Midget submarines; Zaharon fast boats

Naval Infrastructure

Naval bases: 3

- Ashdod, Eilat, Haifa

Ship maintenance and repair facilities

- Repair and maintenance of all naval vessels at Haifa, partly in conjunction with Israel Dockyards

7. JORDAN

GENERAL DATA

Official Name of the State: The Hashemite Kingdom of Jordon
Head of State: King Hussein Ibn Talal al-Hashimi
Prime Minister: Abd al-Salam al-Majali (also Minister of Defense)
Chief of the Joint Staff of the Armed Forces: General Abd al-Hafiz Mar'i al-Kaabana
Chief of Staff of Ground Forces: Major General Tahsin Shurdom
Commander of the Air Force: Major General Muhammad Khair al-Ababna
Commander of the Navy/Coast Guard: Commodore Ali Mahmoud al-Khasawna

Area: 90,700 sq. km
Population: 4,400,000

Demography

Ethnic Groups		
Arabs	4,312,000	98.0%
Circassians and Armenians	88,000	2.0%
Religious Groups		
Sunni Muslims	4,048,000	92.0%
Greek Orthodox and other Christians	352,000	8.0%

Economic Data

		1992	1993	1994	1995	1996
GDP current price, local currency	JD bn	3.493	3.811	4.191	4.560	5.147
GDP (U.S. $)	$ bn	5.137	5.499	5.996	6.524	7.259
GDP per capita	$	1,352	1,341	1,394	1,553	1,650
Real GDP growth	%	11.3	5.8	5.7	6.4	5.2
Balance of payments						
• Exports fob	$ bn	1.219	1.246	1.425	1.780	1.817
• Imports fob	$ bn	2.999	3.145	3.064	3.700	3.818

Economic Data *(continued)*

		1992	1993	1994	1995	1996
• Account balance (Includes services and income)	$ bn	–0.765	–0.628	–0.398	–0.270	–0.222
• External debt	$ bn	7.18	6.905	7.051	7.1	6.92
Government income and expenditure						
• Revenues, local currency	JD bn	1.359	1.406	1.597	1.673	1.764
• Expenditures, local currency	JD bn	1.178	1.337	1.437	1.613	1.518
• Defense expenditures	JD bn	0.221	0.281	0.284	0.308	0.283
• Defense expenditure/ GDP	%	6.3	7.3	6.8	6.7	5.5
• Defense expenditure/ CGE	%	18.8	21	19.8	19	18.6
• Population	m	3.8	4.1	4.3	4.2	4.4
• Official exchange rate	JD: $1	0.68	0.693	0.699	0.699	0.709

Sources: EIU quarterly report, EIU country profile, IMF statistical yearbook, Sipri Yearbook.

Arms Procurement and Security Assistance Received

Country	Type	Details
Iraq	• Financial aid	Oil purchase subsidies (1997)
Germany	• Arms transfers	Ex-GDR PBs for coast guard/police
U.S.A.	• Financial aid	$30 Million (1995); $30 million (1996); $67 million (1997); $250 million (1998)
	• Military training	
	• Advisers	
	• Arms transfers	Combat aircraft (1997), MBTs (1996), helicopters (1996)

Arms Sales and Security Assistance Extended

Country	Type	Details
Palestinians	• Facilities	Camp for Badr unit; PLO and other organizations (offices)
Philippines	• Arms transfers	F-5 aircraft (1997)
Singapore	• Arms transfers	F-5 aircraft (1994)
U.S.A.	• Facilities	Deployment of combat aircraft

Foreign Military Cooperation

	Details
Forces deployed abroad	Small contingency force in Bosnia and Croatia; observers in Angola, Georgia, and Tajikistan; 20 troops in Liberia; a military police company in Cambodia
Joint maneuvers	U.S.A., Britain, France, Oman, Qatar

Defense Production

	M	P	A
Army equipment			
• A plant to produce high explosives under construction (with assistance from India)	√		
• Conversion of M–47 tanks to ARVs	√		
• Badia's APCs and Sangyong vehicles	√		
Electronics			
• Assembly and production of computers (joint venture with companies from U.S.A., Britain, and Singapore)		√	√
• Upgrading of avionics (joint venture)	√		
Optronics			
• Night vision devices		√	

Note: M—manufacture (indigenously developed)
P—production under license
A—assembly

NBC Technology

CW capabilities

• Personal protective and decontamination equipment

ARMED FORCES

Major changes: Since 1996 Jordan received a package of military equipment from the United States. It includes 50 M-60 A3 MBTs, 18 transport helicopters, 5 transport aircraft, and 16 F-16 combat aircraft, the first of which arrived in 1997.

Order-of-Battle

Year	1993	1994	1995	1996	1997
General data					
• Personnel (regular)	90,000–100,000	90,000–100,000	94,000	94,000	94,200
• Divisions	4	4	4	4	4
• Total number of brigades	15	15	15	15	14
Ground Forces					
• Tanks	765	765	765	815	834 (1,226)
• APCs/ARVs	1,480	1,480	1,480	1,480	1,475 (1,575)
• Artillery	400	450	450	450	770 (795)
Air Force					
• Combat aircraft	103	103	85	85	91
• Transport aircraft	18	18	12	12	11 (13)
• Helicopters	54	53	70	60	68
Air Defense Forces					
• Heavy SAM batteries	14	14	14	14	14
• Medium SAM batteries	50	50	50	50	50
• Light SAM launchers	+	+	+	+	50
Navy					
• Combat vessels	10	12	12	12	10

Note: Beginning with data for 1997, we refer to quantities in active service. The number in parentheses refers to the total.

Personnel

	Regular	Reserves	Total
Ground Forces	85,000	60,000	145,000
Air Force	8,500		8,500
Navy	700		700
Total	**94,200**	**60,000**	**154,200**
Paramilitary			
• General security forces (including desert patrol)	25,000		
• Popular Army*		200,000–250,000	

*The Popular Army is not regarded as a fighting force.

GROUND FORCES

Formations

	Divisions	Independent brigade/group	Brigades in division
Armored	2		2 arm., 1 art., 1 AD each
Mechanized	2		1 inf., 2 mech., 1 art., 1 AD each
Infantry/ Royal Guard		1	
Special forces		1	
Artillery		5	
Total	**4**	**7**	

Tanks

Model	Quantity	In service	Since	Notes
High quality				
• Chieftain (Khalid)	365	275	1984	
• M-60 A3	150	150	1980	
Subtotal	515	425		
Others				
• Centurion (Tariq)	290	290	1955	Improved
• M-60 A1	100	100	1977	
• Scorpion	19	19		With desert patrol
• Chieftain	90			From Iran, captured by Iraq, in storage, not serviceable
• M-48 A1	212			In storage, not operational
Subtotal	711	409		
Total	**1,226**	**834**		

APCs/ARVs

Model	Quantity	In service	Since	Notes
High quality				
• BMP-2	35	35		
• M-113 A1/A2	1,240	1,240		
• Engesa EE-11	100	100	1986	With general security forces
Subtotal	1,375	1,375		

APCs/ARVs *(continued)*

Model	Quantity	In service	Since	Notes
Others				
• Ferret	140	approx. 100	1955	Some in storage
• Saracen/Saladin	60	0	1963	Obsolete, in storage
Subtotal	200	approx. 100		
Total	**1,575**	**1,475**		

Artillery

Model	Quantity	In service	Since	Notes
Self-propelled guns and howitzers				
• 203mm M-110 A2	110	110	1980	
• 155mm M-109 A2	220	220	1980	
Towed guns and howitzers				
• 203mm (8") M-115	25			Not in service
• 155mm M-59 (Long Tom)	10	10		
• 155mm M-114	30	30		
• 105mm M-102 A1	50	50		
Mortars, under 160mm				
• 120mm	300	300		
• 107mm	50	50		
Total	795	770		
Artillery/mortar-locating radars				
• AN/TPQ 36/37			1984	
PGMs				
• 155mm Copperhead projectiles (CLGP)	100	100		

Logistic and Engineering Equipment

Mk 2 (D) flail, bridges, mine-clearing plows and bulldozers, UDK-1, AFV transporters (200)

Antitank Weapons

Model	Quantity	In service	Since	Notes
Missiles				
• BGM-71A TOW/ BGM-71C Improved TOW	260	260		
• M-47 Dragon	310	310		
• M-901 ITV SP (TOW under armor)	70	70		
Total	**640**	**640**		
Guns				
• 106mm M40	330	330		

AIR FORCE

Order-of-Battle

Model	Quantity	In service	Notes
• Combat	91	91	
• Transport	13	11	
• Helicopters	68	68	

Combat Aircraft

Model	Quantity	In service	Since	Notes
Strike and multirole aircraft—medium and low quality				
• F-16 (A/B)	6	6	1997	
• Mirage F-1 C/E	30	30	1981	
• F-5 E/F	55	55	1975	
Total	**91**	**91**		
On order				
• F-16 (A/B)	16			Being delivered

Transport Aircraft

Model	Quantity	In service	Since	Notes
• C-130 Hercules	7	5	1972	Some grounded
• CASA C-212	2	2	1975	
• Dove	1	1	1965	

Transport Aircraft *(continued)*

Model	Quantity	In service	Since	Notes
• Gulfstream III	2	2	1986	
• L-1011-500	1	1	1984	
Total	**13**	**11**		

Training and Liaison Aircraft

Model	Quantity	In service	Since	Notes
With ground attack/close air support capability				
• CASA C-101	13	13	1987	
Others				
• AS-202 Bravo	20	20		
• Cessna 318 (T-37)	10	10	1975	
• BAe-SA-3-125 Bulldog	15	15	1978	
Subtotal	45	45		
Total	**58**	**58**		

Helicopters

Model	Quantity	In service	Since	Notes
Attack				
• AH-1G/S Cobra	22	22	1985	
Medium transport				
• UH-60A Black Hawk	3	3	1987	
• AS-332 Super Puma	10	10	1986	
• Bell 205/UH-1H	18	18	1995	
Subtotal	31	31		
Light transport				
• Alouette III	1	1	1977	
• MD 500D	8	8	1980	
• MBB BO-105	3	3		With police
• BK-117	3	3		
Subtotal	15	15		
Total	**68**	**68**		

Miscellaneous Aircraft

On order

TTL BBT-3 Banshee target drones (82), 2 launchers

Advanced Armament

Air-to-air-missiles
AIM-9B/E/J/M/P Sidewinder, R-550 Magique.
Air-to-ground missiles
• AS-30L (R-530)
Bombs
Belouga CBU, Durandal antirunway bombs

Air Force Infrastructure

Aircraft shelters
• For all combat aircraft
Military airfields: 6
• Amman (Marka), Azrak, H-4, H-5, Jaafar, Mafraq

AIR DEFENSE FORCES

Surface-to-Air Missiles (SAMs)

Model	Batteries	Launchers	Since	Notes
Heavy missiles				
• MIM-23B Improved HAWK	14		1976	
Medium missiles				
• SA-8 (Gecko)		50	1982	
Light missiles				
• SA-13 (Gopher)		50	1986	
Shoulder-launched missiles				
• Javelin				
• MIM-43A Redeye		250		
• SA-14 (Gremlin)		300		
• SA-16 (Igla)		240		
Total		**800**		

Other Air Defense Systems

Model	Quantity	In service	Since	Notes
Short-range guns				
• 40mm M-42 SP	218	0		To be phased out
• 23mm ZSU 23×4 SP (Gun Dish)	45	45		

Other Air Defense Systems *(continued)*

Model	Quantity	In service	Since	Notes
• 20mm M-163 A1 Vulcan SP	100	100		
Total	363	145		
Radars				
• AN/TPS-43	2	2		
• AN/TPS-63	5	5		
• S-711	5	5		

NAVY

Combat Vessels

Type	Original Class name	Quantity	Length (m.)/ Displace-ment (t.)	Armament/ special equipment
Patrol craft				
• Feysal class	Bertram	4	11.6/8	2 × 12.7mm MGs
• Al Hussein class	VT Hawk	3	30.5/124	2 × 30mm guns 1 × 20mm gun 2 × 12.7mm MGs
• ARB 65		1	19.8/	2 × 12.7mm MGs
• Al Hashim class	Rotork type 412	3	12.7/9	In Dead Sea 1 × 12.7mm MG
• Patrol boat	Mk-4	2	12.2/	
Total		**13**		

Naval Infrastructure

Naval bases	Aqaba, Hingat al-Ramat

8. KUWAIT

GENERAL DATA

Official Name of the State: State of Kuwait
Head of State: Jabir al-Ahmad al-Sabah
Prime Minister: Saad Abdallah al-Salim al-Sabah (also Crown Prince)
Minister of Defense: Salim al-Sabah al-Salim al-Sabah
Chief of General Staff: Major General Ali al-Mumin
Commander of the Air Force and Air Defense Forces: Brigadier General Sabir al-Suwaidan
Commander of the Navy: Commodore Ahmad Yousuf al-Mualla

Area: 17,820 sq. km., including 2,590 sq. km. of the Neutral Zone
Population: 2,090,000

Demography

Ethnic Groups		
Arabs	1,672,000	80.0%
Persians/Iranians	83,600	4.0%
Southeast Asians	188,100	9.0%
Others	146,300	7.0%
Religious Groups		
Sunni Muslims	1,149,500	55.0%
Shi'ite Muslims	627,000	30.0%
Christians, Parsis, Hindus, and others	313,500	15.0%

Economic Data

		1992	1993	1994	1995	1996
GDP current price, local currency	KD bn	5.520	7.230	7.350	7.950	9.280
GDP (U.S. $)	$ bn	18.840	23.940	24.664	26.678	30.933
GDP per capita	$	14,165	14,509	13,478	13,611	14,800
Real GDP growth	%	75.0	40.3	–4.0	5.5	4.8
Balance of payments						
• Exports fob	$ bn	6.55	10.14	11.13	12.63	14.70
• Imports fob	$ bn	7.24	6.95	6.67	7.15	7.66

Economic Data *(continued)*

		1992	1993	1994	1995	1996
• Account balance (Includes services and income)	$ bn	–0.45	1.94	2.49	4.2	6.77
• External debt	$ bn	9.51	10.03	10.06	7.91	6.21
Government income and expenditure						
• Revenues, local currency	KD bn	2.3637	2.7751	3.1007	3.473	3.000
• Expenditures, local currency	KD bn	3.9363	4.2408	4.193	4.127	4.210
• Defense expenditures	KD bn	1.852	1.088	0.919	0.944	NA
• Defense expenditure/GDP	%	33.55	15.05	12.50	11.87	NA
• Defense expenditure/CGE	%	47.05	25.66	21.92	22.87	NA
• Population	m	1.33	1.65	1.83	1.96	2.09
• Official exchange rate	KD: $1	0.293	0.302	0.298	0.298	0.300

Sources: EIU quarterly report, EIU country profile, IMF statistical yearbook, Sipri Yearbook.

Arms Procurement and Security Assistance Received

Country	Type	Details
Australia	• *Arms transfers*	Patrol craft, APCS
Austria	• *Arms transfers*	Small arms
Britain	• *Arms transfers*	APCs, trainer aircraft, shoulder-launched SAMs, antiship missiles on order
	• *Military training*	Foreign advisers/instructors, trainees abroad
France	• *Arms transfers*	Radars, SAMs, naval craft, antiship missiles
PRC	• *Arms transfers*	SP artillery
Russia	• *Arms transfers*	Spare parts for APCs, MRLs, ATGMs, AIFVs
Singapore	• *Arms transfers*	Two landing craft
South Africa	• *Arms transfers*	Mortars, laser rangefinders, light armament
U.S.A.	• *Arms transfers*	APCs, SAMs, combat aircraft, command and control systems, M-1A2 tanks, ARVs, ATGMs

Arms Sales and Security Assistance Extended

Country	Type	Details
U.S.A.	• *Financial aid*	Annual grant to U.S. ($215 million in 1992) for U.S. force in Kuwait
	• *Facilities*	Facilities for U.S. forces

Foreign Military Cooperation

	Details
• Forces deployed abroad	138 troops in UN forces in Somalia, 1993–1995
• Forces deployed in country	1,300 U.S. soldiers and 4 batteries of MIM-104 Patriot SAMs, 1992–94; prepositioning of U.S. tanks (110), APCs (110) and artillery pieces (quipment for one brigade); 24 U.S.A-10 attack a/c stationed in Kuwait since October 1994; 900 UNIKOM troops and 200 observers
• Joint maneuvers	U.S.A. (amphibious, command post and naval exercises); Britain (marines); GCC countries; France, Egypt, Syria
• Security agreements	U.S.A. Britain, France, Russia, China, Italy

NBC Technology

CW capabilities
- Personal protective equipment; decontamination units

ARMED FORCES

Major Changes: The Kuwaiti ground forces acquired a large quantity of the new ''Desert Warrior'' APCs. Another acquisition is the long-range ''Smerch'' MRL. The Kuwaiti navy's first ''Combattante'' missile patrol boat was launched in 1997 but has not entered service yet.

Order-of-Battle

Year	1993	1994	1995	1996	1997
General data					
• Personnel (regular)	21,000	24,100	32,500	32,500	15,500
• Number of brigades	6	6	6	6	6
• Number of batallions	1	1	1	1	1
Ground Forces					
• Tanks	235	340	472	700	320 (455)
• APCs/ARVs	+	+	50	50	455 (515)
• Artillery incl. MRLs	24	24	24	24	77 (127)
Air Force					
• Combat aircraft	59	78	78	83	40 (83)
• Transport aircraft	3	4	4	6	5
• Helicopters	24	22	22	18–21	24–27

Order-of-Battle *(continued)*

Year	1993	1994	1995	1996	1997
Air Defense Forces					
• Heavy SAM batteries	—	6	6	6	6
Navy					
• Combat vessels	19	35	35	35	68

Note: Beginning with data for 1997, we refer to quantities in active service. The numbers in parentheses refer to the total.
The number of tanks has been changed, due to reassessment of the status of the older models.

Personnel

	Regular	Reserves	Total
Ground Forces	11,000	24,000	35,000
Air Force	2,500		2,500
Navy	2,000		2,000
Total	**15,500**	**24,000**	**39,500**
Paramilitary			
• National Guard	5,000		5,000
• Civil Defense	2,000		2,000

GROUND FORCES

Formations

	Independent brigades/groups	Independent battalions
Armored	2	
Mechanized	2	
Artillery	1	
Border Defense	1	
Royal Guard	1	
Commando		1
Total	**7**	**1**

Tanks

Model	Quantity	In service	Since	Notes
High quality				
• M1A2 Abrams	218	218	1994	
• M-84	200	100	1990	

Tanks *(continued)*

Model	Quantity	In service	Since	Notes
Subtotal	418	318		
Others				
• Chieftain	15	0	1977	In storage
• Vickers Mk 1	20	0		
Subtotal	35	0		
Total	**453**	**318**		

APCs/ARVs (including command vehicles)

Model	Quantity	In service	Since	Notes
High quality				
• BMP-3	55	55	1995	
• BMP-2	46	46	1988	
• M-113	60	60		
• Desert Warrior	254	254	1994	
• M-577 artillery command post vehicle	40	40		
Subtotal	455	455		
Others				
• Fahd	60	+	1994	
Subtotal	60	+		
Total	**515**	**455**		
On order				
• M-113 APCs	approx. 125			Including 30 M-106 mortar carriers
• M-577 artillery command post vehicles	12			
• M-113A3 ambulances	16			
• MOWAG Piranha	some 200			

Artillery

Model	Quantity	In service	Since	Notes
Self-propelled guns and howitzers				
• 155mm M-109 A3 SP howitzer	24	24		

Artillery *(continued)*

Model	Quantity	In service	Since	Notes
• M-109A2	23	0		Were damaged during the Gulf War, being overhauled
• 155mm AMX-13 F-3	18	0		In storage, offered for sale
• 155mm GCT AuF-1	12	0		In storage, offered for sale
Mortars, under 160mm				
• 120mm RTF-1	12–18	12–18		
• 107MM	6	6		
Total	95–101	42–48		
MRLs				
• 300mm Smerch (BM-9A52-2)	27	27	1995	
On order				
• 155mm Norinco 45 caliber	27			Ordered 1997, total requirement for 75
• 120mm SP mortars	30–100			

Logistic and Engineering Equipment

Model	Quantity	In service	Since	Notes
• Mk 3 (D) flail				
• M88 IRVs	14	14	1996	

Antitank Weapons

Model	Quantity	In service	Since	Notes
Missiles				
• AT-4 Spigot				Unconfirmed
• BGM-71A/B Improved TOW	82	82		
• HOT				
• M-901 ITV (TOW under Armor)	8	8		
• M-47 Dragon				
On order				
• Hot; BGM-71F (TOW 2B)				

AIR FORCE

Order-of-Battle

Model	Quantity	In service	Notes
• Combat	83	40	
• Transport	5	5	
• Helicopters	24–27	24–27	

Combat Aircraft

Model	Quantity	In service	Since	Notes
Strike and multirole aircraft—high quality				
• F/A-18C/D	40	40	1992	Number of pilots less than a/c
Strike and multirole aircraft—medium and low quality				
• Mirage F-1B/C	19	0	1976	Not in service
• A-4 KU/TA-4 KU Skyhawk II	24	0	1977	Not in service
Subtotal	43	0		
Total	**83**	**40**		
On order				
• F/A-18C/D	10–20			Under negotiation

Transport Aircraft

Model	Quantity	In service	Since	Notes
• Boeing 737-200	1	1		
• C-130-30 Hercules/ L-100-30	3	3	1971	
• DC-9	1	1	1976	
Total	**5**	**5**		

Training and Liaison Aircraft

Model	Quantity	In service	Since	Notes
With ground attack/close air support capability				
• BAC-167 Strikemaster Mk 83	8	0	1969	
• Hawk	12	0	1985	
Subtotal	20	0		

Training and Liaison Aircraft *(continued)*

Model	Quantity	In service	Since	Notes
Others				
• S-312 (Shorts Tucano)	18	18	1995	
Total	**38**	**18**		

Helicopters

Model	Quantity	In service	Since	Notes
Attack				
• SA-342K Gazelle	16	16	1974	
Transport				
• SA-330 Puma	5–8	5–8	1975	
ASW				
• AS-332 Super Puma	3	3	1985	
Total	**24–27**	**24–27**		
On order				
• SA-365N maritime attack				
• AH-64D Apache Longbow	16	16		
• UH-60A/L Blackhawk	20	20		Under negotiation
• Cougar (SA-532)	20	20		Under negotiation

Advanced Armament

Air-to-air missiles
- AIM-9M Sidewinder, AIM-7F Sparrow, R-550 Magique, Super R-530D/F

Air-to-ground missiles
- AGM-65G Maverick, AS-11, AS-12, HOT

Bombs
- Paveway II laser-guided

On order
- AM-39 Exocet air-to-ship missiles
- AGM-65G Maverick AGMs (300 missiles)—some delivered
- AIM-7 Sparrow AAMs (200 missiles)—some delivered
- AIM-9 Sidewinder AAMS (120 missiles)—some delivered
- AGM-84 Harpoon air-launched antiship missiles

Air Force Infrastructure

Aircraft shelters
- In airfields; for combat aircraft; under reconstruction

Air Force Infrastructure *(continued)*

Military airfields: 3
- al-Ahmadi, al-Jahra (Ali al-Salam AFB), Kuwait International Airport

AIR DEFENSE FORCES

Air Defense Forces

Model	Batteries	Launchers	Since	Notes
Heavy missiles				
• MIM-23B Improved Hawk	6	18	1977	
• Aspide		12		With Skyguard—see below
Total	6	30		
Shoulder-launched missiles				
• FIM-92A Stinger				
• Starburst		48		approx. 250 missiles
Total		48+		

Other Air Defense Systems

Model	Quantity	In service	Since	Notes
Air defense systems (missiles, radars and guns)				
• Skyguard AA system (Egyptian Amoun)	6	6		Each battery with 2 × Aspide launchers, 2 × Oerlikon 35mm guns
Short-range guns				
• 40mm Bofors L-70/L-60				Unconfirmed
• Oerlikon-Buhrle 2 × 35 GDF-002				With Skyguard
• 23mm ZSU 23 × 4 SP (Shilka)				
• 20mm Oerlikon GAI				
Radars				
• AN/FPS-117 (Seek Igloo)				1 system
• AN/TPS-32				1 system
• Tiger (TRS-2100)				1 system

Other Air Defense Systems *(continued)*

Model	Quantity	In service	Since	Notes
• AD command and control unit (ADGE)				
On order				
• MIM-104 Patriot	5			
• SA-10/SA-12	5			Under negotiation
• ADSAMS				Under negotiation
• AN/TPS-63 radars	2			
• Thomson CSF radar	1			
• Crotale SAMs				Unconfirmed
• ZSU 23×4				
• SA-15 (Gauntlet, Tor)				Under negotiation

NAVY

Combat Vessels

Type	Original Class name	Quantity	Length (m.)/ Displace-ment (t.)	Armament/ special equipment
MFPBs				
• Lurssen FPB-57		1	58.1/410	4 × Exocet MM 40 SSM 1 × 76mm gun 2 × 40mm guns mines
• Lurssen TNC-45		1	44.9/255	4 × Exocet MM 40 SSM 1 × 76mm gun 2 × 40mm guns
Subtotal		2		
Patrol craft (mostly with coast guard)				
• Cougar 1300		4	10–12m	12.7mm MG
• Cougar 1200		4	10–12m	12.7mm MG
• Predator 1100		3	10–12m	
• Cougar 1000		3	10–12m	12.7mm MG
• Cougar 900 (CAT-900)		3	10–12m	12.7mm MG
• OPV-310 class		4	31.5/150	1 × 22mm gun 1 × 12.7mm MG

Combat Vessels *(continued)*

Type	Original Class name	Quantity	Length (m.)/ Displace- ment (t.)	Armament/ special equipment
• Simonneau type		12	14.0/10t	1 × 12.7mm MG
• Alshaali class		33	9–10m	
Total		66		
Total		**68**		
On order				
• Magnum Sedan PBs		20		
• Combattante IV MFPBs		8	42.0/245	First launched March 1997
• 2,000-ton OMV corvettes		4		
• P-37 BRL boats				Delivery 1997–99

Landing Craft

Type	Original Class name	Quantity	Length (m.)/ Displace- ment (t.)	Armament/ special equipment
• Al Tahaddy Landing Craft		2	45/215	80 tonnes
• RTK Sea Truck		1	12.7/9	
Total		**3**		

Auxiliary Vessels

Type	Original Class name	Quantity	Length (m.)/ Displace- ment (t.)	Armament/ special equipment
• Logistic support ship		2	32.3/320	170 tonnes
• Logistic support ship		1	27/170	40 tonnes equip.
• Support ship		1	55.4/545	2 × 12.7 MG

Naval Infrastructure

Naval bases (including coast guard): 3

- Kuwait City (Shuwaikh), al-Qulaya (Ras al-Qalaya), Umm al-Hainam

Ship maintenance and repair facilities

- Kuwait City (Shuwaikh harbor)—190-meter floating dock, repair capacity 35,000 dwt

9. LEBANON

GENERAL DATA

Official Name of the State: Republic of Lebanon
Head of State: President Elias al-Hirawi
Prime Minister: Rafiq al-Hariri
Minister of Defense: Mukhsen Dalloul
Commander-in-Chief of the Armed Forces: Lieutenant General Emile Lahoud
Chief of General Staff: Brigadier General Riad Hamed Taki al-Din
Commander of the Air Force: Brigadier General Jouzal Ghassan
Commander of the Navy: Rear Admiral Samir al-Khaddam

Area: 10,452 sq. km.
Population: 3,600,000

Demography

Ethnic Groups		
Arabs	3,420,000	95.0%
Armenians	144,000	4.0%
Others	36,000	1.0%
Religious Groups		
Shi'ite Muslims	1,152,000	32.0%
Sunni Muslims	756,000	21.0%
Druze	216,000	6.0%
Alawis	36,000	1.0%
Christians		
Maronites	756,000	21.0%
Greek Orthodox	288,000	8.0%
Greek Catholics	180,000	5.0%
Armenians (Orthodox and Catholic)	144,000	4.0%
Others	72,000	2.0%

Economic Data

		1992	1993	1994	1995	1996
GDP current price, local currency	L£ bn	9,498.6	13,118.4	15,044.4	17,777.5	20,445

Economic Data *(continued)*

		1992	1993	1994	1995	1996
GDP (U.S. $)	$ bn	5.545	7.535	8.955	10.967	13.014
GDP per capita	$	1,733	2,283	2,634	3,133	3,616
Real GDP growth	%	4.5	7.1	8.5	7.0	4
Balance of payments						
• Exports fob	$ bn	0.601	0.686	0.737	0.827	1.018
• Imports fob	$ bn	3.786	4.939	5.99	7.303	7.559
• Account balance (Includes services and income)	$ bn	–2.768	–3.724	–4.450	–5.546	–5.515
• External debt	$ bn	1.807	1.347	1.718	2.966	3.739
Government income and expenditure						
• Revenues, local currency	L£ bn			2,246	3,280	3,532
• Expenditures, local currency	L£ bn	1,730	2,640	4,106	5,630	7,225
• Defense expenditures	L£ bn	498.541	518.482	703.981	795.168	759.944
• Defense expenditure/GDP	%	5.2	3.9	4.7	4.5	3.7
• Defense expenditure/CGE	%	28.8	19.6	17.1	14.1	10.5
• Population	m	3.2	3.3	3.4	3.5	3.6
• Official exchange rate	L£: $1	1,713	1,741	1,680	1,621	1,571

Sources: EIU quarterly report, EIU country profile, IMF statistical yearbook, SIPRI Yearbook.

Arms Procurment and Security Assistance Received

Country	Type	Details
Arab countries	• Financial aid	$500 million ($274 million in cash, of which $100 million are from Kuwait; this aid program followed Israeli Operation Accountability, July 1993; only part is defense related)
France	• Maintenance of equipment	Helicopters
Qatar	• Financial aid	$1 million grant, possibly for civilian purpose
Saudi Arabia	• Financial aid	$60 million grant (1991)
South Africa	• Military training	Ex–South African officers training the Hizbullah

Arms Procurment and Security Assistance Received *(continued)*

Country	Type	Details
Syria	• Advisers	
	• Military training	Approx. 200 trainees annually
	• Arms transfers	Various items, tanks (1991)
U.S.A.	• Financial aid	Approx. $400,000 in 1995 for training
	• Advisers	
	• Military training	Approx. 200 trainees in U.S.A.
	• Arms transfers	Jeeps, trucks, M-113 APCs (1996), helicopters (1996)

Foreign Military Cooperation

	Details
• Foreign forces in country	Syria (25,000 in Biqa', Tripoli area, and Beirut); Palestinian organizations; Israeli units (in the security zone in South Lebanon, some Iranian Islamic Revolution Guards Corps (IRGC), several instructors in the Syrian-held Biqa', with Hizbullah nongovernment militia; UNIFIL force in South Lebanon (from Fiji, Finland, Ghana, Ireland, Italy, Norway, and Poland)

ARMED FORCES

Major changes: No major change have been recorded in the Lebanese armed forces in 1997.

Order-of-Battle

Year	1993	1994	1995	1996	1997
General data					
• Personnel (regular)	45,100	45,000	52,000	52,000	51,400
• Total number of brigades	12	12	17	17	17
Ground Forces					
• Tanks	350	350	350	350	320 (350)
• APCs/ARVs	500	500	670	670	730 (875)
• Artillery	180	190	190	190	200
Air Force					
• Combat aircraft	14	16	16	16	(16)

Order-of-Battle *(continued)*

Year	1993	1994	1995	1996	1997
• Transport aircraft	1	1	1	1	(2)
• Helicopters	22	22	40	40	16 (34)
Navy					
• Combat vessels	27	36	36	36	39 (43)

Note: Beginning with data for 1997, we refer to quantities in active service. The number in parentheses refers to the total.

Personnel

	Regular	Total
Ground Forces	approx. 50,000	approx. 50,000
Air Force	1,000	1,000
Navy	400	400
Total	**51,400**	**51,400**
Paramilitary		
• gendarmerie/internal security	13,000	

GROUND FORCES

Formations

	Independent brigade/group
Mechanized/Infantry	11
Presidential Guard	1
Special Forces/Airborne/Intervention	5
Artillery	2
Total	**19**

Tanks

Model	Quantity	In service	Since	Notes
Medium and low quality				
• AMX-13/105mm gun	20	20	1982	
• AMX-13/75mm gun	20	20	1981	
• M-48 A1/M-48 A5	130	100	1983	Not all serviceable
• T-55/upgraded T-54	180	180	1985	
Total	**350**	**320**		

APCs/ARVs

Model	Quantity	In service	Since	Notes
High quality				
• AML-90	80	45		
• M-3 (Panhard VIT)	15	15		
• M-113 A1/A2	595	595	1980	
• VAB	75	75	1984	
• V-150 Commando	50			
Subtotal	815	730		
Others				
• Saracen/Saladin	60			Probably not serviceable
Total	**875**	**730**		
On order				
• M-113 A1/A2	500			

Artillery

Model	Quantity	In service	Since	Notes
Towed guns and howitzers				
• 155mm M-198	36	36	1984	
• 155mm M-114	18	15	1980	
• 155mm M-50	12	12		
• 130mm M-46	20	20		
• 122mm D-30	24	24	1985	
• 122mm M-1938	36	36		
• 105mm M 101A1	15	15	1982	
• 105mm M 102	10	10		
Mortars, under 160mm				
• 120mm Brandt M-50 and M-60	130	130		
Total	171	168		
MRLs				
• 122mm BM-21/BM-11	30	approx. 30		

Antitank Weapons

Model	Quantity	In service	Since	Notes
Missiles				
• BGM-71A TOW	24	24		
• Milan			1979	

Antitank Weapons *(continued)*

Model	Quantity	In service	Since	Notes
Total	approx. 80	approx. 80		
Guns				
• 106mm M-40 A2 recoilless rifle				
• 85mm M-1945/D-44	small number	small number		
• Others	small number	small number		

AIR FORCE

Order-of-Battle

Model	Quantity	In service	Notes
• Combat	16	0	
• Transport	2	0	
• Helicopters	34	16	

Combat Aircraft

Model	Quantity	In service	Since	Notes
Interceptors—medium and low quality				
• Mirage III BL/EL	10	0	1963	Grounded
Strike and multirole aircraft—medium and low quality				
• Hawker Hunter F-70/ T-66	6	0	1965	Some grounded
Total	**16**	**0**		

Transport Aircraft

Model	Quantity	In service	Since	Notes
• Falcon 20	1	0	1979	
• Dove	1	0		
Total	**2**	**0**		

Training and Liaison Aircraft

Model	Quantity	In service	Since	Notes
With ground attack/close air support capability				
• CM-170 Fouga Magister	4	0	1966	
Others				
• BAe SA-3-120/126 Bulldog	4	0	1975	
Total	**8**	**0**		

Helicopters

Model	Quantity	In service	Since	Notes
Attack				
• SA-342 Gazelle	3–4	0	1980	In flying condition
Medium transport				
• AB-212	5	0	1973	Questionable serviceability
• SA-330 Puma/possibly IAR-330	5	0	1980	
• UH-1 (Bell 205)	16	16	1995	
Subtotal	26	16		
Light transport				
• Alouette II/III	6–8	0	1960	
Total	**approx. 34**	**16**		
On order				
• UH-1	16–36			

Advanced Armament

Air-to-missiles: Matra R-530

Air Force Infrastructure

Military airfields: 3
Rayaq, Kleiat, Beirut

AIR DEFENSE FORCES

Surface-to-Air Missiles (SAMs)

Model	Launchers	Since	Notes
Shoulder-launched missiles			
• SA-7 (Grail)	small number		

Other Air Defense Systems

Model	Quantity	In service	Since	Notes
Short-range guns				
• 40mm M-42 SP	10–12	10–12		Probably in storage
• 23mm ZU 23 × 2				
• 23mm ZU 23 × 2 SP				On M-113
• 20mm				Probably in storage
Total	**approx. 75**	**approx. 75**		

NAVY

Combat Vessels

Type	Original Class name	Quantity	Length (m.)/ Displace-ment (t.)	Armament/ special equipment
Patrol craft				
• Tracker II class		0	19.3/31	2 × 23mm guns 4 unservicable
• Attacker		7	20/38	2 × 23mm guns
• Aztec class		5	9/5.2	
• Fairey Marine small patrol craft		27	8.2/6	
Total		**39**		

Landing Craft

Type	Original Class name	Quantity	Length (m.)/ Displace-ment (t.)	Armament/ special equipment
• EDIC class LCT		2	59/670	33 troops, 8 APCs 1 × 81mm MRL 2 × 20mm guns 2 × 12.7mm MGs

Naval Infrastructure

Naval bases: 5
Beirut, Junieh, Sidon, Tripoli, Tyre
Ship maintenance and repair facilities
55-meter slipway for light craft repairs in Junieh

NONGOVERNMENTAL PARAMILITARY ORGANIZATIONS

Personnel

	Active	Reserves
• Hizbullah	600–800	3,000–5,000
• Popular Liberation Army (Druz)		10,000
• Lebanese Forces		
• Amal		10,000
• Army of South Lebanon (SLA)	2,600	

Equipment

Organization	Category	System	Number	Notes
Army of South Lebanon	*Tanks*	• Sherman and T-54	45	
	APCs	• M-113	few	
	MRLs	• 107mm		
	Artillery guns	• 155mm (SP)		
		• 130mm		
	Mortars	• 120mm		
	Air defense	• SA-7		
		• ZU 23 × 2	scores	
Hizbullah	*APCs*	• M-113	several	
	Aircrafts	• Ultra-light Air crafts		

Equipment *(continued)*

Organization	Category	System	Number	Notes
	Air Defense	• SA-7		
		• Stinger		
	ATGMs	• AT-3 Sagger		
		• AT-4 Fagot		
	Mortars	• 122mm		
	MRLs	• 240mm		
		• 122mm BM-21		

10. LIBYA

GENERAL DATA

Official Name of the State: The Great Socialist People's Libyan Arab Jamahiriya (*Jamahiriya* is an Arabic term meaning "public" or "polity of the masses.")

Head of State: Colonel Muammar al-Qaddafi (leader, does not hold any other title; in practice also in charge of the Defense Ministry and Commander-in-Chief of the Armed Forces)

Prime Minister: Abd al-Majid Mabrouk al-Qaoud (official title: Secretary-General of the General People's Committee)

Commander-in-Chief of the Armed Forces: Colonel Abu-Bakr Yunis Jaber

Inspector General of the Armed Forces: Colonel Mustapha al-Kharrubi

Commander of the Air Force and Air Defense Forces: Brigadier General Ali Riffi al-Sharif

Area: 1,759,540 sq. km.

Population: 5,330,000 (estimate)

Demography

Ethnic Groups		
Arabs and Berbers	5,170,000	97.0%
Others: Greeks, Maltese, Italians, Egyptians, Pakistanis, Indians, Tunisians, Turks	160,000	3.0%
Religious Groups		
Sunni Muslims	5,170,000	97.0%
Christians and others	160,000	3.0%

Economic Data

		1992	1993	1994	1995	1996
GDP current price, local currency	LD bn	7.540	7.190	6.860	7.174	8.316
GDP (U.S. $)	$ bn	25.050	23.344	22.129	21.1	23.1
GDP per capita	$	5,144	4,641	4,256	4,129	4,333
Real GDP growth	%	–2.5	–4.6	–4.5	2.0	1.5

Economic Data *(continued)*

		1992	1993	1994	1995	1996
Balance of payments						
• Exports fob	$ bn	10.16	8.59	8.38	8.97	9.29
• Imports fob	$ bn	7.52	8.48	7.36	6.21	6.96
• Account balance (Includes services and income)	$ bn	0.39	–1.0	–0.58	1.90	1.18
• External debt	$ bn	4.340	NA	NA	NA	3.768
Government income and expenditure						
• Revenues, local currency	LD bn	2.65	NA	NA	4.38	4.57
• Expenditures, local currency	LD bn	2.84	NA	NA	5.06	4.57
• Defense expenditures	LD bn	0.65	0.468	0.433	NA	NA
• Defense expenditure/GDP	%	8.62	6.51	6.31	NA	NA
• Defense expenditure/CGE	%	22.88	NA	NA	NA	NA
• Population	m	4.87	5.03	5.2	5.11	5.33
• Official exchange rate	LD: $1	0.301	0.308	0.31	0.34	0.36

Sources: EIU quarterly report, EIU country profile, IMF statistical yearbook, SIPRI Yearbook

Arms Procurement and Security Assistance Received

Country	Type	Details
North Korea	• *Arms transfers*	Alleged sales of SSMs
Ukraine	• *Arms transfers*	Alleged sale of SSMs

Note: foreign advisers/instructors/serving personnel—300–500 on individual contracts

Arms Sales and Security Assistance Extended

Country	Type	Details
Niger	• *Arms transfers*	Antonov cargo aircraft

Defense Production

	M	P	A
Army equipment			
• Toxic chemical agent	√		
• Plans to upgrade SSMs, with assistance by foreign experts, and effort to produce an indigenous SSM, al-Fatih, not yet operational	√		
• Tank upgrading facility, with assistance of Czech Republic		√	

Note: M—manufacture (indigenously developed)
P—production under license
A—assembly

NBC Technology

Nuclear capabilities
- Basic R&D; a 5-mw Soviet-made research reactor at Tadjoura

CW capabilities
- Personal protective equipment; Soviet-type decontamination units; ABC protection of SSM sites; stockpile of chemical agents (mustard)

Biological warfare capabilities
- Toxins and other biological weapons (unconfirmed)

ARMED FORCES

Major changes: No major change has been recorded in the Libyan armed forces in 1997.

Order-of-Battle

Year	1993	1994	1995	1996	1997
General data					
• Personnel	100,500	110,000	76,000	76,000	76,000
• Number of brigades	17	17	+	+	5
• Number of battalions	+	+	+	+	46
Ground Forces					
• Tanks	2,600–2,760	2,600–2,760	2,700	2,700	950 (2,700)
• APCs/ARVs	3,000	3,000	3,000	3,000	2,750 (2,970)
• Artillery (incl. MRLs)	2,600–3,000	2,600–3,000	2,600–3,000	2,600 3,000	2,245 (2,325)
• SSM launchers	110	110	110	110	110
Air Force					
• Combat aircraft	528–533	528–533	483	483	361–376 (478–483)
• Transport aircraft	138	141	106	106	85 (90)
• Helicopters	204	204	210	210	164 (212)
Air Defense Forces					
• Heavy SAM batteries	99	99	90	90	25–31
• Medium SAM batteries	+	35	35	35	6+
• Light SAM launchers	80	70	55	55	55

Order-of-Battle *(continued)*

Year	1993	1994	1995	1996	1997
Navy					
• Submarines	6	6	6	6	4
• Combat vessels	49	52	52	52	36

Note: Beginning with data for 1997, we refer to quantities in active service. The numbers in parentheses refer to the total.

Personnel

	Regular	Reserves	Total
Ground Forces	50,000		50,000
Air Force and Air Defense	18,000		18,000
Navy	8,000		8,000
Total	**76,000**		**76,000**
Paramilitary			
• Coast guard			Included in navy
• People's Militia		40,000	40,000
• Revolutionary Guards (part of the People's Militia)	3,000		3,000
• Islamic Pan-African Legion (part of People's Militia)	2,500		2,500

GROUND FORCES

Formations

	Independent brigade/group	Independent battalion
Presidential Security Force	5	
Armored		10
Mechanized/Infantry		21
Artillery		22
Paratroops		15
Air Defense		8
SSM	5	
Total	**10**	**76**

Tanks

Model	Quantity	In service	Since	Notes
High quality				
• T-72/T-72M	360	150	1979	
Others				
• T-62	700–800	300		
• T-55	1,600	500	1974	
Subtotal	2,300–2,400	800		
Total	**2,600–2,760**	**950**		

APCs/ARVs (including command vehicles)

Model	Quantity	In service	Since	Notes
High quality				
• BMP-1/BMP-2	1,050	1,050	1972	
• Engesa EE-9/11	300	200	1977	
• Oto Breda 6614/6616	400	400		
• M-113 A1	50	0–50	1972	
Subtotal	1,800	1,650–1,700		
Others				
• BTR-50/60	750	750	1970	
• BRDM-2	220	220		
• OT-62/OT-64	200	100		
Subtotal	1,170	1,070		
Total	**2,970**	**2,720–2,770**		

Artillery

Model	Quantity	In service	Since	Notes
Self-propelled guns and howitzers				
• 155mm M-109 SP howitzer	20	0		
• 155mm Palmaria SP howitzer	160	160		
• 152mm M-1973 SP howitzer	60	60		

Artillery *(continued)*

Model	Quantity	In service	Since	Notes
• 152mm ZTS Dana SP howitzer	80	80		
• 122mm M-1974 SP howitzer	130	130		
Towed guns and howitzers				
• 130mm M-46	330	330		
• 122mm D-30	270	270		
• 122mm M-1974	60	60		
• 105mm M-101	60	0		
• Other models				
Mortars, over 160mm				
• 240mm	120	120		
• 160mm	24	24		
Mortars, under 160mm				
• 120mm	48	48		
• 107mm	64	64		
Total	1,426	1,346		Partly in storage
MRLs				
• 140mm				
• 130mm M-51				
• 122mm BM-21/RM-70/BM-11	600	600		
• 107mm Type 63	300	300		
Total	2,326	2,246		

Antitank Weapons

Model	Quantity	In service	Since	Notes
Missiles				
• AT-3 (Sagger)	620	620		
• AT-4 (Spigot)	+	+		
• AT-5 (Spandrel)	+	+		
• BRDM-2 carrying AT-3 (Sagger) SP	40	40		
• Milan	400	400		
Total	1,060	1,060		Partly in storage
Guns				
• 106mm recoilless rifle	220	220		
• 84mm Carl Gustav	400	400		

Surface-to-Surface Missiles and Rockets

Model	Launchers	Missiles	Since	Notes
• FROG-7	30			
• SS-1 (Scud B)	80	500	1976	
Total	**110**			
On order				
• Nodong from North Korea, unconfirmed, possibly under negotiation, Scud C (possibly delivered)				

AIR FORCE

Order-of-Battle

Model	Quantity	In service	Notes
• Combat	478–483	361–376	
• Transport	90	85	
• Helicopters	212	164	

Combat Aircraft

Model	Quantity	In service	Since	Notes
Interceptors—high quality				
• MiG-25 and MiG-25R (Foxbat)	65–70	65–70	1980	
Interceptors—others				
• MiG-23 (Flogger G)	170	120–130		
• MiG-21 bis (Fishbed)	70	50		
Subtotal	240	170–180		
Total	305–310	235–250		
Strike and multirole aircraft—high quality				
• Su-24 (Fencer C)	6	6	1989	
Strike and multirole aircraft—medium and low quality				
• MiG-23/27 (Flogger)				Number includes MiG-23G
• Su-20/22 (Fitter C)	90	45		
• Mirage F-1	30	30	1979	
• Mirage 5	40	40	1971	

Combat Aircraft *(continued)*

Model	Quantity	In service	Since	Notes
Subtotal	160	115		
Total	166	121		
Bombers				
• Tu-22 (Blinder)	7	5	1974	
Total	**478–483**	**361–376**		

Transport Aircraft

Model	Quantity	In service	Since	Notes
• An-26 (Curl)	15	10	1983	
• C-130H Hercules/L-100-20/L-100-30	10	10	1970	
• C-140 Jetstar	1	1		
• Fokker F-27-600/F-27-400	9	9	1981	
• G-222L	19	19	1980	
• IL-76 (Candid)	19	19	1979	Including about 4 tankers
• IL-78				Tanker, unconfirmed
• L-410 UVP	15	15		
• Mystère-Falcon 20/50	2	2	1981	
Total	**90**	**85**		

Training and Liaison Aircraft

Model	Quantity	In service	Since	Notes
With ground attack/close air support capability				
• G-2AE Galeb/J-1E Jastreb	120	80	1975	
• L-39 Albatross	165	110	1978	
Subtotal	285	190		
Others				
• SIAI—Marchetti SF-260 M/L/W	55	20	1977	
• Fouga Magistère	12	0	1971	
Subtotal	67	20		
Total	**352**	**210**		

Helicopters

Model	Quantity	In service	Since	Notes
Attack				
• Mi-24/Mi-25/Mi-35	80	45	1978	Hind, number unconfirmed
Heavy transport				
• CH-47C Chinook	15	15	1976	
• SA-321 Super Frelon	10	10	1971	Also employed in ASW role
Subtotal	25	25		
Medium transport				
• AB-212/205	2	2	1974	
• Mi-8/Mi-17 (Hip)	25	25	1975	
Subtotal	27	27		
Light transport				
• Alouette III	14	14	1971	Possibly with police
• Mi-2 (Hoplite)	35	35		
• AB-206	4	4		
• A-109	2	2		
Subtotal	55	55		
ASW				
• Mi-14 (Haze)	25	12	1983	
Total	**212**	**164**		

Advanced Armament

Air-to-air-missiles

• AA-2 (Atoll), AA-6 (Acrid), AA-7 (Apex), AA-8 (Aphid), AA-11 (Archer), R-530, R-550 Magique, Super 530D/F

Air-to-ground missiles

• AS-9 (Kyle), AS-10 (Karen), AS-14 (Kedge), AT-2 (Swatter), AT-6 (Spiral) (unconfirmed)

Air Force Infrastructure

Military airfields: 16

al-Adem (Tobruk), Benghazi (Baninah), Beni Walid, al-Bumbah, Ghurdabiyah (Surt), Jufra, Kufra, Maatan al-Sarra, Misratha, Ouqba ben Nafi (Al-Watiya), Sabhah, Tripoli International (Idriss), Umm al-Tika, 3 additional

AIR DEFENSE FORCES

Surface-to-Air Missiles

Model	Batteries	Launchers	Since	Notes
Heavy missiles				Some in storage
• SA-2 (Guideline)	15–18	90–108		
• SA-3 (Goa)	6–9	24–36		
• SA-5 (Gammon)	4	48	1985	
Total	25–31	162–192		
Medium missiles				Serviceability not clear
• Crotale		10		
• SA-6 (Gainful)	6	24		
• SA-8 (Gecko)	+	20		
Total	6+	54		
Light missiles				
• SA-9 (Gaskin)/SA-13 (Gopher)		55		
Shoulder-launched missiles				
• SA-7 (Grail)		400		
• SA-14 (Gremlin)		+		
Total		400		

Other Air Defense Systems

Model	Quantity	In service	Since	Notes
Short-range guns				
• 57mm S-60	90	90		
• 40mm Bofors L-70	50	0		Possibly phased out
• 30mm 30 × 2 M-53/59 SP	240	0		In storage
• 23mm ZSU 23 × 4 SP (Gun Dish)	250	250		
• 23mm ZU 23 × 2	100	100		
Total	**730**	**440**		

NAVY

Combat Vessels (not all serviceable)

Type	Original Class name	Quantity	Length (m.)/ Displace-ment (t.)	Armament/ special equipment
Submarines				
• F class (Fox-trot)	Type 641	4	91/2,475	10 × 533mm torpe-does 44 mines possibly nonopera-tional
Total		4		
Missile frigates				
• Koni	Type 1159	2	96.4/1,440	4 × SS-N-2C Styx SSMs 2 × SA-N-4 SAMs 4 × 76mm guns 4 × 30mm guns 4 × 406mm torpe-does 1 × RBU 6000 A/S mortar 20 mines
Missile corvettes				
• Nanuchka class		3	59.3/660	4 × SS-N-2C Styx SSMs 2 × SA-N-4 SAMs 2 × 57mm guns
MFPBs				
• Combattante II		9	49.0/311	4 × Ototmat SSMs 1 × 76mm gun 2 × 40mm guns (questionable opera-bility)
• Ossa II		12	38.6/245	4 × SS-N-2C Styx SSMs 4 × 30mm guns
Subtotal		21		

Combat Vessels (not all serviceable) *(continued)*

Type	Original Class name	Quantity	Length (m.)/ Displace- ment (t.)	Armament/ special equipment
Mine wareface vessels				
• Natya class minesweepers	Type 266ME	8	61.0/804	4 × 30mm guns 4 × 25mm guns 2 × RBU 1200 A/S mortars 10 mines Acoustic and mag- netic sweep
Patrol craft (mostly with coast guard)				
• Poluchat		1	29.6/70	2 × 14.5mm MGs used for torpedo recovery
• Thornycroft		1	23.5m	
Subtotal		2		
Total		**36**		

Landing Craft

Type	Original Class name	Quantity	Length (m.)/ Displace- ment (t.)	Armament/ special equipment
• Turkish Type		3	56.0/280	100 troops; 350 tons
• PS-700-class LST		2	99.5/2,800	240 troops; 11 tanks; 6 × 40mm guns helicopter platform
• Polnochny class LCT	Type 773U	3	83.9/1,305	4 × 30mm guns 2 × 140mm MRLs 100 mines
Total		**8**		

Auxiliary Vessels

Type	Original Class name	Quantity	Length (m.)/ Displace- ment (t.)	Armament/ special equipment
• Vosper (Tobruk)		1	54.0/500	1 × 102mm gun 2 × 40mm guns used for training
• Maintenance and repair craft	LSD type	1	98.8/2,200	2 × 40mm guns
• Yelva		1	40.9/300	Diving-support ship
• Spasilac class		1	55.5/1,590	Yugoslav salvage ship 4 × 12.7mm MGs
• Transporters (Ro-Ro)		10	166.5/2,412	

Coastal Defense

Type	Quantity	Notes
• SS-2C Styx		In 3 sites

Naval Infrastructure

Naval bases: 6

• al-Khums, Benghazi, Misratah, Tobruk, Tripoli, Derna

Ship maintenance and repair facilities

• Facilities at Tripoli with foreign technicians for repair of vessels of up to 6,000 dwt; a 3,200-ton lift floating dock; floating docks at Benghazi and Tobruk

11. MOROCCO

GENERAL DATA

Official Name of the State: Kingdom of Morocco
Head of State: King Hassan II (also Minister of Defense, Commander-in-chief of the Armed Forces and Chief of the General Staff)
Prime Minister: Abd al-Latif Filali
Inspector General of the Armed Forces: General Idriss Bin-Issa
Commander of the Air Force: Muhammad Kabaj
Commander of the Navy: Captain Muhammad al-Tariqi

Area: 622,012 sq. km., including the former Spanish Sahara (409,200 sq. km., excluding this territory)
Population: 27,600,000

Demography

Ethnic Groups		
Arabs	16,450,000	59.6%
Berbers	10,900,000	39.5%
Europeans and others	250,000	0.9%
Religious Groups		
Sunni Muslims	27,242,000	98.7%
Christians	303,000	1.1%
Jews	55,000	0.2%

Economic Data

		1992	1993	1994	1995	1996
GDP current price, local currency	Dh bn	243.8	249.8	279.3	281.2	320.9
GDP (U.S. $)	$ bn	28.55	26.86	30.36	32.42	36.88
GDP per capita	$ bn	1,120	1,029	1,141	1,196	1,336
Real GDP growth	%	–4.1	–1	11.6	–7	12
Balance of payments						
• Exports fob	$ bn	5.01	4.936	5.541	6.87	6.89
• Imports fob	$ bn	7.473	7.16	7.185	8.532	9.27

Economic Data *(continued)*

		1992	1993	1994	1995	1996
• Account balance (includes services and income)	$ bn	–0.433	–0.52	–0.724	1.521	–0.628
• External debt	$ bn	21.6	20.7	21.6	22.1	22.1
Government income and expenditure						
• Revenues, local currency	Dh bn	73.46	91.2	105.37	106.21	NA
• Expenditures, local currency	Dh bn	65.93	95.06	110.65	109.81	NA
• Defense expenditures	Dh bn	10.488	11.64	12.565	12.246	NA
• Defense expenditure/GDP	%	4.3	4.65	4.5	4.35	NA
• Defense expenditure/CGE	%	15.9	12.2	11.35	11.15	NA
• Population	m	25.5	26.1	26.6	27.1	27.6
• Official exchange rate	Dh: $1	8.54	9.3	9.2	8.54	8.7

Sources: EIU quarterly report, EIU country profile, IMF statistical yearbook, SIPRI Yearbook

Arms Procurement and Security Assistance Received

Country	Type	Details
Britain	• Arms transfers	Aircraft (1994)
Denmark	• Arms transfers	Patrol craft (1995)
France	• Arms transfers	OPV 64 patrol ships (1997)
U.S.A.	• Financial aid	$95 million grant (1993, and a smaller grant in 1994, approx. $34 million)
	• Arms transfers	Tanks (1994), T-37 aircrafts (1996), supply ship (1994)

Arms Sales and Security Assistance Extended

Country	Type	Details
U.S.A.	• Facilities provided	Use of Sidi Slimane, Marrakech, and Casablanca airfields in emergencies; permission for space shuttle to land at Marrakech AFB; use of communications center at Kenitra; storage and use of naval facilities at Mohammedia

Foreign Military Cooperation

	Details
• Joint maneuvers with:	France, U.S.A.

Defense Production

	M	P	A
Army equipment			
• Small arms ammunition	√		
• Assembly of trucks			√
Aircraft and air ammunition			
• Trainer aircraft, with foreign aid (Portugal)	√		

Note: M—Manufacture (indigenously developed)
P—Production under license
A—Assembly

ARMED FORCES

Major changes: No major change has been recorded in Moroccan armed forces in 1997.

Order-of-Battle

Year	1993	1994	1995	1996	1997
General data					
• Personnel	184,000	138,500	141,000	141,000	196,500
• Number of brigades	11	12	12	12	7
• Number of battalions	21	23	23	23	64
Ground Forces					
• Tanks	400	415	415	415	364
• APCs/ARVs	1,450–1,550	1,450–1,550	1,500	1,500	1,200 (1,537)
• Artillery	336	336	386	386	970 (1,020)
Air Force					
• Combat aircraft	71	65	74	74	70
• Transport aircraft	54	54	48	48	45
• Helicopters	142	142	127	127	129
Air Defense Forces					
• Light SAM launchers	36	36	+	+	37
Navy					
• Combat vessels	24	48	46	65	62

Note: Beginning with data for 1997, we refer to quantities in active service. The number in parentheses refers to the total.

Personnel

	Regular	Reserves	Total
Ground Forces	175,000	150,000	325,000
Air Force	13,500		13,500
Navy and Marines	8,000		8,000
Total	**196,500**	**150,000**	**346,500**
Paramilitary			
• Gendarmerie royale	10,000		
• Force auxilière	25,000		
• Mobile intervention corps	5,000		

Note: Customs and coast guard are included in gendarmerie and navy.

GROUND FORCES

Formations

	Independent brigade/group	Independent battalion
Armored		10
Mechanized	3	8
Infantry		37
Light security	2	
Camel corps		3
Paratroops	2	
Airborne/commando		2+4
Artillery		12
Air defense		1
Total	**7**	**77**

Tanks

Model	Quantity	In service	Since	Notes
High quality				
• M-60 A1/A3	60	60	1981	
Others				
• M-48 A5	224	224	1974	
• SK-105 (Kurassier)	80	80	1985	
Subtotal	304	304		
Total	**364**	**364**		

APCs/ARVs

Model	Quantity	In service	Since	Notes
High quality				
• AMX-10 R/CM	85	85	1981	
• Engesa EE-9/EE-11	50		1981	In storage
• M-113 A1/A2	360	360	1979	
• M-3 (Panhard)	30	30		Unconfirmed
• Ratel 20/90	60	60	1981	
• VAB-VCI/VTT	365	365		
Subtotal	950	900		
Others				
• AML-90/AML-60	230	230	1966	
• EBR-75	16	16	1956	
• M-3 half-track	50	0		
• OT-62	150	0	1968	
• UR-416	55	55		Including 42 equipped with Cobra ATGMs
• BRDM 2	86	0		In storage, 36 carrying AT-3
Subtotal	587	300		
Total	**1,537**	**1,200**		

Artillery

Model	Quantity	In service	Since	Notes
Self-propelled guns and howitzers				
• 155mm M-109 A1	40	40	1981	
• 155mm Mk F-3 (AMX)	100	100		
• 105mm Mk 61	5	5	1963	
Towed guns and howtizers				
• 155mm M-114	20	20		
• 155mm M-198	35	35		
• 155mm FH-70	26	26		
• 130mm M-46	18	18		
• 122mm D-30	50			
• 105mm L-118 Light Gun	36	36		
• 105mm M-1950	35	35		
• 105mm M-101/M-101A1	20	20		
Mortars, under 160mm				
• 120mm	600	600		20 SP mounted on VAB

Artillery *(continued)*

Model	Quantity	In service	Since	Notes
Total	985	935		
MRLs				
• 122mm BM-21	36	36		

Antitank Weapons

Model	Quantity	In service	Since	Notes
Missiles				
• BGM-71A TOW	150	150		
• Cobra	42	42		Mounted on UR-416
• AT-3 (sagger)	36	0		Mounted on BRDM-2, in storage
• M-47 Dragon	480	480		
• MILAN	80	80		
Total	788	750		
Guns				
• 106mm M-40 A2	350	350		
• 90mm M-56	28	28		

AIR FORCE

Order-of-Battle

Model	Quantity	In service
• Combat	70	70
• Transport	45	45
• Helicopters	129	129

Combat Aircraft

Model	Quantity	In service	Since	Notes
Strike and multirole aircraft—medium and low quality				
• Mirage F-1	34	34	1979	
• F-5E/F	20	20	1981	
• F-5A/B	13	13	1967	
• OV-10 Bronco	3	3	1981	
Total	**70**	**70**		

Transport Aircraft

Model	Quantity	In service	Since	Notes
• Beechcraft King Air 100	5	5	1975	
• Beechcraft Super King Air 200	5	5	1983	
• Beechcraft Super King Air 300	1	1	1991	
• Boeing 707	2	2	1982	
• C-130H Hercules	17	17	1974	Including 2 with SLAR employed for electronic surveillance and 2 tankers
• CN-235	7	7	1990	
• Dornier DO-28 D-2	3	3	1981	
• Gulfstream II/III	2	2	1976	
• Mystère-Falcon 50	1	1	1980	
• Mystère-Falcon 20	2	2	1968	Electronic countermeasures
Total	**45**	**45**		

Training and Liaison Aircraft

Model	Quantity	In service	Since	Notes
With ground attack/close air support capability				
• T-37	14	14	1996	
• Alpha jet	22	22	1979	
• CM-170 Fouga magister	22	22	1964	
Subtotal	58	58		
Others				
• AS-202/18A Bravo	10	10	1978	
• Beechcraft T-34C	12	10	1977	
• Cap 10/232	9	9	1983	Aerobatic team
Subtotal	31	29		
Total	**89**	**87**		

Helicopters

Model	Quantity	In service	Since	Notes
Attack				
• SA-342 Gazelle	30	30	1976	Of which 6 with gendarmerie

Helicopters *(continued)*

Model	Quantity	In service	Since	Notes
Heavy transport				
• CH-47C Chinook	7	7	1979	
Medium transport				
• AB-212	5	5	1973	
• AB-205	27	27	1969	
• AS-365 Dauphin II	2	2	1983	With gendarmerie
• SA-330 Puma	30	30	1976	Of which 6 with gendarmerie
Subtotal	64	64		
Light transport				
• Alouette II/III	5	5		With gendarmerie
• AB-206 JetRanger	20	20	1975	
• SA-315B Lama	3	3		With gendarmerie
Subtotal	28	28		
Total	**129**	**129**		

Miscellaneous Aircraft

Model	Quantity	In service	Since	Notes
Tankers				
• KC-130				2 listed under Transport
Standoff ECM				
• Mystère 20F				2 listed under Transport
Surveillance aircraft				
• C-130H				2 listed under Transport
UAVs and mini-UAVs				
• Skyeye R4E-50				
Maritime surveillance aircraft				
• BN-2T Defender		7	1993	Possibly fishery protection

Advanced Armament

Air-to-air-missiles
AIM-9J Sidewinder (320), R-530, R-550 Magique, Super 530D
Air-to-ground missiles:
AGM-65 Maverick (380), HOT

Air Force Infrastructure

Military airfields: 10
Agadir, Casablanca (Nouasseur), Fez, Kenitra, Larache, L'Ayoun, Marrakech, Meknes, Rabat, Sidi Slimane, + additional

AIR DEFENSE FORCES

Surface-to-Air Missiles (SAMs)

Model	Batteries	Launchers	Since	Notes
Light missiles				
• MIM-72A Chaparral		37	1992	
Shoulder-launched missiles				
• SA-7 (Grail)		70		
Total		**107**		

Other Air Defense Systems

Model	Quantity	In service	Since	Notes
Short-range guns				
• 37mm M-1939	100	100		
• 23mm ZU 23×2	90	90		
• 20mm M-163 Vulcan SP	60	60		
• 20mm M-167 SP	40	40		
Total	**290**	**290**		
Radars				
• AN/TPS-43		8		
• AN/TPS-63		8		

NAVY

Combat Vessels

Type	Original Class name	Quantity	Length (m.)/ Displacement (t.)	Armament/ special equipment
Missile frigates				
• Descubierta		1	88.8/1,233	4×MM38 Exocet SSMs 1×8 Aspide SAMs 6×324mm torpedoes 1×SR 375 ASW mortar 1×76mm and 1×40mm guns

Combat Vessels *(continued)*

Type	Original Class name	Quantity	Length (m.)/ Displace-ment (t.)	Armament/ special equipment
MFPBs				
• Lazaga		4	58.1/524	4×MM38 Exocet SSMs 1×76mm, 1×40mm and 2×20mm guns
Gunboats/MTBs				
• Okba class	PR-72	2	57.5/375	1×76mm gun 1×40mm gun
• Cormoran class	P-200D Vigilance	6	58.1/425	1×40mm gun 2×20mm guns
Subtotal		8		
Patrol craft				
• El Wacil class	P-32	6	32/74	6 Elwacil class, 4 Erraid class; 4 with customs/ coast guard 1×20mm gun
• Rais Bargech class	OPV 64	5	64/580	
• Osprey mk I		5	54.8/475	2×20mm guns
• Arcor 46		18	14.5/15	With customs/coast guard 2×12.7mm MGs
• Arcor 53		15	16/17	With customs/coast guard 1×12.7mm MG
Subtotal		49		
Total		**62**		

Landing Craft

Type	Original Class name	Quantity	Length (m.)/ Displace- ment (t.)	Armament/ special equipment
• Batral LSL		3	80/750	140 troops, 12 vehicles Helicopter pod 2×81mm mortars 4×40mm guns
• EDIC LCT		1	59/250	11 vehicles 1×120mm mortar 2×20mm guns
• Newport-class LST		1	159.2/8,450	400 Troops, 500-ton vehicle 4×LCVP/LCPL Boats 1×20mm Phalanx gun
Total		**5**		
On order				
• Batral LSL		3		

Auxiliary Vessels

Type	Original Class name	Quantity	Length (m.)/ Displace- ment (t.)	Armament/ special equipment
• Cargo ship		2	77/1,500	2×14.5mm MGs
• Transport ship		1	784 dwt	
• Agor survey ship	Robert D. Conrad class	1	67.3/1,370	
• SAR craft		3	19.4/40	With coast guard
Total		**7**		

Naval Infrastructure

Naval bases: 7

Agadir, al-Hoceima, Casablanca, Kenitra, Dakhla, Safi, Tangier

Ship maintenance and repair facilities:

156-meter dry dock at Casablanca, repair ships of up to 10,000 dwt, facility for minor repairs at Agadir

12. OMAN

GENERAL DATA

Official Name of the State: Sultanate of Oman
Head of State: Sultan Qabus ibn Said (also Prime Minister and Minister of Defense)
Minister of Defense Affairs: Badr bin Saud bin Harib Al Busaidi
Chief of General Staff: General Khamis al-Kalabani
Commander of the Ground Forces: Major General Ali ibn Rashid al-Kalabani
Commander of the Air Force: Major General Mohammed ibn Mahfoodh al Ardhi
Commander of the Navy: Rear Admiral Shihab al-Said

Area: 212,000 sq. km.
Population: 2,210,000 (including 17% aliens)

Demography

Ethnic Groups		
Arabs	2,002,000	90.6%
Others (Africans, Persians, Southeast Asians)	208,000	9.4%
Religious Groups		
Ibadi Muslims	1,658,000	75.0%
Sunni Muslims	415,000	18.8%
Shi'ite Muslims, Hindus	137,000	6.2%

Economic Data

		1992	1993	1994	1995	1996
GDP current price, local currency	OR bn	4.788	4.804	4.967	5.288	5.854
GDP (U.S. $)	$ bn	12.436	12.478	12.901	13.735	15.205
GDP per capita	$	6,378	6,177	6,173	6,359	6,880
Real GDP growth	%	6.9	7.0	3.8	4.6	6.7
Balance of payments						
• Exports fob	$ bn	5.560	5.370	5.540	6.070	7.340
• Imports fob	$ bn	3.630	4.080	3.840	4.170	4.390

Economic Data *(continued)*

		1992	1993	1994	1995	1996
• Account balance (Includes services and income)	$ bn	–0.592	–1.192	–0.985	–0.979	–0.266
• External debt	$ bn	2.854	2.661	2.592	2.680	2.812
Government income and expenditure						
• Revenues, local currency	OR bn	1.930	1.906	1.915	2.080	1.990
• Expenditures, local currency	OR bn	2.259	2.242	2.253	2.104	2.253
• Defense expenditures	OR bn	0.6795	0.6501	0.699	0.776	NA
• Defense expenditure/GDP	%	14.19	13.53	14.07	14.67	NA
• Defense expenditure/CGE	%	30.08	29.00	31.03	36.88	NA
• Population	m	1.95	2.02	2.09	2.16	2.21
• Official exchange rate	OR $1	0.385	0.385	0.385	0.385	0.385

Sources: EIU quarterly report, EIU country profile, IMF statistical yearbook, SIPRI Yearbook.

Arms Procurement and Security Assistance Received

Country	Type	Details
Britain	• *Arms transfers*	Tanks, Swiss-model MOWAG Piranha APCs, combat aircraft, training aircraft, aircraft radars and navigation systems, upgrade kits for Rapier SAMs, missile corvettes, upgrading Jaguar aircraft
France	• *Arms transfers*	ATGMs, AAMs, naval SSMs, fire control radar, patrol craft
Netherlands	• *Arms transfers*	Surveillance radar, fire control radar
Pakistan	• *Arms transfers*	Light trainer a/c
South Africa	• *Arms transfers*	Artillery
Switzerland	• *Arms transfers*	AA artillery, fire control radar
U.S.A.	• *Arms transfers*	AT guided missiles, AAMs, tanks, SP artillery, a missile frigate
	• *Military training*	Foreign advisers/instructors/serving personnel

Arms Sales and Security Assistance Extended

Country	Type	Details
Britain	• *Facilities*	Use of airfields
U.S.A.	• *Facilities*	Airfields at Masira, Seeb, al-Khasb, Thamarit; storage facilities and prepositioning of U.S. Army and Air Force support equipment; naval facilities at Masira and Ghanam Peninsula; communications center

Foreign Military Cooperation

	Details
• *Joint maneuvers*	Britain, Egypt, GCC countries, USA
• *Security agreement*	U.S.A.

ARMED FORCES

Major Changes: The Omani forces are assimilating the new Challenger II MBTs and the Piranha APCs acquired since late 1995. The Omani Navy is in the process of deploying its new Qahir-class corvettes.

Order-of-Battle

Year	1993	1994	1995	1996	1997
General data					
• Personnel (regular)	27,100	28,500	29,600	29,600	34,000
• Total number of brigades	3	3	4	4	4
• Number of independent battalions	18	18	22	22	18
Ground Forces					
• Tanks	97	106	106	156	178
• APCs/ARVs	62	62	62	142	135 (166)
• Artillery	150	153	177	177	148 (154)
Air Force					
• Combat aircraft	38	37	37	37	31 (47)
• Transport aircraft	41	44	44	44	38 (42)
• Helicopters	37	37	37	37	37
Air Defense Forces					
• Light SAM launchers	52	52	54	54	58
Navy					
• Combat vessels	31	26	26	32	32

Note: Beginning with data for 1997, we refer to quantities in active service. The numbers in parentheses refer to the total.

Personnel

	Regular	Reserves	Total
Ground Forces	25,000		25,000
Air Force	5,000		5,000
Navy	4,000		4,000
Total	**34,000**		**34,000**

Personnel *(continued)*

	Regular	Reserves	Total
Paramilitary			
• Tribal force (Firqat)	5,000		5,000
• Police/border police (operating aircraft, helicopters, and PBs)			7,000
• Royal household (including royal guard, royal yachts, and royal flight)			6,500

GROUND FORCES

Formations

	Independent brigade/group	Independent battalions/ regiments
Royal Guard	1HQ	
Armored	1HQ	2+1 royal guard
Infantry (partly mechanized)	2HQ	8+2 royal guard
Reconnaissance		2 (1 inf.+1 arm.)
Paratroops/Special Forces		1+2 royal guard
Artillery		4
Air Defense		1
Total	**4**	**23**

Tanks

Model	Quantity	In service	Since	Notes
High quality				
• M-60 A3	93	93	1990	
• Challenger 2	18	18	1995	
Subtotal	111	111		
Others				
• M-60 A1	6	6	1980	
• Chieftain	24	24		
• Scorpion	37	37		
Subtotal	67	67		
Total	**178**	**178**		
On order				
• Challenger 2	18			Option for 18 more

APCs/ARVs (including command vehicles)

Model	Quantity	In service	Since	Notes
High quality				
• BTR-80		small number	1994	
• V-150 Commando	20	20		
• VAB	14	14		Number unconfirmed
• VBC-90	6	6		
• GKN-Defense Piranha 8×8	80	80	1995	
Subtotal	120	120		
Others				
• AT-105 Saxon	15	15		
• Fahd	31	+		Unconfirmed
Subtotal	46	15		
Total	**166**	**135**		
On order				
• Option for 40 more Piranha 8×8				

Artillery

Model	Quantity	In service	Since	Notes
Self-propelled guns and howitzers				
• 155mm M-109 A2	15	15	1986	
• 155mm G-6	24	24	1995	
Towed guns and howitzers				
• 155mm FH-70	12	12		
• 130mm Type 59	12	12		
• 122mm D-30	25	25		
• 105mm Light Gun	42	36		
Mortars, under 160mm				
• 120mm	12	12		
• 107mm (4.2") M-30 SP	12	12		
Total	**154**	**148**		

Logistic and Engineering Equipment

Model	Quantity	In service	Since	Notes
• Challenger RV	4	4	1995	

Antitank Weapons

Model	Quantity	In service	Since	Notes
Missiles				
• BGM-71A Improved TOW	18	18		
• MILAN	32	32		

AIR FORCE

Order-of-Battle

Model	Quantity	In service	Notes
• Combat	47	31	
• Transport	42	38	
• Helicopters	37	37	

Combat Aircraft

Model	Quantity	In service	Since	Notes
Strike and multirole aircraft—medium and low quality				
• SEPECAT Jaguar S(O) Mk 1/Mk 2/T2	19	19	1977	To be upgraded to Jaguar 97 standard
• Hawker Hunter FGA-6/FR-10/T-67	16	0		Not in service
• Hawk Mk-203	12	12	1994	
Total	**47**	**31**		
On order				
• F-16	4			From U.S. drawdown (under negotiation)

Transport Aircraft

Model	Quantity	In service	Since	Notes
• BAe-111	3	3		
• Britten-Norman BN-2 Defender/Islander	4	0	1974	
• C-130H Hercules	3	3	1981	
• CN-235	3	3	1993	With police
• DC-8	1	1		
• DC-10	1	1		

Transport Aircraft *(continued)*

Model	Quantity	In service	Since	Notes
• DHC-5D Buffalo	4	4	1982	
• Dornier Do-228-100	2	2	1984	Used by police air wing for maritime surveillance and border patrol
• Gulfstream	1	1	1992	
• Learjet	1	1		In police service
• Mystère-Falcon 20	1	1		
• Mystère-Falcon 10	1	1		
• Mystère-Falcon 900	2	2		
• Short Skyvan Srs 3M	15	15		Seven employed in maritime patrol role
Total	**42**	**38**		
On order				
• CN-235				Unconfirmed

Training and Liaison Aircraft

Model	Quantity	In service	Since	Notes
With ground attack/close air support capability				
• BAC-167 Strikemaster Mk 82	12	12	1967	
• Hawk Mk-103	4	4	1993	
• Mushshak	3	3	1994	
Subtotal	19	19		
Others				
• AS-202 Bravo	4	4	1976	
Total	**23**	**23**		

Helicopters

Model	Quantity	In service	Since	Notes
Medium transport				
• AB-205	19	19	1970	
• AB-212B/Bell 212	3	3	1976	
• AB-214	10	10	1974	
• AS-332 Super Puma/ SA-330 Puma	2	2	1982	
Subtotal	34	34		

Helicopters *(continued)*

Model	Quantity	In service	Since	Notes
Light transport				
• AB-206 JetRanger	3	3	1970	
Total	**37**	**37**		

Miscellaneous Aircraft

Model	Quantity	In service	Since	Notes
Maritime surveillance aircraft				
• Short Skyvan Srs 3M			1970	7 listed under transport
Target drones				
• TTL BTT-3 Banshee	53			Original number supplied (53)

Advanced Armament

Air-to-air missiles
- R-550 Magique, AIM 9P/AIM 9J Sidewinder

Bombs
- BL-755 CBU

Air Force Infrastructure

Aircraft shelters
- For all combat aircraft, at Masira and Thamarit

Military airfields: 6
- Bureimi, Dukha, Masira, Muscat (Seeb), Salala, Thamarit

AIR DEFENSE FORCES

Surface-to-Air Missiles

Model	Batteries	Launchers	Since	Notes
Light missiles				
• Rapier, upgraded to Mk 2/Jernas		28		
• Javelin		30	1989	
• Tigercat				Unconfirmed
Total		**58**		

Surface-to-Air Missiles *(continued)*

Model	Batteries	Launchers	Since	Notes
Shoulder-launched missiles				
• Blowpipe		+	1982	
• SA-7 (Grail)		34		
Total		34		

Other Air Defense Systems

Model	Quantity	In service	Since	Notes
Short-range guns				
• 40mm Bofors L-60	12	12		
• 35mm Oerlikon Contraves	+	+		
• 23mm ZU 23×2	4	4		
• 20mm 20×2 VDAA SP	9	9		
Total	**25**	**25**		
Radars				
• AR-15				
• S-713 Martello 3D	2	2		
• S-600				
• Watchman				
On order				
• Javelin				Unconfirmed

NAVY

Combat Vessels

Type	Original Class name	Quantity	Length (m.)/ Displace- ment (t.)	Armament/ special equipment
Missile corvettes				
• Qahir class	Vosper Thornycroft	2	83.7/1,450	1×helicopter 8×Exocet MM 40 SSMs 1×8 Crotale-NG 1×76mm gun 2×20mm guns 6×324mm torpe- does

Combat Vessels *(continued)*

Type	Original Class name	Quantity	Length (m.)/ Displace-ment (t.)	Armament/ special equipment
MFPBs				
• Dhofar class	Province class	4	56.7/394	6–8 Exocet MM 40 SSM 1×76mm gun 2×40mm guns 2×12.7mm MGs
Gunboat/MTBs				
• Al-Bushra	P-400	3	54.5/475	1×76mm gun 1×40mm gun 2×20mm guns 2×12.7mm MGs 4×406mm torpe-does to be up-graded to MFPB by addition of MM-38 missiles (unconfirmed)
Patrol craft (some in police service)				
• CG-29		3	28.9/84	2×20mm guns with police
• CG-27		1	24/53	1×20mm gun with police
• Seeb	Vosper Thornycroft	4	25/60.7	1×20mm gun 2×7.62mm MGs
• Emsworth type		2	16.0/18	2×7.62mm MGs with police
• Watercraft type		3	13.9/16	2×7.62mm MGs with police
• P-2000		1	20.8/80	1×12.7mm MG with police
• P-1903		1	19.2/26	2×12.7mm MGs with police
• Tyler-Vortex		1	13m	
• Vosper Thornycroft		5	22.9/50	1×20mm gun with police
• D-59116		2	23/65	1×12.7mm MG with police
Total		23		
Total		**32**		

Combat Vessels *(continued)*

Type	Original Class name	Quantity	Length (m.)/ Displace-ment (t.)	Armament/ special equipment
On order				
• Oliver Hazard Perry–class missile frigate		1		
• Al Waffi class		2		
• Vosper Thornycroft Type 83 (Vigilance) missile corvette		1		

Landing Craft

Type	Original Class name	Quantity	Length (m.)/ Displace-ment (t.)	Armament/ special equipment
• Brooke Marine 2,000-ton landing ship—logistics/ tank		1	84.1/2,000	550 tonnes; 188 troops; 2 LCVPs, armament removed
• Brooke Marine 2,500-ton landing ship–logistics/ tank		1	93/2,500	4×40mm guns 2×20mm guns 2×12.7mm MGs 400 tonnes; 240 troops; 2 LCVPs, armament removed
• LCU		1	18.3/30	
• Vosper 230-ton LCM		3	33.0/230	100 tonnes
Total		**6**		
On order				
• Skima 12 hovercraft				Unconfirmed

Auxiliary Vessels

Type	Original Class name	Quantity	Length (m.)/ Displace- ment (t.)	Armament/ special equipment
• Brooke Marine training ship		1	62/900	1×40mm gun 2×20mm guns helicopter deck ex–royal yacht
• Conoship, Gron- ingen		1	65.7m 1,380 dwt	
• Coastal freighter		1		
• Survey craft		1	15.5/23.6	
• Diving craft		1		
• Harbor craft		2	15m	

Naval Infrastructure

Naval bases: 4

- Mina Raysut (Salala), al-Khasb, Muscat, Wuddam

Ship maintenance and repair facilities

- Muscat

13. PALESTINIAN AUTHORITY

GENERAL DATA

This section includes information regarding the Palestinian Authority and Palestinian military organizations inside the Palestinian Authority. It does not cover Palestinians living elsewhere.

Official Name: Palestinian Authority (PA)
Chairman: Yasir Arafat (also Chairman of the PLO)
Chief of security forces: Formally, General Nasser Youssuf (Abd al Rizak al Majaida)

Area: 400 sq. km. (Gaza). By the terms of the Interim Agreement, the West Bank is divided into three areas, designated A, B, and C. The PA has civilian responsibility for Palestinians in all three areas, exclusive security responsibility for Area A, and shared security responsibility for Area B. The size of areas A and B is 1,950 square kilometers; Area C covers 3,850 square kilometers.
Population: Gaza—about 960,000; West Bank—1.4 million

Demography

Religious Groups		
Sunni Muslims	2,124,000	90%
Christians	236,000	10%

Economic Data

		1992	1993	1994	1995	1996
GDP at market prices	Nis bn	6.604	7.454	8.851	10.057	10.835
GDP (U.S. $) (estimate)	$m	2,685.6	2,631.1	2,932.7	3,340.0	3,398.6
GDP per capita	$	1,137.9	1,114.8	1,242.6	1,415.2	1,440.0
Real GDP growth	%	23.1	–1.3	7.3	3.5	–2.5
Balance of payments						
• Exports fob	$m	299.0	236.0	164.5	230.0	400.0
• Imports cif	$m	1,232.0	1,138.0	1,126.0	1,240.0	1,800.0
• Account balance (Exc. Grants)	$m	–224	–282	–402	–721	–1,078
• External debt	$m	NA	NA	NA	800	800

Economic Data *(continued)*

		1992	1993	1994	1995	1996
Government income and expenditure						
• Revenues, local currency	NIS bn	NA	NA	NA	1.207	1.718
• Expenditures, local currency	NIS bn	NA	NA	NA	1.928	2.796
• Defense expenditures	NIS m	NA	NA	NA	511.8	790.6
• Defense expenditure/ GDP	%	NA	NA	NA	5.08	7.29
• Defense expenditure/ CGE	%	NA	NA	NA	26.54	28.27
• Population	m	NA	NA	NA	NA	2.36
• Official exchange rate (AV)	NIS: $1	2.459	2.833	3.018	3.011	3.188

Arms Procurement and Security Assistance Received

Country	Type	Details
Egypt	• Military training	Trainees abroad, police, and civil defense (1997)
European countries	• Financial	
	• Military training	Trainees (police)
Israel	• Financial	$30 million, plus ''nonsecurity assistance,'' as payment for income tax withheld from Palestinian laborers, and now given the Palestinian Authority—about $200 million
Jordan	• Military training	Trainees (police)
Russia	• Arms transfers	Scout cars (BRDM—2)
Saudi Arabia	• Military training	Trainees (police)
U.S.A.	• Financial	$75 million in FY97

Defense Production

	M	P	A
Army equipment			
• Possibly clandestine manufacture of small arms	√		

M=manufacture (indigenously developed)
P=production under license
A=assembly

ARMED FORCES

Major changes: No major change has been recorded in 1997.

Order-of-Battle

Year	1993	1994	1995	1996	1997
General data					
• Personnel (regular)	—	—	21,000–24,000	30,000	34,000+
Ground Forces					
• APCs/ARVs	—	—	45	45	45
Air Force					
• Transport aircraft*	—	—	2	2	2 (3)
• Helicopters	—	—	2	2	2 (4)
Navy					
• Combat vessels	—	—	—	—	7

Notes: *Aircraft are not stationed in PA controlled areas.
Beginning with data for 1997, we refer to quantities in active service. The number in parentheses refers to the total.

Personnel

	Gaza	West Bank	Total
Public security	+	+	+
Preventive security	+	+	+
General intelligence	+	+	+
Military intelligence	+	+	+
Presidential security (including "Force 17")	+	+	+
Total	20,000+	14,000+	34,000+

GROUND FORCES

APCs/ARVs

Model	Quantity	In service	Since	Notes
Low quality				
• BRDM-2	45	45		

AIR FORCE

The PLO-affiliated organizations have no air force. The Fatah air arm is designated Force 14. About 200 Palestinians have reportedly undergone training as fighter and helicopter pilots in Libya, Yemen, Romania, Pakistan, Cuba, North Korea, and the USSR (until 1991); much of this training took place several years ago, and the number of Palestinians at the disposal of the air units is considerably less than 200. Other PLO members learned to fly commercial aircraft several years ago in civilian flight schools in Romania, Yugoslavia, and several Western countries, and have been flying a wide variety of aircraft. In recent years, a concentration of Palestinian pilots and ancillary personnel has reportedly been located in Yemen.

Order-of-Battle

Model	Quantity	In service	Notes
• Transport	3	2	
• Helicopters	4	2	

Transport Aircraft

Model	Quantity	In service	Since	Notes
• Lockheed Jet Star	1	1	1996	
• Fokker 50	2	1	1996	
Total	**3**	**2**		

Note: Aircraft are not stationed in PA controlled areas.

Helicopters

Model	Quantity	In service	Since	Notes
Transport				
• Mi-8	2	0	1996	
• Mi-17	2	2	1996	
Total	**4**	**2**		

Air Force Infrastructure

Airfields: 1
• Dahaniya

NAVY

The naval force is concentrated in Yemen, Libya, and Algeria; some were in Lebanon until January 1994, then moved to Yemen. The Fatah naval force is to be the coast guard of the Palestinian Authority in Gaza.

Combat Vessels

Type	Original Class name	Quantity	Length (m.)/ Displace- ment (t.)	Armament/ special equipment
Patrol craft				
• Volvo		2	8.0/5	7.62 MG
• Zodiak mk 5		5	5.8m	7.62 MG
Total		**7**		

NONGOVERNMENTAL ORGANIZATIONS

- Hamas —Several hundred members
- Islamic Jihad —Several hundred members

14. QATAR

GENERAL DATA

Official Name of the State: State of Qatar
Head of State: Shaykh Hamad ibn Khalifa al-Thani (also Minister of Defense and Commander in Chief of the armed forces)
Prime Minister: Abdallah Ibn Khalifa al-Thani
Chief of General Staff: Major General Mohammad ibn Rashid Sharan al-Khigrani
Commander of the Air Force: Colonel Ahmad Abdallah al-Kuawari
Commander of the Navy: Captain Said al-Suwaydi

Area: 11,437 sq. km.
Population: 575,000

Demography

Ethnic Groups		
Arabs	230,000	40.0%
Pakistanis	103,500	18.0%
Indians	103,500	18.0%
Persians	57,500	10.0%
Others (mostly Southeast Asians)	80,500	14.0%
Religious Groups		
Sunni Muslims	404,000	70.3%
Shi'ite Muslims	140,000	24.3%
Others	31,000	5.4%

Economic Data

		1992	1993	1994	1995	1996
GDP current price, local currency	QR bn	27.8	26.2	26.1	27.5	29.3
GDP (U.S. $)	$ bn	7.637	7.198	7.170	7.555	8.04
GDP per capita	$	14,687	12,853	12,363	12,385	13,982
Real GDP growth	%	5.6	–5.2	1.0	0.8	4.6
Balance of payments						
• Exports fob	$ bn	3.840	3.100	2.980	3.094	4.377
• Imports fob	$ bn	1.800	1.680	1.680	–3.308	–3.805

Economic Data *(continued)*

		1992	1993	1994	1995	1996
• Account balance (Includes services and income)	$ bn	0.200	–0.659	–0.502	–2.681	–2.323
• External debt	$ bn	1.493	2.106	4.803	6.88	10.39
Government income and expenditure						
• Revenues, local currency	QR bn	12.121	10.892	9.614	11.045	13.552
• Expenditures, local currency	QR bn	12.816	12.268	11.679	12.735	14.625
• Defense expenditures	QR bn	1.3	1.2	1.1	1.2	NA
• Defense expenditure/GDP	%	4.68	4.58	4.21	4.36	NA
• Defense expenditure/CGE	%	10.14	9.78	9.42	9.43	NA
• Population	m	0.52	0.56	0.58	0.58	0.575
• Official exchange rate	QR: $1	3.64	3.64	3.64	3.64	3.64

Sources: EIU quarterly report, EIU country profile, IMF statistical yearbook, SIPRI Yearbook.

Arms Procurement and Security Assistance Received

Country	Type	Details
Brazil	• Arms transfers	MRLs (1993)
Britain	• Arms transfers	SAMs (1996), combat vessels (1996), aircraft (1996), APCs (1996)
France	• Arms transfers	APCs (1996), combat aircraft (1997), MBTs (1997), SAMs (1996)
U.S.A.	• Advisers • Trainees abroad	

Arms Sales and Security Assistance Extended

Country	Type	Details
Lebanon	• Financial aid	$1 million grant
Spain	• Arms transfers	F-5 aircraft (1996)
Syria	• Financial aid	
U.S.A.	• Facilities provided	Transportation equipment

Foreign Military Cooperation

	Details
Joint maneuvers with:	USA, GCC countires, Yemen, Britain, France

ARMED FORCES

Major changes: No major change has been recorded in the Qatari ground forces. The Qatari Air Force received the first of its 12 Mirage 2000 combat aircraft. The Navy received two more Vosper Thornycroft ''Barzan-class'' missile patrol boats.

Order-of-Battle

Year	1993	1994	1995	1996	1997
General data					
• Personnel (regular)	8,200	8,200	10,300	10,300	11,800
• Number of brigades					1
• Number of regiments	6	6	1	1	1
• Total number of battalions	7	7	7	7	11
Ground Forces					
• Tanks	24	24	24	24	24
• APCs/ARVs	245	245	310	310	230 (310)
• Artillery (incl. MRLs)	30	30	37	37	52
Air Force					
• Combat aircraft	17	14	14	14	9
• Transport aircraft	7	7	7	7	8
• Helicopters	45	41	41	41	32
Air Defense Forces					
• Light SAM launchers	32	32	32	29	48
Navy					
• Combat vessels	50	50	50	50	51

Note: Beginning with data for 1997, we refer to quantities in active service. The number in parentheses refers to the total.

Personnel

	Regular	Reserves	Total
Ground Forces	8,500		8,500
Air Force	1,500		1,500
Navy (including marine police)	1,800		1,800
Total	**11,800**		**11,800**
Paramilitary			
• Armed police	8,000		

GROUND FORCES

Formations

	Independent brigade/group	Independent battalion	Battalions in brigade
Armored	1		1 arm., 1 mech., 1 art.
Mechanized		4	
Royal Guard	1		3 inf. batt.
Special Forces		1	
Artillery		2	
Total	**2**	**7**	

Tanks

Model	Quantity	In service	Since	Notes
Medium and low quality				
• AMX-30	24	24		
Total	**24**	**24**		
On order				
• Challenger				Under negotiation
• Leclerc	50–100			Under negotiation

APCs/ARVs

Model	Quantity	In service	Since	Notes
High quality				
• AMX-10P/RC/VTT	45	45	1980	
• VAB	158	158	1978	
• VPM 81	4	4		Mortar carrier
• V-150 Commando	8	8		
Subtotal	215	215		
Others				
• Engesa EE-9	20		1978	
• Fahd	10	6–10		
• Ferret	10		1968	
• Saracen	25	6		
• Saladin	30		1970	
Subtotal	95	15		
Total	**310**	**230**		

APCs/ARVs *(continued)*

Model	Quantity	In service	Since	Notes
On order				
• GKN Piranha	48			
• VAB				
• Fahd				

Artillery

Model	Quantity	In service	Since	Notes
Self-propelled guns and howitzers				
• 155mm Mk F-3 (AMX)	22	22	1992	
Towed guns and howitzers				
• 155mm G-5	12	12	1991	
Mortars, under 160mm				
• 120mm Brandt	15	15		
Total	49	49		
MRLs				
• 122mm BM-21				
• 127mm or 180mm SS-30 or SS-40 Astros II	3	3		
Total	52	52		
On order				
• 155mm Mk F-3 SP howitzers				Undergoing upgrading (unconfirmed)

Antitank Weapons

Model	Quantity	In service	Since	Notes
Missiles				
• HOT	48	48		24 are maunted on VAB
• MILAN	60–100	60–100		
Guns				
• 84mm Carl Gustav light recoilless rifle				

AIR FORCE

Order-of-Battle

Model	Quantity	In service	Notes
• Combat	9	9	
• Transport	8	8	
• Helicopters	32	32	

Combat Aircraft

Model	Quantity	In service	Since	Notes
Strike and multirole aircraft—medium and low quality				
• Mirage 2000-5	3	3	1997	Delivery of 12 aircraft commenced
• Mirage F-1E/B	6	6	1984	To be sold—7 planes already sold to Spain
Total	**9**	**9**		
On order				
• Mirage-2000-5	12			Being delivered

Transport Aircraft

Model	Quantity	In service	Since	Notes
• Boeing 707	2	2	1977	
• Airbus 340	1	1	1993	
• Boeing 727	1	1	1979	
• Britten-Norman BN-2 Islander	1	1		
• Mystere-Falcon 900	3	3	1991	
Total	**8**	**8**		

Training and Liaison Aircraft

Model	Quanity	In service	Since	Notes
With ground attack/close air support capability				
• Alpha jet	6	6	1980	
Total	**6**	**6**		
On order				
• Hawk 100	15–18			

Helicopters

Model	Quantity	In service	Since	Notes
Attack				
• SA-342 gazelle	14	14	1983	2 employed as light helicopter with police
Heavy transport				
• Westland Commando mk 2/mk 3	12	12	1982	
Medium transport				
• AS-332 Super Puma/ AS 532 Cougar	6	6		
Total	**32**	**32**		

Miscellaneous Aircraft

Target drones
TTL BTT-3 Banshee: Unconfirmed

Advanced Armament

Air-to-ground missiles: AM-39 Exocet
On order: Mica (50), R-550 Magique 2

Air Force Infrastructure

Military airfields: 2
Doha; Al Ghariyeh

AIR DEFENSE FORCES

Surface-to-Air Missiles (SAMs)

Model	Launchers	Since	Notes
Light missiles			
• Rapier	15		
• Roland 2	9		Number unconfirmed
• Mistral	24		
Total	48		

Surface-to-Air Missiles (SAMs) *(continued)*

Model	Launchers	Since	Notes
Shoulder-launched missiles			
• Blowpipe	6		
• FIM-92A Stinger	12		
Total	18		
On order			
• Shorts Starburst			

NAVY

Combat Vessels

Type	Original Class name	Quantity	Length (m.)/ Displace-ment (t.)	Armament/ special equipment
MFPBs				
• Barzan (new)	Vita Vosper Thornycroft	4	56.3/376	8×MM 40 Excocet SSMs 8×Mistral SAMs 1×76mm gun 1× 30mm gun
• Damsah class	Combattante III	3	56/345	8× MM 40 Exco-cet SSMs 1× 76mm gun 2× 40mm guns 4× 30mm guns
Subtotal		7		
Patrol craft				
• Barzan (old) class	Vosper Thornycroft	4	33.5/120	4× 30mm guns
• Helmatic		3	16/20	
• Damen	Polycat 1450	6	14.5/18	1× 20mm gun
• Keith Nelson class		2	13.5/13	1× 12.7mm MG with police
• MV-45		4	14.5/17	1× 20mm gun with police
• Fairey Marine Spear class		20	9.1/4.3	
• P-1200		4	11.9/4.3	with police
Subtotal		44		
Total		**51**		

Landing Craft

Type	Original Class name	Quantity	Length (m.)/ Displace- ment (t.)	Armament/ special equipment
• Rabha LCT		1	48.8/—	3 tanks or 110 troops

Coastal Defense

Type	Batteries	Notes
• MM-40 Exocet	3–4	

Naval Infrastructure

Naval Bases: Doha, Halul Island

15. SAUDI ARABIA

GENERAL DATA

Official Name of the State: The Kingdom of Saudi Arabia

Head of State: King Fahd ibn Abd al-Aziz al-Saud (also Prime Minister)

First Deputy Prime Minister and Heir Apparent: Crown Prince Abdallah ibn Abd al-Aziz al-Saud (also Commander of the National Guard)

Defense and Aviation Minister: Prince Sultan ibn Abd al-Aziz al-Saud (also Second Deputy Prime Minister)

Chief of General Staff: General Salih ibn Ali al-Muhaya

Commander of the Ground Forces: Lieutenant General Sultan ibn Ali Al-Mutayri

Commander of the Air Force: Lieutenant General 'Abd al-'Aziz ibn Muhammad Hunaydi

Commander of the Air Defense Forces: Lieutenant Gernal Majid ibn Talhab al-Qutaibi

Commander of the Navy: Vice Admiral Talal ibn Salem al-Mufadhi

Area: 2,331,000 sq. km. (approximation; some borders undefined or undemarcated)

Population: 18,510,000

Demography

Ethnic Groups		
Arabs	16,918,000	91.4%
Afro-Arabs	925,000	5.0%
Others	666,000	3.6%
Religious Groups		
Sunni Muslims	17,048,000	92.1%
Shi'ite Muslims	925,000	5.0%
Others (mainly Christians)	537,000	2.9%
Nationality Subdivision		
Saudis	13,457,000	72.7%
Others	5,053,000	27.3%

Economic Data

		1992	1993	1994	1995	1996
GDP current price, local currency	SR bn	461.40	443.80	450.10	468.40	509.3
GDP (U.S. $)	$ bn	123.20	118.50	120.19	125.07	135.99
GDP per capita	$	7,290	6,930	6,868	6,910	7,346
Real GDP growth	%	2.8	–0.6	0.5	–0.8	2.3
Balance of payments						
• Exports fob	$ bn	50.3	42.4	41.8	50.0	56.7
• Imports fob	$ bn	30.2	25.9	21.3	25.7	25.4
• Account balance (includes services and income)	$ bn	–17.7	–17.3	–9.1	–5.5	0.2
• External debt	$ bn	NA	NA	NA	NA	NA
Government income and expenditure						
• Revenues, local currency	SR bn	169.6	141.4	129.0	135.0	132.0
• Expenditures, local currency	SR bn	211.3	187.9	171.1	150.0	150.0
• Defense expenditures	SR bn	57.601	61.692	53.549	50.600	45.300
• Defense expenditure/GDP	%	12.48	13.90	11.90	10.80	8.89
• Defense expenditure/CGE	%	27.26	32.83	31.30	33.73	30.2
• Population	m	16.9	17.1	17.5	18.1	18.51
• Official exchange rate	SR: $1	3.745	3.745	3.745	3.745	3.745

Sources: EIU quarterly report, EIU country profile, IMF statistical yearbook, SIPRI Yearbook

Arms Procurement and Security Assistance Received

Country	Type	Details
Belgium	• Arms transfers	Turrets for LAV APCs
Britain	• Arms transfers	Combat aircraft, trainer aircraft, helicopters, minesweepers, mortars, ARM missiles
	• Military training	Foreign advisers/instructors/serving personnel; trainees abroad
Canada	• Arms transfers	LAV APCs/ARVs
Egypt	• Military training	Foreign advisers/instructors/serving personnel (on individual basis, unconfirmed), trainees abroad (unconfirmed)
France	• Arms transfers	Radars, SAMs, SP artillery, antiship AGMs, upgrading SAMs and missile frigates
	• Military training	Foreign advisers/instructors/serving personnel; trainees abroad for Cougar helicopters
	• Maintenance aid	Naval vessels
India	• Military training	Foreign advisers/instructors/serving personnel
PRC	• Military training	Foreign advisers/instructors/serving personnel for CSS-2 missiles

Arms Procurement and Security Assistance Received *(continued)*

Country	Type	Details
Sweden	• Arms transfers	Early warning system for GCC countries
Switzerland	• Arms transfers	Trainer aircraft coproduced with Britain
U.S.A.	• Arms transfers	AAMs, AGMs, ATGMs, artillery pieces, combat aircraft, helicopters, aircraft engines, SAMs, tanks, transport aircraft, aircraft simulators, integration of air defense system, radio systems, surveillance radars
	• Military training	Foreign advisers/instructors/serving personnel; trainees abroad

Arms Sales and Security Assistance Extended

Country	Type	Details
Bosnia	• Arms transfers	Chinese-made small arms; 26 Russian MI-8 helicopters; French-made Crotale/Shahine SAMs, Rapier SAMs, Stinger SAMs
	• Financial aid	Grant
GCC Peninsula Shield Force	• Facilities	7,000–10,000 man at Hafr al-Batin; mostly Saudis, others from GCC forces except Qatar
Lebanon	• Financial aid	$60 million grant in 1991 and additional grant in 1992
Palestinian Authority	• Financial aid	In 1994 a commitment was made to donate $100 million to the Palestinian Authority in Gaza and Jericho
Syria	• Financial aid	Grants (with other GCC countries)
U.S.A.	• Facilities	HQ at Riyadh, AWACS a/c, U-2 a/c at Taif, approx. 48 F-16s and F-15s at Dhahran with C-130, F-111 EW a/c, and KC-135

Foreign Military Cooperation

	Details
• Joint maneuvers	Britain, Egypt (1997), France, GCC countries, Pakistan, U.S.A.

Defense Production

	M	P	A
Ground forces equipment			
• G-3 ARs		√	
• Small arms ammunition, electronic components	√		
• "Peninsula Shield" APCs	√		
Aircraft and air ammunition			
• Some accessories and components for foreign-made aircraft, flares, and chaff		√	
Electronics			
• Radio transceivers, components of a/c radars, parts for EW equipment			√

Note: M=Manufacture (indigenously developed)
P=Production under license
A=Assembly

NBC Technology

CW capabilities

- Personal protective equipment; decontamination units; U.S.-made CAM chemical detection systems; Fuchs (Fox) ABC detection vehicles

ARMED FORCES

Major changes: The Saudi ground forces are assimilating their newly acquired M-1A1 "Abrams" MBTs and their "Bradley" APCs. The National Guard has deployed its LAV-25 APCs. The Saudi Air Force received its first F-15S combat aircraft, and some more Tornado combat aircraft. The Saudi Navy received another F-2000 frigate from France.

Order-of-Battle

Year	1993	1994	1995	1996	1997
General data					
• Personnel (regular)	125,000–130,000	126,000–136,000	132,000	161,000	159,000
• Number of brigades	15	17	18	18	18
• Number of battalions	20	20	20	20	20
Ground forces					
• Tanks	700	700	900	1,015	865 (1,015)
• APCs/ARVs	3,000	3,400	4,040	4,050–4,100	5,220

Order-of-Battle *(continued)*

Year	1993	1994	1995	1996	1997
• Artillery incl. MRLs	770	770	770	770	405 (575)
• SSM launchers	8–12	8–12	8–12	8–12	8–12
Air Force					
• Combat aircraft	273	270	250	249	322
• Transport aircraft	108	108	77	76	61
• Helicopters	145	171	180	180	175
Air Defense Forces					
• Heavy SAM batteries	17	23	23	23	23
• Medium SAM batteries	+	16	16	16	16
Navy					
• Combat vessels	75	108	109	129	116

Note: Beginning with data for 1997, we refer to quantities in active service. The number in parentheses refers to the total.

Personnel

	Regular	Reserves	Total
Ground Forces	70,000		70,000
Air Force	20,000		20,000
Air Defense	4,000		4,000
Navy (including a marine unit)	12,000		12,000
National Guard	57,000	20,000	77,000
Royal Guard	2,000		2,000
Total	**165,000**	**20,000**	**185,000**
Paramilitary			
• Mujahidun (affiliated with national guard)			30,000
• Coast Guard	4,500		4,500
• Frontier corps	10,500		10,500
Total	**15,000**	**45,000**	

Note: Coast Guard separated from Frontier Corps in 1992.

GROUND FORCES

Formations (Ground Forces and National Guard)

	Independent brigade/group	Independent battalion
Armored (Ground Forces)	3	
Mechanized (5 Ground Forces, 3 Nat. Guard)	8	
Infantry (Royal Guard)	1	
Infantry (National Guard)	5	19
Marines		1
Airborne/Special Forces (Ground Forces)	1	
Independent infantry battalions		
Total	**18**	**20**

Note: Saudi ground forces comprises 9 brigades (5 mechanized, 3 armored, 1 airborne/infantry), plus one royal guard brigade; the national guard has 8 brigades (3 mechanized, 5 infantry)

Tanks

Model	Quantity	In service	Since	Notes
High quality				
• M-1 A2	315	315	1993	
• M-60 A3	400	400	1985	
Subtotal	715	715		
Others				
• AMX-30	300	150	1975	150 in store
Total	**1,015**	**865**		

APCs/ARVs (including command vehicles)

Model	Quantity	In service	Since	Notes
High quality				
• AMX-10/AMX-10P	500	500	1975	
• LAV-25 and other models of LAV/ PIRANHA	1,000	1,000	1992	

APCs/ARVs (including command vehicles) *(continued)*

Model	Quantity	In service	Since	Notes
• M-2/M-3 Bradley	400	400		
• M-113 A1/A2	1,600	1,600	1976/ 1981	
• V-150 Commando	980	980	1977	Number unconfirmed
• Engesa EE-11 Urutu	some	some		
Subtotal	4,480	4,480		
Others				
• AML-60/90	200–250	200–250	1969	
• BMR-600	140	140	1985	With marines
• Fox/Ferret	200	200		Possibly phased out
• M-3 (Panhard)	150	150		
• Peninsula Shield	few	few		Domestically built
Subtotal	740	740		
Total	**5,220**	**5,220**		
On order				
• LAV-25/Piranha and other LAV	some 500			some 600 of 1,117 already supplied
• Peninsula Shield	50			Initial order for 50 is to be followed by a second order for 150

Artillery

Model	Quantity	In service	Since	Notes
Self-propelled guns and howtizers				
• 155mm M-109A2 SP	110	110		
• 155mm GCT SP	51	51		
Towed guns and howitzers				
• 155mm FH-70	72	0		In storage
• 155mm M-198	60	60	1982	
• 155mm M-114	50	50		
• 105mm M-102 Pack howitzer and 105mm M-101	100	0		In storage
Mortars, under 160mm				
• 120mm TDA rifled mortar, SP	73	73		
• 107mm (4.2") M-30 mortar				
Total	516	344		

Artillery *(continued)*

Model	Quantity	In service	Since	Notes
Artillery/mortar-locating radars				
• AN/TPQ-37				
MRLs				
• 180mm SS-40 Astros II }				
• 127mm SS-30 Astros II	60	60		
Total		**10 batteries**		**approx. 60 launchers**

Logistic and Engineering Equipment

- M-123 Viper minefield crossing system, MK 3 (D) Flail, M-69 A1 bridging tanks, bridging equipment, AFV transporters (600)

Antitank Weapons

Model	Quantity	In service	Since	Notes
Missiles				
• AMX-10P SP (carrying HOT)			1982	
• BGM-71C Improved TOW/BGM-71D TOW II			1988	
• M-47 Dragon	1,000	1,000	1977	
Total	1,500 launchers	1,500 launchers		
Guns				
• 106mm M-40 recoilless rifle	50	50		
• 84mm Carl Gustav light recoilless rifle	300	300		
On order				
• BGM-71D	2,000	2,000		TOW II, possibly BGM-71F TOW IIA

Surface-to-Surface Missiles and Rockets

Model	Launchers	Missiles	Since	Notes
• CSS-2 SSM (DF-3, East Wind, IRBM)	8–12	30–50	1988	No. of launchers unconfirmed

AIR FORCE

Order-of-Battle

Model	Quantity	In service	Notes
• Combat	322	322	
• Transport	61	61	
• Helicopters	175	175	

Combat Aircraft

Model	Number	In service	Since	Notes
Interceptors—high quality				
• F-15 C/D Eagle	91	91	1982	
• Tornado ADV (F Mk 3	24	24	1989	
Subtotal	115	115		
Strike and multirole aircraft—high quality				
• F-15S	25	25	1995	75 aircraft were ordered
• Tornado IDS (GR Mk 1/GR-1A reconn. a/c)	93	93	1986	
Subtotal	118	118		
Strike and multirole aircraft—medium and low quality				
• F-5E/F	approx. 64	approx. 64		
• F-5A/B	15	15		Mostly employed as trainer a/c
• RF-5E	10	10		
Subtotal	89	89		
Total	207	207		
Total	**322**	**322**		
On order				
• F-15S	72			Delivery 1998–99 (25 supplied)

Transport Aircraft

Model	Quantity	In service	Since	Notes
• C-130E/H Hercules	46	46	1980	
• CN-235	4	4	1987	
• Gulfstream III	1	1	1983	
• Learjet 35	2	2	1981	Employed in target-towing role
• Mystère-Falcon 20	2	2		
• VC-140 JetStar	2	2	1969	
• HS-125	4	4		
Total	**61**	**61**		

Training and Liaison Aircraft

Model	Quantity	In service	Since	Notes
With ground attack/close air support capabilitiy				
• BAC-167 Strikemaster	30	0		Possibly phased out
• Hawk Mk 65	30	30	1987	
Subtotal	60	30		
Others				
• BAe Jetstream 31	2	2	1987	
• Cessna 172 G/H/L	17	17	1967	
• Pilatus PC-9	50	50	1987	
Subtotal	69	69		
Total	**129**	**99**		
On order				
• Hawk 100/200	20			Under negotiation

Helicopters

Model	Quantity	In service	Since	Notes
Attack (part of ground forces aviation)				
• OH-58D (AHIP)	15	15		Combat Scout
• AH-64A Apache	12	12	1993	
Subtotal	27	27		
Maritime attack				
• AS-365 Dauphin 2/ AS-565MA	27	27	1986	Including small number medical evacuation role
• AS-332 Super Puma	11	11		
Subtotal	38	38		

Helicopters *(continued)*

Model	Quantity	In service	Since	Notes
Heavy transport				
• SH-3 (AS-61A)	3	3		
• KV-107/KV-107 IIA	17	17		
Subtotal	20	20		
Medium transport				
• AB-212/Bell-205	25	25	1977	Number unconfirmed
• Bell 406CS	15	15	1990	
• UH-60A Black Hawk/Desert Hawk/ Medevac	20	20	1990	
Subtotal	60	60		
Light transport				
• AB-206 JetRanger	30	30	1967	
Total	**175**	**175**		
On order				
• British helicopters	80–88			Reportedly WS-70 (UH-60A) or EH-101
• AH-64A	12–24			Under negotiation
• AS-532 Cougar	12			

Miscellaneous Aircraft

Model	Quantity	In service	Since	Notes
AEW/AWACS aircraft				
• E-3A AWACS	5	5	1986	
Tankers				
• KC-130H	7	7	1973	
• KE-3/Boeing 707	8	8	1986	
Target drones				
• TTL BTT-3 Banshee				
• MQM-74C Chukar II UAV				

Advanced Armament

Air-to-air-missiles

- AIM-7F Sparrow (770); AIM-9J/P Sidewinder; AIM-9L/M Sidewinder (1,700); Red Top; Sky Flash

Air-to-ground missiles
- AGM-65A Maverick (2,400); AS-15TT antiship missile; Sea Egale antiship missile

Bombs
- Laser-guided bombs (3,000); CBU (1,000); BL-755 CBU; JP-233 antirunway bombs; Paveway II laser guided

On order
- AS-15TT; AIM-7M AAMs; AIM-9M AAMs; AIM-9S AAMs; AIM-9L AAMs; AIM-9P-4 AAMs; ALARM antiradiation missiles; AM-39 Exocet; AGM-65 AGMs (partly AGM-65D/G); CBU-86; CBU-87; GBU-10/12/15

Air Force Infrastructure

Aircraft shelters:	
for combat aircraft	
Military airfields:	**20–24**

Abqaiq, al-Ahsa, al-Sulayyil, Dhahran, al-Hufuf, Jidda, Jubail, Khamis Mushayt, al-Kharj, Medina, Riyadh, Sharawra, Tabuk, Taif, Gizan, 6–10 additional airfields.

AIR DEFENSE FORCES

Surface-to-Air Missiles

Model	Batteries	Launchers	Since	Notes
Heavy missiles				
• MIM-104 Patriot	5		1991	
• MIM-23B Improved HAWK	17		1982	One used for training
Total	22			
Medium missiles				
• Crotale }	16	93		Some are sheltered mounted for fixed sites
• Shahine I/II			1981	To be upgraded
Total	16	93		
Shoulder-launched missiles				
• FIM-92A/C Stinger		400	1984	
• MIM-43A Redeye		500		
• Mistral		900		
Total		1,800		
On order				
• FIM-92C Stinger SAMs		50		

Surface-to-Air Missiles *(continued)*

Model	Batteries	Launchers	Since	Notes
• Crotale NG II batteries				
• Mistral SAMs				

Other Air Defense Systems

Model	Quantity	In service	Since	Notes
Air defense systems (missiles, radars and guns)				
• 35mm Skyguard AD system (guns, radars and SAMs)	60	60		
Short-range guns				
• 35mm Oerlikon-Buhrle 35×2 GDF	150	150		
• 20mm M-163 Vulcan SP	72	72		
• 30mm×2 Wildcat SP	52	52		
Total	274	274		
Radars				
• AN/FPS-117 (Seek Igloo)	17	17		
• AN/TPS-43G	28	28		
• AN/TPS-59				
• AN/TPS-63	35	35		
Command and control system				
• C³I Peace Shield System				Currently installed
Aerostat with airborne radars				
• LASS				Small number

NAVY

Combat Vessels

Type	Original Class name	Quantity	Length (m.)/ Displace-ment (t.)	Armament/ special equipment
Missile frigates				
• Madina class	F-2000	4	115.0/2,000	In process of up-grading 1×SA–365 heli-copter 8×Otomat SSMs 1×8 Crotale Naval 1×100mm gun 4×40mm guns 4×533mm torpedo tubes
Missile corvettes				
• Badr class	PCG-1 class (Tacoma Boat-building)	4	74.7/870	8×Harpoon 1×76mm gun 2×20mm AA guns 1×20mm Phalanx 6×324mm torpedo tubes
MFPBs				
• Al Siddiq	PGG-1 class (Peterson Builders)	9	58.1/425	4×Harpoon 1×76mm gun 2×20mm AA guns 1×20mm Phalanx
Mine warfare vessels				
• Addriyah	MSC-322 class minesweeper	4	46.6/320	1×20mm AA gun magnetic sweep-ers
• Al Jawf	Sandown class	3	52.7/450	2×30mm guns ECA mine dis-posal system 2 PAP 104 Mk. 5
Subtotal		7		
Patrol craft (Mostly with coast guard)				
• Al-Jubatel	Abeking-Rasmussen	2	26.2/96	1×20mm gun (with coast guard)

Combat Vessels *(continued)*

Type	Original Class name	Quantity	Length (m.)/ Displace-ment (t.)	Armament/ special equipment
• Al Jouf	Blohm & Voss	4	38.6/210	2×20mm guns (with coast guard)
• Halter type		17	23.8/56	2×25mm guns
• Rapier class		12	15.2/26	light armament (with coast guard)
• Sea guard		2	22.5/56	2×MM-15TT SSM 2×20mm guns (with coast guard)
• Simonneau type 51		40	15.8/22	1×20mm gun
• Skorpion class		15	17.0/33	light armament (with coast guard)
Subtotal		92		
Total		**116**		
On order				
• Lafayette-class frigates	Type 3000	2	128/4,100	Delivery in 1999 and 2002 1×AS 365 helicopter 8×MM40 SSMs 8×Crotale Naval 1×100mm gun 2×20mm guns
• Sandown class mine sweepers		3		

Note: Coast Guard has some 650 small patrol craft.

Landing Craft

Type	Original Class name	Quantity	Length (m.)/ Displace-ment (t.)	Armament/ special equipment
• LCM-6 class		4	17.1/62	34 tons or 80 troops

Landing Craft *(continued)*

Type	Original Class name	Quantity	Length (m.)/ Displace-ment (t.)	Armament/ special equipment
• Slingsby SAH 2200 hovercraft		16	10.6/	2.2 tons or 24 troops with coast guard
• US LCU 1610 class LCU		4	41.1/375	170 tons or 120 troops
Total		**24**		
On order				
• Slingsby SAH 2200 hovercraft		4		

Auxiliary Vessels

Type	Original Class name	Quantity	Length (m.)/ Displace-ment (t.)	Armament/ special equipment
• Tabouk training ship		1	60/585	1×20mm gun
• Dammam	Jaguar class	3	42.5/160	ex-gunboat now used for training
• Royal yacht, 1,450 dwt		1		
• Royal yacht, 670 tons		1		
• Royal yacht al-Yamama		1		
• Royal yacht, 112-ton		1		
• Royal yacht Pegasus		1		
• Durance class tanker		2	135.0/ 11,200	4×40mm guns 2 helicopter pads
• Ocean tugs, 680 tons		3		
• Coastal tugs		13		
• Small tankers		3	28.7/233	
• Training ship		1	21.4/75	With coast guard

Auxiliary Vessels *(continued)*

Type	Original Class name	Quantity	Length (m.)/ Displace-ment (t.)	Armament/ special equipment
• Brooke Marine-firefighting craft		1	24.5/82	Firefighting with coast guard

Coastal Defense

Type	Quantity	Notes
• OTOMAT coastal defense missile	4	

Naval Infrastructure

Naval bases (Including Coast Guard): 13
- al-Dammam, Aziziya (Coast Guard), al-Haql (Coast Guard), Jidda, Jizan, Jubayl, Makna (Coast Guard), al-Qatif, Ras al-Mishaab, Ras Tanura, al-Sharma, al-Wajh, Yanbu

Ship maintenance and repair facilities:
- Repair of vessels, dependent on foreign experts; 22,000-ton and 62,000-ton floating docks at Dammam; 45,000-ton and 16,000-ton floating docks at Jidda

16. SUDAN

GENERAL DATA

Official Name of the State: The Republic of Sudan
Head of State: President Lieutenant General Omar Hassan Ahmad al-Bashir
Speaker of Parliament and Secretary General of the National Islamic Front: Hassan Abdallah al-Tourabi (political and religious leader)
Defense Minister: Hassan Abd al-Rahman Ali
Chief of the General Staff: Lieutenant General Said Hamed Siraj
Commander of the Air Force: Major General Ali Mahjoub Mardi
Commander of the Navy: Commodore Abbas al-Said Othman

Area: 2,504,530 sq. km. (dispute with Egypt over the ''Halaib triangle'' area; the government has no effective control over part of the south)
Population: 30,700,000

Demography

Ethnic Groups (exact percentages not known)
Arabs
Nilotics, Negroes, and others
Religious Groups
Sunni Muslims
Animists
Christians (Coptic, Greek Orthodox, Catholic, Protestant)

Economic Data

		1992	1993	1994	1995	1996
GDP current price, local currency	S£ bn	461.7	978.8	3,013.5	5,282.7	13,197.7
GDP (U.S. $)	$ bn	4.73	6.143	10.40	8.62	10.55
GDP per capita	$	182	230	378	304	343
Real GDP growth	%	6.4	0.0	2.0	4.5	4.5
Balance of payments						
• Exports fob	$ m	213	214	257	556	620
• Imports fob	$ m	810	833	840	1,066	1,340

Economic Data *(continued)*

		1992	1993	1994	1995	1996
• Account balance (Includes services and income)	$m	–506.2	–202.2	–600.3	–500.0	–827.0
• External debt	$ bn	16.09	16.56	17.71	18.51	18.1
Government income and expenditure						
• Revenues, local currency	S£ bn	34	78.2	130.8	365.4	679.6
• Expenditures, local currency	S£ bn	118.4	260.1	369.3	1,005.0	2,377.1
• Defense expenditures	S£ bn	13.75	29.50	49.90	51.25	NA
• Defense expenditure/ GDP	%	2.97	3.01	1.65	0.97	NA
• Defense expenditure/ CGE	%	11.61	11.34	13.5	5.09	NA
• Population	m	25.92	26.66	27.47	28.28	30.7
• Official exchange rate (AV)	S£: $1	97.43	159.31	289.61	612.5	1,250.0

Sources: EIU quarterly report, EIU country profile, IMF statistical yearbook, SIPRI Yearbook.

Arms Procurement and Security Assistance Received

Country	Type	Details
Iran	• *Arms transfers*	Small arms, ammunition, EW equipment, vehicles, spare parts for Soviet and Chinese arms, tanks, aircrafts, allegedly CW (1997)
	• *Financial aid*	Grant and loan (approx. $300 million)
	• *Military training*	Technicians and IRGC; trainees abroad
Kyrgyzstan	• *Arms transfers*	Combat helicopter (1997)
PRC	• *Arms transfers*	Combat aircraft (1996)

Arms Sales and Security Assistance Extended

Country	Type	Details
Iran	• *Facilities*	Iranian IRGC, and facilities to Iranian ships at Port Sudan
Lebanon	• *Facilities*	Lebanese militia, camps with the popular defense forces

NBC Technology

CW capabilities

- Personal protective equipment; unit decontamination equipment. Alleged CW from Iran unsubstantiated

ARMED FORCES

Major changes: No major change has been recorded in the Sudanese armed forces in 1997.

Order-of-Battle

Year	1993	1994	1995	1996	1997
General data					
• Personnel	76,500	86,500	86,500	86,500	84,500
• Divisions	10	10	10	10	8
• Number of brigades	30	+	+	+	25
Ground Forces					
• Tanks	430–480	450–500	450	450	290–340
• APCs/ARVs	950	950	950	950	547 (686)
• Artillery (incl. MRLs)	200–250	360	360	360	753 (765)
Air Force					
• Combat aircraft	59	66	45	45	38 (54)
• Transport aircraft	24	24	25	25	27
• Helicopters	59	61	53	53	57 (67)
Air Defense Forces					
• Heavy SAM batteries	5	5	5	5	5
Navy					
• Combat vessels	10	10	10	23	22

Note: Beginning with data for 1997, we refer to quantities in active service. The number in parentheses refers to the total.

Personnel

	Regular	Reserves	Total
Ground Forces	80,000		80,000
Air Force	3,000		3,000
Navy	1,500		1,500
Total	**84,500**		**84,500**

Personnel *(continued)*

	Regular	Reserves	Total
Paramilitary			
• People's Defense Forces (loyal to Hassan Tourabi)	15,000	85,000	100,000
• Border guard	2,500		2,500

GROUND FORCES

Formations

	Divisions	Independent brigades/groups
Armored	1	
Mechanized		1
Infantry	6	24
Airborne	1	
Artillery		3
Reconaissance		1
Total	**8**	**29**

Tanks

Model	Quantity	In service	Since	Notes
High quality				
• M-60 A3	20	20	1981	
Others				
• T-55/Type 59 } • T-54	200–250	200–250		Number unconfirmed
• Type 62	70	70	1972	
Subtotal	270–320	270–320		
Total	**290–340**	**290–340**		

APCs/ARVs (including command vehicles)

Model	Quantity	In service	Since	Notes
High quality				
• M-113	80	36	1982	
• V-150 Commando	100	55	1984	
• BMP-2	6	6		
• BRDM 1/2	60	60		

APCs/ARVs (including command vehicles) *(continued)*

Model	Quantity	In service	Since	Notes
• AMX-VCI	small number	+		
Subtotal	246	157		
Others				
• al-Walid	150	100	1986	
• AML-90	5	5		
• BTR-50	20	20	1970	
• BTR-152	80	80	1960	
• Ferret	60	60	1960	
• Fahd			1989	Unconfirmed
• M-3 (Panhard)			1983	Unconfirmed
• OT-64	55	55		
• OT-62	20	20		
• Saladin	50	50	1961	
Subtotal	440	390		
Total	**686**	**547**		

Artillery

Model	Quantity	In service	Since	Notes
Self-propelled guns and howitzers				
• 155mm Mk F-3 (AMX) SP	10	6	1984	
Towed guns and howitzers				
• 155mm M-114	20	12	1981	
• 130mm Type 59 gun/M-46	75	75		
• 105mm M-101	20	20		
Mortars, under 160mm				
• 120mm	+	+		
Total	125	113		
MRLs				
• 122mm BM-21	90	90		
• 122mm Sakr	50	50		
• 107mm Type 63	500	500		
Total	**765**	**753**		

Antitank Weapons

Model	Quantity	In service	Since	Notes
Missiles				
• BGM-71C Improved TOW	+	+		Not all serviceable
• Swingfire	+	0		Not serviceable
• AT-3 (Sagger)				
Antitank guns				
• 100mm M-1955 field/AT gun				
• 100mm M-1944	50	0		In storage
• 85mm M-1945/D-44 field/AT gun	100	0		In storage
• 76mm M-1942	+	0		
On order				
• 106mm M-40 recoiless	100			

AIR FORCE

Order-of-Battle

Model	Quantity	In service	Notes
• Combat	53–54	37–38	Low serviceability
• Transport	27	27	
• Helicopters	67	55–57	

Combat Aircraft

Model	Quantity	In service	Since	Notes
Interceptors—medium and low quality				
• F-6 Shenyang/J-6	11	11		
• MiG-21 (Fishbed)/ F-7	20	10		
Subtotal	31	21		
Strike and multirole aircraft—medium and low quality				
• A-5 (Fantan)/Q-5	10	10		
• MiG-23	3–4	3–4	1987	
• F-5E/F	9	3	1984/1982	
Subtotal	22–23	16–17		
Total	**53–54**	**37–38**		

Transport Aircraft

Model	Quantity	In service	Since	Notes
• AN-24 (Coke)/An-26	7	7		
• C-130H Hercules	4	4	1978	
• DHC-5D Buffalo	3	3	1978	
• Fokker F-27	1	1		
• Mystère-Falcon 50	1	1	1983	
• Mystère-Falcon 20	1	1	1978	
• C-212	4	4		
• EMB-110P	6	6		
Total	**27**	**27**		

Training and Liaison Aircraft

Model	Quantity	In service	Since	Notes
With ground attack/close air support capability				
• BAC-145 Jet Provost	5	5		
• BAC-167 Strikemaster	5	3		
Total	**10**	**8**		

Helicopters

Model	Quantity	In service	Since	Notes
Attack				
• Mi-24	4	+		
Medium transport				
• Mi-4 (Hound)	3	3		Possibly phased out
• Mi-8 (Hip)	14	6–8		
• SA-330 Puma/IAR-330 Puma	10	10	1985	
• Bell 212/AB-212	5	5	1982	
• AB-412	10	10		
Subtotal	42	36		
Light transport				
• MBB BO-105	18	18	1980	Some serving police
• Bell 206	3	3		
Subtotal	21	21		
Total	**67**	**55–57**		

Helicopters *(continued)*

Model	Quantity	In service	Since	Notes
On order				
• Helicopters from Russia				

Advanced Armament

Air-to-air-missiles
• AA-2 (Atoll)

Air Force Infrastructure

Military airfields: 13
Atbara, al-Fasher, al-Geneina, Juba, Khartoum, Malakal, Merowe, al-Obeid, Port Sudan, Port Sudan (new), Wad Medani, Wadi Sayidina, Wau

AIR DEFENSE FORCES

Surface-to-Air Missiles

Model	Batteries	Launchers	Since	Notes
Heavy missiles				
• SA-2 (Guideline)	5			
Shoulder-launched missiles				
• SA-7 (Grail)		250		
• MIM-43A Redeye		25	1984	
Total		**275**		

Other Air Defense Systems

Model	Quantity	In service	Since	Notes
Short-range guns				
• 40mm	60	60		
• 37mm M-1939	110	110		
• 23mm ZU 23×2	50	50		
• 20mm M-3 VDA	12	12		
• 20mm M-163 A-1 Vulcan SP	8	8	1981	
• 20mm M-167 Vulcan	30	30		
Total	**270**	**270**		

NAVY

Combat Vessels

Type	Original Class name	Quantity	Length (m.)/ Displace- ment (t.)	Armament/ special equipment
Patrol craft				
• Abeking and Rasmussen		2	22.9/70	1×20mm gun YJ-1 SAM
• Ashoora I class		12	8.1/3	
• Sewart class		4	12.9/92	1×7.62mm MG
• Kurmuk	Yugoslav type 15	4	16.9/19.5	1×20mm gun
Total		**22**		

Auxiliary Vessels

Type	Original Class name	Quantity	Length (m.)/ Displace- ment (t.)	Armament/ special equipment
• Small miscellaneous support ships		2		
• Baraka 21 water boat		1		
• Yugoslav supply ships		7	47.3/410	1×20mm gun

Naval Infrastructure

Naval bases: 1
• Port Sudan

NONGOVERNMENTAL MILITARY ORGANIZATIONS

Personnel

	Regular	Reserves	Total	Notes
• Sudan People's Liberation Army (SPLA)	30,000		30,000	The main nongovernmental military organization active in south Sudan

Personnel *(continued)*

	Regular	Reserves	Total	Notes
• South Sudan Independence Movement (SSIM)	10,000		10,000	Also known as SPLA United. In 1996 signed a truce with the government
• Sudan Alliance Forces	1,000–2,000		1,000–2,000	Active in east Sudan
• Beja Congress Forces	500		500	Active in east Sudan
• New Sudan Brigade	2,000		2,000	Recent activity unknown

Equipment

Organization	Category	System	Notes
SPLA	*Tanks*	• T-54/55	
	MRLs	• BM-21	
	Artillery guns	• +	
	Mortars	• 120mm • 60mm	
	Air defense	• SA-7 SAM • 14.5mm AA	

17. SYRIA

GENERAL DATA

Official Name of the State: The Arab Republic of Syria
Head of State: President Hafez al-Assad
Prime Minister: Mahmoud al-Zuabi
Minister of Defense: Lieutenant General Mustafa al-Tlass
Chief of General Staff: General Hikmat Shihabi
Commander of the Air Force: Major-General Muhammad al-Houly
Commander of the Navy: Vice Admiral Wa'il Nasser

Area: 185,180 sq. km.
Population: 14,880,000

Demography

Ethnic Groups		
Arabs	13,437,000	90.3%
Kurds, Armenians, and Others	1,443,000	9.7%
Religious Groups		
Sunni Muslims	11,011,000	74.0%
Alawis, Druze, and Shi'ite Muslims	2,381,000	16.0%
Christians (Greek Orthodox, Gregorian, Armenian, Catholics, Syrian Orthodox, Greek Catholics)	1,488,000	10.0%

Economic Data

		1992	1993	1994	1995	1996
GDP current price, local currency	S£ bn	371.00	434.90	550.60	699.00	695.2
GDP (U.S. $)	$ bn	33.05	38.74	49.05	62.27	61.93
GDP per capita	$	2,550	2,911	3,534	4,349	4,162
Real GDP growth	%	9.6	6.4	6.2	5.8	5.0
Balance of payments						
• Exports fob	$ bn	3.1	3.153	3.555	4	4.298
• Imports fob	$ bn	2.941	3.475	4.57	5.05	4.516
• Account balance (Includes services and income)	$ bn	0.055	–0.607	–0.637	–0.863	0.285
• External debt	$ bn	19	20	20.6	22.2	22.5

Economic Data *(continued)*

		1992	1993	1994	1995	1996
Government income and expenditure						
• Revenues, local currency	S£ bn	NA	123.018	144.162	125.7	156.913
• Expenditures, local currency	S£ bn bn	NA	123.018	144.162	162	188.049
• Defense expenditures	S£ bn	33.412	36.231	36.907	39.98	36.48
• Defense expenditure/ GDP	%	9.01	8.33	6.70	5.7	5.2
• Defense expenditure/ CGE	%	NA	29.45	25.60	24.7	19.3
• Population	m	12.96	13.31	13.88	14.32	14.88
• Official exchange rate	SS£: $1	11.225	11.225	11.225	11.225	11.225

Sources: EIU quarterly report, EIU country profile, IMF statistical yearbook, SIPRI Yearbook.
Note: Economic data is very unreliable. Unrealistic official exchange rate distorts data considerably.

Arms Procurment and Security Assistance Received

Country	Type	Details
Czech Republic	• Arms transfers	T-72MBT (1995)
India	• Arms transfers	Aircraft spare parts; CW chemical components (1996)
Iran	• Financial aid	Promised guarantees for debts to Russia (1997)
	• Arms transfers	Assistance in MBTs upgrade (1997)
North Korea	• Arms transfers	Scud C SSMs (1996), including assistance in production.
Pakistan	• Arms transfers	Trainer aircraft (1994)
PRC	• Advisers	
Russia	• Advisers	approx. 50
	• Arms transfers	No deals have been concluded in past several years
Saudi Arabia and Other GCC Countries	• Financial aid	$350 million promised in 1997

Arms Sales and Security Assistance Extended

Country	Type	Details
Kurds	• Facilities provided	Some facilities also in Syria
Lebanon	• Advisers	

Arms Sales and Security Assistance Extended *(continued)*

Country	Type	Details
	• Military training	approx. 200 trainees annually
	• Arms transfer	T-55 MBTs (1991)
Palestinian "Rejection Front" Organizations	• Financial aid	Grant for Fatah-Intifada, al-Saiqa, PPSF, PLF and PFLP-GC
	• Facilitis provided	Camps

Foreign Military Cooperation

	Details
• Forces deployed abroad in:	Lebanon—25,000 in Biqa', northern Lebanon (Tripoli area), and Beirut

Defense Production

	M	P	A
Army Equipment			
• Ammunition	√		
• Upgrading of tanks		√	
• Production and upgrading of SSMs (in cooperation with North Korea, plant under construction)		√	√
CW and BW:			
• Production of chemical and biological agents, chemical warheads for SSMs	√		

Note: M—Manufacture (indigenously developed)
P—Production under license
A—Assembly

NBC Technology

Nuclear capabilities
- Basic R&D; contract for purchase of a 27-kw research reactor from China; 3-mw research reactor on order from Argentina, deal suspended

CW capabilities
- Personal protective equipment
- Soviet-type unit decontamination equipment
- Stockpiles of nerve gas, including Sarin, mustard gas, VX nerve gas
- Chemical warheads for SSMs
- Chemical armed aerial bombs

Biological warfare capabilities
- Biological weapons and toxins (unconfirmed)

ARMED FORCES

Major changes: No major change has been recorded in the Syrian armed forces in 1997. There have been reports about a major arms deal, but no deal materialized.

Order-of-Battle

Year	1993	1994	1995	1996	1997
General data					
• Personnel (regular)	390,000	390,000	390,000	390,000	380,000
• Divisions	12	12	12	12	12
• Total number of brigades	55	59	59	59	68
Ground Forces					
• Tanks	4,800	4,800	4,800	4,800	3,700 (4,800)
• APCs/ARVs	4,980	4,980	4,980	4,980	4,980
• Artillery (incl. MRLs)	2,500	2,500	2,500	2,500	3,000 (2,600)
• Surface-to-surface launchers	60	62	62	62	62
Air Force					
• Combat aircraft	530	515	515	515	520
• Transport aircraft	23	23	23	23	23
• Helicopters	285	285	285	285	295
Air Defense Forces					
• Heavy SAM batteries	108	108	108	108	108
• Medium SAM batteries	70	70	70	70	65
• Light SAM launchers	+	+	+	+	55
Navy					
• Combat vessels	38	48	48	48	33 (38)
• Submarines	3	3	3	3	0 (3)

Note: Beginning with data for 1997, we refer to quantities in active service. The numbers in parentheses refers to the total.

Personnel

	Regular	Reserves	Total
Ground Forces	306,000	100,000	406,000
Air Force	30,000	10,000	40,000
Air Defense	40,000	20,000	60,000
Navy	4,000	2,500	6,500
Total	**380,000**	**132,500**	**512,500**
Paramilitary			
• Gendarmerie	8,000		8,000
• Workers' Militia		400,000	400,000

Note: Syria can mobilize 750,000 reserves, not organized in units.

GROUND FORCES

Formations

	Corps	Divisions	Independent brigade/ group	Brigades in division
All arms	3			
Armored		7	1	3 arm., 1 mech., 1 art. each
Mechanized		3	1	2 mech., 2 arm., 1 art. each
Infantry/ Special forces		1	3	
Republican Guard		1		3 arm., 1 mech., 1 art. each
Airborne/ Special forces			8–10	
Artillery			2	
SSM forces			3	
Antitank/infantry			2	
Total	**3**	**12**	**20–22**	

Note: One armored division is a reserve unit.

Tanks

Model	Quantity	In service	Since	Notes
High quality				
• T-72/T-72M	1,500–1,600	1,500–1,600	1979/1993	
Others				
• T-62	1,000	1,000	1974	
• T-55/T-54	2,200–2,300	1,100	1957	some upgraded
Subtotal	3,200–3,300	2,100		
Total	**approx. 4,800**	**approx. 3,700**		

Note: 1,200 older models in storage

APCs/ARVs

Model	Quantity	In service	Since	Notes
High quality				
• BMP-1	2,450	2,450		
• BMP-2	approx. 70	approx. 70		
Subtotal	2,520	2,520		

APCs/ARVs *(continued)*

Model	Quantity	In service	Since	Notes
Others				
• BTR-152	560	560	1967	
• BTR-40/50/60	1,000	1,000	1956	
• BRDM-2	900	900		
Subtotal	2,460	2,460		
Total	**4,980**	**4,980**		

Artillery

Model	Quantity	In service	Since	Notes
Self-propelled guns and howitzers				
• 152mm 2S3	50	50		
• 122mm 2S1	400	400		
• 122mm D30	55	55		Syrian
Towed guns and howitzers				
• 180mm S-23	10	10		
• 152mm M-1943	50	50		
• 152mm D-20	20	20		
• 130mm M-46	800	800		
• 122mm D-30	500	500		
• 122mm D-74	400			In storage
• 122mm M-1938	150	150		
Mortars, over 160mm				
• 240mm	10	10		
• 160mm	80	80		
Mortars, under 160mm				
• 120mm				
Total	**approx. 2,500**	**approx. 2,100**		
MRLs				
• 122mm BM-21	250	250		
• 107mm Type 63	200	200		
Total	**450**	**450**		

Logistic and Engineering Equipment

MTU-67 bridging tank/MT-55 bridging tanks (approx. 90), tank-towed bridges, mine-clearing rollers, AFV transporters (800).

Antitank Weapons

Model	Quantity	In service	Since	Notes
Missiles				
• AT-4 (Spigot)	150	150	1980	
• AT-5 (Spandrel)	40	40		
• AT-3 (Sagger) SP	3,000	3,000		Mounted on BRDM-2 and BMP-1
• MILAN	200	200	1984	
Total	**3,390**	**3,390**		

Surface-to-Surface Missiles and Rockets

Model	Launchers	Missiles	Since	Notes
• FROG-7	18		1973	
• SS-1 (Scud B)	18	200		
• SS-1 (Scud C variant from North Korea)	8	60	1992	
• SS-21 (Scarab)	18		1983	
Total	**62**			

AIR FORCE

Order-of-Battle

Model	Quantity	In service	Notes
• Combat	520	520	
• Transport	25	23	
• Helicopters	295	295	

Combat Aircraft

Model	Quantity	In service	Since	Notes
Interceptors—high quality				
• MiG-25 (Foxbat)	35	35	1980	
• MiG-29 (Fulcrum)	20	20	1987	Multirole, employed as interceptor
Subtotal	55	55		

Combat Aircraft *(continued)*

Model	Quantity	In service	Since	Notes
Interceptors—others				
• MiG-21 MF/bis/U (Fishbed)	200–210	200–210		Possibly some upgraded
• MiG-23 ML/MF/MS	100	100	1974	
Subtotal	310	310		
Total	approx. 365	approx. 365		
Strike and multirole aircraft—high quality				
• Su-24 (Fencer)	20	20	1988	
Others				
• MiG-23 U/BN (Flogger)	35	35	1978	
• Su-20/22 (Fitter C/ Fitter D)	100	100	1978	
Subtotal	135	135		
Total	155	155		
Total	**520**	**520**		
On order				
Su-24 (Fencer), MiG-29 (Fulcrum), Su-27				

Transport Aircraft

Model	Quantity	In service	Since	Notes
• An-24/26 (Coke/ Curl)	6	6		
• IL-76 (Candid)	4	4		
• Tu-134	2	2		
• Mystère-Falcon 20/ 900	5	3		
• Piper Navajo	2	2		
• Yak-40 (Codeing)	6	6		
Total	**25**	**23**		

Training and Liaison Aircraft

Model	Quantity	In service	Since	Notes
With ground attack/close air support capability				
• L-39 Albatross	90	90	1980	

Training and Liaison Aircraft *(continued)*

Model	Quantity	In service	Since	Notes
Others				
• MBB 223 Flamingo	40	40		
• Mushshak	6	6	1994	
Subtotal	46	46		
Total	**136**	**136**		

Helicopters

Model	Quantity	In service	Since	Notes
Attack				
• Mi-25 (Hind)	55	55	1980	
• SA-342 Gazelle	45	45	1976	
Subtotal	100	100		
Medium transport				
• Mi-8/Mi-17 (Hip H)	160	160		
• Mi-2	10	10		Limited serviceability
Subtotal	170	170		
ASW				
• Ka-28 (Helix)	5	5		
• Mi-14 (Haze)	20	20		
Subtotal	25	25		
Total	**295**	**295**		

Miscellaneous Aircraft

Model	Quantity	In service	Since	Notes
Reconaissance aircraft MiG-25R	7	7		
UAVs and mini-UAVs				
• Shmel/Malachit				
On order				
Malachit/Pchela-1/ Shmel-1				

Advanced Armament

Air-to-air missiles

AA-2 (Atoll), AA-6 (Acrid), AA-7 (Apex), AA-8 (Aphid), AA-10 (Alamo), AA-11 (Archer)

Air-to-ground missiles
AS-7 (Kerry), AS-9 (Kyle), AS-10 (Karen), AS-11 (Kegler), AS-12, AS-14 (Kedge), AT-2 (Swatter), HOT

Air Force Infrastructure

Aircraft shelters:
in all airfields, for combat aircraft
Military airfields: **21**
Abu Duhur, Afis North, Aleppo, Damascus (international), Damascus (Meze), Dir e-Zor, Dumayr, Hama, Jarah, Khalkhala, Latakia, Marj-royal (Bley), Nassiriyah, Tudmur, al-Qusayr, Rasm al-Aboud, Sayqal, Shayarat, al-Suweida, T-4, Tabaka

AIR DEFENSE FORCES

Surface-to-Air Missiles (SAMs)

Model	Batteries	Launchers	Since	Notes
Long-range missiles				
• SA-2 (Guileline) and SA-3 (Goa)	100	600	1971	
• SA-5 (Gammon)	8	24	1983	
Total	**108**	**624**		
Medium missiles				
• SA-8 (Gecko)	14	56	1982	
• SA-6 (Gainful)	50	200	1973	
Total	64	256		
Light missiles				
• SA-9 (Gaskin)		20	1978	
• SA-13 (Gopher)		35		
Total		55		
Shoulder-launched missiles				
• SA-7 (Grail)			1973	
• SA-14 (Gremlin)				
• SA-16				
On order				
SA-10 (Grumble)				

Other Air Defense Systems

Model	Quantity	In service	Since	Notes
Short-range guns				
• 57mm S-60	700	approx. 400		Partly phased out
• 37mm M-1939	300			In storage

Other Air Defense Systems *(continued)*

Model	Quantity	In service	Since	Notes
• 23mm ZSU 23 × 4 SP	400	400		
• 23mm ZU 23 × 2	600	approx. 300		
Total	**2,000**	**approx. 1,100**		

Radars

Long Track, P-14 (Tall King), P-15 (Flat Face), P-12 (Spoon Rest), P-30, P-35, P-80, PRV-13, PRV-16

NAVY

Combat Vessels

Type	Original Class name	Quantity	Length (m.)/ Displace-ment (t.)	Armament/ special equipment
Submarines				
• R class (Romeo)	Type 633	0	76.6/ 1,830	8 × 533mm torpedoes 28 mines 3 unserviceable
MFPBs				
• Komar		0	27/85	2 × SS-N-2A Styx SSMs 2 × 25mm guns 3 unserviceable
• Ossa I		6	38.6/210	4 × SS-N-2A Styx SSMs 4 × 30mm guns
• Ossa II		10	38.6/245	4 × SS-N-2C Styx SSMs 4 × 30mm guns
Subtotal		16		Some possibly phased out
ASW vessels				
• Petya II submarine chaser frigate		2	81.8/950	3 × 533mm torpedoes 4 × RBU 2500 ASW mortars 22 mines 4 × 76mm guns

Combat Vessels *(continued)*

Type	Original Class name	Quantity	Length (m.)/ Displace- ment (t.)	Armament/ special equipment
Mine warfare vessels				
• Sonya class	Type 1265	1	48/450	2 × 30mm and 2 × 25mm guns
• T-43 class		1	60/580	16 mines 2 × 37mm guns 8 × 14.5mm MGs
• Vanya class		0	40/245	8 mines 2 × 30mm guns 2 unserviceable
• Yevgenia class		5	24.6/77	2 × 25mm guns 2 × 14.5mm MGs
Subtotal		7		
Patrol craft				
• Zhuk class	Type 1400M	8	24/39	4 × 14.5mm guns
Total		**33**		

Landing Craft

Type	Original Class name	Quantity	Length (m.)/ Displace- ment (t.)	Armament/ special equipment
• Polnochny B-class LCT	Type 771	3	75/760	180 troops or 350 tons 2 × 140mm MRLs 4 × 30mm guns
Total		**3**		

Auxiliary Vessels

Type	Original Class name	Quantity	Length (m.)/ Displace- ment (t.)	Armament/ special equipment
• Training ship (al-Assad)		1	105/3,500	

Auxiliary Vessels *(continued)*

Type	Original Class name	Quantity	Length (m.)/ Displace-ment (t.)	Armament/ special equipment
• Natya	Type 226	1	61/804	2 × SA-N-5 grail SAMs 4 × 30mm guns formerly a mine-sweeper, now converted to oceanographic research
• Sekstan class		1	40.8/400	115 ton
• Poluchat tor-pedo recovery vessel		1	29.6/100	2 × 14.5mm MGs
• Rotork Sea Truck		7	14.5/12	
• Survey launch		3	9.5/	
Total		**14**		

Advanced Armament

Surface-to-surface missiles:
SS-N-2 Styx/SS-N-2C

Coastal Defense

Type	Launchers	Missiles	Since	Notes
Missiles				
• SSC-1B Sepal				
• SSC-3	24 × 2		1966	Armed with SS-N-2C missiles
Guns				
• 130mm	36			
• 100mm	12			

Naval Infrastructure

Naval bases: 3
Latakia, Minat al-Baida, Tartus
Ship maintenance and repair facilities:
Repairs at Latakia

18. TUNISIA

GENERAL DATA

Official Name of the State: The Republic of Tunisia
Head of State: President General Zayn al-Abedine Bin Ali (also Minister of Defense)
Prime Minister: Hamid al-Karaoui
Minister of National Defense: Hadid Ben Yahia
Secretary of State for Security: Mohamed Ali Ghenzoui
Minister, Chief of General Staff: Mohamed Jegham
Commander of the Ground Forces: Lieutenant General Muhammad Hadi Bin Hassin
Commander of the Air Force: Major General Rida Hamuda Atar
Commander of the Navy: Commodore al-Shadi Sharif

Area: 164,206 sq. km.
Population: 9,100,000

Demography

Ethnic Groups		
Arabs/Berbers	8,920,000	98.0%
Europeans	72,000	0.8%
Others	108,000	1.2%
Religious Groups		
Sunni Muslims	8,920,000	98.0%
Christians	90,000	1.0%
Others	90,000	1.0%

Economic Data

		1992	1993	1994	1995	1996
GDP current price, local currency	TD bn	13.71	14.60	15.89	17.06	18.96
GDP (U.S. $)	$ bn	15.50	14.55	15.70	18.03	19.49
GDP per capita	$	1,846	1,691	1,784	2,004	2,141
Real GDP growth	%	7.8	2.0	3.3	2.5	6.9
Balance of payments						
• Exports fob	$ bn	4.051	3.748	4.643	5.47	5.51
• Imports fob	$ bn	6.088	5.817	6.217	7.324	7.323

Economic Data *(continued)*

		1992	1993	1994	1995	1996
• Account balance (Includes services and income)	$ bn	–1.089	–1.05	–0.339	–0.349	–0.5
• External debt	$ bn	8.5	8.7	9.3	10.1	9.9
Government income and expenditure						
• Revenues, local currency	TD bn	73.464	91.2	105.37	106.21	
• Expenditures, local currency	TD bn	65.95	95.05	110.65	109.81	
• Defense expenditures	TD bn	0.318	0.346	0.364	0.326	0.343
• Defense expenditure/GDP	%	2.3	2.36	2.3	1.9	1.8
• Defense expenditure/CGE	%	0.48	0.36	0.33	0.3	
• Population	m	8.4	8.6	8.8	9	9.1
• Official exchange rate	TD: $1	0.884	1.004	1.012	0.946	0.973

Sources: EIU quarterly report, EIU country profile, IMF statistical yearbook, SIPRI Yearbook.

Arms Procurement and Security Assistance Received

Country	Type	Details
Czech Republic	• Arms transfers	Trainer and transport aircraft (1996)
Germany	• Arms transfers	Naval vessels (1993)
U.S.A.	• Financial aid	$27 million grant (1993) and a higher grant in 1994

Foreign Military Cooperation

	Details
• Joint maneuvers with:	France, U.S.A., Spain (unconfirmed)

Defense Production

	M	P	A
Naval craft			
• 20-meter patrol craft, with assistance from South Korea		√	

Note: M—Manufacture (indigenously developed)
P—Production under license
A—Assembly

ARMED FORCES

Major changes: No major change has been recorded in the Tunisian armed forces in 1997.

Order-of-Battle

Year	1993	1994	1995	1996	1997
General data					
• Personnel	50,500	35,500	35,500	35,500	35,500
• Total number of brigades	6	8	8	8	5
Ground Forces					
• Tanks	190	192	200	200	139 (144)
• APCs/ARVs	330	316	316	316	316
• Artillery	200	91	91	91	205 (215)
Air Force					
• Combat aircraft	11	14	13	13	12
• Transport aircraft	8	6	11	11	10 (11)
• Helicopters	42	42	35	35	40
Air Defense Forces					
• Light SAM launchers	+	+	+	+	25
Navy					
• Combat vessels	20	33	36	36	47

Note: Beginning with data for 1997, we refer to quantities in active service. The number in parentheses refers to the total.

Personnel

	Regular	Total
Ground Forces	27,000	27,000
Air Force	4,000	4,000
Navy	4,500	4,500
Total	**35,500**	**35,500**
Paramilitary		
• Gendarmerie	2,000	2,000
• National Guard	7,000	7,000

GROUND FORCES

Formations

	Independent brigades/groups	Regiments in brigade
Mechanized/Infantry	3	1 tank, 2 mech., 1 art. each
Commando/Paratroops	1	
Sahara Brigade	1	
Total	**5**	

Tanks

Model	Quantity	In service	Since	Notes
High quality				
• M-60 A3	54	54	1984	
Others				
• M-60 A1	35	30	1975	
• SK-105 (Kurassier)	55	55		
Subtotal	90	85		
Total	**144**	**139**		

APCs/ARVs

Model	Quantity	In service	Since	Notes
High quality				
• Engesa EE-9/EE-11	36	36	1982	
• Fiat Type 6614	110	110	1980	
• M-113 A1/A2/ M-125/M-577	120	120	1980	
Subtotal	266	266		
Others				
• AML-60/AML-90	30	30	1969	
• EBR-75			1958	
• Saladin	20	20		
Subtotal	50	50		
Total	**316**	**316**		

Artillery

Model	Quantity	In service	Since	Notes
Self-propelled guns and howitzers				
• 105mm M-108	10	0	1950	Possibly phased out
Towed guns and howitzers				
• 155mm M-198	48	48	1987	
• 155mm M-114	18	18		
• 105mm M-101	45	45		
Subtotal	111	111		
Mortars, under 160mm				
• 120mm Brandt	18	18		
• 107mm	40	40		
• 107mm SP	36	36		
Subtotal	94	94		
Total	**215**	**205**		
On order				
• 155mm M-109				

Logistic and Engineering Equipment

On order: U.S.-made AFV transporters

Antitank Weapons

Model	Quantity	In service	Since	Notes
Missiles				
• BGM-71A TOW	100	100		
• M-901 ITV SP	35	35		TOW under armor
• MILAN	500	500		
Total	635	635		
Guns				
• 106mm M-40A1		70		Recoilless rifle

AIR FORCE

Order-of-Battle

Model	Quantity	In service
• Combat	12	12
• Transport	11	10
• Helicopters	40	40

Combat Aircraft

Model	Quantity	In service	Since	Notes
Strike and multirole aircraft—medium and low quality				
• F-5E/F-5F	12	12	1984	
Total	**12**	**12**		

Transport Aircraft

Model	Quantity	In service	Since	Notes
• C-130H Hercules	8	7	1985	
• L-410	3	3	1994	
Total	**11**	**10**		

Training and Liaison Aircraft

Model	Quantity	In service	Since	Notes
With ground attack/close air support capability				
• Aermacchi MB-326 B/KT/LT	10	10	1977	
• L-59	12	12	1995	
Subtotal	22	22		
Others				
• SIAI-Marchetti SF-260WT/C	18	18	1978	
• S 208A/M	2	2	1979	
• Piper Cub	10	10		
Subtotal	30	30		
Total	**52**	**52**		

Helicopters

Model	Quantity	In service	Since	Notes
Attack				
• SA-342 Gazelle	5	5		
Medium transport				
• AB-205/Bell-205/UH-1H	19	19	1980	
• AS 365 Dauphin II	1	1		
Subtotal	20	20		

Helicopters *(continued)*

Model	Quantity	In service	Since	Notes
Light transport				
• Alouette II/III	9	9	1964	
• AS-350 Ecureuil	6	6	1980	
Subtotal	15	15		
Total	**40**	**40**		

Advanced Armament

Air-to-air-missiles
AIM-9J Sidewinder

Air Force Infrastructure

Military airfields: 5
Bizerta (Sidi Ahmad), Gabes, Gafsa, Sfax, one additonal

AIR DEFENSE FORCES

Surface-to-air Missiles (SAMs)

Model	Launchers	Since	Notes
Light missiles			
• MIM-72A Chaparral	25	1977	
Shoulder-launched missiles			
• RBS-70	48		
• SA-7 (Grail)	+		
Total			

Other Air Defense Systems

Model	Quantity	In service	Since	Notes
Short-range guns				
• 40mm	12	12		
• 37mm M-1939	15	15		
• 20mm M-55	100	100		
Total	127	127		
Radars				
• TRS-2100 Tiger S				

NAVY

Combat Vessels

Type	Original Class name	Quantity	Length (m.)/ Displace- ment (t.)	Armament/ special equipment
MFPBs				
• Combattante III		3	56/345	8 × MM40 Exocet SSMs 1 × 76mm gun 2 × 40mm guns 4 × 30mm guns
• Bizerte class	P-48	3	48/250	8 × SS-12M SAMs 4 × 37mm guns
Subtotal		6		
Gunsboat/MTBs				
• Shanghai II class		2	38.8/113	4 × 37mm guns 4 × 25mm guns
• Modified Shanghai II class		3	41/170	4 × 14.5mm MGs
Subtotal		5		
Patrol craft				
• Kondor I class		4	51.9/377	2 × 25mm guns formerly a mine-sweeper, now with coast guard
• Coastal patrol craft	Ch. Navals de l'Esterel	4	31.5/60	2 × 20mm guns
• Tazarka class	Vosper Thornycroft	2	31.4/125	with coast guard 2 × 20mm guns 2 × 14.5mm MGs
• Coastal patrol craft	Ch. Navals de l'Esterel	6	25/38	1 × 20mm gun
• Bremse class		5	22.6/42	2 × 14.5mm MGs with coast guard
• Coastal patrol craft	Socomena	11	20.5/32	1 × 12.7mm MG with coast guard
• Gabes class		4	12.9/18	2 × 12.7mm MGs with coast guard
Subtotal		36		
Total		**47**		

Auxiliary Vessels

Type	Original Class name	Quantity	Length (m.)/ Displace-ment (t.)	Armament/ special equipment
• Robert Conrad class		1	63.7/1,370	Survey ship
• Guesette class		1	11/8.5	Survey ship
Total		**2**		
On order				
• T-AGS-33		1		

Naval Infrastructure

Naval bases: 5

Bizerta, Kelibia, Sfax, Sousse, Tunis

Ship maintenance and repair facilities:

4 dry docks and 1 slipway in Bizerta, 2 pontoons and 1 floating dock at Sfax. Capability for maintainance and repair of existing vessels

19. TURKEY

GENERAL DATA

Official Name of the State: Republic of Turkey
Head of State: President Suleyman Demirel
Prime Minister: Mesut Yilmaz
Minister of Defense: Ismet Sezgin
Head of Turkish Chiefs of Staff: General Ismail Hakki Karadayi
Commander of Ground Forces: General Huseyin Kivrikoglu
Commander of the Air Force: General Ilhan Kilic
Commander of the Navy: Admiral Salim Dervisoglu

Area: 780,580 sq. km.
Population: 62,600,000

Demography

Ethnic Groups		
Turkish	50,080,000	80%
Kurdish	12,520,000	20%
Religious Groups		
Sunni Muslims	49,955,000	79.8%
Alevis (Shi'i Muslims)	12,520,000	20.0%
Other (Christians and Jews)	125,000	0.2%

Economic Data

		1992	1993	1994	1995	1996
GDP current price, local currency	TL tr	1,103.6	1,997.4	3,887.9	7,854.9	15,125.1
GDP (U.S. $)	$ bn	160,594	181,830	131,308	171,613	185,800
GDP per capita	$	2,695	3,051	2,163	2,786	2,968
Real GDP growth	%	6.4	8.1	−6.1	8.1	7.4
Balance of payments						
• Exports fob	$ bn	14.89	15.61	18.39	21.98	23.46
• Imports fob	$ bn	23.08	29.7	22.61	35.19	41.94
• Account balance (Includes services and income)	$ bn	–0.98	–6.44	2.63	–2.1	–1.45
• External debt	$ bn	56.5	68.8	66.3	73.8	79.5

Economic Data *(continued)*

		1992	1993	1994	1995	1996
Government income and expenditure						
• Revenues, local currency	TL bn	174,224	351,392	745,116	1,394,023	2,738,148
• Expenditures, local currency	TL bn	221,658	485,249	897,296	1,710,646	2,248,422
• Defense expenditures	TL bn	42,320	77,717	156,724	302,864	569,822
• Defense expenditure/ GDP	%	3.83	3.89	4	3.85	3.76
• Defense expenditure/ CGE	%	19.09	16.02	17.46	17.7	25.34
• Population	m	59.6	59.6	60.7	61.6	62.6
• Official exchange rate	TL: $1	6,872	10,985	29,609	45,771	81,405

Sources: EIU quarterly report, EIU country profile, IMF statistical yearbook, SIPRI Yearbook.

Arms Prodcurement and Security Assistance Received

Country	Type	Details
Britain	• Arms transfers	APCs (1995)
France	• Arms transfers	Helicopters (1997), Circe minesweepers (1998)
Germany	• Arms transfers	Meko frigates (1996), Preveze submarine (1996), aircraft (1993), APCs (1993), tanks (1993), SP artillery (1994), SAMs (1994)
	• maintenance of equipment	Transport aircraft
Israel	• Arms transfers	Upgrade of F-4s and F-5s (1997), guided missiles (1998), radars (1998)
Italy	• Arms transfers	Helicopters (1998), APCs (1995)
Kuwait	• Financial aid	$500 million, from speical Gulf War fund
Netherlands	• Arms transfers	Aircraft (1996)
Russia	• Arms transfers	Mi-17 helicopters (1996), APCs (1992)
Saudi Arabia	• Financial aid	$500 million from speical Gulf War fund
Spain	• Arms transfers	CN-235 aircraft (1997)
U.S.A.	• Financial aid	$122 million U.S. foreign aid
	• Arms transfers	Knox frigates (1997), F-4 aircraft (1994), ATACM SSMs (1997), Seahawk helicopters (1997), MLRS (1992), APCs (1997)

Arms Sales and Security Assistance Extended

Country	Type	Details
Algeria	• Arms transfers	Armored Land Rovers (1996)
Bosnia	• Arms transfers	Artillery (1995)
China	• Cooperation in arms production/assembly/R&D	
Croatia	• Arms transfers	CN-235 aircraft (1998)
Egypt	• Arms transfers	F-16s (1996)
Georgia	• Military training	
Israel	• Facilities provided	Training facilities for IAF (1997)
	• Arms transfers	Armored Land Rovers (1998)
NATO	• Facilities provided	HQ LANDSOUTHEAST, HQ 6 ATAF
Pakistan	• Arms transfers	Armored Land Rovers (1996)
Poland	• Military training	
UAE	• Arms transfers	FMC-Nurol AAPCs (1998)

Foreign Military Cooperation

	Details
• Forces deployed abroad in:	Cyprus (30,000 troops); northern Iraq (1,000 troops); Adriatic sea (Sharp Guard operation); Bosnia (UNPROFOR); Georgia (UNIMIG); Iraq/Kuwait (UNIKOM); Italy (deny flight operation)
• Joint maneuvers with:	U.S.A. NATO states, Israel, Poland, Georgia

Defense Production

	M	P	A
Army equipment			
• ERYX ATGMs		√	
• 35mm Oerlikon antiaircraft guns		√	
• Land Rover APCs, FMC-Nurol AAPCs and AIFVs	√		
• Explosives	√		
• Chines WS-1 SSMs	√		
• MLRs rockets	√		
• Upgrade of 105mm and 155mm SP guns	√		
• 107mm and 122mm MRLs	√		
• Small arms	√		
• M48 tank guns	√		
• Trucks and wheeled tactical vehicles	√		
• 25mm cannons			√
Aircraft and air ammunition			
• UAVs	√		
• Stinger SAMs and SP Stinger systems	√	√	

Defense Production *(continued)*

	M	P	A
• F-16s		√	
• Basic trainers		√	
• Jet engines		√	
• CN-235 light transport aircraft		√	
• Popeye air-launched rockets		√	
• UH-1H helicopters, under negotiations			√
• Cougar helicopters			√
Naval craft			
• Atilay-class submarines			√
• Berk-class missile frigates			√
• Yildiz-class and Dogan-class MFPBs			√
• Osman Gazi landing craft			√
Electronics			
• Land-based EW sets	√		
• Navigation systems	√		
• Ground surveillance radars	√		
• Artillery fire-control systems	√		
• HF/SSB radios		√	
• ALQ-178 EW systems for F-4s and F-16s		√	
• TRS-22 air search radars		√	
• C^{3}I systems		√	
Optronics			
• Optical targeting devices	√		
• Night-vision equipment	√		
• Laser rangefinders	√		

Note: M—manufacture (indigenously developed)
P—production under license
A—assembly

ARMED FORCES

Major changes: The Turkish armed forces have launched a major rearmament project for all military branches. Nevertheless, this procurement program has had no major effect yet on the Turkish order-of-battle in 1997.

Order-of-Battle

Year	1993	1994	1995	1996	1997
General data					
• Personnel	370,000	503,800	507,800	515,800	639,000
• Divisions	2	2–3	2–3	2–3	5
• Total number of brigades	59	64	60	63	67

Order-of-Battle *(continued)*

Year	1993	1994	1995	1996	1997
Ground Forces					
• Tanks	4,069	4,330	4,300	4,280	4,115 (4,190)
• APCs/ARVs	2,900	3,360	4,711	4,046	4,743
• Artillery (incl. MRLs)	4,551	4,275	4,341	4,128	4,113 (4,412)
Air Force					
• Combat aircraft	506	555	374	434	461
• Transport aircraft	102	88	70	62	87
• Helicopters	578	323	305	304	381
Air Defense Forces					
• Heavy SAM batteries	40	40	30	30	24
• Light SAM launchers	24	24	24	24	86
Navy					
• Combat vessels	100	87	88	105	171
• Submarines	15	15	16	16	17

Note: Beginning with data for 1997, we refer to quantities in active service. The number in parentheses refers to the total.

Personnel

	Regular	Reserves	Total
Ground Forces	525,000	259,000	784,000
Air Force	63,000	55,000	118,000
Navy	51,000	65,000	116,000
Total	**639,000**	**379,000**	**1,018,000**
Paramilitary			
• Coast Guard	2,200		
• Gendarmerie/National Guard	180,000	50,000	

GROUND FORCES

Formations

	Corps	Divisions	Independent brigades/ groups	Independent battalions	Battalions in brigade
All arms	4 armies 9 corps				

Formations *(continued)*

	Corps	Divisions	Independent brigades/ groups	Independent battalions	Battalions in brigade
Armored			15		2 arm., 2 mech., 1 art. each
Mechanized		2	18		1 arm., 2 mech., 1 art. each
Infantry		3	9		4 inf., 1 art. each
Commando			4		3 inf., 1 art. each
Presidential Guard			1 (Reg.)		
Border Defense			5 (Reg.)	26	
Coastal Defense (Reserve)			4		
Marines			1		3 inf., 1 art. each
Total		**5**	**57**	**26**	

Tanks

Model	Quantity	In service	Since	Notes
High quality				
• Leopard A1/A3	307	307		
• M-60 A3	658	658		
Subtotal	965	965		
Others				
• M-60 A1	274	274		
• M-48T	2,876	2,876		
• M-47	75	0		In storage
Subtotal	3,225	3,150		
Total	**4,190**	**4,115**		

APCs/ARVs

Model	Quantity	In service	Since	Notes
High quality				
• FMC-Nurol AIFV	280	280		
• FMC-Nurol AAPC	730	730		
• FMC-Nurol ATV	48	48		
• FMC-Nurol AMV	170	170		
• M-113 A1/A2	2,815	2,815		
Subtotal	4,043	4,043		
Others				
• BTR-80	240	240		
• BTR-60	340	340		
• Condor	25	25		
• UR-416	35	35		
• Scorpion (Akrep)	some	some		
• S-55	40	40		
Subtotal	700	700		
Total	**4,743**	**4,743**		

Artillery

Model	Quantity	In service	Since	Notes
Self-propelled guns and howitzers				
• 203mm M-110	219	219		
• 203mm M-55	9	9		
• 175mm M-107	36	36		
• 155mm M-44T	222	222		
• 105mm M-52T	365	365		
• 105mm M-108	26	26		
Towed guns and howitzers				
• 203mm M-115	162	162		
• 155mm M-114	517	517		
• 155mm M-59	171			
• 150mm Skoda	128			
• 105mm M-101/M-102	640	640		
Mortars, under 160mm				
• 120mm	578	578		
• 107mm M-30	1,265	1,265		
• 107mm M-106 SP	some	some		
Total	**4,355**	**4,055**		
Artillery/mortar-locating radars				
• AN/TPQ-37				
• AN/TPQ-36				
• Ranging radars				

Artillery *(continued)*

Model	Quantity	In service	Since	Notes
MRLs				
• 227mm MLRS	12	12		
• 107mm	48	48		
Total	60	60		

Logistic and Engineering Equipment

Mine laying and clearing, bar-mine-clearing system, crossing equipment

Antitank Weapons

Model	Quantity	In service	Since	Notes
Missiles				
• Cobra	186	186		
• Milan	392	392		
• TOW SP	365	365		48 of which are on FMC-Nurol ATV
Subtotal	943	943		
Guns				
• 106mm M-40A1	2,330	2,330		
• 75mm	620	620		
• 57mm M-18	925	925		
Subtotal	3,875	3,875		
Total	**4,818**	**4,818**		

AIR FORCE

Order-of-Battle

Model	Quantity	In service	Notes
• Combat	461	461	
• Transport	87	87	
• Helicopters	381	381	

Combat Aircraft

Model	Quantity	In service	Since	Notes
Interceptors—high quality				
• F-16C/D	175	175	1987	

Combat Aircraft *(continued)*

Model	Quantity	In service	Since	Notes
Strike and multirole aircraft—medium and low quality				
• F-5A/B	63	63	1965	
• F-4E	140	140	1973	
• NF-5A/B	44	44	1965	
• RF-4E (reece)	39	39	1977	
Subtotal	286	286		
Total	**461**	**461**		
On order				
• F-16 C/D	232			Being delivered
• F-5	48			To be upgraded
• F-4E	54			To be upgraded, all others for storage

Transport Aircraft

Model	Quantity	In service	Since	Notes
• C-160D	19	19	1971	
• KC-135R	9	9	1995	Tanker
• C-130	13	13	1964	
• Citation (VIP)	2	2	1985	
• CN-235	44	44	1991	
Total	**87**	**87**		
On order				
• CN-235	62			Being delivered, 6 for maritime patrol

Training and Liaison Aircraft

Model	Quantity	In service	Since	Notes
With ground attack/close air support capability				
• T-38	70	70	1965	
• T-37	62	62	1960	
Subtotal	132	132		
Others				
• SF-260D	40	40	1990	
• T-41	53	53	1972	28 in army aviation
• T-33	34	34	1982	
Subtotal	127	127		
Total	**259**	**259**		

Helicopters

Model	Quantity	In service	Since	Notes
Attack				
• AH-1W/P	38	38	1990	With army aviation
Medium transport				
• AB-212	15	15	1985	13 in the navy, in ASW roll and 3 in army aviation
• AS-352 Cougar	19	19	1995	With army aviation
• Mi-17	19	19	1995	With gendarmeire
• UH-60 Blackhawk	45	45	1988	36 with gendarmeire
• UH-1H/AB-204/AB-205	194	194	1966	160 in army aviation and 3 in Navy
Subtotal	292	292		
Light transport				
• AB 206	20	20	1968	3 with coast guard
• H-300C	28	28	1982	With army aviation
• OH-58B	3	3	1994	With army aviation
Subtotal	51	51		
Total	**381**	**381**		
On order				
• S-70B	4			With navy
• Cougar AS-532	30			

Miscellaneous Aircraft

Model	Quantity	In service	Since	Notes
Reconnaissance aircraft				
• RF-4E			1977	39, listed under Combat Aircraft
ELINT				
• CN 235			1991	2, listed under Transport Aircraft
UAVs and mini-UAVs				
• CL-89				
• Gnat 750				
Maritime surveillance aircraft				
• Maule MX 7	1	1	1993	With coast guard
• S-2A/E Tracker	9	9		

Advanced Armament

Air-to-air-missiles
AIM-120 AMRAAM, AIM-9S Sidewinder, AIM-7E Sparrow
Air-to-ground missiles
AGM-88 HARM, AGM-65 A/G Maverick
Avionics
LANTIRN 24
On order
LANTIRN approx. 10

Air Force Infrastructure

Military airfields: 23
Adnan-menderes, Afyon, Akhisar, Akinci, Ankara-güvercinlik, Balikesit, Bandirma, Dalaman, Diyarbakir, Elazig, Erhac, Erkilet, Erzincan, Eskisehir, Istanbul-Sarigazi, Izmir-Kaklic, Kayseri, Konya, Malatya, Merzifon, Murted, Yalova, Yesilkoy

AIR DEFENSE FORCES

Surface-to-Air Missiles (SAMs)

Model	Batteries	Launchers	Since	Notes
Heavy missiles				
• Nike Hercules	24	72		8 squadrons, 24 batteries
Light missiles				
• Rapier		86		
Shoulder-launched missiles				
• Stinger		108		
• Red-eye		790		
Total		**898**		

Other Air Defense Systems

Model	Quantity	In service	Since	Notes
Short-range guns				
• 40mm L60/70	800	800		
• 40mm T1	40	40		
• M-42 A1	260	260		
• 35mm GDF-003	120	120		

Other Air Defense Systems *(continued)*

Model	Quantity	In service	Since	Notes
• 20mm GAI-DO1	440	440		
Total	**1,660**	**1,660**		
Radars				
• AN/TPS-59				

NAVY

Combat Vessesls

Type	Original Class name	Quantity	Length (m.)/ Displace-ment (t.)	Armament/ special equipment
Submarines				
• Atilay	Type 1200	6	61.2/1,185	8 × 533mm torpedoes
• Cannakkale class	Guppy III	2	99.5/2,450	10 × 533mm torpedoes 40 mines
• Burakreist class	Guppy II A	5	93.2/2,440	10 × 533mm torpedoes 40 mines
• Hizzirreis	Tang	2	87.4/2,700	8 × 533mm torpedoes Mines
• Preveze	Type 1400	2	62/1,586	2 × Sub Harpoon SSMs 8 × 533mm torpedoes Mines
Total		17		

Combat Vessesls *(continued)*

Type	Original Class name	Quantity	Length (m.)/ Displace-ment (t.)	Armament/ special equipment
Destroyers				
• Alcitepe	Carpenter class	2	119/2,425	ASROC Mk112 8 × torpedo launcher 6 × 324mm torpedoes 2 × 127mm guns 2 × 76mm guns 2 × 35mm guns
• Yücetepe	Gearing class	3	119/2,425	Helicopter pad 1 × Harpoon SSM ASROC Mk112 8 torpedo launcher 6 × 324mm torpedoes 4 × 127mm guns 2 × 35mm guns
Subtotal		5		
Frigates				
• Barbaros	Modified MEKO	2	116.7/3,350	AB 212 ASW helicopter 8 × Harpoon SSMs 1 × Seasparrow 8 SAMs 6 × 324mm torpedoes 1 × 127mm gun 3 × Oerlicon 25mm AD guns
• Berk		2	95/1,450	Helicopter pad 2 × hedgehog Mk11 24 ASW rocket launchers 6 × 324mm torpedoes 4 × 76mm guns

Combat Vessesls *(continued)*

Type	Original Class name	Quantity	Length (m.)/ Displace-ment (t.)	Armament/ special equipment
• Muavenet	Knox class	8	134/3,011	AB 212 ASW helicopter 8 × Harpoon SSMs ASROC Mk112 8 torpedo launcher 4 × 324mm torpedoes 1 × 20mm Vulcan Phalanx AD gun 1 × 127mm gun
• Yavuz	MEKO 200	4	115.5/2,414	AB 212 ASW helicopter 8 × Harpoon SSMs 6 × 324mm torpedoes 1 × Seasparrow 8 SAMs 1 × 127mm gun 3 × Oerlicon 25mm AD guns
Subtotal		16		
MFPBs				
• Dogan	Lürssen class	8	58.1/436	8 × Harpoon SSMs 1 × 76mm gun 2 × 35mm guns
• Yildiz		3	57.8/433	8 × Harpoon SSMs 1 × 76mm gun 2 × 35mm guns
• Kartal	Jaguar class	8	42.5/160	2–4 Penguin SSMs 2 × 533mm torpedoes 2 × 40mm guns 4 mines
Subtotal		19		

Combat Vessesls *(continued)*

Type	Original Class name	Quantity	Length (m.)/ Displace-ment (t.)	Armament/ special equipment
Mine warfare vessels				
• Nurset		1	77/1,880	4 × 76mm guns 400 mines
• Mersin	Modified ECM-1	1	61.9/743	6 × 40mm guns 6 × 20 mm guns 400 mines
• Mehmecik class	YMP class	1	39.6/540	
• Karamürsel	Vegasack class	6	47.3/362	Active mine detectors 2 × 20mm guns
• Seymen	Adjutant class	11	43/320	sonar sweep 2 × 20mm guns
• Fona	Clove class	4	34/180	1 × 12.7mm MG
• Dalgic mine-hunters		8	21.8/80	1 × 20mm gun
• Samandira minelayer		3	19.6/72	
Subtotal		35		
Patrol craft (mostly with Coast Guard)				
• Grine class		1	58.1/341	2 × Mousetrap Mk 20 4 ASW rocket launchers 2 × 40mm guns 2 × 20mm guns
• Bora class	Ashville	1	50.1/225	1 × 76mm gun 1 × 40mm guns 4 × 12.7mm MG
• Hisar class	PC-1638	6	53/325	1 × Hedgehog Mk 15 24 ASW rocket launcher 1 × 40mm gun 4 × 20mm guns
• Trabzon class		4	50/370	1 × 40mm gun 2 × 12.7mm MG

Combat Vessesls *(continued)*

Type	Original Class name	Quantity	Length (m.)/ Displace-ment (t.)	Armament/ special equipment
• Turk class		12	40.2/170	1 × Mousetrap Mk 20 4 ASW rocket launcher 1–2 × 40mm guns 1 × 20mm gun 2 × 12.7mm MGs
• PGM-71 class		4	30.8/130	2 × Mousetrap Mk 22 8 ASW rocket launchers 1 × 40mm gun 4 × 20mm guns
• Coast Guard type		4	25.3/63	2 × Mousetrap Mk 20 8 ASW rocket launchers 2 × 20mm guns
• Large patrol craft		20	40.7/187	1 × 40mm gun 2 × 12.7mm MGs
• Sar 33 Type		10	34.6/180	1 × 40mm gun 2 × 12.7mm MGs
• Sar 35 Type		4	36.6/210	1 × 40mm gun 2 × 12.7mm MGs
• KW 15 class		8	28.9/70	1 × 40mm gun 2 × 20mm guns
• Coastal patrol craft	KW 15 class	1	26.7/56	2 × 20mm guns
• Coastal patrol craft	US Mk5	6	16.8/25	1 × 12.7mm gun
• Coastal patrol craft		12	14.6/29	1 × 25mm gun or 1 × 12.7mm MG
• Inshore patrol craft		1	11.6/10	1 × 12.7mm MG
• Harbour patrol craft		2	17/15	
Subtotal		96		
Total		**171**		
On order				
• Prevese-class submarines		2		
• Oliver Perry–class frigates		3		

Combat Vessesls *(continued)*

Type	Original Class name	Quantity	Length (m.)/ Displace-ment (t.)	Armament/ special equipment
• Circle-class minesweepers		5		
• Meko-class Frigates		2		To be supplied 1998
• Yildiz class		2		To be supplied 1998

Landing Craft

Type	Original Class name	Quantity	Length (m.)/ Displace-ment (t.)	Armament/ special equipment
• Osman Gazi		1	105/3,773	900 troops, 15 tanks 4 LCVPs 3 × 40mm guns 2 × 35mm guns
• Sarucabey		2	92/2,600	600 troops, 11 tanks 2 LCVPs 2 × 40mm guns 4 × 20mm guns
• Akabey		1	77.3/1,600	400 troops, 9 tanks 2 LCVPs 4 × 40mm guns 4 × 20mm guns
• Ertugan	Terrebonne Parish class	2	117.1/5,800	395 troops, 2,200 tons 4 LCVPs 6 × 76mm guns
• LCM-8		22	22/113	160 troops or 60 tons 2 × 12.7mm MGs
• LCT		28	59.6/600	100 troops, 5 tanks 2 × 20mm guns 2 × 12.7mm MGs
• Edic Type		7	57/580	100 troops, 5 tanks 2 × 20mm guns 2 × 12.7mm MGs

Landing Craft *(continued)*

Type	Original Class name	Quantity	Length (m.)/ Displacement (t.)	Armament/ special equipment
• Bayraktar	LST	2	100/1,653	6 × 40mm guns
• LCU		2	44.3/405	2 × 20mm guns
Total		**67**		

Auxiliary Vessels

Type	Original Class name	Quantity	Length (m.)/ Displacement (t.)	Armament/ special equipment
• Tankers		6	1,400–19,000	2 × 20mm guns
• Water tankers		15	300–1,200 tons	
• Salvage/ rescue		3	1,200–1,600 tons	2–4 20mm, 76mm, or 40mm
• Survey		3	680 tons	2 × 20mm guns
• Intelligence vessel		1	1,497 tons	
• Training ships		2	2,370 tons	2 × 100mm, 4 × 40mm guns
• Transport		34	Various sizes	
• Tugs		10	750, 1,235 tons	
• Repair		12		400–16,000-ton lift
• Boom defense		3	560–780 tons	3–4 20mm, 76mm, or 40mm

Naval Infrastructure

Naval bases: 14

Aksaz, Aksaz Bay, Ankara (HQ), Çanakkala, Erdek, Ereğli, Foça, Gölcük, Iskanderun, Istanbul, Izmir, Karamürsel (training), Marmaris, Mersin, Samsun, Trabzon

Ship maintenance and repair facilities: 2

Gölcük, Taskiçak

Naval aviation bases: 4

Antalia, Cigli, Topel, Trabzon

NONGOVERNMENTAL PARAMILITARY FORCES

Personnel

	Active
• PKK	8,000

Equipment

Organization	System	Model	Number	Notes
PKK	*Air defense*	• SA-7 (Garil)		

20. UNITED ARAB EMIRATES (UAE)

GENERAL DATA

Official Name of the State: United Arab Emirates*

Head of State: President Shaykh Zayid ibn Sultan al-Nuhayan, Emir of Abu Dhabi (also Supreme Commander of the Armed Forces)

Prime Minister: Shaykh Maktum ibn Rashid al-Maktum, Emir of Dubai (also Vice President)

Minister of Defense: Shaykh Muhammad ibn Rashid al-Maktum

Chief of General Staff: HRH Lieutenant General Muhammad ibn Zayid al-Nuhayan

Commander of the Air Force and Air Defense Forces: Brigadier General Atik Gum'a al-Hamli

Commander of the Navy: Captain Muhammad al-Muhairi

Area: Approximately 82,900 sq. km. (borders with Oman, Saudi Arabia, and Qatar partly undemarcated and/or disputed)

Population: 2,440,000 (estimate)

Demography

Ethnic Groups		
Arabs	1,220,000	50.0%
Southeast Asians	1,069,000	43.8%
Others (Europeans, Persians)	151,000	6.2%
Religious Groups		
Sunni Muslims	1,525,000	62.5%
Shi'ite Muslims	366,000	15.0%
Others	549,000	22.5%
National Groups		
UAE nationals	464,000	19.0%
Alien Arabs	561,000	23.0%
Southeast Asians (Indians, Pakistanis, Thais, Filipinos)	1,220,000	50.0%
Others (Europeans, Iranians)	195,000	8.0%

*The UAE consists of seven principalities: Abu Dhabi, Dubai, Ras al-Khaima, Sharja, Umm al-Qaiwain, Fujaira, and Ajman.

Economic Data

		1992	1993	1994	1995	1996
GDP current price, local currency	Dh bn	130.100	131.000	134.800	144.000	163.8
GDP (U.S. $)	$ bn	35.440	35.685	36.720	39.226	44.619
GDP per capita	$	17,630	16,598	16,466	16,482	18,286
Real GDP growth	%	1.8	0.4	−1.7	1.1	1.0
Balance of payments						
• Exports fob	$ bn	24.27	23.65	25.06	29.37	33.22
• Imports fob	$ bn	15.83	17.75	19.11	21.05	23.52
• Account balance (includes services and income)	$ bn	3.21	1.01	1	3.16	6.66
• External debt	$ bn	10.81	10.14	11.02	11.56	11.72
Government income and expenditure						
• Revenues, local currency	Dh bn	15.91	15.90	16.85	16.92	20.58
• Expenditures, local currency	Dh bn	17.38	17.63	17.82	17.94	17.02
• Defense expenditures	Dh bn	7.6	7.7	7.0	7.1	14.3
• Defense expenditure/GDP	%	5.84	5.88	5.19	4.93	8.73
• Defense expenditure/CGE	%	43.73	43.68	48.01	48.04	84.01
• Population	m	2.01	2.15	2.23	2.38	2.44
• Official exchange rate	Dh: $1	3.671	3.671	3.671	3.671	3.671

Sources: EIU quarterly report, EIU country profile, IMF statistical yearbook, SIPRI Yearbook.

Arms Procurement and Security Assistance Received

Country	Type	Details
Britain	• *Arms transfers*	AFV transporters, PGMs, sonar
France	• *Arms transfers*	Combat aircraft (Mirage 2000-9), helicopters, AGMs, Leclerc tanks (1996), radio sets, thermal imaging night-vision systems, shoulder-launched SAMs, ARVs, torpedoes
Germany	• *Arms transfers*	Trainer a/c (1997)
	• *Military training*	Trainees abroad
Indonesia	• *Maintenance of equipment*	Transport a/c (1993)
Italy	• *Arms transfers*	Helicopters

Arms Procurement and Security Assistance Received *(continued)*

Country	Type	Details
Netherlands	• *Arms transfers*	Frigates, artillery surveillance radar, CIWS
	• *Military training*	Trainees abroad
Norway	• *Arms transfers*	Navy simulator
Romania	• *Arms transfers*	Romanian-built French-model helicopters
Russia	• *Arms transfers*	BMP-3 APCs, MRLs, ATGMs
South Africa	• *Arms transfers*	Artillery (1995)
Sweden	• *Arms transfers*	Early warning system
Switzerland	• *Arms transfers*	Trainer aircraft
U.S.A.	• *Military training*	Foreign advisers/instructors/serving personnel (some civilians); trainees abroad
	• *Arms transfers*	Aircraft training simulator, transport aircraft, SAMs, light reconnaissance vehicles, radio systems, AH-64A Apache helicopters, AGM missiles, two missile frigates; early warning system, LANTIRN on order; reconnaissance satellite, under negotiation

Arms Sales and Security Assistance Extended

Country	Type	Details
Bosnia	• *Arms transfers*	AMX-30 MBTs
Britain	• *Facilities*	Logistical facilities
Netherlands	• *Arms transfers*	Artillery (1997)
U.S.A.	• *Facilities*	Storage facilities, for naval equipment at Jebel Ali and Fujaira, and prepositioning of equipment for an armored brigade under negotiation

Foreign Military Cooperation

	Details
• *Forces deployed abroad*	In Saudi Arabia (part of GCC Peninsula Shield Force)
• *Joint Maneuvers*	France, GCC countries, U.S.A., India
• *Security agreement*	France, Germany

Defense Production

	M	P	A
Naval equipment			
• Construction of patrol boats at Ajman (with British cooperation)		√	

Note: M=manufacture (indigenously developed)
P=production under license
A=assembly

NBC Technology

CW capabilities

- Personal protective equipment; unit decontamination equipment

ARMED FORCES

Major changes: The ground forces of the United Arab Emirates are in the process of deploying the Leclerc MBT (deliveries are in progress) and M-109 155mm SP howitzers. No changes have been recorded in the Air Force in 1997, although orders for the new Mirage 2000-9 have been placed. The navy received its first Kortenaer missile frigate, from the Netherlands.

Order-of-Battle

Year	1993	1994	1995	1996	1997
General data					
• Personnel	48,400	48,000	46,500	46,500	63,500
• Number of brigades	6	6	6	6	9
Ground forces					
• Tanks	216	216	212	216	366
• APCs/ARVs	665	893	1,100	1,100	955(1,115)
• Artillery	222	270	264	264	326(343)
Air Force					
• Combat aircraft	76	76	65	66	54(66)
• Transport aircraft	33	40	36	36	31(34)
• Helicopters	59	69	85	85	93(95)
Air Defense Forces					
• Heavy SAM batteries	7	7	5–7	5–7	5–7
• Medium SAM batteries	+	3	3	3	+

Order-of-Battle *(continued)*

Year	1993	1994	1995	1996	1997
• Light SAM launchers	+	+	+	+	113
Navy					
• Combat vessels	78	60	60	131	131

Note: Beginning with data for 1997, we refer to quantities in active service. The number in parentheses refers to the total.

Personnel

	Regular	Reserves	Total
Ground Forces	57,000		57,000
Air Force	4,500		4,500
Navy	2,000		2,000
Total	**63,500**		**63,500**
Paramilitary			
• Coast Guard			+
• Frontier Corps			+

GROUND FORCES

Formations

	Independent brigade/group
Armored	2
Mechanized	2
Infantry	4
	(including two brigades under Dubai National Command)
Royal Guard	1
Artillery	1
Total	**10**

Tanks

Model	Quantity	In service	Since	Notes
High quality				
• Leclerc	150	150	1995	Out of a total order of 436
Subtotal	150	150		
Medium and low quality				
• AMX-30	100	100		
• OF-40 Lion Mk2	36	36	1984	

Tanks *(continued)*

Model	Quantity	In service	Since	Notes
• Scorpion	80	80	1979	
Total	**366**	**366**		
On order				
• Leclerc tanks	436 (total order)			

APCs/ARVs (including command vehicles)

Model	Quantity	In service	Since	Notes
High quality				
• AMX-VCI	10	10		
• AMX-10P	20	20	1980	
• BMP-3	250	250		
• Engesa EE-11 Urutu	+	30	1985	
• Engessa EE-9 Cascavel	+	100		
• M-3 (Panhard)	300	300		
• VAB	20	20	1980	
• VBC-90				
• VCR				
Subtotal	730+	730		
Others				
• AML-60/AML-90	105	105		
• Fahd	100	100		
• Ferret	60	0		In storage
• Saladin	70	0		In storage
• Saracen	30	0		In storage
AT-105 Saxon	20	20		Possibly with police
Subtotal	385	225		
Total	**1,115**	**955**		
On order				
• M-2/M-3 Bradley	200			
• BMP-3	120			Status uncertain
• AIFV	136			From Turkey, delivery 1999

Artillery

Model	Quantity	In service	Since	Notes
Self-propelled guns and howitzers				
• 155mm Mk F3 (AMX-13)	20	20		
• 155mm G-6	78	78		
• 155mm M-109A3	some	some	1995	Deliveries in progress
Towed guns and howitzers				
• 155mm M-198	+	12		
• 130mm Type 59	+	30		
• 105mm L-118 light gun	81	81		
• 105mm M-102	50	50		
• 105mm M-56 Pack howitzer	18	18		
Mortars, under 160mm				
• 120mm	12	12		
Total	301+	301		
MRLs				
• 122mm Firos-25/30	48	25		
On order				
• 227mm MLRS				
• 155mm M-109A3	85			Used Dutch M-109A2 being upgraded. Deliveries in progress

Logistic and Engineering Equipment

- Matenin automatic mine layers, Mk 3(D) Flail

Antitank weapons

Model	Quantity	In service	Since	Notes
Missiles				
• BGM-71B Improved TOW	24	24	1983	
• HOT	50	50		Launchers
• Milan	230	230		
Total	approx. 300	approx. 300		Launchers
Guns				
• 120mm BAT L-4 recoilless rifle				

Antitank weapons *(continued)*

Model	Quantity	In service	Since	Notes
• 84mm Carl Gustav M-2 light recoilless rifle	250	250		

AIR FORCE

Order-of-Battle

Model	Quantity	In service	Notes
• Combat	66	54	
• Transport	30	27	
• Helicopters	95	93	

Combat Aircraft

Model	Quantity	In service	Since	Notes
Strike and multirole aircraft—high quality				
• Mirage 2000	36	36	1989	8 are reconnaissance
Strike and multirole aircraft—others				
• Mirage V—AD/ RAD/DAD	18	18	1974	
• Mirage III	12	0		
Subtotal	30	18		
Total	**66**	**54**		
On order				
• Mirage 2000-9	30			14 new and 13 ex–French AF. The existing aircraft are to be upgraded to the same standard.

Transport Aircraft

Model	Quantity	In service	Since	Notes
• Bae 125	1	1		
• Boeing 747	3	3	1985	

Transport Aircraft *(continued)*

Model	Quantity	In service	Since	Notes
• Boeing 737	1	1	1976	
• Boeing 707	2	2	1976	
• Britten-Norman BN-2 Islander	1	1	1983	
• C-130H Hercules/L-100-30	6	6	1975/ 1981	
• CASA C-212	4	4	1982	Employed in EW role
• CN-235	7	7	1993	Some in maritime partrol role
• DHC-4 Caribou	3	0		Possibly not serviceable
• G-222	1	1		Number unconfirmed
• IL-76	4	4	1994	On lease
• Mystère-Falcon 20	1	1		
Total	**34**	**31**		
On order				
• C-130				
• CN-235				Under negotiation

Training and Liaison Aircraft

Model	Quantity	In service	Since	Notes
With ground attack/close air support capability				
• Aermacchi MB-326 KD/LD	8	8	1974	
• Aermacchi MB-339	5	5	1984	
• Hawk Mk 102	26	26	1993	
• Hawk Mk 61/63	22	22	1983/ 1984	
Subtotal	61	61		
Others				
• Cessna 182 Skylane	1	1		
• Pilatus PC-7	23	23	1982	
• G-115T (Grob)	12	12	1997	
• SIAI-Marchetti SF-260 WD	5	5	1983	
Subtotal	41	41		
Total	**102**	**102**		
On order				
• G-115T (Grob)				Option for additional 12

Helicopters

Model	Quantity	In service	Since	Notes
Attack				
• AH-64A Apache	20	20	1993	
• SA-342K Gazelle	12	10	1980	
• Alouette III	7	7		
Subtotal	39	37		
Medium transport				
• A-109	3	3	1995	Possibly with police
• AB-205/Bell 205	8	8	1969	
• AB-212	3	3	1977	
• AB-214	4	4	1981	
• AB-412	5	5	1994	Possibly with police
• SA-330 Puma/possibly IAR-330	11	11	1972	
Subtotal	34	34		
Light transport				
• AB-206 JetRanger/ Bell 206L	10	10	1984	
• BO-105	5	5	1992	Employed in liaison role, number unconfirmed
Subtotal	15	15		
Maritime attack				
• AS-332/532 Super Puma/Cougar	7	7	1982	Some in maritime attack role
Total	**95**	**93**		
On order				
• AH-64A	10			Total order 30
• AS-565 Panther	7			Maritime attack
				All the AS-332/532s are to be upgraded to maritime attack and ASW role

Miscellaneous Aircraft

Model	Quantity	In service	Since	Notes
AEW/AWACS aircraft				
• C-130 EW				

Miscellaneous Aircraft *(continued)*

Model	Quantity	In service	Since	Notes
Target drones				
• TTL BTT-3 Banshee				
UAVs and mini-UAVs				
• Beech MQM-107A UAV	20	20		

Advanced Armament

Air-to-air-missiles
- AIM-9L Sidewinder, R-550 Magique

Air-to-ground missiles
- AS-11, AS-12, AS-30L, AM-39, Exocet, al-Hakim (PGM-1/PGM-2)

Bombs
- BAP-100 antirunway

On order
- al-Hakim PGM-1/PGM-2, British-made, possibly delivered; PGM-3, PGM-4 (long-range al-Hakim under development); AS-15TT air-to-surface (antiship) missiles; AM-39, AIM-120 (under negotiation)

Air Force Infrastructure

Aircraft shelters
- for combat aircraft at Abu Dhabi and Jabil (Jebel) Ali AF bases

Military airfields: **7**
- Abu Dhabi (international), al-Dhafra (Sharja), Bateen (Abu Dhabi), Dubai (international), Fujaira, Sharja, Mindhat

AIR DEFENSE FORCES

Surface-to-Air Missiles

Model	Batteries	Launchers	Since	Notes
Heavy missiles				
• MIM-23B Improved HAWK	5–7	30–40	1989	

Surface-to-Air Missiles *(continued)*

Model	Batteries	Launchers	Since	Notes
Medium missiles				
• Crotale	+	9		
• Rapier	+	12		
Total	+	21		
Light missiles				
• RBS-70		13	1980	
• Mistral		100	1993	
• Javelin		+		
• Tigercat		+		Probably phased out
Total		113		
Shoulder-launched missiles				
• Blowpipe		20+		Probably phased out
• FIM-92AStinger		+		
• SA-7 (Grail)		+		
• SA-14 (Gremlin)		+		
• SA-16 (Gimlet)		10		
Total		30+		
On order				
• MIM-104 Patriot				Under negotiation
• SA-10				
• SA-12 (S-300V)				Under negotiation

Other Air Defense Systems

Model	Quantity	In service	Since	Notes
Air defense systems (missiles, radars, and guns)				
• Skyguard AA system	7	7		
Short-range guns				
• 30mm × 2 M-3 SP				
• 20mm × 2 GCF-BM2 SP				
Radars				
• AN/TPS-70	3	3		
• Watchman				
On order				
Westinghouse air defense command, control and communication system; LASS; Crotale-NG SAMs (under negotiation); Mistral SAMs; Oerlikon ADATS (under negotiation); Starburst (under negotiation)				

NAVY

Combat Vessels

Type	Original Class name	Quantity	Length (m)/ Displace- ment (t)	Armament/ special equipment
Missile frigates				
• Kortenaer class		2	130.5/ 3,050	2 × helicopters 8 × Harpoon SSMs 4 × 324mm torpe- does 8 × Sea Sparrow 1 × 76mm gun
Missile corvettes				
• Muray-Jib	Lurssen 62	2	63/630	1 × Alouette heli- copter 8 × Exocet SSMs 8 × Crotale Nava- les 1 × 76mm gun 1 × 30mm Goal- keeper
MFPBs				
• Ban-Yas	Lurssen TNC-45	6	44.9/260	4 × Exocet MM40s 1 × 76mm gun
• Mubarraz class	Lurssen	2	44.9/260	4 × Exocet MM40s 1 × 6 Mistral SAM 1 × 76mm gun
Subtotal		8		
Patrol craft (some with coast guard)				
• Ardhana	Vosper Thornycroft type	6	33.5/110	2 × 30mm guns 1 × 20mm gun
• Camcraft		5	23.4/70	2 × 20mm guns with coast guard
• Camcraft		16	19.8/50	1 × 20mm gun with coast guard
• Watercraft		8	13.7/25	

Combat Vessels *(continued)*

Type	Original Class name	Quantity	Length (m)/ Displacement (t)	Armament/ special equipment
• Boghammar		3	13m	With police
• Baglietto GC-23		6	24/50.7	1 × 20mm gun with coast guard
• Baglietto		3	18.1/22	With coast guard
• Baglietto		2		With police
• Arctic		8	8.5/4	
• Al-Shaali		12	8.5/4	
• Harbor partrol craft		40	6/6–10m	With coast guard
• Dhafeer + Spear (coast guard)		10	9–12m	With police
Subtotal		119		
Total		**131**		
On order				
• Oliver Hazard Perry missile frigates		2		From U.S. draw-down

Landing Craft

Type	Original Class name	Quantity	Length(m)/ Displacement(t)	Armament/ special equipment
• al-Feyi	Siong Huat LSL	3	50/650	
• LCM		1	40/100	
• LCT		2		
• Serana class		2	26.3/105	45 tons or 100 troops
Total		**8**		

Auxiliary Vessels

Type	Original Class name	Quantity	Length(m)/ Displacement(t)	Armament/ special equipment
• Diving tender		1	31.4/100	
• Coastal tug		1	35.0/795	
• Diving tender (coast guard)		2		

Auxiliary Vessels *(continued)*

Type	Original Class name	Quantity	Length(m)/ Displace-ment(t)	Armament/ special equipment
On order				
• Crestitalia 30-meter diver support vessels		2		

Coastal Defense

Type	Quantity	Notes
• MM-40 Exocet		Unconfirmed

Naval Infrastructure

Naval bases: **11**

Including Coast Guard

- Ajman, Dalma (Abu Dhabi), Fujaira, Mina Jabil (Jebel) Ali (Dubai), Mina Khalid (Sharja), Mina Khor Fakkan (Sharja), Mina Rashid (Dubai), Mina Saqr (Ras al-Khaima), Mina Sultan (Sharja), Taweela, Mina Zayd (Abu Dhabi)

Ship maintenance and repair facilities

- Dubai wharf for maintenance and repair of merchant and naval vessels; two dry docks available, a new ship repair facility from the U.S.A. on order

21. YEMEN

GENERAL DATA

Official Name of the State: Republic of Yemen
Head of State: President Lieutenant Ali Abdallah Salih
Prime Minister: Faraj said bin Ghanim
Minister of Defense: Major General Muhammad Dayfallah (also Chief of Staff)
Commander of the Air Force: Colonel Muhammad Salih al-Ahmar
Commander of the Navy: Captain Ali Qasim Talib

Area: 527,970 sq. km. (borders with Saudi Arabia partly undemarcated and/or disputed)
Population: 13,620,000

Demography

Ethnic Groups		
Arabs	12,490,000	91.7%
Afro-Arabs	858,000	6.3%
Others	272,000	2.0%
Religious Groups		
Sunni Muslims	8,444,000	62.0%
Shi'ite Zaydi Muslims	4,903,000	36.0%
Shi'ite Ismaili Muslims	68,000	0.5%
Others	204,000	1.5%

Economic Data

		1992	1993	1994	1995	1996
GDP current price, local currency	YR bn	134.710	169.790	218.280	385.800	487.00
GDP (U.S. $)	$ bn	4.036	3.484	2.710	3.355	3.799
GDP per capita	$	323	268	201	239	278
Real GDP growth	%	4.2	4.3	–0.8	3.6	4.7
Balance of payments						
• Exports fob	$ bn	1.1	1.17	1.81	2.09	2.22
• Imports fob	$ bn	1.94	2.13	1.86	1.83	2.28

Economic Data *(continued)*

		1992	1993	1994	1995	1996
• Account balance (Includes services and income)	$ bn	–1.119	–1.289	–0.07	–0.90	–0.09
• External debt	$ bn	9.636	8.825	8.861	8.781	NA
Government income and expenditure						
• Revenues, local currency	YR bn	38.1	42.9	88	155.9	NA
• Expenditures, local currency	YR bn	69	87.1	124.1	181.4	NA
• Defense expenditures	YR bn	16.812	19.752	NA	NA	NA
• Defense expenditure/ GDP	%	12.48	11.63	NA	NA	NA
• Defense expenditure/ CGE	%	24.37	22.67	NA	NA	NA
• Population	m	12.5	12.99	13.49	14.02	13.62
• Official exchange rate	YR: $1	33.38	48.73	80.55	115	128.18

Sources: EIU quarterly report, EIU country profile, IMF statistical yearbook, SIPRI Yearbook.

Arms Procurement and Security Assistance Received

Country	Type	Details
Bulgaria	• *Arms transfers*	T-62 tanks, small arms
France	• *Military training*	Trainees abroad
Moldova	• *Arms transfers*	MiG-29, of Russian origin, MRLs
U.S.A.	• *Arms transfers*	Spare parts for American-made systems (1996)

Arms Sales and Security Assistance Extended

Country	Type	Details
Iraq	• *Facilities*	Refuge to a few Iraqi aricraft (unconfirmed)

ARMED FORCES

All figures are rough estimates, due to 1994 civil war. No major change has been recorded in the Yemeni armed forces in 1997.

Order-of-Battle

Year	1993	1994	1995	1996	1997
General data					
• Personnel	62,500–66,500	62,500–66,500	62,500–66,500	62,500–66,500	60,000–64,000
• Number of brigades	33	41	30	30	33
Ground Forces					
• Tanks	1,300	1,300	1,000	1,040	575 (1,040)
• APCs/ARVs	950	950	870	1,320	480 (1,165)
• Artillery (incl. MRLs)	1,000	1,130	1,020	1,020	659 (1,019)
• SSM launchers	22	22	22	22	22
Air Force					
• Combat aircraft (some in storage)	175	170	166	166	55 (147)
• Transport aircraft	23	23	23	23	18 (23)
• Helicopters	97	77	67	67	27 (67)
Air Defense Forces					
• Heavy SAM batteries	21	25	25	25	25
• Medium SAM batteries	–	+	+	+	+
• Light SAM launchers	+	+	+	+	120
Navy					
• Combat vessels	35	31	23	20	18

Note: Beginning with data for 1997, we refer to quantities in active service. The numbers in parentheses refers to the total.

Personnel

	Regular	Reserves (only partly trained)	Total
Military forces*			
Ground Forces	55,000–59,000	40,000	95,000–99,000
Air Force	3,000		3,000
Navy	2,000		2,000
Total (possibly 10% less due to casualties and desertion)	**60,000–64,000**	**40,000**	**100,000–104,000**

Personnel *(continued)*

	Regular	Reserves (only partly trained)	Total
Paramilitary			
Central Security Force (for internal purposes)	50,000		50,000

*Combination of personnel of former YAR and PDRY; no information regarding reorganization.

GROUND FORCES

Formations

	Independent brigade/group	Independent battalion
Armored	7	
Mechanized	5	
Infantry (mostly skeleton or undermanned units)	18	
Artillery	4	
SSM	1	
Air Defense		2
Commando/Paratroops	1	
Special Forces	1	
Central Guards	1	
Total	**38**	**2**

Tanks

Model	Quantity	In service	Since	Notes
Medium and low quality				
• T-62	200	75	1979	
• M-60 A1	140	50	1979	
• T-54/55	700	450	1979	
Total	**1,040**	**575**		

APCs/ARVs (including command vehicles)

Model	Quantity	In service	Since	Notes
High quality				
• BMP-1/BMP-2	250	100		
• M-113 A1 and its derivatives	70	70	1979	
Subtotal	320	170		
Others				
• AML-90/AML-60	125	80	1975	
• BRDM-2	150	50		
• BTR-40/50/60	500	180		
• BTR-152				
• al-Walid				
• Ferret	10	+		Possibly phased out
• Saladin	60	+		Possibly phased out
Subtotal	845	310		
Total	**1,165**	**480**		

Artillery

Model	Quantity	In service	Since	Notes
Self-propelled guns and howitzers				
• 122mm M-1974	+	+		
• 100mm SU-100	30	0		Obsolete
Towed guns and howitzers				
• 155mm M-114	12	12	1980	
• 152mm D-20	10	+		
• 130mm M-46	75	60		
• 122mm D-30	150	130		
• 122mm M-1938	100	40		
• 122mm M-1231/7	30	30		
• 105mm M-101	30	25		
Mortars, over 160mm				
• 160mm mortar	100	100		
Mortars, under 160mm				
• 120mm	100	100		
• 107mm	12	12		
Total	**649**	**509**		
MRLs				
• 240mm BM-24	35	+		Unconfirmed
• 140mm BM-14	30	+		

Artillery *(continued)*

Model	Quantity	In service	Since	Notes
• 132mm BM-13	15	+		
• 122mm BM-21	290	150		

Antitank Weapons

Model	Quantity	In service	Since	Notes
Missiles				
• AT-3 (Sagger)	+	+		
• BGM-71A Improved TOW	12	+	1979	
• M-47 Dragon	24	+	1982	
Guns				
• 107mm B-11 recoilless rifle	+	+		
• 100mm M-1955 field/ AT gun	20	+		
• 85mm M-1945/D-44 field/AT gun	100	90		
• 82mm recoilless rifle	+	+		
• 76mm M-1942 divisional gun	100	70		
• 75mm recoilless rifle	+	+		
• 57mm gun				

Surface-to-Surface Missiles and Rockets

Model	Launchers	Missiles	Since	Notes
• FROG-7	12			
• SS-1 (Scud B)	6			
• SS-21 (Scarab)	4		1988	
Total	**22**			

AIR FORCE

Order-of-Battle

Model	Quantity	In service	Notes
• Combat	147	55	Some in storage
• Transport	23	18	
• Helicopters	67	27	

Combat Aircraft

Model	Quantity	In service	Since	Notes
Interceptors—high quality				
• MiG-29 (Fulcrum)	4–5	+	1994	
Interceptors—medium and low quality				
• MiG-21 (Fishbed)	82	30	1979	A few in storage
Total	**87**	**30**		
Strike and multirole aircraft—medium and low quality				
• MiG-23/27 (Flogger B/D)	15	+	1980	
• Su-20/22 (Fitter C)	35	15	1980	
• F-5E/B	10	10	1980	
• MiG-17 (Fresco)/ MiG-15 (Faggot) Midget				In training role, some not serviceable
Total	60	25		
Total	**147**	**55**		
On order				
• Su-20/22	12			
• MiG-29	30			Possibly some delivered

Transport Aircraft

Model	Quantity	In service	Since	Notes
• An-24/An-26 (Coke/ Curl)	15	10	1984/ 1985	
• C-130H Hercules	2	2	1979	
• IL-14 (Crate)	4	4		
• Short Skyvan Srs. 3	2	2		
Total	**23**	**18**		

Training and Liaison Aircraft

• YAK-11	15	10		

Helicopters

Model	Quantity	In service	Since	Notes
Attack				
• Mi-24 (Hind)	12	6	1980	

Helicopters *(continued)*

Model	Quantity	In service	Since	Notes
Medium transport				
• AB-212	5	3	1980	
• AB-204	2	2		
• AB-205	2	2		
• Mi-8/Mi-17 (Hip)	40	10		
Subtotal	49	17		
Light transport				
• AB-206 JetRanger	6	4		
Total	**67**	**27**		

Advanced Armament

Air-to-air-missiles
• AA-2 (Atoll)
Air-to-ground missiles
• AT-2 (Swatter)

Air Force Infrastructure

Military airfields (approx. 18)
• Aden (Khormaksar), al-Anad, Ataq, Bayhan, al-Qasab, Ghor Ubyad, al-Hudaydah, Ir-Fadhl, Kamaran Island, Lawdar, al-Mukalla, Nugaissa, al Riyan (Rayane), San'a, Socotra, approx. three others

AIR DEFENSE FORCES

Surface-to-Air Missiles

Model	Batteries	Launchers	Since	Notes
Heavy missiles				
• SA-2 (Guideline)				
• SA-3				
Total	25			
Medium missiles				
• SA-6	+			
Light missiles				
• SA-9 (Gaskin)		120		
Shoulder-launched missiles				
• SA-7 (Grail)		100–200		

Other Air Defense Systems

Model	Quantity	In service	Since	Notes
Short-range guns				
• 57mm ZSU 57×2 SP	+	+		
• 57mm S-60	150	100		
• 37mm M-1939	150	150		
• 23mm ZSU 23×4 SP (Shilka)	10	+		
• 23mm ZU 23×2	30	30		
• 20mm M-163 Vulcan SP	20	20		
• 20mm M-167 Vulcan	52	20		
Total	**412**	**320**		

NAVY

Combat Vessels

Type	Original Class name	Quantity	Length (m.)/ Displace-ment (t.)	Armament/ special equipment
Missiles corvettes				
• Tarantul	Type 1241	2	56.1/385	4 × Styx SS-N-2C SSMs 4 × SA-N-5 Grail SAMs 1 × 76mm gun 2 × 30mm guns
MFPBs				
• Huang-Feng		3	33.6/171	4 × YJ-1 (C-801) SSMs 4 × 25mm guns
Mine warfare vessels				
• Yevgenia class	Type 1258	5	24.6/177	2 × 25mm guns or 2 × 14.5mm MGs
• Natya class	Type 266ME	1	61/804	Acoustic and Magnetic sweeps 4 × 30mm guns 4 × 25mm guns 2 × RBU 1200 ASW mortars 10 mines
Subtotal		6		

Combat Vessels *(continued)*

Type	Original Class name	Quantity	Length (m.)/ Displace-ment (t.)	Armament/ special equipment
Patrol craft				
• Broadsword class (customs)		3	32/90.5	2 × 25mm guns 2 × 14.5mm MGs 2 × 12.7mm MGs
• Zhuk class	Type 1400M	4	24/39	4 × 14.5mm MGs
Subtotal		7		
Total		**18**		
On order				
• CMN-15-60 patrol craft		6		

Landing Craft

Type	Original Class name	Quantity	Length (m.)/ Displace-ment (t.)	Armament/ special equipment
• Ondatra LCU	Type 1176	2	24/145	1 tank
• Ropucha LST	Type 775	1	112.5/4,080	4 × SA-N-5 SAMs 4 × 57mm guns 2 × 122mm MRLs 92 mines 10 tanks and 190 troops
Total		**3**		

Auxiliary Vessels

Type	Original Class name	Quantity	Length (m.)/ Displace-ment (t.)	Armament/ special equipment
• Toplivo class		2	53.7/1,029	50 tonnes
• Shabwah YTM		2		
• 14m hydrographic craft		1	14m	

Coastal Defense

Type	Launchers	Notes
• Land-based SS-N-2 Styx	8	

Naval Infrastructure

Naval bases: 6

- Aden, al-Hudaydah; anchorage at Kamaran Island (unconfirmed); al-Mukalla, Perim Island, Socotra

Ship maintenance and repair facilities

- National dockyards, Aden; 4,500-ton floating dock and 1,500-ton slipway

PART III

DATA AND DOCUMENTATION

COMPARATIVE TABLES

Table 1. Major Armies of the Middle East

		Personnel (thousands)			Divisions			Indep. Brigades			Indep. Battalions			Tanks						
Country	Year	Reg.	Res.	Total	Armor	Mech.	Inf./ Para./ Com./	Armor	Mech.	Inf./ Para./ Com./	Armor	Mech.	Inf./ Para./ Com./	High Quality	Others	Total	APCs and ARVs	Guns and Mortars	ATGM Launchers	SSM Launchers
Egypt*	96–97	300	150	450	4	7	1	4	4	10	—	—	—	1,250	1,800	3,050	5,100	2,850	2,950	21
	95–96	320	600	920	4	7	1	3	2	9	—	—	—	1,100	1,800	2,900	5,180	2,750	1,750–1,950	24
Iran**	96–97	450	350	800	8	—	24	1	—	10	—	—	—	200	1,300	1,500	1,200	1,600–2,600	+	26–36
	95–96	340	+	340	6	3	23	1	—	6	—	—	—	200	1,300	1,500	1,000	1,750	+	15
Iraq***	96–97	350	650	1,000	6	4	13	—	—	2	—	—	—	1,000	1,200	2,200	3,300	1,950	1,500	34
	95–96	350	+	350	6	4	13–15	—	—	14	—	—	—	900	1,200	2,100	3,300	1,800	1,500	34
Israel	96–97	141	380	521	12	—	4	—	8	5	—	—	—	2,120	1,780	3,900	8,010	1,900	+	12
	95–96	141	360	501	12	—	4	—	—	13	—	—	—	2,050	1,820	3,870	8,010	1,280	+	+
Jordan	96–97	85	60	145	2	2	—	—	—	2	—	—	—	515	711	1,230	1,580	800	640	—
	95–96	85	60	145	2	2	—	—	—	3	—	—	—	375	692	1,070	1,570	450	550	—
Libya	96–97	50	—	50	—	—	—	—	—	5	10	21	15	360	2,350	2,710	2,970	1,430	1,060	110
	95–96	50	—	50	—	—	—	+	+	+	—	—	—	360	2,350	2,710	3,000	2,200	1,500	110
Saudi	96–97	127	20	147	—	—	—	3	8	7	—	—	20	715	300	1,015	5,220	515	1,500	8–12
Arabia#	95–96	129	—	129	—	—	—	3	7	8	—	—	20	715	300	1,015	4,040	700	1,500	8–12
Syria	96–97	306	100	406	8	3	1	1	1	11–13	—	—	—	1,550	3,250	4,800	4,980	2,500	3,400	62
	95–96	306	100	406	8	3	1	1	1	9	—	—	—	1,500	3,250	4,800	4,980	2,400	2,000	62

Note:

+ precise number unknown

—no entry

* due to change in estimate

** army and IRGC, excluding Baseej reserves

*** excluding Popular Army

\# army and national guard

For classification of tanks according to quality, see introductory note, part 2.

All figures represent total quantity.

Table 2. Major Air Forces of the Middle East (including Air Defense Forces)

		Personnel (thousands)			Interceptors		Strike and Multirole Aircraft					Helicopters				
Country	Year	Reg.	Res.	Total	High Quality	Others	High Quality	Others	Bombers	Total Combat a/c	Transport a/c	Attack	Transport +ASW	Total	Military Airfields	Heavy SAM Batteries*
Egypt	96–97	105	80	185	148	224	—	133	—	505	35	101	122	223	29	105
	95–96	95	80	175	153	205	—	139	—	497	47	94	117	211	28	122
Iran	96–97	30	—	30	95	25	24	174	—	318	114	100	453	553	20	30–35
	95–96	35	—	35	60	50	24	85	—	219	119	70	205	275	20+	30–35
Iraq	96–97	40	+	40	30	160	6	130	5	331	+	150	330	480	38	60
	95–96	40	+	40	35	185	+	150	5	380	+	150	250	400	38	60
Israel	96–97	36.5	54	90.5	73	—	245	462	—	780	93	140	148	288	11	21
	95–96	36.5	54	90.5	73	—	246	465	—	784	83	135	150	285	11	+
Jordan	96–97	8.5	—	8.5	—	—	—	91	—	91	13	22	46	68	6	14
	95–96	8.5	—	8.5	—	—	—	85	—	85	12	22	46	68	6	14
Libya	96–97	18	—	18	65–70	240	6	160	7	478–483	90	80	132	212	16	25–31**
	95–96	18	—	18	65–70	240	6	160	7	478–483	106	80	130	210	16	90
Saudi	96–97	20	—	20	115	—	118	89	—	322	61	27	148	175	20–24	22
Arabia	95–96	18	—	18	116	—	45	89	—	249	76	27	153	180	20–24	23
Syria	96–97	70	30	100	55	310	20	135	—	520	25	100	195	295	21	108
	95–96	80	40	120	55	310	20	150	—	515	23	100	185	285	21	108

Note:

\+ precise number unknown —no entry

For classification of combat aircraft according to quality, see Introductory Note, part 2.

*For classification of heavy SAMs, see introductory note.

**due to change in estimate

All figures represent total quantity.

Table 3. Major Navies of the Middle East

Country	Year	Personnel (thousands) Reg.	Res.	Total	Submarines	MFPBs	Missile Destroyers, Frigates, Corvettes	SSMs	Gun Destroyers, Frigates, Corvettes	ASW Vessels	Mine Warfare Vessels	MTB and Gunboats	Patrol Craft	Landing Craft	Hover-craft	Naval Bases
Egypt	96–97	16	14	30	6	24	8	Harpoon, Otomat, Styx, HY-2	1	—	13	18	83	17	—	8
	95–96	16	14	30	8	22	6	Harpoon, Otomat, Styx, HY-2	1	—	12	18	70	17	—	8
Iran*	96–97	38	—	38	3	21	5	Harpoon, Sea Killer, C-801, C-802	2	—	5	—	136+	18	10	19
	95–96	38	—	38	2	21	5	Harpoon, Sea Killer, C-801, C-802	2	—	5	—	176	19	14	19
Iraq	96–97	1.8	—	1.8	—	1	2	Styx	—	—	2	—	83	—	—	4
	95–96	1.9	—	1.9	—	1	—	Styx	—	—	5	1	86	3	—	4
Israel	96–97	9.5	10	19.5	4	18	3	Gabriel, Harpoon	—	—	—	—	35	7	—	3
	95–96	9.5	10	19.5	3	19	3	Gabriel, Harpoon	—	—	—	—	36	8	—	3
Libya	96–97	8	—	8	4	21	5	Otomat, SS-12, Styx	—	—	8	—	2	8	—	6
	95–96	8	—	8	6	24	10	Otomat, SS-12, Styx	1	—	7	3	9	8	—	6
Saudi Arabia	96–97	12	—	12	—	9	8	Harpoon, Otomat 2	—	—	7	—	92	8	16	13
	95–96	12	—	12	—	9	8	Harpoon, Otomat 2	—	—	7	3	102	8	16	13
Syria	96–97	4	2.5	6.5	—	16	—	Styx, SS-N-2C	—	2	7	—	8	3	—	3
	95–96	4	2.5	6.5	3	21	—	Styx, SS-N-2C	—	2	9	—	16	3	—	3

Note: —indicates no entry

*including IRGC

Table 4. The Israel-Syria Military Balance

Army

Country	Personnel (thousands)			Divisions			Indep. Brigades				APCs and	Guns and		
	Reg.	Res.	Total	Armor	Mech.	Inf.	Armor	Mech.	Inf./Para./Com./Terr.	Tanks	ARVs	Mortars	ATGM Launchers	SSM Launchers
Israel	141	380	521	12	—	4	—	8	5	3,900	8,010	1,900	+	12
Syria	306	100	406	8	3	1	1	1	11–13	4,800	4,980	2,500	3,400	62

Air Force and Air Defense

Country	Personnel (thousands)			Interceptors		Strike and Multirole Aircraft		Total		Helicopters				Heavy
	Reg.	Res.	Total	High Quality	Others	High Quality	Others	Combat a/c	Transport a/c	Attack	Transport+ ASW	Total	Military Airfields	SAM Batteries
Israel	36.5	54	90.5	73	—	245	462	780	93	140	148	288	11	21
Syria	70	30	100	55	310	20	135	520	25	100	195	295	21	108

Navy

Country	Personnel (thousands)			Submarines	MFPBs	Missile Destroyers, Frigates Corvettes	SSMs	ASW Vessels	Mine Warfare Vessels	Patrol Craft	Landing Craft	Hovercraft	Naval Bases
	Reg.	Res.	Total										
Israel	9.5	10	19.5	4	18	3	Gabriel, Harpoon	—	—	35	7	—	3
Syria	4	2.5	6.5	—	21	—	Styx, SS-N-2C	2	7	8	3	—	3

Note:
+ precise number unknown
—no entry
For classification of tanks, long-range SAMs, and combat a/c according to quality, see Introductory Note, part 2.
All figures represent total quantity.

Table 5. Eastern Front–Israel Military Balance

This is only one of several possibilities, assuming that Egypt and Jordan remain out to the war.
Full participants: Israel, Syria, Palestinian volunteers from the "rejection front."
Partial participants: Saudi Arabian land (three brigades) and air units (four combat a/c squadrons, one transport squadron, and one helicopter squadron); Kuwaiti air units (one squadron); Iraqi land (five divisions, 10 SSM launchers) and air units (100 combat a/c, 100 helicopters); Libyan land (three armored brigades, three mechanized brigades. 20 SSM launchers); and air units (two combat a/c squadrons, one squadron attack helicopters), and the entire Libyan Navy. Iran would contribute arms, weapons systems, and spare parts.

Army

Country	Personnel (thousands)			Divisions			Indep. Brigades					APCs and	Guns and	ATGM	SSM
	Reg.	Res.	Total	Armor	Mech.	Inf.	Armor	Mech.	Inf./Para./ Com./Terr.	Total	Tanks	ARVs	Mortars	Launchers	Launchers
Eastern Front	461	110	571	10	4	2	6	5	15	26	6,100	7,000	3,600	4,250	100
Israel	141	380	521	12	—	4	—	8	5	13	3,900	8,010	1,900	+	12
Ratio, 96–97	3.3:1	0.3:1	1.1:1	0.8:1	*	0.5:1	*	0.6:1	3:1	2:1	1.6:1	0.9:1	1.9:1	*	*
Ratio, 95–96	3.2:1	0.3:1	1.1:1	0.8:1	*	0.5:1	*	*	1:1	1.8:1	1.6:1	0.9:1	2.7:1	*	*

Air Force and Air Defense

Country	Personnel (thousands)			Interceptors		Strike and Multirole a/c			Total		Helicopters				Heavy
	Reg.	Res.	Total	High Quality	Others	High Quality	Others	Bombers	Combat a/c	Transport a/c	Attack	Transport +ASW	Total	Military Airfields	SAM Batteries
Eastern Front	127	20	147	155	550	80	235	4	1,024	50	200	212	412	38	120
Israel	36.5	54	90.5	73	—	245	462	—	780	93	140	148	288	11	21
Ratio, 96–97	3.4:1	0.4:1	1.6:1	2.1:1	*	0.3:1	0.5:1	*	1.3:1	0.5:1	1.4:1	1.4:1	1.4:1	3.5:1	*
Ratio, 95–96	3.7:1	0.6:1	1.8:1	2.1:1	*	0.3:1	0.5:1	*	1.3:1	0.6:1	1.5:1	1.3:1	1.4:1	3.5:1	*

Navy

Country	Personnel (thousands)			Submarines	MFPBs	Missile Detroyers, Frigates, Corvettes	SSMs	Gun Destroyers, Frigates Corvettes	ASW Vessels	Mine Warfare Vessel	Patrol Craft	Landing Craft	Naval Bases
	Reg.	Res.	Total										
Eastern Front	13	2.5	15.5	4	37	5	Styx, Otomat	—	2	1	6	11	9
Israel	9.5	10	19.5	4	18	3	Gabriel, Harpoon	—	—	—	35	7	3
Ratio, 96–97	1.4:1	0.3:1	0.8:1	1:1	2:1	1.7:1		*	*	*	0.2:1	1.6:1	3:1
Ratio, 95–96	1.4:1	0.3:1	0.8:1	3:1	2.4:1	3.3:1		*	*	*	0.7:1	1.4:1	3:1

Note:

The constellation of full and partial participants presented here is only one of several reasonable possibilities; it reflects neither an absolute certainty nor the maximum force which the countries involved are thought to be capable of deploying.

\+ precise number unknown

—no entry

* no basis for calculation

For classification of tanks, long-range SAMs, and combat a/c according to quality, see Introductory Note, part 2.

All figures represent total quantity.

Table 6. Arab-Israel Military Balance (Israel vs. Arab Coalition, including Egypt and Iraq)

Full participants: Israel, Syria, Palestinian volunteers, Egypt, Libyan Navy.
Partial participants: Saudi Arabian land (three brigades) and air units (three squadrons); Iraqi land (five divisions, 10 SSM launchers) and air units (100 combat a/c, 100 helocopters); Kuwaiti air units (one squadron); Algerian land (two brigades); air (two combat a/c squadrons), and naval units (three vessels); Moroccan land (one brigade) and air units (one squadron); Libyan land (three armored brigades, three mechanized brigades, 20 SSM launchers) and air units (two combat a/c squadrons, one squadron of attack helicopters). Iran would contribute arms and weapons systems.

Army

	Personnel (thousands)			Divisions				ndep. Brigades								
Country	Reg.	Res.	Total	Armor	Mech.	Inf.	Total	Armor	Mech.	Inf./Para./ Com./Terr.	Total	Tanks	APCs and ARVs	Guns and Mortars	ATGM Launchers	SSM Launchers
Arab Coalition	827	660	1,487	16	15	3	34	12	10	28	50	10,550	13,870	6,930	6,470	127
Israel	141	380	521	12	—	4	16	—	8	5	13	3,900	8,010	1,900	+	12
Ratio, 96–97	5.9:1	1.7:1	2.9:1	1.3:1	*	0.8:1	2.1:1	*	1.3:1	5.6:1	3.8:1	2.7:1	1.7:1	3.6:1	*	*
Ratio, 95–96	6:1	1.8:1	3:1	1.3:1	*	0.8:1	2.1:1	*	*	1.8:1	3.3:1	2.7:1	1.7:1	5.3:1	*	*

Air Force and Air Defense

	Personnel (thousands)			Interceptors		Strike and Multirole a/c					Helicopters				
Country	Reg.	Res.	Total	High Quality	Others	High Quality	Others	Bombers	Total Combat a/c	Transport a/c	Attack	Transoprt +ASW	Total	Military Airfields	Heavy SAM Batteries
Arab Coalition	244	100	344	325	739	95	453	4	1,256	100	328	378	706	74	239
Israel	36.5	54	90.5	73	—	245	462	—	780	93	140	148	288	11	21
Ratio, 96–97	6.6:1	1.8:1	3.8:1	4.5:1	*	0.4:1	1:1	*	1.6:1	1.1:1	2.3:1	2.5:1	2.5:1	6.7:1	*
Ratio, 95–96	6.7:1	2.1:1	4.1:1	4.5:1	*	0.4:1	1:1	*	1.6:1	1.3:1	2.4:1	2.4:1	2.4:1	6.6:1	*

Navy

Country	Personnel (thousands)			Submarines	MFPBs	Missile Destroyers, Frigates, Corvettes	SSMs	Gun Destroyers, Frigates, Corvettes	ASW Vessels	Mine Warfare Vessels	Patrol Craft	Landing Craft	Naval Bases
	Reg.	Res.	Total										
Arab Coalition	31	16.5	47.5	12	61	13	Styx, HY-2 Harpoon, Otomat	—	2	12	98	28	18
Israel	9.5	10	19.5	4	18	3	Gabriel, Harpoon	—	—	—	35	7	3
Ratio, 96–97	3.3:1	1.7:1	2.4:1	3:1	3.4:1	4.3:1	*	*	*	*	2.8:1	4:1	6:1
Ratio, 95–96	3.3:1	1.7:1	2.4:1	6.3:1	3.5:1	5.3:1	*	*	*	*	2.9:1	3.5:1	6:1

Note:
The constellation of full and partial participants presented here is only one of several reasonable possibilities; it reflects neither an absolute certainty nor the maximum force that the countries involved are thought to be capable of deploying.
+ precise number unknown
—no entry
* no basis for calculation
For classification of tanks, long-range SAMs, and combat a/c according to quality, see Introductory Note, part 2.
All figures represent total quantity.

Table 7. Arab-Israel Military Balance 1984–1997

Participants: See table 6

Army

	Divisions								Independent Brigades		Tanks		APCs and ARVs		Guns and Mortars		ATGM Launchers		SSM Launchers	
	Armor		Mechanized		Infantry		Total													
	84	97	84	97	84	97	84	97	84	97	84	97	84	97	84	97	84	97	84	97
Arab coalition	10	16	10	15	3	3	23	34	51	50	8,065	10,550	8,470	13,870	6,050	6,930	5,150	6,470	54	127
Israel	11	12	—	—	—	4	11	16	20	13	3,650	3,900	8,000	8,010	1,000	1,900	+	+	+	12
Ratio	0.9:1	1.3:1	*	*	*	0.8:1	2.1:1	2.1:1	2.5:1	3.8:1	2.2:1	2.7:1	1.1:1	1.7:1	6.1:1	3.6:1	*	*	*	*

Air Force and Air Defense

	Interceptors				Strike and Multirole a/c				Total Combat a/c		Helicopters						Military Airfields		Heavy SAM Batteries	
	High Quality		Others		High Quality		Others				Attack		Transport +ASW		Total					
	84	97	84	97	84	97	84	97	84	97	84	97	84	97	84	97	84	97	84	97
Arab Coalition	130	325	620	739	496	95	354	453	1,635	1,256	161	328	324	378	485	706	48	74	304	239
Israel	40	73	—	—	445	245	185	462	670	730	55	140	133	148	188	288	11	11	+	21
Ratio	3.3:1	4.5:1	*	*	1.1:1	0.4:1	1.9:1	1:1	2.4:1	1.3:1	2.9:1	2.3:1	2.4:1	2.6:1	2.4:1	2.5:1	4.4:1	6.7:1	*	11.3:1

Navy

	Submarines		MFPBs		Missile Destroyers, Frigates, Corvettes		Gun Destroyers, Frigates, Corvettes		Landing Craft		Naval Bases	
	84	**97**	**84**	**97**	**84**	**97**	**84**	**97**	**84**	**97**	**84**	**97**
Arab Coalition	18	12	67	61	8	13	8	—	36	28	17	18
Israel	3	4	24	18	—	3	—	—	13	7	3	3
Ratio	6:1	3:1	2.8:1	3.4:1	*	4.3:1	*	*	2.8:1	4:1	5.7:1	6:1

Note:
+ precise number unknown
—no entry
* no basis for calculation
All figures represent total quantity.

Table 8. The Iran-Iraq Military Balance

Army

Country	Personnel (thousands)			Divisions			Indep. Brigades				Tanks	APCs and ARVs	Guns and Mortars	ATGM Launchers	SSM Launchers
	Reg.	Res.	Total	Armor	Mech.	Inf.	Armor	Mech.	Inf./Para./Com./Terr.	Total					
Iran*	350	350	700	8	—	24	1	—	10	11	1,500	1,200	1,600–2,600	+	26–36
Iraq**	350	650	1,000	6	4	13	—	—	2	2	2,200	3,300	1,950	1,500	20–30

Air Force and Air Defense

Country	Personnel (thousands)			Interceptors		Strike and Multirole a/c		Bombers	Total Combat a/c	Transport a/c	Helicopters			Military Airfields	Heavy SAM Batteries
	Reg.	Res.	Total	High Quality	Others	High Qualtiy	Others				Attack	Transport +ASW	Total		
Iran*	30	—	30	60	25	24	117	—	226	93	70	240	310	20	30–35
Iraq**	40	+	40	30	160	6	130	5	331	+	150	330	480	38	60

Navy

Country	Personnel (thousands)			Submarines	MFPBs	Missile Destroyers, Frigates, Corvettes	SSMs	Gun Destroyers, Frigates, Corvettes	ASW Vessels	Mine Warfare Vessels	MTBs and Gunboats	Patrol Craft	Landing Craft	Hovercraft	Naval Bases
	Reg.	Res.	Total												
Iran	38	—	38	3	21	5	Harpoon, Sea Killer, C-801, C-802	2	—	5	—	136	19	10	19
Iraq	1.8	—	1.8	—	1	2	Styx	—	—	2	—	83	—	—	4

Note:

+ precise number unknown

—no entry

* Army and IRGC; only serviceable a/c incl. in total

** excluding popular army

For classification of tanks, long-range SAMs, and combat a/c according to quality, see Introductory Note part 2.

Table 9. The U.S.A. in the Middle East: Financial Aid (Military), Arms Sales, Advisers, Trainees, and Facilities

Country	Financial Aid ($ millions)			Arms (major items)	Advisers	Trainees in U.S.	Facilities Provided to U.S.	Joint Maneuvers
	Grants	Loans	Total	Granted or Sold				
Bahrain	—	—	—	ATGMs combat a/c, helicopters, tanks, APCs, SAMS, landing craft, a missile frigate	+	+	naval, storage, and intelligence facilities, prepositioning of army equipment; HQ	+
Egypt	1,300+	—	1,300+	tanks, APCS, artillery, UAVs, helicopters, combat a/c, SAMs, naval SSMs, early warning a/c, radars, fire control for submarines, sonars, ATGMs, communication and ECCM equipment	+	+	use of airfields	+
Israel	1,800+	—	1,800+	APCs, artillery, combat a/c, SAMs, naval SSMs, tank transporters, attack helicopters, corvettes	—	+	prepositioning of equipment	+
Jordan	100	—	100	terminally guided artillery shells, spare parts for U.S.-made arms, F-16 a/c, MBTs	+	+	—	+
Kuwait	—	—	—	SAMs, APCs, patrol boats, combat a/c, command and control systems, night–vision equipment, tanks	+	+	naval and ground forces, prepositioning of equipment	+
Lebanon	c. 4 (in 1995)	—	c. 4	Jeeps, trucks, helicopters, M-113 APCs	+	+	—	+
Morocco	34 (in 1994)	—	34	tanks, T-37 aircraft, supply ship	+	+	use of airfields, naval communications, storage	+

Country	Financial Aid ($ millions)			Arms (major items) Granted or Sold	Advisers	Trainees in U.S.	Facilities Provided to U.S.	Joint Maneuvers
	Grants	Loans	Total					
Oman	—	—	—	SP artillery, AAMs, tanks, a missile frigate on order	+	—	use of airfields, naval communications, storage	+
Qatar	—	—	—	upgrading of air defense	+	+	prepositioning agreed upon, not yet implemented	+
Saudi Arabia	—	—	—	tanks, APCs, artillery, ATGMs, combat a/c, transport a/c, SAMs, AAMs, AGMs, AD systems, radio systems	+	+	air, ground, naval forces, and logistical facilities, including prepositioned equipment, HQ	+
Tunisia	27 (in 1993)	—	27	tanks, SAMs, transport a/c, artillery spares	+	+	—	+
UAE	—	—	—	transport aircraft, SAMs, a/c training simulator, light reconnaissance vehicles, radio systems, combat a/c and AH-64 helicopters, AGM missiles, frigates, early warning systems	+	+	storage facilities	—

Note:
+ precise number unknown
—no entry

Table 10. Russia in the Middle East: Arms Sales, Advisers, and Trainees

Country	Arms (major items) Sold	Advisers	Trainees in Russia
Algeria	helicopters, air defense equipment	—	—
Egypt	APC turrets, spare parts	—	—
Iran	APCs, SAMs, combat aircraft, tanks, submarines	+	+
Kuwait	APCs, MRLs, ATGMs, AIFVs	—	+
Syria	No deals have been concluded in the past several years	+	—
UAE	BMP-3 APCs, MRLs, ATGMs	—	—

Note:
+ precise number unknown
—no entry

Table 11. France in the Middle East: Arms Sales, Advisers, and Trainees

Country	Arms (major items) Granted or Sold	Advisers	Trainees in France
Algeria	helicopters	—	—
Iran	Socata training a/c	—	—
Israel	Socata Trinidad a/c, protective vest	—	+
Kuwait	radars, naval vessels SAMs, antiship missiles	+	+
Lebanon	maintenance of helicopters	+	—
Morocco	OPV-64 patrol craft	+	+
Oman	ATGMs, naval SSMs, AAMs, fire-control radar, patrol craft	—	+
Qatar	APCs, artillery, combat aircraft, MFPBs, naval SSMs, antiship AGMs	+	+
Saudi Arabia	radars, SAMs, antiship AGMs, SP artillery, upgrading of SAMs and missile frigates, missile frigates on order	+	+
UAE	combat aircraft, AAMs, AGMs, Leclerc tanks, helicopters, shoulder-launched SAMs, ARVs, torpedoes, thermal-imaging night-vision systems	+	+

Note:
+ precise number unknown
—no entry

Table 12. Britian in the Middle East: Arms Sales, Advisers, Trainees, and Cooperation in Arms Production

Country	Arms (major items) Granted or Sold	Advisers	Trainees in Britain	Cooperation in Arms Production
Algeria	naval vessels	—	—	naval vessels
Bahrain	patrol craft, electronics	+	+	
Egypt	naval radars, mortar-locating-radar upgrading	—	+	ATGMs, radio transceivers, electronics
Israel	spare parts	—	+	—
Kuwait	APCs, trainer aircraft, shoulder-launched SAMs, antiship missiles on order	+	+	—
Oman	Swiss-model MOWAG Piranha APCs, tanks, combat and training aircraft, a/c radars and navigation systems, upgrading Jaguar a/c, missile corvettes, uprading kits for Rapier SAMs	seconded and hired personnel	+	—
Qatar	helicopters, SAMs, drones, ship	+	+	—
Saudi Arabia	mortars, combat and trainer aircraft, helicopters, AAMs, minesweepers	+	+	assembly of electronics
UAE	AFV transporters, PGMs, sonar	—	—	—

Note:
+ precise number unknown
—no entry

Table 13. China in the Middle East: Arms Sales, Advisers, Trainees and Cooperation in Arms Production

Country	Arms (major items) Granted or Sold	Advisers	Trainees in PRC	Cooperation in Arms Production
Egypt	spare parts for F-7 combat a/c	—	—	
Iran	coastal defense SSMs, F-7 combat a/c, SAMs, MFPBs, transport aircraft	+	+	cooperation in nuclear research; SAM production MRLs
Saudi Arabia	—	connected to CSS-2 SSMs purchased in 1988	—	—
Sudan	combat a/c (A-5 Fantan, F-7, F-6)	+	—	—
Syria	—	+	—	—

Note:
+ precise number unknown
—no entry

Table 14. North Korea in the Middle East: Arms Sales, Advisers, Trainees, and Technology Transfers

	Present				
Country	Arms Sales	Advisers	Trainees in North Korea	Technology Transfers	Past (last years)
Egypt		—	—	cooperation in SSM technology	cooperation in SSM technology (1989 and earlier)
Iran	SSMs	+	+	SSM technology	artillery, AAGs, naval mines, midget submarines, AAMs, SSMs (1989)
Libya	SSMs	—	—	—	advisers/instructors
Syria	SSMs	—	+	cooperation in SSM technology	instructors

Note:
+ precise number unknown
—no entry

Table 15. Surface-to-Surface Missiles and Rockets in Service of Middle Eastern Armies (by number of launchers)

Country	Model							Total
	Frog 7	SS-1 Scud B	al-Hussein	Scud C	SS-21 Scarab	CSS-2	Other	
Egypt	12	9	—	—	—	—	—	21
Iran	—	+	—	+	—	—	+	26–36
Iraq	29	+	5	—	—	—	—	34
Israel	—	—	—	—	—	—	MGM-52C Lance, Jericho I, II*	12+
Libya	30	80	—	—	—	—		110
Saudi Arabia	—	—	—	—	—	8–12	—	8–12
Syria	18	18	—	8	18	—	—	approx. 62
Yemen	12	6	—	—	4	—	—	22

Note:

+ precise number unknown

—no entry

* according to foreign sources

GLOSSARY OF WEAPONS SYSTEMS

AA Guns, Short-Range

(caliber; designation; NATO codename, if relevant; SP, tracked or wheeled, when relevant; country of origin)

57mm ZSU 57×2 SP, tracked, Russia

57mm S-60, Russia

40mm M-42 (twin 40mm) SP, tracked, U.S.A.

40mm Bofors L-70, Sweden

40mm Bofors L-60, Sweden

37mm M-1939, Russia

35mm Contraves Skyguard; *see* Air Defense Systems

35mm Gepard SP, FRG

35mm Oerlikon-Buhrle 35×2 GDF-002, Switzerland; may be part of 35mm Skyguard system

30mm AMX DCA 30 (twin 30mm) SP, tracked, France

30mm Artemis (twin 30mm), Greece, based on 30mm Mauser AAG, FRG

30mm 30×2 M-53/59 SP, wheeled, Czechoslovakia

30mm Oerlikon, Switzerland

30mm 30×2 Wildcat SP, wheeled, FRG

30mm 30×2 M-3, SP, France

23mm ZSU 23×4 (Gun Dish) SP, tracked, Russia (Russian designation Shilka)

23mm ZU 23×2, Russia

20mm 20×2 VDAA SP (on VAB APC), France

20mm TCM-20×2 SP (Israeli mounting of French gun on U.S.-made M-3 halftrack)

20mm Oerlikon GAI, Switzerland

20mm Hispano-Suiza, France

20mm M-163 A1 Vulcan SP, U.S.A.

20mm M-167 Vulcan, U.S.A.

20mm 20×2mm SP (mounted on Panhard VCR 6×6), France

20mm 20×3 M-55 A4, Yugoslavia

20mm VDAA SP (mounted on VAB 6×6), France

Air Defense Systems, Short-Range

(caliber of gun, designation, missiles, SP when relevant, country of origin)

ADAMS, based on naval Barak missile, Israel; not yet operational

35mm Skyguard (Contraves Skyguard) 2×35, Aspide or RIM-7M Sparrow SAM, SP, Italy (gun – Switzerland, SAM – Italy or

U.S.A., chassis and radar – Italy or Austria); Egyptian designation Amoun

23mm Sinai 23, 23mm×2, 4×SA-7, SP, Egypt (gun + SAM – Russia or Egypt, chassis – U.S.A., radar – France)

Antitank Guns

(caliber, designation, recoilless if relevant, country of origin)

120mm BAT L-4 recoilless rifle, Britain

107mm B-11 recoilless rifle, Russia

106mm M-40 A1C/A2 recoilless rifle, U.S.A./Israel

100mm M-1955 gun (field/AT gun), Russia; *see* Guns and Howitzers

90mm light gun, low recoil gun, Belgium; used on AFVs

85mm M-1945/D-44 field/AT gun, Russia; *see* Guns and Howitzers

84mm Carl Gustav light recoilless rifle, Sweden

82mm B-10 recoilless rifle, Russia

76mm M-1942 divisional gun (ZIS-3), Russia (field/AT gun, *see* Guns and Howitzers)

75mm M-20 recoilless rifle, U.S.A.

57mm AT gun, Czechoslovakia

APCs/ARVs

(designation, tracked or wheeled, APC or ARV, amphibious if relevant, ATGM equipped if relevant, country of origin)

Achzarit APC, Israel (with foreign components); based on chassis of T-55 tank

al-Walid, wheeled APC, Egypt

AML-60, wheeled ARV, France

AML-90, wheeled ARV, France

AMX-10 RC/P, tracked, amphibious APC (P) reconnaissance vehicle (RC), France

AMX-VCI, tracked APC, France

AT-105 Saxon, wheeled APC, Britain

BMP-1, tracked, amphibious, ATGM-equipped APC (usually AT-3 Sagger), with 73mm gun, Russia

BMP-2, tracked, amphibious, ATGM-equipped APC (usually AT-5 Spandrel), with 30mm cannon, Russia

BMP-3, tracked, amphibious APC with a 100mm gun, Russia

BMR-600, wheeled, amphibious APC, Spain

BRDM-2, wheeled, amphibious, ATGM-equipped ARV, Russia

BTR-40, wheeled, amphibious ARV, Russia

BTR-50, tracked, amphibious APC, Russia

BTR-60, wheeled, amphibious APC, Russia

BTR-80, wheeled, amphibious APC, Russia, other former Russia states

BTR-152, wheeled APC, Russia

Desert Warrior, tracked APC, Britain; variant of British Warrior, produced for Kuwait

EBR-75, wheeled ARV, France

Eland, wheeled ARV, South Africa/licensed production of French AML-90/AML-60

Engesa EE-3 Jararaca, wheeled ARV, Brazil

Engesa EE-9 Cascavel, wheeled ARV, Brazil

Engesa EE-11 Urutu, wheeled, amphibious APC, Brazil

Engesa EE-17 Sucuri, wheeled, amphibious tank destroyer, Brazil

Fahd, wheeled APC, Egypt (FRG collaboration)

Ferret, wheeled ARV, Britain

Fiat Type 6614, wheeled, amphibious APC, Italy

Fiat Type 6616, wheeled, amphibious ATGM-equipped ARV, Italy

Fox, wheeled, amphibious ARV, Britain

FUG-70/PSZH-IV, *see* above, BRDM-2, usually without ATGM, Hungary (licensed production of Soviet BRDM-2)

K-63, tracked, amphibious, APC, PRC

LAV-25, wheeled, amphibious APC, Canada; licensed production of Swiss MOWAG Piranha 8×8; produced by GM of Canada, subsidiary of U.S. GMC

Magachon, tracked APC, Israel; on chassis of a foreign tank

M-2/M-3 Bradley, tracked amphibious APC/Rec. vehicle, U.S.A.

M-2, half-tracked APC, U.S.A.

M-3, half-tracked APC – *see* M-2

M-3 (Panhard, VTT), wheeled, amphibious APC (occasionally 4×HOT are added; *see* Antitank Missiles), France

M-60P, APC, Yugoslavia

M-901 ITV (TOW under armor), tracked, amphibious ATGM-equipped ARV (tank destroyer) (based on M-113 APC), U.S.A.; *see also* under ATGM

M-113 A1/A2/A3, tracked, amphibious APC, U.S.A./Italy (licensed production)

M-125, derivative of M-113, 81mm mortar carrier, U.S.A.

M-577/M-577 A1, tracked artillery command post vehicle (based on M-113 APC), U.S.A.

MOWAG Piranha 8×8, wheeled, amphibious APC, Switzerland

MT-LB, Russia; *see* under Artillery Ammunition Carriers

Nagmashot, tracked APC, Israel; on chassis of a foreign tank

OT-62, APC, Czechoslovakia; *see* BTR-50

OT-64, wheeled APC, Czechoslovakia
PSZH-IV, wheeled, amphibious APC, Hungary; derived from FUG-70/BRDM-2
RAM, wheeled ARV, Israel; improvement of RBY-2
Ratel 20, wheeled APC, South Africa
Ratel 90, same as Ratel 20 with a 90mm gun and turret, South Africa
RBY/RBY-2, wheeled ARV, Israel
Saladin, wheeled ARV, Britain
Saracen, wheeled APC, Britain
Steyr 4K 7FA tracked APC, Austria
Type 77, PRC, copy of Soviet BTR-50, PRC; *see* BTR-50
UR-416, wheeled APC, FRG
V-150 Commando, wheeled, amphibious ATGM-equipped ARV/APC, U.S.A.
V-300, wheeled APC, U.S.A.
VAB, wheeled, amphibious APC, France
VBC-90, wheeled ARV, France; derivative of VAB, with 90mm gun
VCR/TH, wheeled, amphibious ATGM-equipped APC/tank destroyer (*see* Antitank Missiles), France
VPM 81 mortar carrier, wheeled amphibious derivative of VAB, France
YPR-765, license produced U.S. M 113 APC variant, The Netherlands
YW-531, tracked, amphibious APC, PRC

Army AA Defense – Missiles

(designation, NATO codename if relevant, Russian designation if relevant, SP when relevant, man-portable if relevant, range, country of origin)
ADATS, SP AA and AT system, 8km., Switzerland/Canada
Ain al-Saqr (Egyptian-improved version of Soviet SA-7, man-portable, 4.4 km., Egypt/some French technical assistance
AdSAMs, surface-to-air variant of AIM-120 AMRAAM AAM, USA; *see below*
Blowpipe, man-portable, Britain
Crotale NG (New Generation) SP, 11 km., France
Crotale SP, 9 km., France; *see also* Shahine 2
FIM-92A Stinger, man-portable, 5.4 km., U.S.A.
Javelin, man-portable, Britain
HN-5, man-portable, 4 km., PRC; improved version of Soviet SA-7
MIM-43A Redeye, man-portable, 3 km., U.S.A.
MIM-72A Chaparral SP, 8 km., U.S.A.

Mistral (Matra Mistral), man-portable, 6 km., France
Rapier, 6 km., Britain
RBS-70, 5 km., Sweden
Roland, I/II 6.3 km., SP, France and FRG
SA-6 Gainful, 3M9 Kub, SP, 3–21 km., Russia
SA-7 Grail, 9M32 Strella, man-portable, 3.5 km., Russia
SA-8 Gecko, 9M33 Osa Romb, SP, 1.4–9.9 km., Russia
SA-9 Gaskin SP, 0.6–8 km., Russia
SA-11 Gadfly, 9M38, SP, 3–28 km., Russia
SA-13 Gopher, 9M37, Strella-10, SP, 0.5–5 km., Russia
SA-14 Gremlin, Strella 3, man-portable, 0.6–6 km. (unconfirmed), Russia
SA-15 Gauntlet, Tor, Russia
SA-16, Gimlet, 9M313, Igla-1, man-portable, 0.6–5 km., Russia; improvement of SA-7
Shahine 1, SP, France
Shahine 2/Crotale Shahine 2, SP, 13km., France; improvement of Crotale listed above
Shahine 2 ATTS (Air Transportable Towed System); a towed version of Shahine 2
Starburst, man-portable, 4 km., Britain
Tigercat, Britain

Artillery Ammunition Carriers

(designation, tracked or wheeled, armored, country of origin)
M-992, tracked, U.S.A.
MT-LB, tracked, armored, Russia; also serves as prime mover for towed artillery and APC

Artillery/Mortar Locating Radars

(designation, country of origin)
AN/TPQ-37, U.S.A.
AN/PPS-15, U.S.A.
Blindfire, Britain
Elta Shilem, Israel

ATGMs

(antitank guided missiles, designation, NATO codename if relevant, SP if relevant, range, Soviet designation if relevant, country of origin)
AT-1 Snapper, 500–2,300 m., Russia
AT-2 Swatter, 600–2,500 m., 9M17 Falanga, Russia

AT-3 Sagger, 500–3,000 m., Malyutka, Russia
AT-4 Spigot, 2,000 m., Russia
AT-5 Spandrel, 3,600 m., Russia
AT-6 Spiral, 5,000 m., 9M114 Shturm V, Russia
BGM-71A TOW/BGM-71C Improved TOW, 65–3,750 m. (range of Improved TOW), U.S.A.
BGM-71D TOW II, U.S.A.; improvement of BGM-71C, U.S.A.
BGM-71E TOW IIA, U.S.A.
BGM-71F TOW IIB, programmed for top attack, U.S.A.
BRDM-2 carrying AT-3 (Sagger) SP, 500–3,000 m., Russia
Dragon III, 1,500 m., U.S.A.; improved M-47A
HOT, 75–4,000 m., France/FRG
HOT Commando, HOT mounted on a Peugeot P-4 4×4 jeep-like vehicle, France
Israeli BGM-71C Improved TOW SP, 65–3,750 m.; derivative of M-113 APC, U.S.A.; missile and APC, U.S.A.; mounting and hydraulics, Israel
M-3 (Panhard) carrying HOT SP, 75–4,000 m., France; *see also* APC
M-47A Dragon, 1,000 m., U.S.A.
M-901 ITV SP (TOW under armor), BGM-71A TOW, 65–3,750 m., derivative of M-113 APC, U.S.A.; *see also* APC/ARV
Mapats, 5,000 m., Israel; laser-beam-riding Israeli improvement of U.S.-made BGM-71A TOW
MILAN, 25–2,000 m., France/FRG
Nimrod, land-based variant of Nimrod AGM, 26,000 m., laser guided, Israel
SS-11, 500–3,000 m., France
SS-12, 6,000 m., France (can be employed as ATGM or as antiship missile launched from ground, helicopter or ship)
Swingfire, 300–4,000 m., Britain/Egypt
T-1/T-16 SP, ATGM system/tank destroyer (unconfirmed), Russia
VCR/TH carrying HOT SP, 75–4,000 m., France; *see also* APC

Automatic Grenade Launchers
(caliber, designation, country of origin)
30mm AGS-17, Russia
40mm Mk 19, U.S.A.

Engineering Equipment
(designation, type, country of origin)
Bar-mine-laying system, Britain
EWK pontoon bridge (Faltschwimmbrucke), FRG

Gilois motorized bridge, France
GSP self-propelled ferry, Russia
Matenin SA autonomous, automatic mine layers, France
Mk 3(D) flail, antimine vehicle, France
M-60 AVLB bridging tank, U.S.A.
M-69 A1 bridging tank, U.S.A.
M-123 Viper minefield-crossing system, U.S.A.
MT-55 bridging tank, Russia
MTU-55 bridging tank, Russia
MTU-67 bridging tank, Russia
PMP pontoon bridge, Russia
Pomins II, portable (infantry) mine neutralization system, Israel
PRP motorized bridge, Russia
Puma, a combat vehicle carrying a squad of combat engineers and some equipment, Israel (improvement of existing foreign tank chassis)
TAB, tactical assault bridge, Israel
TLB, trailer-launched bridge, Israel
TPP pontoon Bridge, Russia
TWMP, tread-width mine ploughs, Israel
UDK-1, bridge, Britain

Guns and Howitzers, SP

(caliber, designation, gun or howitzer, range, country of origin)
210mm al-Faw, 57 km. (with base bleed and RAP ammunition), Iraq (with assistance of companies from Belgium and Britain)
203mm/8" M-110 A1 SP howitzer, 16.8 km., U.S.A.
175mm M-107 SP gun, 32.7 km., U.S.A.
155mm Mk F-3 (AMX) SP howitzer, 18 km., France
155mm G-6 SP howitzer, 30.8 km. (39 km. with base bleed ammunition), South Africa
155mm GCT SP howitzer, 23.5 km., France
155mm L-33 (Sherman/Soltam) SP howitzer, 21 km., Israel; gun, Israel: chassis – obsolete U.S.-made tanks
155mm M-44 SP howitzer, 14.6 km., U.S.A.
155mm M-50 (Sherman) SP howitzer, 17.5 km., Israel (gun – France; chassis – USA, improved in Israel)
155mm M-109 A1/A2/A6 SP howitzer, 21 km., U.S.A.
155mm M-109 Doher, U.S.A., Israel, upgrading of M-109
155mm Majnoon SP howitzer, Iraq, with assistance from a company in Belgium
155mm Palmaria SP howitzer, 24 km., Italy

152mm M-1973 SP howitzer, 18 km., Russia
122mm M-1974 SP howitzer, 15.3 km., Russia
122mm AR-122 SP howitzer, 15.4 km., Russia (gun)/Egypt (conversion to SP with U.S. aid), gun Russia or Egypt
122mm ISU SP gun, 16 km., Russia
105mm M-108 SP howitzer, 11.5 km., U.S.A.
105mm M-52 SP howitzer, 11.3 km., U.S.A.
105mm Mk 61 SP howitzer, 15 km., France
100mm SU-100 SP gun, Russia

Guns and Howitzers, Towed

(caliber, designation, gun or howitzer, range, country of origin)
203mm/8" M-115 howitzer, 16.8 km., U.S.A.
180mm S-23 gun, 32 km., Russia
155mm M-41 gun, 30 km., Iraq/Austria; a combination of the 130mm gun and Austrian 155mm tubes
155mm FH-70 howitzer, 24 km., FRG
155mm G-5 gun/howitzer, 30 km., South Africa
155mm GHN-45 howitzer/gun, 17.8 km., Austria
155mm M-198 A1 howitzer, 18.1 km., U.S.A.
155mm M-114 A2 howitzer, 14.6 km., U.S.A.
155mm M-1950 howitzer, 17.5 km., France
155mm M-71 gun/howitzer, 24 km., Israel
155mm M-59 (Long Tom) gun, 22 km., U.S.A.
152mm D-20 howitzer/gun, 18 km., Russia
152mm M-1946 2A36 howitzer, 27km., Russia
152mm M-1943 (D-1) howitzer, Russia
130mm M-46 gun, 27.1 km., Russia
130mm Type-59 gun, 27.4 km., PRC; copy of Soviet 130mm M-46
122mm M-1938 howitzer, 11.8 km., Russia
122mm D-30 howitzer, 16 km., Russia
122mm D-74 gun, 24 km., Russia
122mm Saddam, Iraq/Russia (Soviet 122mm D-30 produced in Iraq, with assistance from Yugoslavia)
105mm L-118 Light Gun, 17.2 km., Britain
105mm M-102 A1 howitzer, 11.5 km., U.S.A.
105mm M-101 A1 howitzer, 11.3 km., U.S.A.
105mm M-56 pack howitzer, 10.6 km., Italy
100mm M-1955 gun, 21 km. (field/AT gun), Russia
25 lb. (87mm) howitzer, 12.2 km., Britain
85mm M-1945/D-44 gun, 15.8 km. (field/AT gun), Russia
76mm M-1942 divisional gun (ZIS-3), 13.3 km., Russia

Light ATRLs

(designation, effective range, country of origin)
al-Nasira, Iraq; copy of Soviet RPG-7
APILAS (APILAS Manurhin), 330 m., France
B-300, Israel
LAW-80, 500 m., Britain
M-72 A1/A2 LAW, 300 m., U.S.A.
Panzerfaust 3LR, 800 m., with laser guidance, FRG with Israel
RPG-2, 150 m., Russia
RPG-7, 500 m., Russia
89mm M-65, Spain
89mm Strim-89, 360 m., France
3.5" M-20 (Bazooka), 110 m., U.S.A.

Machine Guns

(caliber, designation, type, country of origin)
14.5mm KPV HMG, Russia
14.5mm ZPU 14.5×4 HMG, Russia; employed in antiaircraft role
14.5mm ZPU 14.5×2 HMG, Russia; employed in antiaircraft role

Mortars, Heavy, 160mm and Over

(caliber, designation, SP if relevant, range, country of origin)
240mm M-240, 9.7 km., Russia
160mm M-43/53, 5.1 km., Russia
160mm M-66 SP, 9.3 km., Israel

Mortars, Heavy, Under 160mm

(caliber, designation, SP if relevant, range, country of origin)
120mm M-43, 5.7 km., Russia
120mm Brandt M-50/M-60, 6.6 km. (unconfirmed), France
120mm Brandt SP on LAV chassis, France (mortar)/Canada (vehicle)
120mm M-65, 6.3 km., Israel; also available as SP, mounted on U.S.-made M-2 halftrack
120mm TDA SP rifled, 13 km., France; mounted on Mowag Piranha 8×8 APC
120mm × 4 SP, 11.5 km., Iraq; mounted on Soviet-made MT-LB carrier
107mm (4.2") M-30 SP/towed (SP on M-106 A2 carrier, a derivative of M-113 APC), 5.6 km., U.S.A.

MRLs

(caliber, designation, number of launchers, range, country of origin)

400mm Ababil-100, 4, 100 km., Iraq; improved version of Yugoslavia's 262mm LRSV M-87

355mm Nazeat, 90 km. (unconfirmed), Iran

333mm Shahin 2, 20 km. (unconfirmed), Iran

300mm SS-60, 4, 68 km., Brazil

300mm Sajeel 60, Iraq; copy of Brazilian 300mm SS-60

300mm BM-9A52-2 Smerch, 12, 70km., Russia

290mm (MAR 290), 4, 25 km. (unconfirmed), Israel

262mm Ababil-50, 12, 50 km., Iraq; copy or production under license of Yugoslavia's 262mm LRSV M-87

240mm BM-24, 12, 10.2 km., Russia

240mm Fajr 3, Iran

230mm Oghab, 3, 80 km. (unconfirmed), Iran; improved version of PRC's Type-83 273mm rocket

227mm MLRS, 12, 30km., U.S.A.

180mm SS-40 Astros II, 16, 35 km., Brazil

180mm Sajeel 40, Iraq; copy of Brazilian 180mm SS-40

140mm BM-14-16, 16, 9.8 km., Russia

140mm RPU-14, 16, 9.8 km., Russia

140mm Teruel, 40, 18.2 km., Spain

132mm BM-13-16, 16.9 km., Russia

130mm M-51 (=130mm RM-130), 32, 8.2 km., Romania/Russia

130mm M-51, 32, 8.2 km., Czechoslovakia

130mm Type 63, 19, 10.4 km., PRC

128mm M-63, 32, 8.5 km., Yugoslavia

127mm SS-30 Astros II, 32, 30 km., Brazil

127mm Sajeel 30, Iraq; copy of Brazilian 127mm SS-30

122mm BM-11, 30, North Korea; a variant of Soviet BM-21

122mm BM-21, 40, 20.8 km., Russia

122mm Firos-25, 40, 25 km., Italy

122mm RM-70, 40, 20.4 km., Czechoslovakia; similar to Soviet BM-21

122mm Saqr 36, similar to Saqr 30, with 36 launchers, Egypt

122mm Saqr 30, 22.5 km., Egypt

122mm Saqr 10 and Saqr 18, short-range versions of Saqr 30, Egypt

107mm RM-11, 8.1 km., North Korea

107mm, Iraq; copy of 107mm from PRC or RM-11 from North Korea

107mm Type 63, 12, 8.5 km., PRC

Kachlilit, antiradar rocket, Israel

Keres antiradar rocket, a derivative of US RGM-66D, which is derived from Standard ARM and Standard RIM-66 shipborne SAM, 40 km., Israel

Recovery Vehicles

(designation, APC/tank chassis, country of origin)

M-578 A1 APC, U.S.A.

M-88 A1 recovery tank, U.S.A.

T-55 recovery tank, Russia

T-62 recovery tank, Russia

SS Missiles and Rockets

(designation, NATO codename if relevant, Russian designation if relevant, range, circular error probability [CEP], payload, country of origin)

al-Hussein (Iraqi modified SS-1), 590–640 km., 300kg, Russia/Iraq Iraqi TELs (transporter erector launchers) and MELs (mobile erector launchers) al-Nida and al-Walid

CSS-2 (East Wind) IRBM, 1,500 km., 2,045 kg (with conventional warhead), PRC

CSS-8, also M-7, 150 km., 190 kg, PRC; this is derived from HQ-2 SAM, for export

FROG-7 (Soviet designation Luna-M or 9K52), 60 km., 450 kg, 500m, Russia

Jericho I, 450 km., 500 kg (according to foreign publications), Israel

Jericho II, 800 km., 500 kg (according to foreign publications), Israel

Laith 90, 90km., Iraq; copy of Soviet FROG-7, with range improvement, probably still experimental

MGM-52C Lance, 75 km. (with conventional warhead), 225 kg, 225m, U.S.A.

M-9, 600 km. (unconfirmed), PRC

M-11, 150 km. (unconfirmed), PRC

Nodong, 960–1,000 km., North Korea (still under development, on order by countries in the Middle East)

Saqr 80, 80 km., 200 kg, Egypt; launched from FROG-7 launcher

SS-1 Scud B, R-17 or 9K72, 280 km., 800–1,000 kg, 1,000m, Russia

SS-21 Scarab, OTR-21 or Tochka, 70 km., 160m, 120 kg, Russia; Tochka U has a range of 120 km.

SS-1 Scud C, 550 km., 500–700 kg., 2,000–3,000m, North Korea (similar to Scud C made in Russia, upgrading of Soviet SS-1 Scud B)

Tamuz 1, 2,000 km., Iraq (with assistance from German, Italian, and French experts, not operational)

Tanks

(designation, caliber of gun, weight, country of origin)

AMX-13 LT, 75mm/105mm, 14.5 tons, France

AMX-30 MBT, 105mm, 36 tons, France

Assad Babil, Iraqi designation for locally assembled T-72

Centurion MBT, 105mm, 52 tons, Britain

Challenger 2 MBT, 120mm, 62 tons, Britain

Chieftain Mk 3/Mk 5 MBT, 120mm, 52.3 tons, Britain

Khalid – Jordanian designation for Chieftain; *see above*

Leclerc MBT, 120mm, 53 tons, France

Magach 7, Israel; upgraded M-60 MBT, 105mm, U.S.A., upgraded by Israel

M-1 A1 MBT, 120mm, 57 tons, U.S.A./Egypt (assembly)

M-1 A2, same as M-1 A1 with improved fire control, U.S.A.

M-41 LT, 76.2mm, 24 tons, U.S.A.

M-47 A1/2/5 MBT, 90mm, 44 tons, U.S.A.

M-48 A1/A3/A5 Patton MBT, 90mm/105mm, 46.6 tons, U.S.A.

M-60/M-60 A1/A2/A3 MBT, 105mm, 49 tons, U.S.A.

M-77 MBT (improved Soviet T-55), Romania

M-84 MBT, Yugoslavia; licensed production of Soviet T-72

Merkava Mk 1/Mk 2 MBT, 105mm, 56 tons, Israel

Merkava Mk 3 MBT, 120mm, 59 tons, Israel

OF-40 Lion MBT, 105mm, 43 tons, Italy; heavily reliant on FRG's Leopard 1 in design and components

Osorio (EE-T1) MBT, 105mm/120mm, Brazil

PT-76 amphibious LT, 76mm, 14 tons, Russia

Ramses II MBT, 105mm, 36 tons (unconfirmed), Egypt; Soviet T-54/T-55 upgraded with U.S.A. model gun and U.S.A. stabilizer, laser range finder, fire control and night vision

Scorpion LT, 76mm, 7.8 tons, Britain

SK-105 (Kurassier) LT/tank destroyer, 105mm, 18 tons, Austria

T-34 medium tank, 85mm, 32 tons, Russia

T-54 B/C MBT, 100mm, 36 tons, Russia

T-55 B/C/D MBT, 100mm, 36 tons, Russia

T-62 MBT, 115mm, 37.5 tons, Russia

T-72 MBT, 125mm, 41 tons, Russia

T-72M MBT, same as T-72 with upgraded fire control and jammer, Russia

Type-59 (=T-55), PRC

Type-62 medium tank, 85mm, 21 tons, PRC

Type-69, improved Type-59, above, PRC

Vickers Mk 1 MBT, 105mm, 38.1 tons, Britain

Zulfikar, Iranian tank, with gun from Russia

Air Force

AA Guns, Long-Range

(caliber, designation, country of origin)
100mm M-49, Russia
85mm M-44, Russia

AEW/AWACS Aircraft

(designation, NATO codename if relevant, derivation if relevant, function, speed, endurance, radar range, country of origin)
Adnan I/II, Iraq, using Soviet IL-76 aircraft and French radar
E-3A Sentry, AWACS, Boeing 707, 853 km./h., 6 hrs., 370 km., U.S.A.
E-2C Hawkeye, AEW, 602 km./h., 6 hrs. 6 min., 250 km., U.S.A.
TU-126 Moss, AWACS, TU-114, 850 km./h., 12,550-km. range, Russia

Air-to-Air Missiles (AAMs)

(designation, NATO codename if relevant, Russian designation if relevant, guidance systems, effective range, country of origin)
AA-1 Alkali, R-5, semiactive radar guidance, 6–8 km., Russia
AA-2 Atoll, R-13, infrared homing, 5–6.5 km., Russia
AA-2 Advanced Atoll, active radar homing, 5–6.5 km., Russia
AA-6 Acrid, infrared guidance, 37 km., Russia
AA-7 Apex, R-23, infrared or semiactive guidance, 27 km., Russia
AA-8 Aphid, R-60, 5–7.4 km., Russia
AA-10 Alamo, R-27, semiactive radar homing, 20–34 km., Russia; there is an R-27T1 infrared-guided version
AA-11 Archer, R-73, active terminal radar, 39–68 km., Russia
AA-12, Russia
AIM-7/AIM-7E/F Sparrow III, semiactive radar guidance, 44 km., U.S.A.
AIM-9B Sidewinder, infrared homing, now obsolete, U.S.A.
AIM-9E/F Sidewinder, infrared guidance, U.S.A.; improved AIM-9B
AIM-9J Sidewinder, U.S.A.; advanced version of AIM-9E with enhanced dogfight capability
AIM-9L Sidewinder, infrared guidance and active laser fuse, 18 km., U.S.A.
AIM-9M Sidewinder, similar to AIM-9L, with improved target acquisition and lock-on capabilities, U.S.A.
AIM-9P/P4 Sidewinder, improved AIM-9B, U.S.A.

AIM-54A Phoenix, semiactive radar guidance and fully active radar during terminal guidance, 44 km., U.S.A.

AIM-120 AMRAAM, command, inertial and active radar, 50 km., U.S.A.

Mica, command, inertial and active radar imaging on infrared, 50 km., France

Firestreak, infrared homing, 1.8 km., Britain

Python 3, infrared guidance, 15 km., Israel

Python 4, derived from Python 3, Israel

Red Top, infrared homing, 12 km., Britain

R-530 (Matra R-530), infrared guidance version/semiactive radar version, 18 km., France

R-550 Magique, infrared guidance, 10 km., France

Shafrir, infrared guidance, 5 km., Israel

Sky Flash, semiactive radar, 40 km., Britain

Super 530D/F (improved R-530), semiactive homing radar, 25 km., France

Air-to-Ground Missiles (AGMs)

(designation, NATO codename if relevant, Russian designation if relevant, function, guidance, range, country of origin)

AGM-45A/B Shrike, antiradar/SAM sites, radar-guidance, 12–16 km., U.S.A.

AGM-62A Walleye, antiship/airbase/bridge, TV-guided, U.S.A.

AGM-65A/B Maverick, antitank/hard target, TV-guided, U.S.A.

AGM-65C/D/G Maverick (=65A/B guided by Laser designator), U.S.A.

AGM-78D Standard ARM antiradar/SAM site, passive radar homing, U.S.A.

AGM-84, antiship missile, air-launched variant of RGM-84A Harpoon SSM, U.S.A.; *see* Navy

AGM-114 Hellfire, helicopter-borne, ATGM, guidance by Laser designator, U.S.A.

al-Hakim, PGM-1/2/3/4, Britain, ordered by UAE

ALARM, air-launched antiradar missile, Britain

AM-39, antiship, radio and radar guided, 50–70 km., France; air-launched derivative of the MM-38 and MM-40 Exocet SSMs

Armat, air-launched antiradar missile, homing on radar emission, France; enhanced successor version of French-British AS-37

AS-1 Kennel, KS-1, antiship/hard target, radar guidance, 90 km., Russia

AS-2 Kipper, autopilot command override, active terminal homing, 160 km., Russia

AS-4 Kitchen, Kh-22, inertial guidance with radar terminal homing, 400 km., Russia

AS-5 Kelt, KSR-2, antiship and hard target, radar guidance, 160 km., Russia

AS-6 Kingfish, KSR-5, inertial guidance, 240 km., Russia

AS-7 Kerry, Kh-66, 9.6 km., Russia

AS-9 Kyle, Kh-28, passive radar, 90km., Russia; designated Nisan in Iraq

AS-10 Karen, Kh-25, semiactive laser guidance, 9.6 km., Russia

AS-11, antiship, wire-guided (optical/tracked navigation), 3 km., France, helicopter-launched antiship and antitank version of SS-11 ATGM

AS-11 Kilter, Kh-58, 30 km., Russia

AS-12, antiship, wire-guided (optical/tracked navigation), 6 km., France; helicopter-launched antiship version of the SS-12 ATGM

AS-14 Kedge, Kh-29 antitank/hard target, midcourse guidance and electro-optical homing, 30km. (unconfirmed), Russia

AS-15TT, antiship, radar and radio-guided, 14.4 km., France; helicopter-launched

AS-30, radio-guided, 11.2 km., France

AS-30L, laser-guided, France

AT-2 antitank missile launched from helicopter, Russia

AT-6 antitank missile launched from helicopter, Russia

C-601, antiship, semiactive radar, active radar terminal guidance, 80km., PRC; similar to Hai Ying-2 (HY-2, Silkworm) shipborne SSM

LX, antiship missile (unconfirmed), Russia

Nimrod, antitank missile, semiactive laser, 25 km., Israel

PGM-1/PGM-2/PGM-3/PGM-4 – *see* al-Hakim, above

Popeye (also designated Have Nap, AGM-142), inertial and TV, 80km., Israel/Israel in cooperation with U.S.A.

Sea Eagle, antiship missile, inertial navigation and radar homing, 100 km., Britain

X-23, antiradiation missile (unconfirmed), Russia

Aircraft, Bombers

(designation, NATO codename, maximum speed, range, armament, country of origin)

H-6 (B-6D), copy of Soviet Tu-16, can carry C-601 antiship missile, PRC

IL-28 Beagle, 900 km./h., 2,260 km., 2,040 kg. bombs, 4×23mm gun, Russia

Tu-16 Badger, 945 km./h., 4,800 km., Kelt AGM/9,000 kg. bombs, 2×2×23mm gun, Russia

Tu-22 Blinder, Mach 1.4, 2,250 km., Kitchen AGM and bombs, 1×23mm gun, Russia

Aircraft, Counter-Insurgency

OV-10 Bronco (also Rockwell OV-10 Bronco), counterinsurgency/surveillance aircraft, FLIR sensor, laser designator, 272 kg. weapon pods/20mm guns/bombs, 463 km./h., 367 km. (combat radius with weapon load), U.S.A.

Aircraft, Interceptors

(designation, NATO codename if relevant, maximum speed, combat radius, armament, country of origin)

F-6 Shenyang (=MiG-19), PRC; *see also* Aircraft, Strike and Multirole, and MiG-19, below

F-7 Shenyang (=MiG-21), PRC; *see* MiG-21, below

F-14A Tomcat, Mach 2.4, 4×AIM-7 or 4×AIM-54A Phoenix + 4×AIM-9, 1×20mm gun, U.S.A.

F-15A/B/C/D Eagle, Mach 2.5+, 1,000 km., 4×AIM-7/4×AIM-9, 1×20mm gun, U.S.A.

FT-6, PRC; two-seater training version of F-6; also JJ-6, copy of Soviet MiG-19 UTI

MiG-19 PF/PFM Farmer C/D, 1,452 km./h., 685 km., 2×AA-2 Atoll AAM, 2 or 3×30mm gun, Russia

MiG-21 MF/S/U Fishbed, Mach 2.1, 1,100 km., 2×AA-2 Atoll AAM/Advanced Atoll, 1×23mm gun, Russia

MiG-23 ML/MF/MS Flogger B/E/G, Mach 2.3, 1,200 km., 5×AA-7 Apex/AA-8 Aphid AAM, 1×23mm gun, Russia

MiG-25 Foxbat A/B/E/U, Mach 2.8, 1,450 km., 4×AA-8 Aphid/AA-6 Acrid AAM, Russia

MiG-25R, reconnaissance version of MiG-25

Mirage III C/E/BL/EL, Mach 2.2, 1,200 km., 1×R530/2×AIM-9, 2×30mm gun, France

Su-27 Flanker A, Mach 2.3, 1,500 km., 6–8×AA-10 AAM, 23mm gun, Russia

Tornado (Panavia Tornado) ADV, (F Mk 3) Mach 2.2, radius 620 km., AIM-9L, Sky Flash AAM, 1×27mm Mauser cannon, Britain, FRG and Italy (joint production); *see also* Aircraft, Strike and Multirole

Xian J-7, copy of MiG-21, PRC; export version designated F-7 Shenyang, *see above*

Aircraft, Maritime Surveillance

(designation, jet/turboprop, speed, endurance, range, sonar, radar, country of origin)

EMB-111N Bandeirante, based on EMB-110 transport aircraft, turboprop, 360 km./h., 2,940 km., sea patrol radar, Brazil

P-3 Orion, turboprop, 608 km./h., 3 hours on station, 3,835 km., sonar (ARR-72), APS-115 radar, U.S.A.; may carry depth charges

Westwind I/Sea Scan/1124 Sea Scan, based on Westwind 1124, maritime reconnaissance aircraft, 872 km./h., 6 hrs. 30 min., equipped with search radar, Israel

Beechcraft 1900C, derivative of commuter/light transport aircraft employed in Egypt in ELINT and/or maritime surveillance role, U.S.A.; *see* Aircraft, Transport and Executive

BN-2T Defender turboprop, 315 km./h., 1,090 km., Bendix/King RDR-1400 radar, Britain/Switzerland (derived from BN-2A Islander/Pilatus light transport aircraft; BN is a British subsidiary of Swiss Pilatus)

Aircraft, Strike and Multirole

(designation, NATO codename if relevant, maximum speed, combat radius/range, armament, country of origin)

A-4 A/B/D/E/J/KU Skyhawk, 1085 km./h., 3,200 km., 2×20mm gun, 4,500 kg. bombs, U.S.A. (A-4E data)

A-5 Fantan, also designated J-6, Mach 1.1, 600 km., up to 2,000-kg. bombs or rockets, 1×23mm gun, PRC

F-4 D/E Phantom, Mach 2+, 1,145 km., 4×AIM-7 + 4×AIM-9, 1×20mm gun, 7,250-kg. bombs, U.S.A.

F-4 Shenyang (=MiG-17), PRC, *see* MiG-17

F-5 A/B/E/F (Tiger II), Mach 1.64, 890 km., 2×AIM-9, 2×20mm gun, 3.17-ton bombs, U.S.A. (F-5E data)

F-6 Shenyang, PRC (copy of Soviet MiG-19 interceptor); *see* Aircraft, Interceptors, MiG-19

F-15I, a variant of U.S.-made F-15E for Israel; *see* Interceptors F-15C, U.S.A.

F-15S, a variant of U.S.-made F-15E for Saudi Arabia; *see* Interceptors F-15C, U.S.A.

F-16 A/B/C/D Fighting Falcon, Mach 1.95, 925 km., 2×AIM-9, 1×20mm gun, 6.8-ton bombs, U.S.A.

F/A-18C/D Hornet, Mach 1.7+, 2×AIM-9, AIM-120, AGM-84, AGM-65F, various bombs; combinations of armament to a maximum of approx. 7 tons, U.S.A.

Hawker Hunter FGA-6/F-70/FR-10/T-66/T-67, Mach 0.8, 4×30mm gun, 0.5-ton bombs, Britain

J-1 Jastreb, light attack version of SOKO G-2 Galeb; *see* Aircraft, Training

J-6, *see* A-5 Fantan

Kfir C-2/TC-2/C-7/TC-7, Mach 2.3, 768 km., 2×Shafrir AAM, 2×30mm gun, 3,150-kg. bombs, Israel

MiG-15 Faggot, 1,070 km./h., 1,400 km., 1×37mm gun, 2×23mm gun, Russia; also employed as advanced trainer

MiG-17 Fresco, 1,145 km./h., 1,400 km., 1×37mm gun, 2×23mm gun, 500-kg. bombs, Russia

MiG-23 S\BN\U Flogger A/BL/F/C/S/G, Mach 2.3, 1,200 km., AA-7 Apex & AA-8 Aphid AAMs, 1×23mm twin barrel gun, Russia; *see also* Aircraft, Interceptors

MiG-27 Flogger D, Mach 1.6, approx. 500 km., AA-7 Apex & AA-8 Aphid AAMs, 1×23mm twin barrel gun, Russia

MiG-29 Fulcrum, Mach 2.8 (unconfirmed), Russia

Mirage 5/50, Mach 2.2, 1,300 km., 2×AIM-9 AAM/2×R-530, 2×30mm gun, up to 4,000-kg. bombs, France

Mirage F-1 B/C/D/E, Mach 2.2, AIM-9/R-530 and R-550 Magique, AS-30 AGM, 2×30mm gun, 3,600-kg. bombs, France

Mirage F-1 2000-5 EQ5/EQ2/EQ4 = F-1 E equipped to fire AM-39 Exocet ASM, France

Mirage 2000, Mach 2.2+, 1,480 km. with external tanks and bombs, 2×Super R-530 AAM and 2×R-550 Magique AAM, 2×30mm gun, up to 5,000-kg. bombs, France

Mirage 2000-5, multirole upgrade of Mirage 2000, France

Phantom 2000, an Israeli upgrade of F-4E, above

RF-4E Phantom, reconnaissance version of F-4E

RF-5E Northrop Tiger II, reconnaissance/photography version of F-5E (unarmed), U.S.A.

SEPECAT Jaguar S/E-01, Mach 1.6, 1,408 km., 2×R-550 Magique or 2×AIM-9 AAM or AS-37 AGM, 1-2×30mm gun, 3,600-kg. bombs, Britain and France

Su-7 BM/U Fitter A/B, Mach 1.6, 480 km., 2×30mm gun, 1-ton bombs, Russia

Su-20/22 Fitter C, Mach 2.17, 630 km., AA-2 Atoll AAMs, 2×30mm gun, 4,000-kg. bombs, Russia

Su-24 Fencer C, Mach 2.18, 1,800 km., 11,000-kg. bombs/AGMs including AS-7 Kerry AGM, one gun, Russia

Su-25 Frogfoot, 880 km./h., 556 km., AA-2 Atoll/AA-8 Aphid

AAMs, 30mm guns, maximum armament and bomb load 4 tons, Russia

Su-27 Flanker, Mach 2.35, 1,500 km. (radius) AA-10, AA-11, 30mm gun, Russia

TA-4 KU, USA – *see* A-4; designation of advanced two-seater training aircraft for Kuwait

Tornado (Panavia Tornado) IDS, (GR Mk 1) Mach 2.2, 1,390 km. with heavy weapons load, AIM-9, AGM-65/AS-30 AGM/CBU-15, 2×27mm gun, maximum armament and bomb load 8.1 tons, Britain, FRG and Italy (joint production); *see also* Aircraft, Interceptors

Aircraft, Tanker (aerial refueling)

(designation, derivation, fuel load, country of origin)

Boeing 707 Tanker, U.S.A. – *see* KC-135; also a Boeing 707 made in U.S.A., converted to aerial refueling role in Israel

KC-135A Stratotanker, Boeing 707, U.S.A.

KC-130H, C-130H Hercules, 23,923 liter, U.S.A.

KE-3A, similar to KC-135A, U.S.A.; designation of aircraft for Saudi Arabia

Aircraft, Training and Liaison

(designation, jet, turboprop or piston engine, ground attack capability if relevant, country of origin)

Aermacchi MB-326 B/KT/LT, jet, ground attack capability, Italy

Aermacchi MB-339, jet, ground attack capability, Italy

al-Gumhuriya, piston, Egypt (German/Spanish model)

Alpha Jet, jet, ground attack capability, France and West Germany/Egypt – assembly

Alpha Jet MS-2, same as Alpha Jet, licensed production in Egypt with improved ground attack and naval attack capabilities

AS-202/18A Bravo and AS-202/26A, piston, Switzerland

BAC-145 Jet Provost, jet, ground attack capability, Britain

BAC-167 Strikemaster Mk 82/Mk 83, jet, ground attack capability, Britain; development of BAC-145

BAe Jetstream 31, turboprop, Britain; a transport aircraft employed for cockpit training for Tornado aircrews

BAe-SA-3-120 Bulldog series 125/126, piston, Britain (formerly Scottish Aviation B-125 Bulldog and Beagle B-125 Bulldog)

Beechcraft Bonanza F-33A and V-35B, piston, U.S.A.

Beechcraft T-34C Turbo Mentor, turboprop, U.S.A.

Broussard, piston, France

CASA-101 Jet, Spain
Cessna 150, U.S.A.
Cessna 180, U.S.A.
Cessna 172 G/H/L, piston, U.S.A.
Cessna 182 Skylane, piston, U.S.A.
Cessna 185 Skywagon, piston, U.S.A.; same as Cessna U-206
Cessna 318 (T-37), jet, U.S.A.
Cessna U-206 Skywagon, piston, U.S.A.
CM-170 Fouga Magister, jet, ground attack capability, France/Israel (assembly)
Embraer EMB-312 (T-27), turboprop, Brazil; produced under license by Egypt and Britain; also designated Tucano T-27
FT-6, trainer, two-seat version of F-6 (interceptor), PRC; *see* Aircraft, Interceptors
G-115T (Grob), piston, FRG
Galeb – *see* SOKO
Gepal IV (AMIN Gepal IV), turboprop, Morocco
Grob G-109B, ultralight, FRG
Hawk, jet, ground attack capability, Britain
L-29 Delfin, jet, ground attack capability, Czechoslovakia
L-39 Albatross, jet, ground attack capability, Czechoslovakia
L-59, advanced variant of L 39, above, Czech Republic
MBB-223 Flamingo/MBB-Flamingo, piston, FRG/Spain; produced in FRG by MBB or SIAT, and in Spain by CASA
MiG-15 UTI – *see* Aircraft, Strike and Multirole
Mushshak (Saab Safari Supporter, Saab MF-17, also designated PAC Mushshak), piston, Pakistan; produced under license from Sweden (Saab)
Pilatus PC-6 Turbo-Porter, turboprop, Switzerland
Pilatus PC-7 Turbo-Trainer, turboprop, Switzerland
Pilatus PC-9, turboprop, Switzerland
Piper Cub/Piper/PA-18 Super Cub, piston, U.S.A.
Piper PA-44, U.S.A.
PZL-104 Wilga 35/80, piston, Poland
Rockwell T-6 (Texan, Harvard), piston, U.S.A.
S-312, same as Brazilian Embraer EMB-312, assembled in Britain
SIAI-Marchetti SF-260M/WD\WT\C/L Warrior, piston, Italy
SIAI-Marchetti S-208A, piston, Italy
SOKO G-2A/G-2AE Galeb, jet, ground attack capability, Yugoslavia; J-1 Jastreb derived from G-2A for light attack roles and advanced training
Strikemaster – *see* BAC-167 Strikemaster

T-33, jet, ground attack capability, U.S.A.

Tzukit, (French) CM-170 Fouga Magister upgraded by Israel (strengthened frame and new avionics)

YAK-11 Moose, piston, Russia

YAK-18 Max, piston, Russia

Aircraft, Transport and Executive

(designation, NATO codename if relevant, piston, turboprop or jet engine, maximum cruising speed, range, load, accommodation, paratroop dropping capability if relevant, country of origin)

Aero Commander 690

An-2 Colt, piston, 200 km./h., 905 km., 1,240 kg./14 paratroopers, Russia

An-12 Cub, turboprop, 670 km./h., 3,600 km., 20 tons/100 paratroopers, Russia

An-24 Coke, turboprop, 450 km./h., 640 km., 5,700 kg./38 passengers or 30 paratroopers, Russia

An-26 Curl, turboprop, 440 km./h., 1,100 km., 5,500 kg./38–40 passengers, Russia

Arava (IAI 101/201/202 Arava), turboprop, 319 km./h., 630 km., 2,351 kg./24 passengers/16 paratroopers, Israel (IAI 202 data)

BAe-111 (BAC-111), jet, 870 km./h., 3,013 km., 10,733 kg./119 passengers, Britain

BAe-125 (also known as HS-125), jet, 845 km./h., 5,318 km., 1,088 kg./2 pilots + 14 passengers, Britain

Beechcraft Bonanza A-36, piston, 326 km./h, pilot + 4–6 passengers, U.S.A.; an executive aircraft

Beechcraft 1900C, turboprop, 435 km./h., 1,469 km., 19 passengers/EW/CEW equipment, U.S.A.; a commuter aircraft employed in EW/CEW and/or maritime surveillance role in Egypt

Beechcraft King Air B-100, turboprop, 486 km./h., 2,232 km., 13 passengers, U.S.A.

Beechcraft Queen Air, turboprop, 370 km./h., 2,520 km., 1,599 kg./9 passengers, U.S.A.; an executive aircraft

Beechcraft Sierra, U.S.A.

Beechcraft Super King Air, turboprop, 536 km./h., 3,658 km., 14 passengers, U.S.A.

Boeing 707/707-200/707-320, jet, 973 km./h., 7,700 km., 43 tons; 180 passengers, U.S.A.

Boeing 707KE, aerial refueling aircraft, based on Boeing 707, U.S.A.

Boeing 720/720B/720B-023B, jet, 897 km./h., 6,690 km., 112 passengers, U.S.A.

Boeing 727, jet, 960 km./h., 14,740 kg./131 passengers, U.S.A.
Boeing KC-135 – *see* Boeing 707, aerial refueling aircraft
Boeing 737/737-200, jet, 943 km./h., 3521 km., 15 ton/115 passengers, U.S.A.
Boeing 747/747-200B/747-200C, jet, 967 km./h., 10,562 km., 160 tons/450 passengers, U.S.A.
Britten-Norman BN-2A Islander/Pilatus BN-2B Islander II, piston, 251 km./h., 1,530 km., 10 passengers, Britain/Switzerland
C-47 – *see* DC-3 Dakota
C-130H-30, stretched version of C-130H, *see* L-100-30
C-130 E/H Hercules, turboprop, 621 km./h., 3,791 km. (maximum payload), 19,685 kg./92 paratroopers, U.S.A.
C-140 Jetstar, jet, 885 km./h., 3,185 km., 1,360 kg./10 passengers, U.S.A.
C-212 – *see* CASA C-212 Aviocar
Caravelle Super B, 835 km./h., 2,725 km., 9,265 kg./104 passengers, France
CASA C-212-5 series 100/C-212 series 200 Aviocar, turboprop, 365 km./h., 408 km., 2,770 kg./24 passengers/23 paratroopers, Spain/Indonesia (licensed production)
Cessna 310, piston, 361 km./h., 2,842 km., 6 passengers, U.S.A.
CN-235 (CASA/Nurtanio CN-235, also Airtech CN-235), turboprop, 454 km./h., 796 km., 3,575 kg./39 passengers/30 paratroopers, Spain/Indonesia; Airtech is company jointly owned by CASA (Spain) and Nurtanio (Indonesia)
DC-3 Dakota (C-47), piston, 220 km./h., 500 km., 2.5 tons/24 paratroopers, U.S.A.
DC-8, jet, Mach 0.8, 11,410 km., 30,240 kg./189 passengers, U.S.A.
DC-9, jet, 907 km./h., 3,095 km., 14,118 kg./119 passengers, U.S.A.
DC-10, jet, 925 km./h. 7,400 km., 43.3 tons/380 passengers, U.S.A.
DHC-4/DHC-4A Caribou, piston, 293 km./h., 2,103 km., 3,965 kg./32 passengers/26 paratroopers, Canada
DHC-5/DHC-5D Buffalo, turboprop, 467 km./h., 1,112 km., 8,164 kg./41 passengers, Canada
DHC-6 Twin Otter, turboprop, 338 km./h., 1,297 km., 1,940 kg./20 passengers, Canada
Dornier Do-28 D/Do-28 D2 Skyservant, piston, 286 km./h., 2,875 km., 1,000 kg./13 passengers, FRG
Dornier Do-228-100, turboprop, 428 km./h., 600–1,740 km., 2.2 ton/15–20 passengers, FRG
Dove, piston, 338 km./h., 620 km., 670 kg./11 passengers, Britain

EMB-110/EMB-110 P2 Bandeirante, turboprop, 417 km./h., 1,900 km., 1,681 kg./21 passengers, Brazil

EMB-121 Xingu, turboprop, 450 km./h., 2,352 km., 1,477 kg./9 passengers, Brazil; an executive aircraft

Falcon 20 – *see* Mystère-Falcon 20

Fokker F-27 Mk 400/F-27 Mk 600, turboprop, 480 km./h., 1,926/1,935 km., 5,727/5,696 kg./40/44 passengers, Netherlands

Fokker F-27 Mk 400M, military version of F-27 Mk 400, 46 paratroopers, Netherlands

Fokker F-28, jet, 843 km./h., 1,900 km., 10,478 kg./85 passengers, Netherlands

G-222L, turboprop, 439 km./h., 2,409 km., 9,000 kg./53 passengers/42 paratroopers, Italy

Gulfstream II, jet, 0.85 Mach, 6,579 km., 8 passengers, U.S.A.; an executive jet

Gulfstream III, executive jet, U.S.A.

HS-125, a business jet, Britain

IL-14 Crate, piston, 358 km./h., 2,600 km., 5.3 tons/18 passengers/paratroopers, Russia

IL-18 Coot, turboprop, 675 km./h., 4,700 km., 13,500 kg./122 passengers, Russia

IL-76 Candid, jet, 800 km./h., 6,700 km., 40 tons/more than 100 passengers, Russia

Jetstar, executive jet, 917 km./h., 10 passengers, U.S.A.

L-100-20, turboprop, 581 km./h., 3,889 km. (maximum payload), 21,130 kg./92 paratroopers (optional), U.S.A.; civilian or military stretched Hercules

L-100-30, turboprop, 583 km./h., 3,326 km. (maximum payload), 23,014 kg./passengers – not less than L-100-20, U.S.A.; civilian or military stretched Hercules

L-410 UVP, turboprop, 360 km./h., 540km., 1,300 kg./2 crew + 19 passengers, Czechoslovakia

L-1011, basically a civilian aircraft, U.S.A.

Learjet 35, jet, 872 km./h., 4,200 km., 8 passengers, U.S.A.

MD-315 Flamant, piston, 147 km./h., 10 passengers, France

Merlin IV (corporate version of Metro III), turboprop, 524 km./h., 1,805 km., 13–16 passengers, U.S.A.

Mystère-Falcon 10, jet, 900 km./h., 3,370 km., 7 passengers, France; an executive jet

Mystère-Falcon 20, jet, 855 km./h., 4,170 km., 1,180 kg./7 passengers, France; an executive jet

Mystère-Falcon 50, jet, 800 km./h., 6,480 km., 8 passengers, France; an executive jet

Mystère-Falcon 900, jet, 927 km./h., 6,412 km., 1,045 kg./15–18 passengers, France; an executive jet

Piper Navajo, turboprop, 386 km./h., 1,742 km., 6–8 passengers, U.S.A.; an executive aircraft

Sabreliner 75A, jet, Mach. 0.80, 3,173 km., 10 passengers, U.S.A.; an executive jet

Short SC-7 Skyvan Srs. 3M, turboprop, 327 km./h., 1,075 km., 2,358 kg./22 passengers/16 paratroopers, Britain

Tu-124/Tu-134 Crusty, jet, 885 km./h., 3,020 km., 8,200 kg./84 passengers, Russia

Turbo-Commander 690B, turboprop, 532 km./h., 11 passengers, U.S.A.

Westwind I/Westwind 1124, jet, 872 km./h., 4,490 km., 10 passengers, Israel; an executive jet

Yak-40 Codling, jet, 550 km./h., 2,000 km., 2,720 kg./32 passengers, Russia

Bombs, Advanced

(designation, function, weight, country of origin)

ATA-1000, Cluster Bomb Unit (CBU), antipersonnel and AFV, 450 kg., Israel

ATA-500, CBU, 225 kg., Israel

Belouga Dispenser Weapon (BLG-66) Cluster Bomb Unit (CBU), antipersonnel and AFV, 290 kg., France

BL-755, cluster bomb, France

Cardoen CBU, cluster bomb, Chile

CBU-7A, cluster bomb, U.S.A.

CBU-55, cluster bomb, antipersonnel, U.S.A.

CBU-87, cluster bomb, U.S.A.

CBU Mk 20, cluster bomb, U.S.A.

CBU-10

GBU-12

Durandal Penetration Bomb, antirunway bomb, 195 kg., France

FAE, fuel air explosive bomb, various countries

Griffin, laser-guided bomb (attached to the GBU-12 Mk 82, 241-kg., GBU-11 Mk 84,900-kg., and GBU-16 Mk 83, 450-kg. bombs), Israel

Guillotine, laser-guided bomb, Israel

JP-233 antirunway bomb, Britain

Opher terminal guidance bomb, an infrared homing kit added to U.S. GBU-12 Mk 82, 241 kg. bomb, Israel

Paveway 2

Pyramid, antipersonnel, with terminal TV guidance, Israel

Rockeye Cluster Bomb Mk 20, antitank CBU, U.S.A.

Tal, cluster bomb unit (CBU), 220 kg., Israel

Helicopters, ASW

A-109/AS-109 – *see* Helicopters, Attack

AB-212/Bell 212 – *see* Helicopters, Medium Transport

Kamov Ka-25 Hormone – *see* Helicopters, Medium Transport

Ka-28 Helix, Russia

Mi-14 Haze, Russia

SH-2G, (Kaman), ASW and SAR, U.S.A.

SH-3D (=Westland S-61), U.S.A. – *see* Helicopters, Heavy Transport

Westland Sea King HAS Mk 1/S-61A/AS-61A – *see* Helicopters, Heavy Transport

Westland Sea King Mk 47 – nearly identical to Westland Sea King HAS Mk 1

Helicopters, Attack

(designation, NATO codename if relevant, maximum speed, range, armament, country of origin)

Agusta A-109A, 311 km./h., 583 km., 4–8 BGM-71C Improved TOW, 2–3×7.62mm MG, 1×12.7mm HMG, 12×68mm rockets, Italy; a variant employed in ASW and/or naval attack role

AH-1S/AH-1G/AH-1J/AH-1Q Huey Cobra, 333 km./h., 577 km., 8×BGM-71C Improved TOW, 2×20mm minigun pod/68mm rockets/grenade dispensers, U.S.A.

AH-64A Apache, 300 km./h., 689 km., 8×AGM-114 Hellfire, 30mm gun, 68mm rockets, U.S.A.

Alouette III – *see* Helicopters, Light Transport; armed with AS-12 AGMs

500MG Defender/TOW Defender/Advanced Scout Defender, 244 km./h., 589-km. range, 4×BGM-71C Improved TOW, 30mm chain gun, U.S.A. (derivative of Hughes 500D light transport helicopter, renamed McDonnell Douglas 500MD)

530MG, armament equivalent to Hughes 500MD, U.S.A. (military derivative of Hughes 530F, renamed McDonnell Douglas 530MG); *see above* and Helicopters, Light Transport

MBB BO-105, 6×HOT – *see* Helicopters, Light Transport

Mi-24 Hind D/E 330 km./h., 4×AT-2 Swatter ATGM, 1×12.7mm MG, 4×32 57mm rockets, 8 troops, Russia

Mi-25 Hind, improved version of Mi-24, Russia

Mi-35, export version of Mi-24, Russia

NAS-330, SA-342 assembled in Indonesia

OH-58D, Combat Scout (AHIP), 22 km./h., 556 km., BGM-71C Improved TOW, LGM/or 2 AAMS, U.S.A.; derived from Bell 206 light helicopter, also designated Bell 406

SA-342/SA-342K/L/M Gazelle, 310 km./h., 360 km., 4×HOT/6×HOT/4×AS-11/2×AS-12, 2×7.62 mm MG, France

Westland Lynx, 259 km./h., 630 km., 8×BGM-71C Improved TOW/8×HOT/6×AS-11 AGM, 2×20mm gun/7.62mm MG, 18×68mm rockets, 10 troops, Britain; also employed as medium transport

Helicopters, Heavy Transport

(designation, NATO codename if relevant, speed, range, accommodation, load, country of origin)

AS-61A/A4, Italy (licensed production of U.S.-made S-61A); *see* S-61A

CH-47C/D Chinook, 304 km./h., 185-km. radius (ferry range 2,142 km.), 44 troops/9,843 kg., U.S.A./Italy (licensed production)

CH-53/CH-53D, 315 km./h., 413 km., approx. 50 troops/5.9 tons/9-ton external payload, U.S.A.

CH-53-2000, CH-53D (U.S.A.) upgraded in Israel

KV-107/KV-107 IIA-17, 270 km./h., 1,097 km., 25 passengers/12 passengers and 2,268 kg., Japan (licensed production of U.S.A.-Boeing Vertol 107, Model II)

Mi-6 Hook, 300 km./h., 1,450-km. ferry range, 65 passengers/12,000-kg. internal payload/9,000-kg. external payload, Russia

RH-53 maritime CH-53, U.S.A.

S-61 A/S-61 A4 (Sikorsky SH-3 Sea King), 267 km./h., 1,005 km., 25 passengers/3,630 kg., U.S.A.; employed mainly in ASW role, and in search and rescue with sonar, Doppler navigation radar

SA-321 Super Frelon (SA-3200 – earlier aircraft), 275 km./h., 1,020 km., 27–30 troops/5,000-kg. external/internal load, France; can carry AM-39 Exocet AGM

SH-3 (AS-61A) VIP version of S-61 or AS-61, Italy; licensed production of S-61

Westland Commando Mk 2 (=S-61A and Westland Sea King transport version), 28 troops, Britain

Westland Sea King HAS Mk 1, 211 km./h., 1,110 km., 22 passengers/2,720-kg. internal load/3,630-kg. external load, Britain; employed mostly in ASW role or in search-and-rescue role; equipped with Plessey dipping sonar, Doppler navigation radar system and search radar (licensed production of S-61A)

Helicopters, Light Transport

(designation, NATO codename if relevant, speed, range, accommodation, country of origin)

AB-47G/3B-1, 196 km./h., 367 km., pilot + 3 passengers, U.S.A./ Italy; licensed production of Bell 47

AB-206 (=Bell 206), Italy

Alouette II (early versions designated Sud-Aviation SE 313/3130; later version designated Aerospatiale SA-318), 205 km./h., 720 km., pilot + 4 passengers/600 kg., France

Alouette III (early version designated Sud-Aviation SE-316/3160; later version designated Aerospatiale SA-316/319), 210 km./h., 540 km., pilot + 6 passengers/750 kg., France

AS-350 Ecureuil, 230 km./h., 700 km., pilot + 5 passengers, France

Bell 206/206B JetRanger II/III, 225 km./h., 608 km., 2 pilots + 4 passengers, U.S.A.

Bell 206L LongRanger, improved Bell 206, 2 pilots + 5 passengers, U.S.A.

BK-117 (MBB/Kawasaki BK-117), 248 km./h., 493 km., pilot + 6 passengers, FRG/Japan

Hiller UH-12E, 154 km./h., 565 km., pilot + 3 passengers, U.S.A.

Hughes 500D, 282 km./h., 531 km., pilot + 4 passengers, U.S.A. (=Hughes 500MD attack helicopter for civilian or observation tasks); renamed 500D (McDonnell Douglas)

Hughes 530F, improvement of 500D, renamed 530F (McDonnell Douglas), U.S.A.

Hughes 300C, 169 km./h., 370 km., pilot + 2 passengers, U.S.A.

IAR-316, Romania; license-produced French SA-316 Alouette III, *see above*

MBB B0-105, 270 km./h., 1,112 km., pilot + 4 passengers /approx. 300 kg., FRG (=Nurtanio MBB NBO 105, Indonesia); can be fitted with HOT ATGM and used as attack helicopter; licensed production in Spain and Indonesia

SA-315B Lama, France

Helicopters, Maritime Attack

(designation, maximum cruising speed, range, armament, country of origin)

AS-365 Dauphin=SA-365

HH-65A Dolphin, 257 km./h., U.S.A. (licensed production of French Aerospatiale SA-366 Dauphin 2)

SA-365N/365F Dauphin 2, 252 km./h., 4×AS-15TT air-to-ship missiles, France

SA-366 – improved SA-365

Helicopters, Medium Transport

(designation, NATO codename if relevant, speed, range, accommodation, load, country of origin)

AB-205 (=Bell 205), Italy; production under U.S.A. license

AB-212 (=Bell 212), Italy; production under U.S.A. license

AB-214/214A (Bell 214), 250 km./h., 654 km., 16 passengers, Italy; production under U.S.A. license

AB-412 (=Bell 412), 226 km./h., 461 km., 14 troops, Italy; production under U.S.A. license

AS-332 Super Puma, 296 km./h, 644 km., 20 passengers, France

AS-532, also AS-532 Cougar, improved version of AS-332, *see above*, France

Bell 205, 204 km./h., 511 km., 14 troops/1,759 kg., U.S.A. (AB-205 in Italy)

Bell 212/212B, 259 km./h., 420 km., 10 troops/2,268 kg. external load/1,814-kg. internal load, U.S.A. (AB-212 in Italy)

Bell 214, U.S.A.

Bell 222, 259 km./h., 532 km., 8–10 passengers/3,810-kg. external load/3,742-kg. internal load, U.S.A.

Bell 412, 259 km./h., 695 km., 14 troops/2,268 kg. external load/1,814 kg. internal load, U.S.A.; a four blade derivative of the Bell 212

HH-34F (S-58), 158 km./h., 450 km., 16 troops, U.S.A.

IAR-330 Puma, Romania; licensed production of French SA-330 Puma (*see below*) Kaman HH-43F Huskie (also Kaman model 600-3/5/43B), 193km./h., 445 km., 10 passengers/1,760 kg., U.S.A.; employed as maritime rescue or VIP helicopter

Kamov Ka-25 Hormone, 209 km./h., 650 km., in ASW role – search radar and dipping sonar, 12 passengers in search-and-rescue role, Russia; *see* Helicopters, ASW

Mi-2 Hoplite (also PZL Swidnik), 210 km./h., 580 km., 8 troops/2,372 kg., Poland (designed in Russia)

Mi-4 Hound, 210 km./h., 400 km., 14 troops/1,740 kg., Russia

Mi-8/17 Hip, 250 km./h., 425 km., 24 troops/4,000-kg. internal/3,000-kg. external load, Russia

S-76, 269 km./h., 1,112 km., 12 troops/1,814-kg. external payload, U.S.A.

SA-330 Puma, 263 km./h., 550 km., 16 equipped troops/3,200 kg., France

UH-60A Black Hawk (also designated S-70), 268 km./h., 600 km., 14 troops/3,630-kg. external load, U.S.A.

Westland Lynx – *see* Helicopters, Attack

Westland Whirlwind Series 3, 159 km./h., 480 km. (ferry range – 834 km.), 10 troops/approx. 1,000 kg., Britain

Radars

(designation, effective range, country of origin)

AN/FPS-100, U.S.A.

AN/FPS-110, U.S.A.

AN/FPS-117, 350 km., U.S.A.

AN/TPS-32, 556 km., U.S.A.

AN/TPS-43, 408 km., U.S.A.

AN/TPS-59, 370 km., U.S.A.

AN/TPS-63, 296 km., U.S.A.

AN/TPS-70, 350 km., U.S.A.

AR-3 D, 24 km., Britain

AR-15, Britain

Cossor SSR, also Cossor monopulse secondary surveillance system, Britain

ELTA-2220/2206 148 km., Israel

LASS, aerostat with radar, U.S.A.

Long Track, 150 km., Russia; associated with SA-6 and SA-8

P-12 Spoon Rest, 275 km., Russia

P-14 Tall King, 500–600 km., Russia

P-15 Flat Face, 210–250 km., Russia

P-15M Squat Eye, 200 km., Russia

P-35/37 Barlock, 390 km., Russia

S-713 Martello 3-D, 500 km., Britain

S-711, Britain

Square Pair, Russia

S-600, Britain

TRS-2100 (Tiger S), 110 km., France

TRS-2215, France

TRS-2230, France

Watchman, Britain

SAMs, Long-Range

(designation, NATO codename if relevant, Russian designation if relevant, SP if relevant, range, country of origin)
HAWK, 35 km., U.S.A.
HQ-2J (CSA-1), PRC; copy of SA-2
MIM-23B Improved HAWK, 40 km., U.S.A.
MIM-104 Patriot, 68.5 km., U.S.A.
SA-2 Guideline, V-75 Dvina/Volkhov, 34.8 km., Russia
SA-3 Goa, S-125 Neva, 2.4–18.2 km., Russia
SA-5 Gammon, S-200 Volga/Angara, 250 km., Russia
SA-10 Grumble, S-300P/S-300 PMU-1 Buk, 70 km., Russia, a SAM with alleged ATBM capability
SA-12 Gladiator, S-300V, 150 km., SAM, ATBM, Russia
Note: SA-6, SA-7, SA-8, SA-9, Crotale, Crotale/Shahine, Rapier, Redeye, Stinger – *see* Army AA Defense – Missiles

Target Drones

(designation, type, country of origin)
Aerospatiale CT-20, target drone, France
Beech AQM-37A, target drone, U.S.A.
Beech MQM-107B, target drone, U.S.A.
MQM-74C Chukar II (also Northrop MQM-74C), target drone, U.S.A.
TTL BTT-3 Banshee, target drone, Britain

UAVs and Mini-UAVs

(designation, type, country of origin)
DRC-30, Russia
Heron, UAV, Israel; still experimental
Hunter, mini-UAV, Israel
Mastiff, mini-UAV, Israel
Mirach-100, mini-UAV, Italy; can serve as target drone, or tactical cruise missile
MQM-74C Chukar II, UAV, U.S.A.
Pioneer, mini-UAV, Israel
Qadr
R4E-50, Skyeye, mini-UAV, U.S.A.
Scout, mini-UAV, Israel
SD-3 UAV, Russia
Searcher, mini-UAV, Israel
Teledyne Ryan model 124 Firebee, mini-UAV, U.S.A.
Teledyne Ryan model 324 Scarab, UAV, U.S.A.

CHRONOLOGY OF MAJOR EVENTS

January

Date	*Major Events*
1	Seven Palestinians wounded in Hebron as an IDF soldier opens fire in the marketplace.
	Turkish Army kills 83 PKK men in an army operation in northern Iraq.
	Nine killed in bomb explosion on a bus in Damascus, Syria.
	Five killed by unknown assailants in Algeria.
1–15	Dennis Ross visits the Middle East in an attempt to conclude the agreement on Hebron.
2	Four soldiers from the South Lebanon Army (SLA) wounded in Hizbullah attack in southern Lebanon.
	Six officers and 2 civilians are condemned as spies for U.S. and executed in Libya.
3	Two IDF soldiers and five Lebanese wounded in exchanges of fire in southern Lebanon.
	Sixteen killed by unknown assailants in the village of Banashur, southern Algeria.
4	Eighteen killed by unknown assailants in Blida region in southern Algeria.
5	Netanyahu confers with Arafat at Erez checkpoint, in order to conclude the agreement on Hebron.
	Three IDF soldiers wounded in exchanges of fire in southern Lebanon.
	A car explosion in northern Syria, near Latakiya. Syrian government holds Israel responsible.
	Iran's Foreign Minister declares his country's wish to form military alliance with Turkey.
	Egypt discloses that an attempt to assassinate President Mubarak was thwarted in November 1996.
	Eighteen killed by unknown assailants in Banashur, south of Algiers.
7	Syrian President Assad had undergone an operation, possibly connected to his heart problems.
	Five wounded in terrorist attack in Baghdad.
	Seven killed and 48 wounded at car-bomb explosion in Algiers, Algeria.

8 One IDF soldier killed and eight wounded in exchanges of fire in southern Lebanon. Three Amal activists killed.

9 Thirteen wounded when two bombs explode in the old bus station in the center of Tel Aviv.

11 An SLA soldier wounded in bomb explosion in southern Lebanon.

12 Nineteen killed by unknown assailants in Blida region in southern Algeria.

13 Israeli and Palestinian negotiation teams meet in Jerusalem to conclude the Hebron agreement.

Syrian Vice President Abd al-Halim Khadam and Foreign Minister Faruk al-Shar'a visit Iran.

14 Twelve killed and 80 wounded in a car-bomb explosion near Algiers. Police forces kill 12 Muslim militants in Algiers.

An Israeli employer is killed by his Palestinian worker in Jerusalem.

15 Rebels occupy military outposts in southern Sudan.

Israel and the Palestinians sign the agreement on redeployment in Hebron.

16–17 IDF withdraws its troops from parts of Hebron, in accordance with the Hebron agreement.

19 A Palestinian woman attempts to stab an Israeli policeman in Jerusalem.

Forty-two killed and 60 wounded in car-bomb explosion in the capital, Algiers. Forty-eight killed by unknown assailants in Meda region in southern Algeria.

20 Oman declares the renewal of its relations with Israel, as consequence of the Hebron agreement.

21 Seven killed and 44 wounded in car-bomb explosion in Algiers.

22 Seventeen killed in car-bomb explosions in Blida region in southern Algeria.

25 Forty killed by unknown assailants near Algiers.

26 An anti-Islamic activist assassinated in the capital Algiers.

28 A union leader, Abd Bin Hamuda, is assassinated in the capital Algiers.

29 Three IDF soldiers killed and one wounded in bomb explosion in southern Lebanon.

30 Ex-general is assassinated and eight civilians killed in Algiers.

February

Date	*Major Events*
2	Thirty-one killed by Muslim militants in Media region in southern Algeria.
3	Sixteen killed by Muslim militants south of Algiers.
4	Seventy-three IDF soldiers killed on Israel's northern border as two helicopters collide on their way to southern Lebanon. This is the worst aerial accident in Israel's history.
8	Seven IDF soldiers wounded by Hizbullah fire in southern Lebanon.
11	Israeli Air Force attacks bases of terrorist organizations in the Beka' Valley in Lebanon, seven wounded.
12–17	Israeli Prime Minister Netanyahu visits the U.S., confers with President Clinton about negotiations with Syria.
12	Nine Copts killed and five wounded in Muslim militant attack in southern Egypt.
13–17	Iranian Defense Minister visits Syria to strengthen the Syrian-Iranian alliance.
13	An Israeli guard is stabbed and wounded by Qatari citizen in Rafiah checkpoint, near Gaza Strip.
14	Three Copts killed by Muslim militants in southern Egypt.
15	Syrian Vice President Abd al-Halim Khaddam and Foreign Minister Faruk al-Shar'a confer with Egyptian President Mubarak in Cairo.
17	Egyptian court indicts Israeli citizen Azzam Azzam of spying for Israel.
	Thirty-three killed by unknown assailants in Blida region in southern Algeria, police kill eight of the terrorists.
18	A Lebanese woman killed and two civilians wounded in exchanges of fire in southern Lebanon.
22	President Assad confers with Egyptian President Mubarak in Damascus about Israeli-Syrian negotiations.
	The two Kurdish leaders Jalal Talabani and Mohammed Barazani visit Iran.
23	Netanyahu confers with King Hussein in Amman.
	Security forces kill four Muslim militants in Algiers.

25 Israeli soldiers kill one Palestinian and injure three others in Bethlehem.

26 Israeli government authorizes the building of a new neighborhood at Har Homa near Jerusalem. Loud protests in the Arab world.

A Hizbullah activist killed and a civilian wounded in exchanges of fire in southern Lebanon.

28 An IDF soldier killed and another wounded in Hizbullah attack in southern Lebanon.

Turkish National Security Council demands that Prime Minister Erbakan act to curb the rise of Islamic fundamentalism.

March

Date	*Major Events*
1	Arafat confers with Mubarak in Cairo, speaks to a special session of the Arab League, and states intention to declare the establishment of an independent Palestinian state.
3–5	French Foreign Minister visits Israel, Syria, and Lebanon.
4–7	German Foreign Minister visits Jordan, Gaza, and Israel.
4–5	Israel conducts an airborne exercise.
5	Netanyahu confers with Mubarak in Cairo about the peace process.
	Turkish Prime Minister Erbakan signs orders to curb Islamic fundamentalism after a week of political pressure.
8	Israeli government approves a first further redeployment in the West Bank.
9–11	Mubarak visits Washington and confers with President Clinton.
9	Assad confers with Iranian Foreign Minister Velayati in Damascus, Syria, in order to restore good relations between the two states.
	Turkish armed forces launch an operation against the Kurdish PKK movement in northern Iraq that goes on until the end of the year.
10	Twelve Palestinians wounded by IDF soldiers while trying to stop road construction near Hebron.
	An IDF soldier wounded in car-bomb explosion near the Israeli border in southern Lebanon. Two Lebanese policemen wounded by another car-bomb explosion in Jezzine enclave in southern Lebanon.
	Iranian Foreign Minister Velayati visits Turkey in order to restore good relations with the Islamic government.
11	An IDF soldier is wounded in a terrorist attack by two Palestinians on a settlement south of Hebron.
	Successful test launch of Arrow-2 missile.
13	Seven Israeli school girls killed and six wounded by a Jordanian soldier in Naharayim, on the Israeli-Jordanian border.
	UN General Assembly passes resolution denouncing the building at Har Homa, near Jerusalem.

15 Velayati visits Saudi Arabia for the first time since 1993.

Policemen kill 51 Islamic militants in southern Algeria.

18 Work begins on Har Homa project. Palestinian demonstrations in the West Bank. Security cooperation between Israel and the Palestinian Authority (PA) is halted.

19 An IDF soldier killed and three wounded in Hizbullah attack on military convoy in southern Lebanon.

Thirty-two killed by unknown assailants in the village Kasar Bukhari, south of Algiers.

21 Three Israelis killed and 61 wounded when Palestinian terrorist blows himself up in a restaurant in the center of Tel Aviv. Israeli government orders a total closure on the West Bank and Gaza Strip.

21–31 Demonstrations continue in Hebron and Bethlehem.

27 A meeting of ''Jerusalem Committee'' in Morocco, with envoys from 14 Islamic states, including the Palestinian Authority, denounces Israel's ''expansionist'' policy in the West Bank and Gaza Strip.

28 One Palestinian killed and 40 wounded during violent demonstrations in the West Bank.

31 Arab Foreign Ministers meet in Cairo and decide to freeze the normalization process with Israel.

April

Date	*Major Events*
1	Two Palestinians killed and eight wounded in attempted suicide-bomb attack on buses of Israeli settlers.
	Two Palestinians killed by IDF soldiers during violent demonstrations in the West Bank.
	Lebanese girl wounded in bomb explosion in a village in southern Lebanon.
2	Thirteen IDF soldiers wounded when their truck is attacked by Molotov cocktail in the West Bank.
6	Seventeen killed by Muslim militants in Tihara region, in southern Algeria.
7–8	Netanyahu visits the U.S., agrees with President Clinton on the need to fight terror.
7	Thirteen killed by Muslim militants in Marshish in western Algeria.
	Two Palestinians are shot and wounded by an Israeli settler.
8	Three Palestinians killed, seven wounded in violent demonstrations in Hebron, following the killing of a Palestinian by Jewish settlers.
	Israeli Foreign Minister David Levy confers with Prime Minister Erbakan in Turkey.
9–21	Continued demonstrations in Hebron.
10	A German court accuses Iranian leadership of ordering assassinations and terrorist attacks. The EU expels Iranian ambassadors and withdraws its ambassadors from Tehran.
	Israeli and Palestinian security services uncover a terrorist unit responsible for several deadly attacks.
13	Closure is eased, Palestinian workers allowed to enter Israel.
	An SLA soldier killed and three civilians wounded in bomb explosions in southern Lebanon.
	Iraqi ships shoot at Kuwaiti Coast Guard boats across their joint border.
	Three wounded in shooting by a Palestinian woman at Allenby Bridge checkpoint, on the border between Israel and Jordan.

14 The Iraqi Parliament authorizes a major oil deal with Russia.

Iranian students demonstrate in front of the German embassy in Tehran following the court ruling in Germany.

15 European-Mediterranean forum convenes in Malta.

The closure of the West Bank is renewed.

IDF elite unit kills three Hizbullah activists in southern Lebanon.

16 David Levy confers with Yasir Arafat in Malta. Arafat promises to renew security cooperation with Israel.

17 Netanyahu confers with Dennis Ross in Jerusalem.

11–17 Russian Undersecretary of State visits Damascus, Beirut, Amman, and Gaza, where he meets with Chairman Arafat.

20 Two SLA soldiers killed by Hizbullah bomb in southern Lebanon.

22 Ninety-three killed by unknown assailants in a village near Bugara, south of Algiers.

22–25 Iran concludes a land and naval exercise of the Revolutionary Guard in the Straits of Hormuz.

23 Arafat confers with King Hussein in Akaba about ways to promote the peace process.

24–25 United Nations General Assembly concludes a special meeting, denounces Israel on the decision to build a settlement in Har Homa.

24 Two Lebanese wounded by Israeli helicopter fire in southern Lebanon.

Palestinians demonstrate in Gaza Strip against the enlargement of settlements.

Forty-two killed by unknown assailants in Umariya village, south of Algiers.

Two Israeli women killed by a Palestinian shepherd in Wadi Kelt, near Jerusalem.

25 Two IDF soldiers wounded in Hizbullah bombardment in southern Lebanon.

26 Turkish Security Council forces Erbakan to curb the spread of Islam in Turkey.

27 General elections in Yemen. Victory for the ruling party.

One Palestinian killed and two wounded by IDF soldiers during violent demonstrations in a village near Hebron.

30 An Israeli woman wounded in a stabbing attempt in Umm Qais, in northern Jordan.

Israeli security forces kill a Palestinian during a car chase in Jerusalem.

30/4–2/5 Turkish Defense Minister visits Israel to discuss strategic cooperation.

May

Date	*Major Events*
1	Assad confers with Mubarak in Cairo. Assad declares that Arab states are willing to abandon WMD if Israel abandons nuclear weapons.
	Israeli police evacuate two caravans near a settlement near the West Bank city of Jericho.
5	An Israeli businessman, Nahum Manbar, is indicted for alleged sale of chemical military technology to Iran.
	Iran's Foreign Minister visits Egypt for the first time since the revolution.
	Two SLA soldiers and three Lebanese civilians wounded by Hizbullah bomb in southern Lebanon.
6	Israeli police demolish three illegal buildings in a settlement near Nablus, in the West Bank.
	Arafat confers with President Weitzman at Erez checkpoint. They promise to renew Israeli-Palestinian security cooperation.
	Two Lebanese civilians killed and two wounded by Hizbullah bomb in southern Lebanon. Two Hizbullah activists killed by IDF ambush.
	Head of Hamas's political wing, Musa Abu Marzuq, is deported from U.S. to Jordan under restricted conditions.
	Five killed and 32 wounded in bomb explosion in Algiers.
8	Netanyahu confers with King Hussein in Akaba about implementation of the water agreement.
	Israel accuses the Palestinian Authority (PA) of responsibility for the murder of the real estate dealer Farid Bashiti in Ramallah.
10–14	Pope John visits Lebanon and calls for support of Lebanese independence.
11–17	Iran concludes a large military exercise in the Gulf of Oman.
12	Four Hizbullah activists killed during abortive attack on SLA outpost in southern Lebanon.
14	A Hizbullah activist killed in an engagement with IDF soldiers in southern Lebanon.

15 Three IDF soldiers killed and seven wounded in a clash with Hizbullah in southern Lebanon. Two Hizbullah activists killed.

17 A Palestinian real estate dealer is killed in Ramallah.

19 Syrian business delegation visits Iraq for the first time in 17 years.

Israeli navy boat foils attempted suicide attack by Amal activist near Israel's northern border.

21 An IDF soldier is wounded by bomb in southern Lebanon.

22.5–9.6 Jordan and U.S. conduct joint ground exercises in Jordan.

23 General elections for the presidency in Iran. A moderate candidate, Muhammad Khatami, is elected.

Israeli government ratifies the water agreement with Jordan, negotiated by Infrastructure Minister Ariel Sharon.

A Hizbullah activist killed and three others wounded in a clash with IDF soldiers in southern Lebanon.

24 PA comptroller issues report on embezzlement by high-ranking officials in the PA. Chairman Arafat orders the establishment of committee of inquiry.

27 Mubarak confers with Netanyahu in Sharm al-Shaikh, Egypt agrees to begin to mediate an initiative.

29 Two Hizbullah activists killed and three wounded in an ambush by IDF soldiers in southern Lebanon.

30 An IDF soldier killed and four Lebanese wounded in Hizbullah bombardment in southern Lebanon.

31 One killed and 24 wounded by a bomb explosion in Algiers.

Qatari Foreign Minister has conditioned Israel's participation in the economic conference in Doha on progress in the peace process.

A third Palestinian real estate dealer is killed in Ramallah for selling land to settlers.

June

Date	*Major Events*
1	IDF special unit kidnaps three Hizbullah activists in Lebanon, for interrogation in Israel. Four Lebanese wounded in IDF bombardment of Hizbullah infrastructure.
2	Eighteen killed and 100 wounded in a bomb explosion in Algiers.
	Syria opens three checkpoints on its border with Iraq, after 17 years of closed borders.
4	Israeli and U.S. delegations meet for strategic dialogue in Israel.
	Netanyahu presents to cabinet his plan for permanent status agreement with the Palestinians, reserves 60 percent of the West Bank for Israel.
	A Lebanese civilian killed by Hizbullah bomb in southern Lebanon.
5	Three international elections supervisors wounded in a bomb explosion in a village near the capital Algiers.
6	National elections are held in Algeria, progovernment parties win majority in Parliament.
7	Syria and Iraq sign a trade agreement.
8	Israeli and Palestinian negotiation teams meet in Cairo for the first time in four months.
	Arafat holds a secret meeting with Iraqi ambassador to Jordan, his first meeting with an Iraqi diplomat in five years.
10	Turkish Army dismisses 61 officers and 100 enlisted men for supporting Muslim fundamentalism.
12–21	Violent demonstrations near Israeli settlements in Gaza Strip, some Palestinians wounded.
12	Israeli government agrees to forgo $50 million of American foreign assistance in favor of Jordan.
13	Iraqi trade delegation visits Syria for the first time in 17 years.
14	An Israeli woman wounded in a terrorist ambush in Har Hadar settlement, near Jerusalem.
	An IDF soldier wounded in Hizbullah bombardment in

southern Lebanon. Three UNIFIL soldiers held by Hizbullah for several hours in Beirut.

15 Police kill three Muslim militants in southern Egypt

An IDF soldier killed and three wounded when their tank is hit by Hizbullah bomb in southern Lebanon.

Arafat announces in Ramallah that the Egyptian mediation initiative is finished.

18 Turkish Prime Minister Erbakan resigns after pressure from the army to contain the Islamic Welfare Party.

19 Syrian Foreign Minister al-Shar'a and Vice President Khaddam visit Tehran and confer with Khatami on Israel's threat to Syria. Khatami invites Iraq to participate in the Islamic conference to be held in November.

20 A terrorist attack foiled when bomb is found on a beach in Tel Aviv.

21 Six UNIFIL soldiers wounded by Israeli mines in southern Lebanon.

UN Security Council warns Iraq of more stringent sanctions after Iraqi soldiers obstruct UNSCOM operations

22–24 Israel conducts major military exercise on the Golan Hights.

25–26 Foreign Ministers of the Damascus Declaration states (Syria, Egypt, and the GCC states) denounce Turkey's military links with Israel, decide to create a common market.

26 The PA foils suicide-bombing attempt in Jerusalem by arresting the bomber.

27 Two Hizbullah activists killed by IDF ambush in southern Lebanon.

A pamphlet depicting Prophet Muhammad as a pig is distributed in Hebron by right-wing activist, igniting violent demonstrations in the West Bank.

28 An IDF soldier wounded in Hizbullah bombardment on Israeli outpost in southern Lebanon.

29 Two Hizbullah activists killed in a clash with IDF soldiers in southern Lebanon.

Israel and PA agree to resume security cooperation under American supervision.

Mesut Yilmaz is appointed Prime Minister of Turkey.

July

Date	*Major Events*
1	Two IDF soldiers wounded by bomb thrown during violent demonstrations in Hebron.
	A Hizbullah activist killed in IDF ambush in southern Lebanon.
2	A Palestinian boy killed during violent demontrations held in Gaza Strip and Hebron to protest "Pig Pamphlet."
3	A SLA soldier killed and three wounded by Hizbullah bomb in southern Lebanon.
	Two killed and 10 wounded in a terrorist attack by PKK on a military ammunition factory in central Turkey.
4	Lebanese Army arrests 100 in demonstrations in Ba'albek led by an ex-Hizbullah leader, Subhi Tufaili.
5	Islamic leaders in Egypt issue a call for a cease-fire with authorities.
5–7	Iranian Vice President visits Damascus to discuss strategic cooperation with Syria.
6	An IDF soldier killed in Hizbullah attack. Three Lebanese civilians wounded in exchanges of fire between IDF and Hizbullah, which include firing Katyusha rockets toward Israeli border.
7	Iraq ceases propaganda transmissions of a Syrian opposition radio station.
	Seven Lebanese civilians wounded in Hizbullah bombardment in southern Lebanon.
9	Turkey announces a unilateral moratorium on exercises in the Aegean Sea, as a confidence-building measure with Greece.
	Two IDF soldiers wounded in bomb explosion near Nablus.
	An IDF soldier wounded from Hizbullah bombardment in southern Lebanon.
10–14	Violent demonstrations and rock throwing against IDF soldiers in Hebron.
11	Hizbullah fire Katyusha rocket into Israeli territory from Lebanon.

12 A Lebanese civilian killed by IDF in exchanges of fire with Hizbullah in southern Lebanon.

Twenty-one killed and 11 wounded by unknown assailants in southern Algeria.

13 Forty-four killed by unknown assailants in southern Algeria.

Two IDF soldiers and one Lebanese civilian wounded in exchanges of fire in southern Lebanon.

14 Twenty-one killed and 40 wounded in a bomb attack at a market place near Algiers.

Three Palestinian policemen arrested for attempt to attack an Israeli settlement near Nablus.

Two Lebanese civilians killed and two SLA soldiers wounded in exchanges of fire in southern Lebanon.

15 UN Security Council passes a very harsh resolution against Israeli settlements.

Hizbullah fires Katyusha rockets on IDF outposts in southern Lebanon and into Israeli territory.

Algerian authorities release the former leader of the outlawed "Islamic Salvation Front" from jail.

16 Hizbullah fire Katyusha rockets into Israeli territory from southern Lebanon.

20 Palestinian police uncover a bomb factory near Bethlehem.

21 One hundred killed during a raid by security forces on Muslim militant meeting, south of Algiers.

22 Ten wounded when a Palestinian from Nazareth runs his car into a group of tourists in Jaffa.

A policeman is wounded in a stabbing attack in the Gaza Strip.

SLA Commander Gen. Antoine Lahad expresses his willingness to discuss a withdrawal from the Jezzine enclave in southern Lebanon.

23 An IDF officer wounded in Hebron.

Three SLA soldiers wounded by Hizbullah bomb in Jezzine enclave in southern Lebanon.

Mubarak urges Arab countries to implement an agreement on Arab Economic Market, acknowledges an Iranian effort to launch military cooperation with Egypt.

Six policemen killed and two civilians wounded in a terrorist attack in southern Egypt.

Palestinian Airlines begins commercial flights from El-Arish to Amman.

Algerian security forces kill the leader of the most violent Muslim militant group, the Armed Islamic Group.

24 Twenty-nine killed by Muslim militants west of Algiers.

25 Palestinian policemen detain 11 Israeli settlers who were hiking in Area B, which is under Israeli security control.

Thirteen killed and seven wounded by Muslim militants in southern Algeria.

26 A Lebanese woman killed in exchanges of fire in southern Lebanon.

27 A plan is revealed to build Jewish housing in on Arab neighborhood in Ras al-Amud, Jerusalem.

IDF blows up a smuggler's tunnel connecting Gaza Strip with Egypt.

A Lebanese woman and an SLA soldier wounded in exchanges of fire in southern Lebanon.

Several bombs are thrown at Israeli outposts in Hebron.

Two kidnapped Italians are released by Yemeni tribesman.

28 Sixty-six killed by unknown assailants in southern Algeria.

David Levy confers with PA Economic Cooperation Minister Nabil Shaath; joint committees to resume their work.

29 Mubarak confers with Assad in Damascus, and King Hussein in Amman.

Israeli soldier wounded in stabbing attack near Nablus; the Palestinian attacker is killed.

Forty-one killed by unknown assailants in southwestern Algeria.

30 Thirteen killed and 168 wounded when two suicide-bombers blow themselves up in Mahaneh Yehuda Market in Jerusalem. IDF imposes closure of the West Bank, government decides to demolish illegally built Arab houses in Jerusalem.

Eight killed and 25 wounded in a car-bomb explosion in Algiers.

31 Assad visits Iran and confers with former President Rafsanjai.

Eighty-eight killed and 12 badly wounded by unknown assailants in southern Algeria.

Moroccan government and the Polisario Front agree on a preliminary peace proposal.

August

Date	*Major Events*
1	Assad confers with President-elect Khatami in Tehran. In a speech in the Iranian Majlis, calls for Israeli withdrawal from the Golan Heights.
2	Arafat confers with Mubarak in Cairo.
	Twenty killed by unknown assailants, south of Algiers.
	Supreme Military Council in Turkey discharges 73 officers on charges of being Islamic activists.
	Two policemen wounded in car-bomb attack in central Turkey.
3	A Palestinian is shot dead south of Hebron, in the West Bank.
	Mohammad Khatami sworn in as President of Iran.
4–6	Israel conducts a three-day airborne exercise.
4	IDF kills five members of Hizbullah in southern Lebanon.
	Twenty-six killed and 15 wounded by unknown assailants in southern Algeria
5	Three killed in southern Lebanon by Israeli Air Force attack.
	Police kill seven Muslim militants in southern Algeria
6	Netanyahu confers with Jordan's Crown Prince Hassan and Prime Minister Abd al-Salam Majali.
	U.S. Secretary of State Madeleine Albright announces a new American proposal for peace in the Middle East.
	Arafat calls Palestinians to prepare for the next battle
7	An SLA soldier and three civilians killed in southern Lebanon by Hizbullah bombs.
8	Hizbullah fires Katyusha MRLs from Lebanon into Israel's territory.
	Thirty-two killed and 40 wounded by unknown assailants in southern Algeria.
8–14	A delegation of 50 Israeli Arabs visits Syria.
9–13	Dennis Ross visits Israel, Jordan, and Gaza in an attempt to revive the peace process.
9	One civilian killed and three wounded by Israeli aircraft in southern Lebanon.

10 One IDF soldier killed in Hizbullah attack in southern Lebanon, two civilians wounded by Hizbullah rockets.

11 Italian tourist released after being held hostage for two days by Yemeni tribesmen.

12 PLO offices in U.S. are closed after the expiration of Middle East Peace Facilitation Act.

Dennis Ross completes an Israeli-Palestinian agreement to resume full security cooperation. Security cooperation committee set up with Israeli, Palestinian, and U.S. representatives.

Lebanese government sends 700 soldiers and policemen to the Beka' Valley against Hizbullah guerrillas.

13 Netanyahu confers with King Hussein in Akaba.

14 Israel apprehends Palestinian policeman who shot at an IDF patrol in the Gaza Strip.

15 Iraq resumes exports of crude oil.

17 An attempt made to assassinate Turkish Prime Minister Mesut Yilmaz in central Turkey.

Seven killed by unknown assailants in southern Algeria.

Security forces in Jordan arrest five Jordanians who planned terrorist attack in Israel.

An Israeli attempts to shoot at a Palestinian car near Jerusalem.

18 Three Lebanese children killed by Hizbullah bomb. Six Lebanese killed and 35 wounded by SLA bombardment of Sidon.

Tunisia will send an envoy to maintain its interest office in Israel. Oman's interest office remains open. Envoy allowed to return to Israel.

Thirteen Islamic activists killed and 100 arrested by security forces in an operation in southern Egypt.

Nine killed and three wounded by unknown assailants in southern Algeria.

19 Hizbullah fires 30 Katyusha rockets from southern Lebanon into Israel's northern front. One civilian wounded and a few houses in Kiryat Shemona are damaged.

20 Fifth test launch of the Arrow-2 antiballistic missile fails.

Israeli Air Force attacks several targets in Lebanon. A power line is bombed as a signal to Lebanese government.

The Iranian Parliament approves the new government headed by President Khatami.

Palestinian Authority holds a National Unity Conference in Gaza, which includes all the opposition organizations in Gaza Strip.

Sixty-three killed and 12 women kidnapped by Muslim militants in Algeria.

21 Israeli Infrastructure Minister Sharon decides to change the location of Adasiya Dam on the Yarmuk River. The new location will be on former Syrian-controlled territory in el-Hama.

23 Three Hizbullah men killed by IDF during an attack on IDF outpost in southern Lebanon. Two Amal men killed in Beirut in car explosion. One SLA soldier killed by bomb in southern Lebanon.

Ten Palestinians wounded during demonstrations in Bethlehem.

23–28 Netanyahu visits Japan and South Korea. Japan rejects Israeli proposal to invest in Arrow project.

24 Netanyahu confers with Chinese Deputy Prime Minister in Beijing.

Israel denounces Russia for helping the Iranian nuclear program.

24–26 Iran conducts major exercise near the border with Afghanistan.

25 Arafat confers with Mubarak in Cairo, declares that five Arab countries will donate funds to the PA.

Exchanges of fire in southern Lebanon. One SLA officer wounded in bomb explosion.

Three Palestinians wounded during demonstrations in Bethlehem against closure.

A Druze woman from Golan Heights is arrested for spying for Syria.

Four killed and 60 wounded in car-bomb explosion in the market in Algiers.

26 Four Palestinians wounded by IDF soldiers during demonstrations in Bethlehem.

Sixty-four killed by unknown assailants in Blida region in southern Algeria.

28 Four IDF soldiers killed and six wounded in a fire in southern Lebanon. Four Amal activists are killed as well.

Eight killed and 50 wounded in car-bomb explosion in Algiers.

29 Three hundred killed by unknown assailants in Blida region in southern Algeria.

31 Egyptian court sentences the Israeli Azzam Azzam to 15 years in jail with hard labor for spying for Israel.

September

Date	*Major Events*
1	IDF eases the closure on the West Bank and Gaza Strip and allows 4,000 workers to enter Israel.
	Iranian President Mohammed Khatami declares hard-line posture toward Israel.
	An Islamic opposition leader is put under house arrest in Algeria.
	Islamic opposition organizes demonstrations in Turkey against restrictive new laws.
2	Two civilians wounded in bomb explosion in southern Lebanon.
	Police kill 47 Islamic militants in southern Algeria.
3	Twenty-two killed by unknown assailants in El Arbi in southern Algeria.
4	Four killed and 200 wounded when three Palestinian suicide-bombers strike at the center of Jerusalem. Israeli government renews full closure on the West Bank and Gaza Strip. Netanyahu declares that Israel will not honor commitments to further redeployments until the Palestinians fulfill all obligations.
	Five killed and 20 wounded in a bomb explosion in Algiers.
	Iraq opens its border to pilgrims from Iran for the first time in 17 years.
5	Eleven IDF soldiers killed and four wounded when elite commando unit confronts an ambush by Hizbullah in southern Lebanon.
	Eighty killed and 100 wounded in attack by Muslim militants near Algiers.
7	One IDF soldier killed in Hizbullah bombardment, in southern Lebanon.
	Arafat confers with Mubarak and King Hussein in Cairo, calls for swift resumption of Israeli-Palestinian talks.
9	Algerian security forces kill 78 Islamic militants, including the leader of the Armed Islamic Group.
	Palestinian security forces arrest four Palestinians suspected of planning to assassinate Chairman Arafat.

10–14 US Secretary of State Madeleine Albright visits the Middle East in an attempt to revive the peace process.

Two Hizbullah activists killed by IDF soldiers in southern Lebanon.

Nine killed by unknown assailants in Laraba region in southern Algeria, four killed in explosion in a suburb of Algiers.

12 Four Hizbullah activists and six Lebanese soldiers killed in an engagement with IDF soldiers in southern Lebanon.

14 Two IDF soldiers killed in bomb explosion in southern Lebanon.

Four Israeli families try to establish a new settlement in Ras al'Amud neighborhood in Jerusalem.

19 Fifty-three killed by Muslim militants in Galeb Al-Kabir, south of Algiers.

20–22 Arab Foreign Ministers convene in Cairo, Egypt.

21–23 Israeli security forces make sweeping arrests of Hamas activists in the West Bank, following the investigation of the recent terrorist attacks in Jerusalem.

22 Two Israeli security men are shot and wounded near the house of the Israeli cultural attaché in Amman, Jordan.

22–28 Iran conducts major military exercise near the city of Qom.

23 Two hundred killed by unknown assailants near Algiers.

24 Netanyahu announces enlargement of Efrat settlement near Jerusalem, announcement condemned by the Palestinian Authority and U.S.

25 Two SLA soldiers and a Lebanese woman wounded by Hizbullah bombardment in southern Lebanon.

Two Mossad agents are caught during an assassination attempt on Hamas leader, Khaled Masha'al, in Amman. Israel releases Hamas spiritual leader, Sheikh Ahmad Yassin, and other Palestinian prisoners in return for their release.

27 Thirty killed by unknown assailants in El Haj village, in southern Algeria.

28 Army aircraft attack a group of men from the Armed Islamic Group in Old Elal village, south of Algiers.

29 David Levy confers with PLC Speaker Abu Ala'a and Mad-

eleine Albright. An agreement is reached to resume the work of the joint bilateral committees.

One IDF soldier is killed by Hizbullah bombardment of Israeli outposts in southern Lebanon.

Iranian aircraft bomb bases of Mujahedin el-Khalk in northern Iraq.

Eighty-four killed by unknown assailants in Blida region, south of Algiers.

October

Date	*Major Events*
2	Twenty killed by unknown assailants in Oran region, western Algeria.
3	Seventy-two killed by unknown assailants in Blida region south of Algiers.
	Syria and Iran mass armed forces on the border with Turkey in order to contain the Turkish operation in Iraq.
4	Fifty-four killed by unknown assailants in Ouled Sidi Yahia, in southern Algeria.
5	Two Lebanese civilians are killed by Hizbullah bomb in southern Lebanon.
	Twenty killed by unknown assailants near Algiers.
6	Eleven Muslim militants killed by security forces near Algiers.
	President Weizman confers with Clinton in Washington, raises the idea of a Camp David – like conference.
8	Two IDF soldiers killed and six other, wounded by Hizbullah bombs near Israeli border, in southern Lebanon.
10	IDF soldiers kill an infiltrator from Jordan near the Dead Sea.
11–20	Iran conducts major military exercises in the Persian Gulf.
12	Forty-three killed by unknown assailants in Oran region, western Algeria
13	Ten policemen killed in terrorist attack in Minya Province in southern Egypt.
18	An IDF soldier killed and two others wounded by Hizbullah missile attack on Israeli outpost in southern Lebanon.
19	Two civilians killed by Hizbullah bomb in southern Lebanon.
19–20	Twenty-eight killed by unknown assailants across southern Algeria. Security forces kill 17 Muslim militants.
20	Two nephews of a Palestinian terrorist leader Abu Nidal assassinated in Beirut, Lebanon.
21	Two IDF soldiers wounded by Hizbullah rocket attack on Israeli outpost in southern Lebanon.

25–28 Lebanese Prime Minister Rafiq Hariri visits Iran and is offered free oil in exchange for direct airline routes.

26 Joint American-Egyptian exercise begins west of Alexandria.

Sixteen killed by unknown assailants in Medea province south of Algiers. At least 30 found dead in a well in Bentalah region south of Algiers.

28 Two Hizbullah activists killed by IDF soldiers in southern Lebanon.

29 Iraqi government orders all American citizens working for the UN inspection teams to leave the country within a week. US threatens military operation against Iraq.

30 Two SLA soldiers killed by bomb in Jezzine enclave in southern Lebanon.

November

Date	Major Events
1–7	Turkey conducts a week-long military exercise off the shores of Cyprus.
2	Mesut Yilmaz visits Greece for the first time in 10 years.
2–6	Negotiations between Israeli and Palestinian teams on the implementation of the Interim Agreement are held in Washington.
4	General elections for the Jordanian Parliament boycotted by Muslim Brotherhood.
5	U.S. decides to enforce sanctions on Sudan for sponsoring terrorism.
	U.S. buys 25 MiG-29 aircraft from former Soviet Republic of Moldova in order to prevent their sale to Iran.
7	Two SLA soldiers wounded in Hizbullah bombardment in southern Lebanon.
	Twenty-three killed by unknown assailants near the town of Silssen in northwestern Algeria.
8	Syrian President Assad confers with Iranian Foreign Minister on Turkey's military operations in northern Iraq.
	Twenty-seven killed by unknown assailants in Blida region, south of Algiers.
10	Saudi Arabia formally announces that it will boycott the Economic Conference in Qatar, in 16–18 November.
	Iranian Parliament ratifies the new Chemical Weapons Convention.
11	Egypt announces formally that it will boycott the Economic Conference in Qatar.
	A Palestinian boy wounded by IDF soldiers in Bethlehem.
12	UN Security Council denounces Iraqi behavior and sets a travel ban on Iraqi officials to UN member states.
	Three soldiers killed and two civilians wounded in a terrorist attack by Islamic militants on a train in Upper Egypt.
13	All UN inspectors leave Iraq following government decision to expel American inspectors from the country.
	European Community decides to send ambassadors back to Tehran, following their recall to Europe last April.

Demonstrations in Algiers by opposition parties accusing the Algerian government of election fraud.

14 General elections are held in Morocco for the first time since its independence.

15 Russians arrest an Iranian diplomat for buying secret information from Russian experts.

IDF soldiers kidnap two Hamas activists who are held by Palestinian security forces. Palestinian demonstrators claim the two activists were handed over to Israel.

Kuwait begins a month-long exercise with U.S., Britain, and Italy.

16 Several arrested by Yemeni security forces in connection with a series of bombings and terrorist attacks in San'a.

16–18 The Middle East Economic Conference held in Doha, Qatar, despite Arab leaders' objections to Israeli presence. The conference calls upon Israel to respect the principle of land for peace.

17 Sixty-eight killed, including 58 tourists, in a suicide attack by members of Al Gama'a Al Islamia, in Luxor, Egypt.

Israeli security forces arrest a wanted Hamas activist in Jenin.

19 An Israeli killed and another badly wounded by gunfire near the walls of the Old City of Jerusalem. Israel sets up new police posts in the Old City.

Lebanon rejects an Israeli offer of military agreement prior to Israeli withdrawal from southern Lebanon.

Large demonstrations in the city of Qom in support of the Islamic leadership of Iran.

Netanyahu confers with King Hussein in London.

20 After Russian mediation, Iraqi government agrees to the return of UN inspectors, including Americans, to Iraq. Iraq still denies the UN inspectors access to many "presidential sites."

21–22 Iraqi Deputy Prime Minister Tariq Aziz visits Syria and Jordan at the end of a two-week tour of the Middle East aimed at pressuring the UN Security Council to lift sanctions from Iraq.

22 A Palestinian killed by IDF soldiers at a roadblock near Bethlehem, in the West Bank.

23 Eight civilians killed and 2 IDF soldiers wounded in bombardments by Hizbullah and Amal in southern Lebanon.

24 Three Hizbullah activists killed by IDF forces in southern Lebanon.

Israel and Jordan conduct joint naval exercise in the Red Sea.

28 Three SLA soldiers killed and five IDF soldiers wounded by bomb explosions in southern Lebanon.

29 Twenty Palestinians wounded by IDF fire during demonstrations in Bethlehem.

30 Israeli government decides on the principle of conditional withdrawal from more territory in the West Bank.

December

Date	*Major Events*
1	An IDF soldier wounded in shooting incident on the Egyptian border in Gaza Strip.
	Seventy Muslim militants killed by Algerian security forces in a 10-day operation south of Algiers.
2	Three IDF soldiers wounded in Hizbullah rocket attack on Israeli outpost in southern Lebanon. One Hizbullah activist killed by IDF soldiers.
5	Thirty Palestinians wounded by IDF soldiers in violent demonstrations in Rafiah.
8–10	Israeli Defense Minister Yitzhak Mordechai visits Turkey in order to enhance military and strategic cooperation.
9–11	The Islamic Conference Organization meets in Tehran. The kings of Jordan, Saudi Arabia, and Morocco as well as Egyptian President Mubarak do not attend. The final declaration calls for an international conference on terrorism, sponsored by the UN.
10	Jordanian government orders the expulsion of 17 Iraqi diplomats, after the execution of four Jordanian citizens in Iraq.
	Five killed and seven wounded in a bomb explosion inside a mosque in Algiers.
12	One Hizbullah activist killed and three wounded by IDF soldiers in southern Lebanon.
14	Iranian President Khatami calls for a dialogue with the Americans.
	Fifteen killed by gunmen at a roadblock near Khemis Meliana, southwest Algeria.
15	Sixteen killed by unknown assailants in Cheraga, a suburb of Algiers.
18	Ten found dead in Mitijda region south of Algiers.
20	Eight killed and four wounded in a bomb explosion in Algiers.
22	A shooting incident at Israeli military outpost in Hebron.
	Thirty killed by unknown assailants in El Bordj village in western Algeria.

23 Three IDF soldiers wounded in bomb explosion in southern Lebanon.

Four hundred and twenty killed by unknown assailants in Tiaret region in western Algeria.

25 Two SLA soldiers wounded in Hizbullah bombardment of IDF and SLA outposts in southern Lebanon.

29 Thirty-four killed in southern and western regions of Medea and Bel Abbes in Algeria.

30 Four hundred and twelve killed by unknown assailants in Relizane Province, western Algeria.

31 An Israeli woman killed by Palestinian terrorists in a roadside ambush near Ariel, in the West Bank.

Abbreviations

AA	antiaircraft
AAG	antiaircraft gun
AAM	air-to-air missile
AEW	airborne early warning
AFB	air force base
AFV	armored fighting vehicle
AGM	air-to-ground missile
AP	antipersonnel
APC	armored personnel carrier
AR	assault rifle
ARV	armored reconnaissance vehicle
ASW	antisubmarine warfare
AT	antitank
ATGM	antitank guided missile
ATRL	antitank rocket launcher
AWACS	airborne warning and control system
batt.	battalion
bil.	billion
CAS	close air support
CBU	cluster bomb unit
CEW	counter – electronic warfare
CLGP	cannon-launched guided projectile
CW	chemical warfare
div.	division
dwt	deadweight tons
ECM	electronic countermeasures
ECCM	electronic counter-countermeasures
ESM	electronic surveillance measures
EW	electronic warfare
FAE	fuel air explosive
FLIR	forward-looking infrared
ft.	feet
GBU	glide bomb unit
GCC	Gulf Cooperation Council
GDP	gross domestic product
GHQ	general headquarters
GPMG	general purpose machine gun
grt	gross registered tons

h.	hours
HMG	heavy machine gun
HQ	headquarters
HUD	head up display (in combat a/c)
IAF	Israel Air Force
IAI	Israel Aircraft Industries
IDF	Israel Defense Forces
kg.	kilograms
km.	kilometers
laser	light amplification by stimulated emission of radiation
LCM	landing craft, mechanized
LCT	landing craft, tank
LCU	landing craft, utility
LMG	light machine gun
LSM	landing ship, mechanized
LST	landing ship, tank
LT	light tank
m.	meters
MBT	main battle tank
MFPB	missile fast patrol boat
MG	machine gun
mil.	million
MLRS	multiple-launch rocket system
mm	millimeter
MMG	medium machine gun
MRL	multiple-rocket launcher
MTB	motor torpedo boat
Naval SSM	sea-to-sea missile
NCO	noncommissioned officer
PGM	precision-guided munition
PKK	Kurdish Workers Party
PLA	Palestine Liberation Army
PLO	Palestine Liberation Organization
port.	portable
PRC	People's Republic of China
reg.	regular
res.	reserve
R&D	research and development
RPV	remotely piloted vehicle; *see also* UAV
SAR	semiautomatic rifle

SAM	surface-to-air missile
SDV	swimmer delivery vehicle
SLAR	sideways-looking airborne radar
SMG	submachine gun
SP	self-propelled
sq.	square
SSB	single side band (radio transceiver)
SSM	surface-to-surface missile
Sys.	system
STOL	short takeoff/landing
TALD	tactical air-launched decoy
TEL	transporter-erector-launcher (for SSMs or SAMs)
TOE	table of organization and equipment
TOW	tube-launched, optically wire-guided (antitank) missile
UAV	unmanned aerial vehicle; RPV is remotely piloted, UAV is either remotely piloted or flies according to preplanned computerized program
unconf.	unconfirmed

MAPS

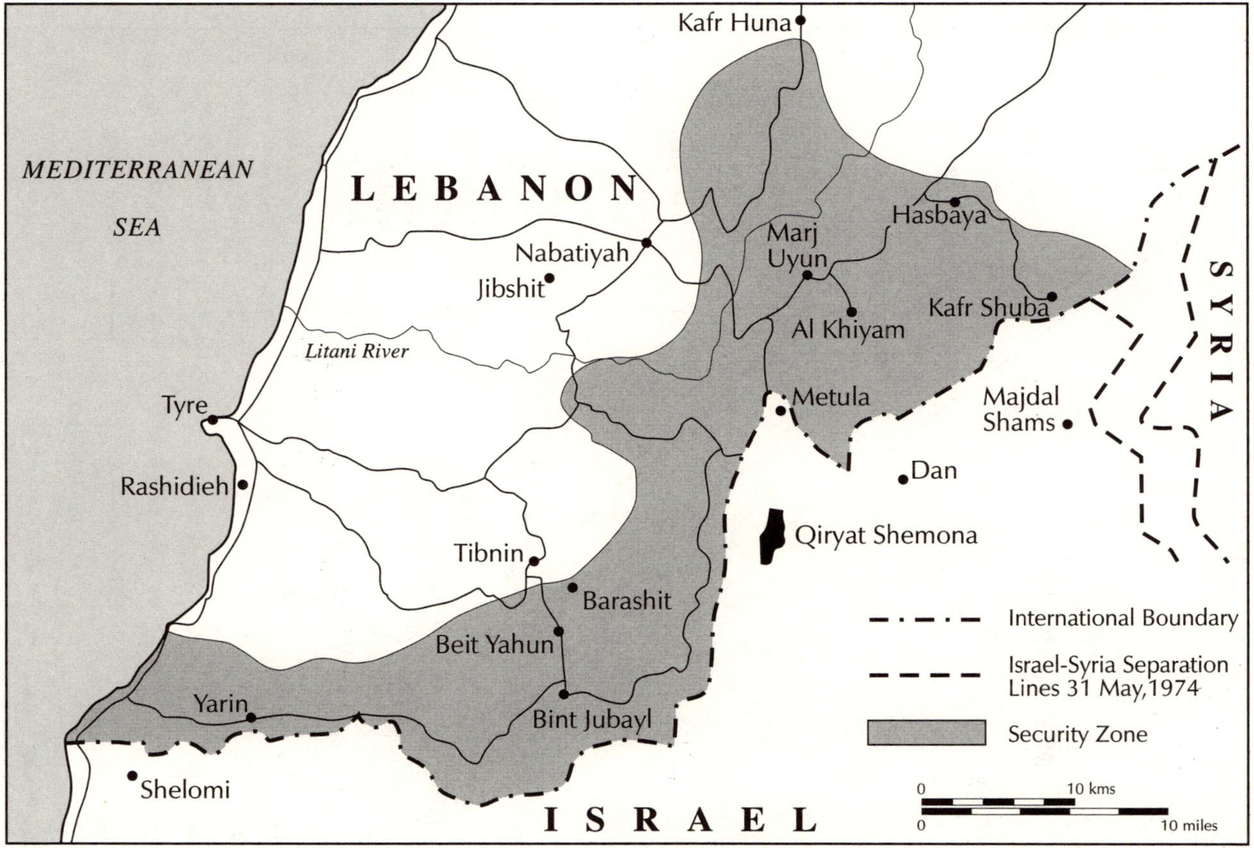

1. South Lebanon

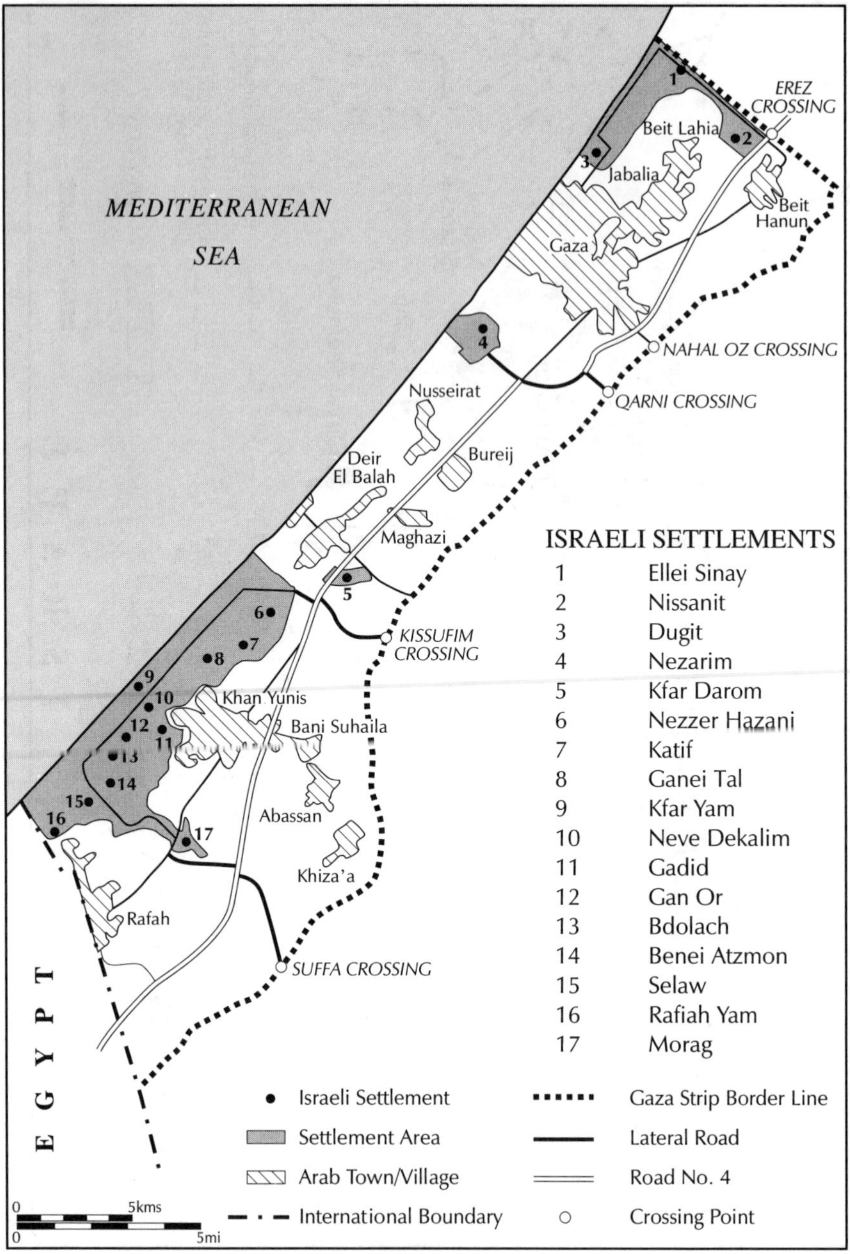
MEDITERRANEAN SEA
EGYPT
EREZ CROSSING
NAHAL OZ CROSSING
QARNI CROSSING
KISSUFIM CROSSING
SUFFA CROSSING
Beit Lahia
Jabalia
Beit Hanun
Gaza
Nusseirat
Bureij
Deir El Balah
Maghazi
Khan Yunis
Bani Suhaila
Abassan
Khiza'a
Rafah
1
2
3
4
5
6
7
8
9
10
11
12
13
14
15
16
17
ISRAELI SETTLEMENTS
1 Ellei Sinay
2 Nissanit
3 Dugit
4 Nezarim
5 Kfar Darom
6 Nezzer Hazani
7 Katif
8 Ganei Tal
9 Kfar Yam
10 Neve Dekalim
11 Gadid
12 Gan Or
13 Bdolach
14 Benei Atzmon
15 Selaw
16 Rafiah Yam
17 Morag
Israeli Settlement
Settlement Area
Arab Town/Village
International Boundary
Gaza Strip Border Line
Lateral Road
Road No. 4
Crossing Point
0 5kms
0 5mi

2. Gaza Strip

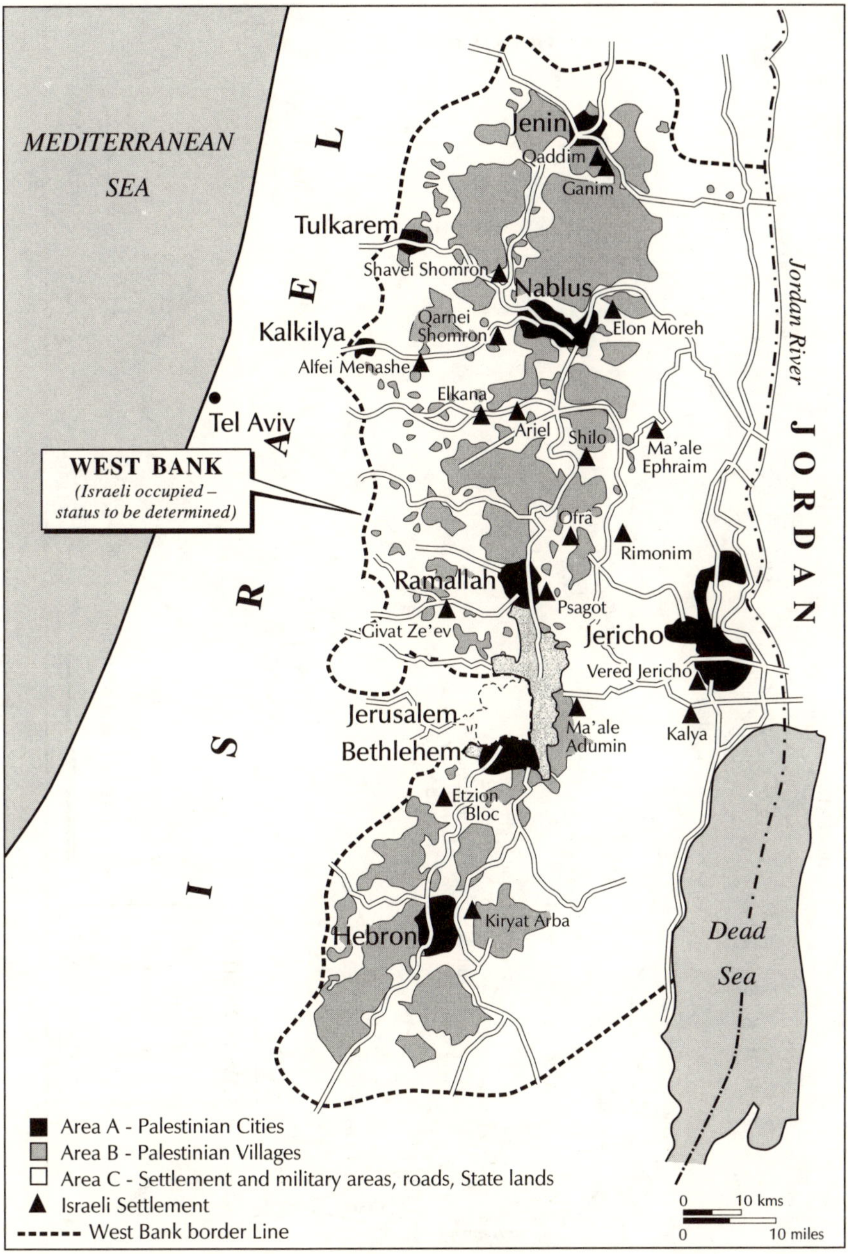

3. Oslo II: The West Bank

4. Iran and Iraq

About the Editors

Mark A. Heller

Mark A. Heller holds an M.A. in Middle Eastern Studies and a Ph.D. in Political Science from Harvard University. He joined the JCSS in 1979 and served as Deputy Director of the Center from 1984 to 1986. His publications include *A Palestinian State: The Implications for Israel* (1983) and *The Dynamics of Soviet Policy in the Middle East* (1991). He edited and coauthored the first three editions of *The Middle East Military Balance* (1983–1985), and has written numerous monographs, book chapters, and journal articles on Middle Eastern political-strategic affairs.

Yiftah Shapir

Yiftah Shapir joined JCSS in 1993 as an associate of the Center's project on Security and Arms Control, where he followed proliferation of weapons of mass destruction in the Middle East. Before joining the Center, Mr. Shapir served as an officer in the Israel Air Force, in various instructional and analytical postings. He holds a B.Sc. degree in physics and chemistry from the Hebrew University of Jerusalem and an M.B.A. (specializing in information technology and operation research) from Tel Aviv University.

Additional Contributors

Amos Gilboa

Brigadier-General (Res.) Amos Gilboa was head of the Research and Estimate Division in IDF Military Intelligence, IDF attaché in Washington D.C., and chief of the Israeli delegation to talks with Lebanon in 1984–85. From 1986 to 1989 he was the Prime Minister's Adviser on Israeli-Arab Affairs. He writes on security issues for the daily *Ma'ariv*.

Aharon Levran

Brigadier-General (Res.) Aharon Levran served for thirty years in the IDF. His service began in armor and infantry reconnaissance units and his last postings include assistant for operational intelligence to the Chief of Intelligence, deputy commandant of the National Defense College, and IDF attaché in Tokyo and Seoul. He is a graduate of the Hebrew University of Jerusalem in Middle East

Studies and Political Science and has written extensively on Israeli strategic affairs. His most recent publication is *Israeli Strategy After Desert Storm* (1997).

Anat Kurz

Anat Kurz studies low-intensity conflict, with special emphasis on organizational aspects of insurgency, and directs the Project on Low Intensity Warfare at JCSS. She is coauthor of *ASALA: Irrational Terror or Political Tool* (1985), editor of *Contemporary Trends in World Terrorism* (1987), and editor and coauthor of *Islamic Terrorism and Israel: Hizbullah, Palestinian Islamic Jihad, and Hamas* (1993).

Gerald L. Sorokin

Gerald L. Sorokin is Assistant Professor of Political Science at the University of Iowa. In 1996 and 1997–98, he was Visiting Fellow at the JCSS. His research focuses on alliances and conflict management. He has published articles in such journals as *International Studies Quarterly*, *Journal of Conflict Resolution*, and *Journal of Strategic Studies*.